BENITA PARRY

Delusions and Discoveries

STUDIES ON INDIA
IN THE BRITISH IMAGINATION
1880–1930

UNIVERSITY OF CALIFORNIA PRESS

Berkeley and Los Angeles

University of California Press
Berkeley and Los Angeles, California

Copyright © Benita Parry, 1972

ISBN 0–520–02215–7

Library of Congress Catalog Card Number 70–186786

Printed in Great Britain

20th C SHORT STORY EXPL.

Contents

Acknowledgements

I want to thank Gay Clifford, Douglas Johnson and William Parry for reading and commenting on sections of the book, David Thomson for his critical and sympathetic editing, Mrs T. Thompson for allowing me to consult and quote from her husband's papers, and Mrs Indira Gandhi for permission to quote from Nehru's letters to E. J. Thompson.

NOTES

1. 'Anglo-Indian' is used to designate the British community in India. After 1916 the term was officially applied to persons formerly known as Eurasians, but it continued to be used in its original meaning both colloquially and in writing until independence.

2. Because Indian words are variously transliterated by the authors discussed, the different forms have been retained in quotations. Thus both spellings of sahib/saheb, Shiva/Siva etc. appear.

3. In trying to understand the Indian traditions I have used and deferred to the commentaries of several scholars whose different insights and interpretations provide for those unfamiliar with the subject a glimpse into the complexity and subtlety of Indian thought. To the uninitiated, Heinrich Zimmer is an inspired guide through the world of the Indian intellect and sensibility and I have drawn most heavily on his expositions of Indian ideas, myths and legends.

Those who are shut in within one society, one nation, or one religion, tend to imagine that their way of life and their way of thought have absolute and unchangeable validity and that all that contradicts their standards is somehow 'unnatural', inferior or evil. Those, on the other hand, who live on the borderlines of various civilizations comprehend more clearly the great movement and the great contradictoriness of nature and society.

Isaac Deutscher, *The Non-Jewish Jew and Other Essays*

India – as Life brooding on itself – thinks of the problem of time in periods comparable to those of our astronomy, geology, and paleontology. India thinks of time and of herself, that is to say, in biological terms, of the species, not of the ephemeral ego. . . . We of the West, on the other hand, regard world history as a biography of mankind, and in particular of Occidental Man, whom we estimate to be the most consequential member of the family. . . . We think of egos, individuals, lives, not of Life. Our will is not to culminate in our human institutions the universal play of nature, but to evaluate, to set ourselves against the play, with an egocentric tenacity.

Heinrich Zimmer,
Myths and Symbols in Indian Art and Civilization

Every doctrine of imperialism devised by man is a consequence of their second thoughts. . . . Imperialist ideas are less ideas than instincts.

A. P. Thornton, *Doctrines of Imperialism*

Introduction

'CIVILIZATION' is necessarily an abstraction. Contact is made not between abstractions, but between real, live, human beings.[1]

Mannoni's observation on relationships within a colonial society is relevant to the British connexion with India. The various ideas on India's government conceived in London during the century of direct rule were based on the belief that it rested with the British to supervise the functioning of Indian society and to guide India's future. These theories and projects were translated by Anglo-Indians and it is interesting to know not only what they claimed their role to be, but also what they felt about India, and what were their inclinations, frustrations and satisfactions. Because analyses of the British in India focus on the magnitude of the impact which they made on the country and its peoples, the British tend to appear as catalysts in a situation which they dominated. This was the impression which as rulers they sought to give in official declarations, personal reminiscences and individual behaviour, and it was their posture of unlimited self-confidence which both undermined the educated Indian's self-esteem and stimulated him into rebellion.

There was something fascinating about the British approach to the Indian problem, even though it was singularly irritating. The calm assurance of always being in the right and of having borne a great burden worthily, faith in their racial destiny and their own brand of imperialism, contempt and anger at the unbelievers and sinners who challenged the foundations of the true faith – there was something of the religious temper about this attitude. Like the Inquisitors of old, they were bent on saving us regardless of our desires in the matter.[2]

There were thoughtful and humane men in the Anglo-Indian community as well as mindless authoritarians, and generalizations

I

must inevitably shrink the range of experiences which they knew as individuals. Yet if we listen to the voices of those who were committed to Anglo-India and set these off against the ironic commentaries of the dissidents in the community who protested at their companions' dispositions and attitudinizing – and, given the pressures to conform, the extent of criticism is remarkable – it is apparent that, whatever the individual variations, the usually self-assured and often arrogant British, whose trade as rulers was to deal in moral certainties, were displaced persons in India, victims of that destiny which influential and articulate elements in their nation exhorted them to obey.

> Fair is our lot – O goodly is our heritage!
>   (Humble ye, my people, and be fearful in your mirth!)
> For the Lord our God Most High
> He hath made the deep as dry,
> He hath smote for us a pathway to the ends of all the Earth![3]

When British rule over India in the late nineteenth century took on the ideology of an Anglo-Saxon mission to the dark peoples of the globe, the British–Indian encounter became a battle expressed as a political struggle and experienced as a psychological crisis.

The greater part of British literature on India, reminiscences, commentaries and fiction, was written by Anglo-Indian officials and their wives, men and women from a section of British society which identified with the prevailing national beliefs and trusted that their already praiseworthy social order was evolving towards an even higher excellence. At the turn of the century it was conceivable that Englishmen could have a robust faith in Western civilization and would therefore speak without saving clauses about the ignorance and backwardness of peoples who were not white, Anglo-Saxon and Christian. Such confidence was exaggerated in those who saw themselves as divinely elected to rule over the peoples of Asia and Africa who had failed to develop the white world's principles and rules of life.

But while they spoke loudly and often of their high calling, their proficiency and success, India's resident rulers were troubled by India. From its beginnings, the British–Indian relationship was a confrontation between philosophical systems, ethical doctrines and styles of life which were sufficiently different to imperil mutual understanding; in the context of imperialist domination the growth of British tolerance towards Indian norms and the sympathetic exploration of her ideals was inhibited. Physically removed from Britain but remaining assertively British, purveyors of policies framed according to Western ideas and priorities, the Anglo-Indians did not join in Indian society, were unresponsive to its values and uneasy about the peoples they dominated. As a prominent administrator remarked in a melancholy tale he wrote, 'The Englishman in India has no home, and he leaves no memory.'*

From the pedestal of a predominantly Protestant middle-class ethic, with its belief in work, restraint and order, the British looked down on the codes and habits of Indians as aberrations from a human norm which they defined in terms of their own standards. Their picture of India, therefore, which could be accurate in its details, was invariably false in its essence. Once people are segregated because of race, class or religion, delusions and fantasies about each other will grow rampant, and the British in India were obsessed not only with those Indian customs which seemed to them to invite licence and debase men, but with religious goals which demanded superhuman effort and promised ecstasy. They saw in India vestiges of a primordial, dark and instinctual past which their own society had left behind in its evolution to civilization, as well as intimations of spiritual experiences more inclusive and transcendent than any known to the West and which in their bewilderment they included as part of India's mystery.

It was inevitable that both the speculative, experimental traditions of India's religious and those more popular forms of worship which regard the sexual energies as creative and destructive forces, as the differentiated representations of the Absolute, should have impinged themselves so forcefully on the British imagination. The Tantric tradition, for example, whose texts 'do not teach to subdue the senses, but to increase their power and then to harness them in

---

* Sir William Wilson Hunter, *The Old Missionary* (1896), p. 133. Hunter (1840–1900) joined the Indian Civil Service in 1862 and spent twenty-five years in India.

3

the achievement of lasting enstasy',* was frequently invoked by the British as evidence of Indians' earthly depravity and intimacy with the forces of darkness. The rites of this system, in which sex plays a central symbolic role, give a metaphoric expression to inclinations which were rigorously suppressed in imperial Britain; to Anglo-Indians a religion which could accommodate such concepts and practices appeared as a road to God paved by devils and aroused the wildest surmises about Indian proclivities. Many of the British ideas and images of India suggest that Indians were feared not only as subjects who had once rebelled and who could do so again, but as perverts threatening to invade and seduce the white world. A visitor to India during the 1930s was warned by a seasoned Anglo-Indian lady, 'You'll never understand the dark and tortuous minds of the natives . . . and if you do I shan't like you – you won't be healthy.'† The safest course was to barricade themselves within their own community, to shield their consciousness against India's encroachment:

> Hold ye the Faith – the Faith our Fathers sealed us;
> Whoring not with visions – overwise and overstale.[4]

This study is an attempt to understand something of the interior British experience of India in a period which covers the age of imperial confidence and the setting in of disenchantment. British images of India can be found in a great number of written and visual forms; among written sources travellers' tales, antiquarian studies, histories, political treatises, administrative records, missionaries'

---

* Agehananda Bharati, *The Tantric Tradition* (1965), p. 290. Heinrich Zimmer explains that the goal of the Tantric student is 'to incorporate the excluded forces as well as those accepted generally, and experience by this means the essential non-existence of the antagonistic polarity – its vanishing away, its nirvana; i.e. the intrinsic purity and innocence of the seemingly dark and dangerous sphere. In this way he breaks within himself the tension of the "forbidden", and resolves everything in light.' *Philosophies of India* (1967), p. 579.

† J. R. Ackerley, *Hindoo Holiday: An Indian Journal* (1952), pp. 23–4. This is an account of the short period which Ackerley spent as private secretary to the Maharajah of Chhatarpur. Ackerley (1896–1967) was literary editor of the *Listener* from 1935 until 1959; he wrote novels and a memoir, *My Father and Myself*.

4

reports, newspapers, periodicals, diaries, letters, memoirs, poetry and fiction, will all suggest what the British thought and felt about India. The approach chosen here, and one which makes no claim to arriving at a definitive account, is to consider how writers reordered their ideas and perceptions in fiction. The emphasis is on what they saw or discovered in and through India, on how they reacted to the new demands for understanding which India made on their imaginations and intellects. It is not therefore the actuality of India's civilization which is being examined, nor the identity of her peoples or how they responded to the British, but the reflections of India as these were distorted and in those rare instances illuminated through the lens of the British imagination.

The chapters on the writers of fiction are preceded by an outline of the British connexion with India from about 1880 to 1930, and a survey of Anglo-Indian attitudes drawn from their own writings. Overwhelmingly intended as hagiology, the memoirs and exegeses of the British in India are in their own way imaginative recreations where the authors set out to render good accounts of themselves to their contemporaries and to posterity. These writings imply the mental and emotional climate which was either reproduced or scrutinized in fiction; they also suggest what actual Englishmen and women made of their opportunity to know India. The historical context cannot explain why British literature about India can claim only two important writers and a single masterpiece. But since most of the fiction was written by those who had lived as Anglo-Indians, an understanding of their society can help to account for the limitations on empathy and the poverty of imagination which characterize such writing.

From the vast volume of fiction about India,[5] romantic novelettes, problem novels and the works of the two major artists, Kipling and Forster, offer an obvious selection, suggesting as they do the different concerns and perceptions which writers brought to their transfigurations of the Indian experience.* Certain themes and scenes repeatedly find their way into the fiction, spanning the writings of

* With one exception, all the novels and stories discussed deal with situations contemporaneous with the author's lifetime and historical recreations have been excluded.

those with different outlooks and temperaments,[6] and this variation on motifs underscores the difficulty of discussing within the same framework fiction which ranges from the trivial to the profound. An attempt has therefore been made to approach all the writings as imaginative inventions but to assess them on different levels – the fiction of little or no literary significance for what it uncovers of a community's social norms and psychological existence, and the works of the important writers, whose insights transcend their personal preoccupations and their own society's established modes of thought, for their explorations of experience in all its complexity and ambiguity.

The romantic writers, whose novelettes are grouped together because they are virtually indistinguishable, reveal themselves rather than India, and are principally interesting as symptomatic of Anglo-Indian attitudes. The received opinions and automatic responses of the conformist Anglo-Indians are naïvely recorded, as is the neurotic concern with protecting their identity from pollution by strange, unwholesome and deviant India. What they did not know about India – and they knew very little – these writers guessed, and these guesses and half-truths uncover their obsessions and fantasies. Drawn from Anglo-Indian mythology and ministering to the community's conceit, theirs is both a calculated self-portrait and an unintended confession.

Many of the lady-romancers' characteristics can equally be applied to Flora Annie Steel, but she has been treated separately both because she was earnestly concerned with verisimilitude in her portrayals of India and because she had considerably more insight into the Anglo-Indian dilemma. During a long period of residence in India she met the people whom her husband, a member of the Indian Civil Service, administered. Even such limited associations as she formed with Indians were assiduously avoided by most ladies of Anglo-India. Mrs Steel's India, which is simultaneously clear-sighted and obstinately blind, accurate and preposterous, tolerant and self-righteous, suggests the chasm between empirical observation and the discernment of subjective truth.

It is immediately obvious that the versions of India reported by the romancers and Flora Annie Steel come from the same stratum of

the Anglo-Indian mind which expresses itself in so many reminiscences. With Edmund Candler and Edward Thompson we move to
self-aware and introspective writers who distanced themselves from
Anglo-India and attempted to interpret their response to India. In
their different ways Candler, who established a reputation as a
travelling journalist in the East, and Thompson, who became known
as an authority on Indian history and affairs, express the confusions
of intelligent and sensitive men at a time when the Raj was being
challenged and undermined by Indian nationalism. Their thoughtful novels about the British–Indian problem are overtly concerned
with the virtues and deficiencies of British rule, with race prejudice
and the gulf between British and Indian. Heretical about the
imperial mission, they assess the cost in decency and dignity of belonging to an alien ruling class, and cast a critical eye on Anglo-India.
At the same time, they advance both conventional and idiosyncratic
defences of the white man's role in India. Both tried to explain the
opacities of India and both were defeated. Candler's quest to know
the East ended in disillusion when the adventurer chose the certainties of Home. For Thompson, a Christian and a liberal, empathy
and estrangement remained locked in battle. The cord between their
feelings and their imaginative creations had not been cut and both
men failed to transform their impressions, observations and sensations into art. But the stuff of their writings, the images they received
of India, the feelings they recorded and buried, communicates an
experience of India and reveals how India seeped into their
consciousness.

The arrangement of the chapters is not chronological and is
intended to suggest an ascending order in complexity of vision.
Where the other writers told of the ways India disturbed and pleased
them and attempted to explain the Indian mind and outlook, Kipling
and Forster assimilated India into their art. Where the other writers
saw India as a frieze, they knew her as a spirit.* For the romancers
and Flora Annie Steel, as for Candler and Thompson, India essentially remained an area of darkness which some feared to enter and
where others were lost. In Kipling's tales there are discoveries of
India, a bringing to light of an alien but authentic world. The

* The phrase is Forster's in *A Passage to India*.

ambiguities of the Indian-born Englishman whose inspiration derives simultaneously from love of India and identification with the white man's pretensions in the age of imperialism, whose spite as a contemptuous outsider coexists with compassion as an initiate, makes Kipling's Indian fiction the richest single source for understanding the paradoxical hold which India could exercise on the British mind.

It was a conceit of Anglo-Indians to invoke their years of residence in India as proof of knowing the real India. Ironically, the one great novel in British writing about India is the work of a writer who had spent only short periods in the sub-continent. India for Forster opened out his growing vision of man's experiential range. Through speculating on the historical and cultural being of India Forster recreated this as the symbol of man's spiritual history and his experiments in self-understanding. His perception of the flux of India's existence and the variousness of the Indian sensibility poses the possibility that her life-styles respect truths about man's nature which the West has suppressed, liberating his potential for sensuous and transcendent experiences; and in *A Passage to India* there are intimations of what the British might have learned from their long association with India.

CHAPTER I

The British–Indian Encounter

The Official Creed

IN an era when overseas possessions were a status symbol and Empire was acquiring a mystique, India manifested Britain's position as a European power and a great nation. India's more tangible importance was in providing the territorial and military base for Britain's Far and Middle Eastern policies, and in serving as a satellite of the home economy. The instrument of Britain's Eastern policies was the Indian Army. Commanded by some 3,000 British officers and financed from Indian revenues, its peace-time strength of about 150,000 Indian soldiers could in times of war swell to 670,000.* After the 1857 rebellion the proportion of Indian to British soldiers was laid down as two to one, and in addition to the Indian Army there were some 75,000 troops of the British Army stationed in India who came under the commander-in-chief of the Indian Army and were also paid for out of Indian revenues.

While the expansion of British rule in India proceeded in a pragmatic and haphazard way, the government of India grew out of the definite purpose of ensuring British commercial undertakings and persisted in large part to protect investments and other economic advantages.[1] The development of indigo plantations in Bengal during the eighteenth century had been followed in the mid nineteenth

* Colin Cross, *The Fall of the British Empire, 1918–1968* (1968), p. 44, gives the peace-time strength as 200,000; the figure in 1863 when the Army was reorganized is given in *The Oxford History of Modern India* (1964) as 140,000 Indian to 65,000 European troops (p. 235).

James Morris in *Pax Britannica: The Climax of an Empire* (1968) lists the places where the Indian Army had served in the nineteenth century: China, Persia, Ethiopia, Singapore, Hong Kong, Egypt and East Africa: 'It was the possession of India that made the Empire a military power – "an English barrack in the Oriental seas", Salisbury had once called it' (p. 263). During the First World War the Indian Army served in Mesopotamia and on the European Front.

9

century by the rapid growth of the jute, tea and coffee industries and by the establishment in the twentieth century of rubber plantations. In the latter half of the nineteenth century the government of India undertook the construction of railways and, apart from the decade between 1869 and 1879, provided incentives for private companies to operate in the field. The British presence in India was an important factor in encouraging investment as there was rarely a default and it has been estimated that, during the 1880s, about one fifth of British overseas capital, some £270 million, was invested in India.[2]

A modern Indian historian has summed up the damaging impact of British rule on the Indian economy:

The British had given an impetus to the destruction of the old economy but did not permit the rise in its place of one more suited to the modern age. India was made to serve as the supplier of raw materials to Britain's new industries and as the market for her manufactured goods.[3]

This interdependence of the British and Indian economies stimulated the home economy and operated to the detriment of India's own handicraft industries – textiles, glass, paper, metal and iron smelting. Through this relationship India's tendency to an overwhelmingly agricultural economy was intensified: the 1931 census returns showed that 11 per cent of the population was urban, that 2·7 per cent lived in the large cities and that only 9·7 per cent was dependent on industry for its livelihood.[4]

In Britain, various economic interests benefited from British control of India. Within India, British businessmen organized into Chambers of Commerce, and the broader body of non-officials – planters, members of the professions – calling themselves the European Association, were able to exert pressure on the government in defence of their privileged position.* Even if, as has been suggested, British policy was divided between self-interested measures and

* M. Kidron in *Foreign Investment in India* (1965) writes that 'British business enjoyed almost sole access to the Government in the early years and a disproportionate weight in the legislatures from 1909' (p. 12). In *Eastern Interlude: A Social History of the European Community in Calcutta* (1930), R. Pearson suggests that one of the main social trends in Calcutta during the nineteenth century was the increase in the power and influence of limited liability companies who organized themselves into the powerful Bengal Chamber of Commerce. Through this body, he writes, 'the Directors of these companies came to

those like famine relief, sanitation and irrigation where Indian needs were primary,[5] British rule was hardly the altruistic undertaking advertised by mission-happy Anglo-Indian officials. The cost of foreign rule and of Britain's imperial ventures in Asia and the Middle East was borne by the Indian people and a significant part of the elaborate administration's functions was the collection of taxes to which every Indian peasant contributed in direct or indirect form. The revenues drawn from the Indian people financed the administration, the Indian Army and the organization of Indian affairs in England.*

The ultimate control of the Indian Empire was exercised from London by a Secretary of State for India who sat in the Cabinet and was responsible to the British Parliament. Local knowledge was provided by the Council of India, which also sat in London and consisted of fifteen members, usually ex-officials of the Indian Services, nominated by the British government for a period of ten to fifteen years. Within India, government was supervised by the Governor-General or Viceroy who ruled with an Executive Council of five members† and was advised by a Legislative Council of six to twelve members nominated by the Viceroy and holding office for two years. At least half the membership was drawn from the non-official British community and the few Indians included were invariably princes and retired government officials. Defence, foreign

---

voice their opinion on every subject, economic, moral and political which in any way affected the commercial interests of the English in India, and won for the leading members of the business community considerable influence over the decisions of the Government' (p. 216). One of the most notable victories of the non-official community was their defeat of the Ilbert Bill, 1882, which proposed extending full rights of jurisdiction to Indian judges in the country districts, thereby cancelling an Act of 1872 limiting their powers. This victory they shared with the majority of officials who had also opposed the measure.

* These 'Home Charges' also paid the dividend on the East India stock, the interest on the Home Bond Debt and the furlough and retirement pay of British officials in the Indian Services.

† Under the Councils Act of 1861 the composition of the Executive Council was to contain two members of the Civil Service and two who might be chosen from outside the Services, one as financial expert and one as law member. There was also to be one military member and the commander-in-chief of the Army was to serve as extraordinary member. Subsequently additional members were added.

affairs, finance, railways, posts and telegraphs were the responsibility of the central government, that is of the Viceroy and his Executive Council. Regional administration was exercised by the provincial governments headed by a Governor, a Lieutenant-Governor or a Chief Commissioner assisted by an executive body of civil servants, and a legislative council of nominated members.

The provinces were divided into districts, the basic unit of the administrative system devised by the British to rule India. At the head of each district, which could contain a hundred villages and a population of about half a million, was a Collector or Deputy Commissioner who was served by members of the Indian Civil Service. Between 1858 and 1935 this service numbered about 1,000 men, while membership of the other civilian services – public works, police, education, telegraphs, forestry, engineering and the medical services – was about 4,000. Until 1925 when enlarged Indian recruitment to both the Civilian and the Military Services was permitted, Indianization was very gradual indeed and it was the proud and repeated claim of Anglo-India that a small number of officials together with an equally small number of army officers ruled over some 400,000,000 Indians.

After 1853, recruitment to the I.C.S. was through competitive examinations. Those seeking a career in the service were graduates of British universities, in the main Oxford and Cambridge with a few from the Scottish universities and in later years London. In 1875 the I.C.S. had been divided into the judicial and the administrative branches, the judicial section dealing with county court and sessions work and with civil and criminal appeals from the magistrates' courts which formed part of the administrative branch. One third of the judges were members of the I.C.S., while the rest were British and Indian barristers.*

The administrative section was responsible for the actual running of the district, collecting revenues and scrutinizing agricultural records, supervising schools, roads, hospitals, famine relief, and overseeing the police and petty justice, duties which entailed exten-

* Cross, *op. cit.*, writes that the 'judiciary was the only public service in which Indians commonly reached high posts but the chief justices of the high courts were always British' (p. 39).

sive tours of the area. A recruit in his early twenties would serve as an assistant for about five years before becoming a Collector or District Officer. Civilians tended to retire in their early forties; if they then returned to Indian service it would be to the secretariat of the various government departments or to membership of the Viceroy's Councils.

By the later decades of the nineteenth century the reforming zeal of the Utilitarians and Evangelicals, who had believed that British intervention could fundamentally change and improve Indian society, had been dissipated.[6] The disenchantment of these elements who had influenced official thinking about India, coincided with the government's pragmatic change of policy after the 1857 revolt. Interference with Indian customs and traditions, they now considered, had alienated the land-owning classes and the princes; in some areas it had generated hostility in the peasantry. The decision now was to conciliate the natural leadership of old India, the princes and landlords, and to organize India's modernization through material improvement, while avoiding interference with the social system. Thus the Widows Remarriage Act – a head-on assault on Hindu tradition – which had been initiated during Dalhousie's viceroyalty, was dropped and while officials hoped that education would stimulate Indians to change their social customs, the policy of reform was abandoned.*

But every measure ever imposed by the British before and after 1857 stemmed from British evaluations of what was necessary and desirable for India and did interfere with Indian society. The Penal Code of 1860 and the Code of Criminal Procedure, 1861, which incorporated the British concepts of equality before the law, of law deriving from the legislative authority of the state and not from religion, of uniformity in statutes and procedures and readily available justice, became the basis of the Indian legal system. The decision taken under Bentinck's administration in 1835 to introduce Western education – 'the great objects of the British government ought to be the promotion of European literature and science' – remained the purpose of the government's education policy. Grants in

* Some measures impinging on social practices were passed, e.g. the Age of Consent Act of 1891 which raised the age for consummation of marriage to twelve.

aid to private institutions run by Indians were given and more government schools and colleges were established in the latter part of the nineteenth century. The emphasis on higher education – conceived as the knowledge of English literature, history and institutions – meant that education was available to a minority, while vocational training lagged behind and mass education was virtually neglected.

Until the end of the century, when some adjustments in policy were made, it was assumed that India's economy should be governed by the same methods as those operating in the Western capitalist countries. Because India was basically an agrarian society, the most devastating impact of this approach was on land tenure and the village communities. The aim during the nineteenth century had been to introduce a free enterprise, competitive agrarian system by granting proprietary titles to individuals where previously the land had been communally held. Revenues were fixed in money and, if the assessments were not paid, the sale of land was forced. The purpose of this was to dismember the petrified corporate structure so that it could be rebuilt on Western lines. The outcome was the weakening of the village community, traditionally the heart of the Indian social system, peasant indebtedness and massive land alienation from the cultivators into the hands of absentee landlords and money-lenders. Only after the peasant riots in the Deccan in 1876 was there an implicit reversal of policy in the Deccan Agriculturists Relief Act of 1879 which laid down that the courts could award only reasonable interest in the case of debt but not confiscation of land. Towards the end of the century the tendency evolving was that measures should be devised to preserve rural society in its static, traditional form, a reversal of former policy. Eviction from the land because of debt and the sale of land to non-cultivators was forbidden by the Punjab Land Alienation Act of 1900, and the Land Resolution of 1902 advocated greater flexibility in assessments and recommended that any expansion of revenues should be sought elsewhere than from the land.[7]

Raghavan Iyer[8] distinguishes four interacting doctrines informing British ideas on India's government: the Roman element of good government and peace under the law; the Semitic element of racial exclusiveness and destiny, the calm belief that the British were an elect, divinely appointed to rule; the aggressive Prussian element of militancy and firmness, expressed as pride in military power and demanding the docility of the ruled; and the nonconformist radical element which stressed the need for atonement and penance.

The diversities among the men who ruled India and the contradictions between the various doctrines that they invoked must not make us forget the nature of the system that was set up and eventually had to be abandoned. It was a centralized, enlightened despotism that was transformed in time into an elaborate, autocratic bureaucracy.[9]

It is in the light of Iyer's remarks that the public works creed of the administrators in the later nineteenth century should be viewed. This was how they would impose Western influence on India, whether or not the people wanted or appreciated the gift; this was how service would be thrust on a people unable to initiate material improvements on their own. By 1900 the extensive railway system was completed, essential for policing the sub-continent and for transporting raw materials and distributing goods. Roads were built, bridges, canals and dams constructed. After the famine of 1876–8, the Famine Code of 1883 was formulated which aimed at detecting symptoms of food shortages and at planning the distribution of relief, a system which was further improved in 1901.

Disillusion in the prospect of India's rapid moral regeneration was joined with the conviction that India would always require Britain's benevolent despotism. In *The English Utilitarians and India* Eric Stokes describes James FitzJames Stephen as the political philosopher of the Indian Civil Service, the man who provided a reasoned doctrine for its prejudices. Stephen spent only two and a half years in India as Legal Member of the Council, between 1869 and 1872, but his analysis of the foundations of British rule in India had a lasting influence on the administrators. The government of India, he argued, was essentially an absolute government founded not on consent but on conquest and representative not of the Indian people but of ideas totally different from theirs, ideas derived from English and European morality: 'our government implies at every point the superiority of the conquering race'.

The British task, he argued, was to revolutionize Indian ideas and institutions, to introduce

the essential parts of European civilization into a country densely peopled, grossly ignorant, steeped in idolatrous superstitions, unenergetic, fatalistic, indifferent to most of what we regard as the evils of life, and preferring the repose of submitting to them to the trouble of encountering and trying to remove them.[10]

These essential parts of European civilization he defined as peace, order, supremacy of law, enforcement of contracts, development of the state's military force and public works, these to be implemented with as little interference as possible with the wealth and comfort of the people. The alternative, which was to leave India in its original condition, was abhorrent on moral and economic grounds.

Stephen's reasoning and assertions were to persist as the foundations of the Anglo-Indian officials' creed. Writing in the 1880s, Sir John Strachey* declared:

The real foundations of our power do not rest on the interested approval of the noisy few but on justice and on the contentment of the silent millions ... we ... to use Sir James Stephen's expression, are the representatives of a belligerent civilization which has to wage constant warfare against strange barbarisms, horrid customs and cruel superstitions, ancient survivals, ready at any moment to start into activity.[11]

Such premises, sometimes crudely expressed, sometimes subtly, were for generations repeated in the determined public expressions of determined public men engrossed in administration and tending to view Indians as objects to be ruled and India as the raw material on which policies were to be imposed. Even Sir Alfred Lyall,† whose respectful interest in 'the subtle and searching mind of India'

* Born in 1823, Strachey joined the I.C.S. in 1842, was Chief Commissioner of Oudh, 1866–8, a member of the Viceroy's Council, 1868–74, and again from 1876 until 1880, Lieutenant-Governor of the North-West Provinces, 1874–6, and a member of the India Council, 1885–95. He died in 1907.

† Lyall (1835–1911) joined the I.C.S. in 1856 and had a distinguished career in the government of India. He was Home Secretary, 1873–4, Foreign Secretary, 1878–81, and Lieutenant-Governor of the North-West Provinces, 1882–7. From 1887 until 1902 he was a member of the India Council. A scholar and poet, Lyall published books of verse and studies of Asian civilization.

separated him from his colleagues, expressed a like confidence in Britain's ability to influence India for the good technically, intellectually and morally, and he applauded British rule for conferring great and permanent blessings on India. In his treatise, *The Rise and Expansion of British Dominion in India*, he argued that since the fall of the Roman Empire civilization had been receding from the East and that the only important ground recovered for centuries by civilization had been won in India by the English, 'foremost as harbinger of light and liberty', whose Empire 'must necessarily give an enormous impulse and totally new direction to the civilization of that continent'.[12]

But other prominent officials were less confident of India yielding to the beneficent influence of Western civilization as embodied in her rulers and stressed instead the need to keep order with the threat of military force. In the 1890s Lord Roberts,* who had recently retired as commander-in-chief of the Indian Army, recommended these remedies against any challenge to permanent British dominion:

> By rendering our administration on the one hand firm and strong, on the other tolerant and sympathetic . . . by doing all in our power to gain the confidence of the various races, and by convincing them that we have not only the determination but the ability to maintain our supremacy in India against all assailants.[13]

The ways in which the British described their purpose in India depended on the prevailing assumptions in England about the Anglo-Saxon destiny as a governing race. In the last decades of the nineteenth century, trusteeship as a calling to the advanced and powerful nations of the West to govern the weaker, backward peoples dominated both Tory and Liberal thinking about colonial possessions.[14] Racialism was the justification for modern imperialism and its primary expression. Racist theories seeking to prove the inferiority of non-white peoples had been current in Europe since the eighteenth century. Polygenism had attributed differences between peoples to the separate creation of the races and, when this theory was ousted by Darwinism, racism found in 'natural selection' a new

* Roberts (1832–1914) was born in India. He joined the Indian Army in 1851. From 1885 until 1893, when he retired, he was commander-in-chief in India.

explanation for the different stages of development of the various races.[15] Although the propagandists for Britain's national mission – Carlyle, Dilke, Seeley and Froude – did not proclaim the permanent inferiority of particular races,* their teachings fed the British middle classes' belief in their own superiority, provided a respectable basis for politicians' dogmas and helped to create an intellectual climate in which the grandiose assertions of the Indian Services could pass for proven facts. When Chamberlain, addressing the Imperial Institute on 11 November 1895, declared, 'I believe in the British Empire, and ... I believe in the British race. I believe that the British race is the greatest of governing races that the world has ever seen',[16] he was reiterating what had for decades been received opinion amongst Anglo-Indians. In 1883, Sir Lepel Griffin,† a prominent civilian, writing in a British journal, stated that it would be unwise for the British

to descend from the high place which the genius of Englishmen has rightfully won, and endeavour to persuade the people of India what, indeed, only the most credulous among them would believe – that they are intellectually or morally our equals, and that to them have been confided by fortune those secrets of government which in the modern world, are the inheritance of the Anglo-Saxon race alone.[17]

While official policy had abandoned the active weaning of Indian people away from their customs and traditions, India's rulers continued to present the purpose of British rule as the improvement of both the physical fabric and the moral fibre of Indian society. Distinguished administrators stated that the task was nothing less than that of activating and succouring an inert and degenerate people.

---

* John Seeley in *The Expansion of England* (1883) supported the aims of Britain's mission to India, but not because of Indian inferiority: 'We are not cleverer than the Hindu; our minds are not richer or larger than his. We cannot astonish him, as we astonish the barbarian, by putting before him ideas that he never dreamed of. He can match from his poetry our sublimest thoughts; even our science perhaps has few conceptions that are altogether novel to him' (p. 244).

† Griffin (1838–1908) joined the I.C.S. in 1859, was Chief Secretary to the Punjab government, 1878, Political Adviser in Afghanistan, 1880, and Agent to the Governor-General in Central India, 1881–9.

Writing in the 1880s of his thirty years in India, Sir Richard Temple*
defined the object of British rule as moulding 'the character as well
as the intellect' of the Indian, and claimed that

the English or Western education has greatly elevated the character of
the Natives who have come within its influence. It has taught them
truthfulness and honour both morally and intellectually. It has made
them regard with aversion that which is false and dishonest... They will
no longer tolerate any superstitions or any absurdity whatsoever.[18]

A sanguine conclusion, if one is to judge from the virulence of subsequent British statements on the character of the Western-educated
Indian. The corollary of conviction in the Anglo-Saxon genius for
government was belief in Indian defects: 'There may be flashes of
light here and there in exceptional cases, but it is darkness that prevails among the non-Christian peoples whom I have known... In
the elevating and civilizing power of Christianity the hope of India
seems to lie,'[19] wrote Sir Andrew Fraser,† Lieutenant-Governor of
Bengal at the time of his retirement in 1908.‡

So ingrained was the claim that the British were rendering a selfless and magnificent service to India that sentiments current among
officials were echoed by Anglo-Indians notorious for abusing the
Indian labour they employed:

They [the planters] did the rough hard work that all pioneers must face;
they changed the wilderness and the jungle into fields yearly ripening for
the harvest; they trained the natives of India to aid them in their great
endeavours; they conferred untold blessings on generations past and yet

* Temple (1826–1902) joined the I.C.S. in 1847, held posts in the Punjab from
1851 until 1856, was Chief Commissioner in the Central Provinces, 1862–7, a
member of the Viceroy's Council, 1868–74, Lieutenant-Governor of Bengal,
1874–7, Governor of Bombay, 1877–80, and a Member of the British Parliament,
1885–95.

† Fraser (1848–1919) joined the I.C.S. in 1871, spent twenty-eight years in the
Central Provinces and was Lieutenant-Governor of Bengal from 1903 until 1908.

‡ Discussing British conceptions of Indian character Hutchins, *op. cit.*, suggests that the Victorians 'pictured the decadence and disarray of Indian society
as a reflection of Indian racial character rather than the primary deterrent to its
true expression' (p. 72). Already existing climatic explanations of Indian depravity 'were amplified by racial notions which conceived that, whether the result
of climate or not, Indians constituted a distinct and inferior race' (p. 69).

unborn... In the case of indigo whole provinces have been enriched and the land covered with a contented peasantry, yearly growing in comfort, in health, in happiness, and in such wealth as never before in the history of India was scattered so widespread among the classes immediately depending on a living from the land. In the case of tea, the planter had entered the trackless, fever-breeding jungles, and where dark, deadly vapours and impenetrable forest covered the land, there has arisen under his magic touch vast tracts of country drained, cleared, smiling with periodic harvests and peopled by races of men yearly increasing in intelligence and wealth.[20]

The Anglo-Indian rhetoric of the 1880s and 1890s trumpets the fact of British power, discloses the gratifications which this brought to the ruling race and offers a moral justification for the British presence in India. At the Jubilee celebrations of 1887 Sir Rivers Thompson, then Lieutenant-Governor of Bengal, spoke of the advent of a higher civilization taking over in India through the peaceful coercion and moral ascendancy of the British. The Viceroy, Lord Dufferin, referred to the gratitude of the entire Indian population, to improvements in all spheres and to the mysterious decrees of Providence which had ordered Britain to undertake the Supreme Government of India.[21]

Ironically, the most extravagant expressions of benevolent paternalism were voiced by Lord Curzon during his viceroyalty, 1898–1905, at a time which was to be the turning-point in Britain's ability to govern India without consulting the wishes of the articulate strata of the Indian people. After the 1857 rebellion the British government had looked on the traditional aristocracy, the princes and the large land-owners, as the natural leadership whose authority was to be affirmed and bolstered and whose interests were to be conciliated. The Indian middle classes, whose growth had been stimulated by the government's need for minor officials, clerks in the administration and commerce, school-teachers and pleaders in the courts, and who had assimilated elements of Western consciousness through their education, were disowned by the British as being unrepresentative and as claiming rights which were inimical to the interests of the 'real India', the unchanging India of the rural masses, martial races and the princes.

The political expression of this emergent class was the Indian National Congress which first met in 1885 and reflected the trend away from regionalism and towards the possibility of an Indian political awareness. The refusal of the British to take these moderate men into partnership hastened the development of more militant tendencies which during the last decade of the nineteenth century and the early years of the twentieth century was intimately associated with the assertion of traditional values from within Indian civilization.*

After 1905 the political relationship between Britain and India was dominated by small concessions grudgingly given in answer to increasing demands for independence from the Indian political movement. By 1904 the demand for self-government within the Empire had been put forward from the Congress platform. Within Congress two tendencies were crystallizing: the moderates who retained faith in the good intentions of British democracy and the efficacy of negotiating, and the militants, calling themselves the New Party or the Nationalists and dubbed by their opponents as the Extremists, who advocated passive and active resistance against their masters. An Indian historian of this period has written: 'The older Congressmen believed that the continuance of British rule was the indispensable condition of India's progress and prosperity. The Nationalists argued that political freedom was an essential preliminary to all national progress.'[22] Amongst the militants were those like Aurobindo Ghose and Bipin Chandra Pal who rejected the goal of colonial self-government and others like Tilak who were prepared to accept self-government within the Empire as the political aim.

The years between 1905 and 1910 saw political unrest expressed in protests, demonstrations and in a few sporadic acts of terrorism. In 1905, in the teeth of protracted opposition from the Hindus of Bengal, who objected to the dismemberment of the province and feared the setting up of an administrative area with a Moslem

* In west India, Bal Gangadhar Tilak (1856–1920) instituted the revival of Shivaji-worship as a means of arousing political consciousness and instilling national pride. Shivaji (1627–80) had challenged the Moghul Empire and built a Maratha state in west India. In Bengal the agitation over partition was associated with a revival of Kali-worship and the reverence of national heroes.

majority, the partition of Bengal was carried out by a Liberal Secretary of State, John Morley. Although this disregard of peaceful petitioning undermined the moderates' tactics, Gopal Krishna Gokhale, their main spokesman, persisted in the method of protest through discussion. In 1906 he informed Morley that it was the aim of Congress to win for India the status of a self-governing colony, only to be told that 'for many a day to come – long beyond the short span of time that may be left to me – this was a mere dream'.[23]

The response of the then Viceroy, Lord Minto, to Indian militancy was to conciliate the 'loyalist' elements in Indian society and to remind Indians that Britain held India by the sword. Morley's inclination was to grant some concessions to defuse a potentially explosive situation,* and the outcome of their joint thinking was the Morley–Minto reforms, incorporated in the Indian Councils Act of 1909. This opened membership of the provincial executive councils to Indians, whereas previously Indians had been appointed only to the Viceroy's Council and to the Council of India in London. The aim of these measures, as Mehrotra, quoting from the Morley–Minto correspondence, shows, was a scheme of administrative improvement designed to win over the loyal and moderate elements, and with their help as a bridge to the native mind, to strengthen the government of India.

They were both convinced that the safety and welfare of India depended on the permanence of the British administration, that the Government of India was always to remain autocratic, and that the sovereignty must be vested in British hands and could not be delegated to any kind of representative assembly.[24]

Although these measures were not intended as a stepping-stone to representative government, the Congress moderates initially welcomed them as an advance towards self-government.

With the outbreak of war in 1914 both the moderates and the militants in Congress pledged themselves to stand by the Empire. In

* In reply to Morley's remark that Reforms might not save the Raj but that if they didn't, nothing would, Minto wrote, 'The *Raj* will not disappear in India as long as the British race remains what it is, because we shall fight for the *Raj* as hard as we have ever fought, if it comes to fighting, and we shall win as we have always won.' Quoted by Mehrotra (*op. cit.*, p. 47) from the Minto Papers.

the period since the 1909 reforms, sections of educated opinion had been pacified by such acts as the revoking of Bengal's partition in 1911 and the conciliatory attitudes of Hardinge's administration. An Indian expeditionary force was sent to the Western Front and Indian soldiers were dispatched to East Africa and the Middle East. In all, about one million Indians fought in the war and £146 million was contributed from Indian revenues. Politically active Indians awaited a firm declaration of British policy and were disappointed. By 1916 the militants, who had in the intervening years left Congress, now re-entered and together with the Moslem League demanded a proclamation declaring 'that it is the aim and intention of British policy to confer self-government at an early stage'.[25] Agitation was intensified; when Annie Besant was interned in 1917 for her Home Rule activities, there were nation-wide protests.

The Montagu–Chelmsford Report of 1917 cautiously declared that the policy of the British government and the government of India 'is that of the increasing association of Indians in every branch of the administration, and the gradual development of self-governing institutions, with a view to the progressive realization of responsible government in India as an integral part of the British Empire'.[26] Congress welcomed the proposals but asked for details and guarantees as to the precise steps contemplated to implement the policy. By 1918 Congress stated that the actual proposals were disappointing and unsatisfactory, while reiterating their loyalty and their willingness to be patient. By the time the constitution proposed by the Montagu–Chelmsford Reforms was implemented as the Government of India Act, 1921, political feeling amongst Indians had outstripped the concessions.

The action of General Dyer in shooting on an unarmed crowd holding a prohibited meeting at Amritsar in April 1919 epitomized the strong-arm methods which British rule persisted in using. This, together with the effect of the war and the Russian Revolution, was to harden the attitudes of politically conscious Indians. But the most powerful new element in the Indian political scene was Gandhi, who was able to appeal to the imaginations of the Indian masses and evoke their latent capacity for action, a development which the British had not foreseen and which defied their pronouncements on the immutable pathetic contentment of the people. Ravindar Kumar has said of Gandhi's impact: 'From outside the range of British intellectual experience, and alien to its traditions, a new force had arisen in the political cosmos which spoke to the masses in familiar accents and evoked symbols and ideals deeply ingrained in their consciousness.'[27]

Gandhi, at the start of his political activities a moderate and loyalist, appealed to the people to cooperate with the Reforms and make them work, but after Amritsar and the harsh treatment of Turkey by the terms of the Treaty of Sèvres, he redirected his energies to organizing the non-cooperation movement of 1920–22. This programme was adopted by Congress in 1920, who declared that *Swaraj*, self-government, was their goal, to be attained by all legitimate and peaceful means. These developments led to a break between Congress and the moderates, who now concentrated on developing the National Liberal Federation of India and who at future negotiations with the British were, like the Moslem League, separately represented.

For Gandhi, *Swaraj* meant full dominion status, but others like Nehru were moving towards a position demanding independence outside the Empire. Until 1927, Gandhi was able to hold the progress of the radicals in check, but when the British government appointed the all-white Simon Commission to inquire into India's constitutional future, Congress passed a resolution declaring that the goal of the Indian people was complete national independence. Still Gandhi continued to urge discussion and cooperation with the British, and he persuaded Nehru, president-elect of the next Congress session, to sign a manifesto agreeing to a round table conference which would frame a dominion status constitution for India. The assurances of the Viceroy, Irwin, that constitutional progress would be made in the direction of dominion status, led to a furore in England, and caused Irwin to qualify his statements. Congress then withdrew its support from the conference.

Gandhi now mobilized the people in peaceful protests, leading a march in opposition to the salt tax which in turn generated a large-scale campaign of civil disobedience. During the next five years Gandhi used the people's militancy to win negotiating concessions

24

from the British government. Between 1930 and 1932 round table conferences were begun in London, broke down and were reconstituted. Within Congress the left wing was gaining ground and disillusion with civil disobedience and legalism was growing, a tendency which Gandhi adroitly worked to contain. In England the 1935 Government of India Act was being formulated, a measure which accepted in principle the need to establish parliamentary institutions as India's form of government.

The challenge from their wards led some Anglo-Indians to question the British presence in India, but the dominant response of officials was to reaffirm even more belligerently the old basis for their power. Few new ideas were formulated, the Anglo-Indian creed was again intoned: the British had won India by the sword; British rule was impartial and efficient and ensured peace and prosperity for the mutually hostile peoples; British rule functioned in the interests of the masses, of the poor, the silent millions, the real India. Writing in 1911 Sir Andrew Fraser insisted that the people were concerned only about the just government which the British provided, and that anarchy and sedition were to be firmly suppressed so that the 'old principles of rectitude, firmness and sympathy might prevail'.[28] In the 1920s Sir Michael O'Dwyer* seemed unable to contemplate the possibility that Indians were questioning the Raj and declared that the discontent came solely from the Hindu intelligentsia who were anxious to exploit the masses in their own interests; the Indian people, from which he excluded the Western-educated middle class, had no political aspirations and were not interested in change.[29]

Sir Evan Maconochie† voiced his disgust at the India of the 1920s,

---

* O'Dwyer (1864–1940) joined the I.C.S. in 1885, served in the Punjab, Central India and Hyderabad and was Lieutenant-Governor of the Punjab from 1913 until 1919 when he retired. After his retirement he was active in journalism and the India Defence League opposing concessions to Indian political demands.

† Maconochie (1868–1927), who came from a family represented on both sides in the Indian Services, joined the I.C.S. in 1889. He was Under-Secretary in the Department of Revenue and Agriculture of the government of India from 1897 to 1900. Subsequently he was private secretary to the Maharajah of Mysore, Collector of a district in Bombay and agent to the Governor in Kathiawar. He retired in 1922.

filled as it was with racial and political feelings and disturbing for men 'connected with India for generations, accustomed to regard the Indian Service as their birthright and India as their second home'.[30] His statement of the British role was classical:

We have no need to apologise for our position in India or to adopt the attitude of humanitarian cranks, usually profoundly ignorant of the facts of history, who regard our Indian Empire as a crime, and while concentrating on the more questionable dealings of a less scrupulous age, ignore the rescue of hundreds of millions of their fellow men from chaotic misery and the peace and prosperity that we have established.[31]

Though in some ways more ironic than his fellow-officials, Sir Walter Lawrence* wholly identified with the anxieties which the changing situation brought to Anglo-Indians:

These splendid men working like slaves, their wives encouraging them, telling them that it was the greatest of England's missions and endeavours, well worth the exile, the separation from children, and the certainty of the scrapheap at an age when many are at their best – what must they feel in this strange new world, when they are told that they were all wrong and sinners against the new world Rousseau and his law of self-determination? Their mission was clear; it was to secure the welfare of the millions, to prevent corruption and tyranny, to prevent and to fight famine, plague and pestilence and to ensure that every Indian should have the free right to enjoy unmolested the rites and rules of his religion, his caste and his tribe.[32]

The most inflamed assertion of Britain's continuing right to rule India was made in 1924 in *The Lost Dominion*, which appeared under the pseudonym, Al. Carthill. The author was Bennet Christian Huntingdon Calcraft-Kennedy,† a high-ranking official in the

---

* Lawrence (1857–1940) joined the I.C.S. in 1879 and was posted initially to the Punjab. After six years in Kashmir, he served in the Secretariat, returning to England in 1894. In 1898 he returned to India as Curzon's private secretary, a post he retained until 1903. In 1905 he was Chief of Staff for the Indian tour of the Prince of Wales, after which he was for some years a member of the India Council.

† Calcraft-Kennedy (1871–1935) entered the I.C.S. in 1889 and went to India in 1891. He served as assistant-collector and magistrate and rose to be a judge; by the time of his retirement in 1926 he had served as Judicial Commissioner of

THE OFFICIAL CREED

Indian administration. Calcraft-Kennedy voices his loathing of the Indian character and makes a murderous attack on British left-wingers and humanitarians who opposed the Raj:

It was perhaps wrong to say of these extremists that they thought it a sin to kiss a white girl's mouth, and a virtue to kiss a black man's – foot. But it is perhaps no exaggeration to say that their humanity never slumbered save when an Englishman was murdered, or an Englishwoman violated by a Negro or an Asiatic.[33]

Deriding the British government for its readiness to abandon a valuable possession on moral grounds, he advises the government of India on what it should boldly have said in the face of Indian agitation:

Our mission is a high and holy mission. We are here to govern India as delegates of a Christian and civilized power. We are here as representatives of Christ and Caesar to maintain this land against Shiva and Khalifa. In that task we shall not falter, we will oppose ideal to ideal, force to force, constancy to assassination. We shall maintain the directorate and the chief executive in our own hands for the workman must have confidence in his tools. If you agitate, you will be punished; if you preach sedition, you will be imprisoned; if you assassinate, you will be hanged; if you rise, you will be shot down.[34]

Hypnotized by belief in their Messianic role or infatuated with vanity at wielding great power, Anglo-Indians expunged from their writings the material interests which Britain had in India and detached the idea of a mission from the complex and equivocal motives which had brought them to India and which were gratified in ruling over Indians.* It was, recalls Sir Walter Lawrence, 'a

---

Sind and as a High Court Judge in Bombay. In addition to *The Lost Dominion* he wrote, also under the pseudonym of Al. Carthill, *The Garden of Adonais: A Review of the Effects of British Rule in India* (1927) and *Madampur: Experiences of a District Officer in India* (1931), as well as polemics on the iniquities of liberalism. In the *Dictionary of Anonymous and Pseudonymous English Literature*, Vol. 6 (1932), Al. Carthill is identified as Sir John Perronet Thompson, another high-ranking government official, an error which was corrected in Vol. 9 (1962).

* 'The British Empire was not some mystical structure, rooted (according to one's taste) in geology or in metaphysics, above and beyond mundane matters of money, whose officials were devoid of self-interest. It reflected the social

27

splendid happy slavery. . . Looking back it seems a divine drudgery, and we all felt that the work was good. We were proud of it; we were knights-errant.'[35] Whatever the different temperaments and tastes of the men in the Indian Services there is a uniformity to their rhetoric when they are celebrating the great tradition to which they belonged. Writing in the late 1920s Sir Walter Lawrence declared that India remained the greatest and noblest field of British endeavour, that the glorious task of helping Indians to manage their own affairs was a far higher mission than had fallen to the lot of the British in the previous century.

After the war, the implementation of the Reforms and the activities of the Indian political movement made a career in the Indian Services less attractive. 'Retired officials visited the universities to encourage recruitment by painting idyllic pictures of Anglo-Indian life in some remote Punjab district in the late 'eighties,'[36] wrote Dennis Kincaid* who followed the family tradition in joining the I.C.S. During the 1930s two studies of the I.C.S. were written by retired civilians extolling the British achievement in India made possible by a small body of dedicated men and urging young men to choose a career in the Service because it continued to afford a splendid opportunity for doing valuable work.[37]

The times changed but the tradition of advertising the exceptional qualities nurtured in the Indian Services persisted, and the most interesting, because the most sophisticated, instance of this survival is Philip Mason's† *The Men who Ruled India*.[38] Published in 1953–4,

---

gradations of England, and repeated the assumptions accompanying them. The entire English connection with India, with all that had sprung from it, was the direct product of commercial imperialism. No reading of the record could make it otherwise, however much it irritated the civilian and military officers of the *Raj* to have this drawn to their attention.' A. P. Thornton, *Doctrines of Imperialism* (1965), p. 108.

* Dennis Kincaid (1905–37) joined the I.C.S. in 1928 and was assistant collector in Bombay. He wrote a number of novels about Indian life.

† Born in 1906 Mason joined the I.C.S. in 1927 and had a varied and distinguished career in the Service until his retirement in 1947. From its foundation in 1958 until 1969 Mason was Director of the Institute of Race Relations in London. He has written a number of books and essays on race attitudes and relations.

this study is distinguished from the turgid memoirs and expositions of most Anglo-Indians by Mason's irony and wit and by his disarming admission of the many foibles and failings of his heroes. Nevertheless, it is hagiography and as such it views the administrators as guardians of the Indian masses whose entire concern was dedicated to serving India. Yet Mason understood how convoluted were the white man's satisfactions in colonial situations. In his Foreword to the English translation of *Prospero and Caliban* he accepts Mannoni's thesis that the homage of dependants meets a psychological need in the colonial European:

M. Mannoni suggests that the colonial administrator, the missionary and the pioneer show themselves, by choosing a colonial career, particularly prone to this weakness, of which the germ is present in every member of a competitive society and flourishes with peculiar luxuriance in the warm broth of the colonial situation... Prospero at his best stands for many a man conscious of powers he cannot exert to the full among his peers, a magnificent leader among people who give him unquestioning homage and do not compete with his greatness. Livingstone springs to mind – but colonial history is full of them and none of us are quite free from the Prospero complex. I, at least, since I first read Mannoni, have caught myself again and again.[39]

The second volume of Mason's work on the British ruling caste in India includes the period in which he served as an administrator and is pervaded by the assumption that the civil servants were indeed Platonic guardians of the Indian millions. To reprimand for inconsistency a man who so patently understands the tangled web of human motivation and rationalization, not least when he is examining his own responses, would be impertinent. Yet in accepting the public image as identical with the private experience, Mason dissociates his insights into the behaviour of colonial rulers from his celebration of British virtue in India.*

* One wishes, too, for those layers of consciousness which Mason articulated in his novels about the British–Indian relationship – *Call the Next Witness* (1945) and *The Wild Sweet Witch* (1947) – where he tells of the sense of British displacement in India and the emotional suffering this brought. This is Mason's account of his hero, a District Magistrate: 'there came suddenly over him a despair of his work, a contempt for the sand of his daily ploughing, a baffled feel-

Certainly a career which demanded and encouraged independence was a large factor in attracting recruits into the Indian Services. But there were other spheres in which enterprise and responsibility were essential, yet few corporate bodies have written of themselves with quite the same self-congratulation as did the Indian Civil Service. It is because of this inflated self-regard couched in flatulent prose that one is bound to remark on how many Anglo-Indian officials were preoccupied with rank and advancement.* They were, indeed, no more than men doing a job, yet at a cost to themselves which did not ostensibly figure in their book-keeping but was sometimes buried in their recollections. Sensitive Anglo-Indians were uneasy about their position in India, sometimes even troubled by guilt, but one looks in vain for the clarity of vision and the moral decisiveness which led two servants of British Imperialism in other colonies to renounce their roles as imperial masters.

In his autobiography, Leonard Woolf, who was in the Ceylon Civil Service from 1904 until 1911, traces the development of his awareness from being 'an innocent, unconscious imperialist' slightly disconcerted by the atmosphere surrounding a ruling caste in a strange Asiatic country, to a full knowledge of what his position as a ruler over subject peoples entailed. With this came his first doubts as to 'whether I wanted to rule other people, to be an imperial proconsul'.[40] When he was falsely accused by a lawyer of whipping him in the street, an accusation readily believed by the people of

ing that he was on a surface beneath which he could not see, playing always with guesses to which he never knew the certainty. Passionately he longed for England; he wanted to deal with people who would say what they thought and who were not the slaves of passion and intrigue; he wanted to feel beneath his feet a soil that was friendly to him.' *Call the Next Witness*, p. 217.

* Sir Edward Wakefield, in his recollections *Past Imperative: My Life in India 1927–1947* (1966), writes entertainingly of the eccentricities and pettiness of some officials. When he was secretary to the Resident for the Punjab States he heard that the Resident was so concerned with his status that he had asked the author's predecessor to arrange for his washerwoman to have a stone above rather than below that used by the Commissioner's *dhobi* at the *ghat*. Wakefield, born in 1903, joined the I.C.S. in 1927 and transferred to the Political Department in 1930. He served in the Punjab, Rajputana, Kathiawar, Baluchistan, Central India and Tibet. In 1946 and 1947 he was Joint Secretary to the Political Department in Delhi. After his retirement in 1947 he entered British politics.

Jaffna, Woolf entertained the possibility that they were 'right in feeling that my sitting on a horse arrogantly in the main street of their town was as good as a slap in the face'.[41] By the time he re-signed, the prospect of the Europeanized life of Colombo and the 'dreary pomp and circumstance of imperial government, filled me with misgiving and disgust'.[42]

George Orwell was from 1922 until 1927 a member of the Imperial Police in Moulmein, Burma, where he was 'hated by large numbers of people'. He disliked his job, in which he saw 'the dirty work of Empire at close quarters', and had already made up his mind 'that imperialism was an evil thing'. His crucial moment came when he had to kill an elephant which had gone berserk and was threatening the villagers:

And it was at that moment, as I stood there with the rifle in my hands, that I first grasped the hollowness, the futility of the white man's dominion in the East. . . I perceived in this moment that when the white man turns tyrant it is his own freedom that he destroys. He becomes a sort of hollow, posing dummy, the conventionalized figure of a sahib.[43]

Anglo-Indian Attitudes

The British-born population of India in 1881 was about 100,000; in 1911 it was estimated as 123,000.[44] The 1931 census gave the number of Europeans as 168,000, of which 60,000 were in the army, 21,000 in business or private occupations and 12,000 in the civil services and other government employment. The presence of the civil and military officials set the tone of Anglo-Indian life but European society was not homogeneous and included merchants, planters, entrepreneurs, bankers, managers, agents for trading and shipping firms, commercial travellers, members of the professions, missionaries,* artisans, unskilled workers, soldiers, adventurers, remittance men and loafers.

'India is the paradise of the middle classes and the land of snobs,' wrote A. Claude Brown, a one-time editor of a Calcutta newspaper, the *Empress*, in a book which set out to present the viewpoint of the

---

* Missionaries, who came from Britain, France, Scandinavia, Germany and the United States, generally numbered about 5,000.

non-official community. 'One's occupation, not one's birth, breed-ing, education or even financial standing, determines one's place in the Indian scheme of things.'[45] In this hierarchy, government circles were the aristocracy, and civilian and military officials the *élite* to whose exclusive social set planters, business and professional men were admitted. There was, however, considerable prejudice towards the lower rungs of the commercial community, the 'box-wallahs', 'the untouchables of the white caste system of the Raj', as they have been described by Michael Malim who was employed by a trading company during the 1930s.[46] The division within the community observed by a visitor during the 1920s was that between the first-class people who went to the Club and called on each other, and the second-class people made up of European and Eurasian subordin-ates in various spheres who gathered at the Railway Institute.[47] It was with this group that the British troops mingled, sometimes tak-ing employment in India after leaving the Army and intermarrying with the second-class people, many of whom were permanent residents.[48] Within the upper stratum there were subtle gradations which appalled Sir Edward Wakefield when he arrived in India in 1927: 'never, I am sure, has there existed in England such an elaborate structure of class distinction as British exiles erected for themselves in up-country clubs in India'.[49]

But if Anglo-India was internally stratified it was united in main-taining caste *vis-à-vis* the peoples of India. White men in India con-tinued to patronize Indian prostitutes and keep Indian mistresses, but intermarriage with Indians and Eurasians had by the mid nineteenth century become a symptom of degeneration, and in popular fiction Eurasians were shown as debased and without dig-nity, as shrill and cringing, a warning against the mixing of the races. 'Going native' was an abandonment of true standards: 'The man who sinks to the level of the East is not the man for India, where he is expected to help to benefit and elevate its peoples,' declared Sir Andrew Fraser.[50] Sir Walter Lawrence, who regarded white loafers with greater worldliness, though he thought them to be on the whole a feckless, hopeless lot, observed that the vagrant was often a man of good family and education who had gone downhill: 'India suits him: he hates the strenuous life of the West. He is often a philosopher, a cynic, but he knows much that is hidden from us.'[51]

It was more difficult for Anglo-Indians to explain the behaviour of those few well-educated Englishmen and women of good family who adapted to Indian ways without taking to drink, drugs and debauchery. Such people, if mentioned at all, were dismissed as cranks: Annie Besant, a luminary in the Theosophist movement, settled in India and lived as a high-caste Indian in an esoteric community;* Margaret Noble, as Sister Nivedita, proselytized for Hinduism;† Madeleine Slade became a Hindu and Gandhi's intimate associate, taking the name of Mira Behn.‡

Anglo-Indians did not directly control the government of India and only a small minority settled there permanently, but if the community is considered as a diverse whole their position in India and their relationship to the Indian people approximates to that of white settlers in other British colonies.[52] The British went to India for many reasons, some to realize the ideal of service, others to follow a career, some hoping to save souls, others to amass a fortune, some to escape the intense competitiveness of the metropolitan society, others to play roles not available at home. Both for officials and for many in the commercial and plantation community, India offered a higher material standard of living than they would have enjoyed in Britain. Colin Cross in *The Fall of the British Empire* refers to the lavish terms of employment offered to Indian officials as the best available under the British Crown:

The young Civilian between the wars started on a salary of £540 (equivalent in 1968 values to about £1,600) rising by annual increments of £45. At the age of about 30, when he got a substantial appointment, he went up to a scale rising from £1,300 to £2,385. Every competent

* Annie Besant (1847–1933) was converted to Theosophy by Madam Blavatsky in 1893 and left to live in India in 1895. She was active in Indian politics as a propagandist and wrote many essays on Indian thought and custom. See Arthur H. Nethercot, *The Last Four Lives of Annie Besant* (1963).

† Sister Nivedita, who died in 1911, was a follower of Swami Vivekananda who established the Ramakrishna Mission in San Francisco. She wrote *The Web of Indian Life* (1904).

‡ See her autobiography, *The Spirit's Pilgrimage* (1960). An admiral's daughter, born in 1892, Mira Behn went to India in 1925.

official could rely on reaching this maximum and after 23 years' service he was entitled to a £1,000-a-year pension.[53]

The pay for officers in the Indian Army was higher than that in the British Army, starting at £500 a year, and because of this attracted those in the upper middle class who were without private means.

Apart from the material rewards, India for significant numbers meant a radical transformation of their social status. In a thinly fictionalized account of a visit to India by O. Douglas, *Olivia in India*, published in 1913, the author records her heroine's impressions of the position occupied by the first-class Europeans with whom she associated: 'Everybody in India is, more or less, somebody. It must be a very sad change to go home to England and be (comparatively) poor and shabby, and certainly obscure.'[54]* For all white men India brought promotion to membership of a master race. In the memoirs of Private Frank Richards, one of the very few accounts of life in India written by one in a lowly position, he tells of the harsh conditions borne by Tommies. But they too had their compensations and Richards, who gives advice on how best to beat natives without leaving evidence, tells of one soldier who assaulted an Indian servant for claiming to be his brother and equal.

Self-importance and specialized standards of excellence were bound to grow in colonial societies, fed by the lower material standards of the indigenous peoples and by their customs which to the European appeared bizarre and primitive. Thus the notoriously philistine Anglo-Indians – Sir Malcolm Darling† described a col-

* This did not prevent Anglo-Indians from publicizing their sacrifice, a tendency which A. Claude Brown deplored: 'Of course it is fashionable in most European circles throughout India to damn the country, and the life there, on all possible occasions. But, if the objections are dealt with quite honestly, it will be found in most cases that the life in England which is held up in regretful comparison with the life in India is not the life which individuals were used to in the days before they came out to India. . . The status of certain classes of Europeans goes up very considerably when they come to India.' *op. cit.*, pp. 37, 39.

† Born in 1880, Darling served in the I.C.S. from 1904 until 1940, holding various posts including that as Vice-Chancellor of Punjab University. He wrote a number of studies of the peasantry in the Punjab.

league as 'that *rara avis* in Anglo-India, a lover of books'[55] – blandly represented themselves as transmitters of a higher civilization. An aristocracy in India, the Anglo-Indians often felt themselves regarded as redundant men and quaint outsiders when they returned Home* and this feeling of relegation added to their insistence that the society which they had established for themselves in India was one of surpassing excellence. It is to this society with its corporate mentality and mythology that we now turn.[56]

In *Bound to Exile: The Victorians in India*, Michael Edwardes describes the various physical environments of Anglo-Indians. Calcutta, until 1911 the capital of British India and the most European of Indian cities, had a great number of lavishly furnished palatial houses built in the style of the classical mansion. Even the modest bungalows in the city were built with pillars. A feature of the Bombay bungalow was the wide veranda, 'its shady overhanging roof supported on low arches and open to the garden'.[57] Senior civilians of that city lived in stately-looking mansions. In Delhi, the style of European houses combined the Palladian pattern with elements borrowed from Moghul mansions and tombs – a large central chamber and a high domed roof. The houses of Madras 'were usually of one storey, with a flat roof and an elegant portico in the neo-classical style'.[58]

The sparsely furnished bungalows of the up-country stations were 'white-washed, and had columns holding up the projecting verandah ... their roofs were high and thatched... In the hot weather, the doorways would be filled in with grass curtains which, when doused with water, produced a slightly cooled breeze.'[59] The Anglo-Indian stations were situated a few miles from the Indian towns or settlements: 'A low wall surrounded each bungalow, enclosing what was known in the special language of Anglo-India as "the compound". Inside the compound, as well as the bungalow there was the servants'

---

* Commenting on the changing status of the community during the 1930s, Dennis Kincaid drew attention to their marked characteristics distinguishing them from other Englishmen: 'One may hazard that in the future the British in India may be less noticeable for their eccentricities, their conscious superiority, but it is extremely unlikely that anyone will ever mistake them for citizens of any nation but their own.' *op. cit.*, p. 292.

quarters, the stables, and a cow-house. There was also the garden, to which a great deal of attention was devoted.'[60]

The social life of the large cities and the hill stations – Simla, to which the government retired in the hot weather, was the principal of these – was centred around balls, private dances and dinners, theatres, concerts and gymkhanas. In up-country stations, community life revolved around the Club and the Regimental Mess. Here Anglo-Indians had to make their own entertainments and recreation was found in mild sport such as tennis and riding as well as in hunting game and pig-sticking, diversions which feature prominently in Anglo-Indian reminiscences.

Dennis Kincaid's account of the ceaseless round of entertainment during the Poona season in the early years of the century draws on notes supplied by his mother:*

While the ladies drove to the Gymkhana soon after tea, the gentlemen drove there straight from the office so as to be able to put in a full hour or two hours at tennis or croquet. Many of the ladies played croquet too, but others preferred to sit in the basket chairs in the veranda and sew. . . They would visit the Club library but would be unlikely to find any books there. It boasted of very few books and those were in constant demand. . . So they would content themselves with gossip about the last ball at Government House, the delinquencies of the servants, and the health of their children. And indeed, what else should they talk about? There were no theatres or cinemas and only an occasional concert.[61]

Night after night people attended each other's elaborately formal dinner parties, after which there would be music, guessing games and competitions.

Anglo-Indian hospitality and the European style of life to which they clung was made possible by the employment of armies of servants. Anglo-Indian writing devotes a good deal of attention to the servant problem: Maud Diver† in *The Englishwoman in India* considered them to be mostly excellent, though of course it was essential that children be protected from 'promiscuous intimacy'[62]

* Kincaid's father, Charles A. Kincaid, was a judge in Poona from 1905 to 1910 and again between 1913 and 1915. See *Forty-Four Years a Public Servant* (1934).

† For information on Maud Diver, see Chapter 2.

with them. The worst charges that could be brought against them as employees were uncleanliness and a propensity to petty theft and lies; but, she added, they were amazingly adaptable, compared favourably with their English counterparts and, if treated kindly, could be turned into devoted slaves, never demanding an evening out and rarely taking a holiday. O. Douglas quickly learned how to deal with servants: '*Lao* means "bring" and *jao* "go". You never say "please", and you learn the words in a cross tone – that is, if you really want to be an Anglo-Indian.'[63] She records with hilarity seeing a nice old globe-trotting lady having a cup of chocolate at Peliti's – the famous hotel at Simla – and insisting 'on sending on to see if the tikka-gharry wallah would like a cup!'[64]

A writer in the *Indian Planter's Gazette* inveighed against the iniquities of Indian servants – ' "the vasty deeps" of the duplicity, incompetence and general "cussedness" of the Aryan domestic. Dirty, plausible, extravagant, useless, provoking, incompetent and, in short, unspeakable' – and suggested that the benign government which yearly manufactures B.A.s, M.A.s and other alphabetical imitations of the cultured West might instead do 'something to help helpless Europeans towards securing a passable supply of fairly honest and capable domestics'.[65]

As late as 1937 Sir Edward Blunt, in a book written to explain the I.C.S. to the English and to recruit suitable young Englishmen into the service, gave this information on the domestic arrangements a young civilian would need to make:

He will have to provide himself with a bearer, who looks after his clothes and rules his household, and (if his bearer is a Hindu) also a Muhammedan table servant (kidmatgar) for no Hindu will wait at table except to serve drinks; a dhobi to wash his clothes, and a sweeper [who emptied and cleaned the latrines or where these existed looked after the lavatories]. When he sets up a house of his own, he will need more servants: a cook and possibly a bhishti, who fetches water; also a garden staff, consisting of a gardener (mali) and a coolie or two. If he is living in a place where electricity is not available, he will also need coolies to pull his fans (punkhas).

The young man would also require transport, 'and a horse involves two more servants: a groom (syce), and a grass cutter, though if he purchases two horses, one syce and two grass cutters should suffice'.[66]

In the large cities, the hill stations, the cantonments and the up-country stations, the hospitality of the British community, Anglo-Indians explained, was in marked contrast to the formality prevailing in England. India for the British, wrote Maud Diver, was the land of the open door: 'Englishmen and women are, as it were, members of one great family, aliens under one sky. Their social conditions have been handed down to them from the days when Indian service practically meant life-long banishment; and so long as they hold by these, India will be a pleasant and friendly land, even though it be a land of exile.'[67] Like Maud Diver, Sir Michael O'Dwyer was familiar with the Punjab and he recalled the breezy, friendly and optimistic social life which the Anglo-Indians enjoyed in the 1880s and 1890s. Also writing of the same period, Major-General L. C. Dunsterville* remembered that 'Lahore clung to the spacious ideas of hospitality that added so much to the charm of life in India in the old days'.[68]

Anglo-India came to be hailed by its members as a better society than the comparable one in England, and Sir Robert Baden-Powell† considered that the close intercourse between Europeans in the small cantonments nourished a form of friendliness and hospitality which could not be equalled in any other part of the world; because troubles came more often, home was far away and dangers were always close, there were stronger sympathies, more lasting friendships and greater personal pluck and self-sacrifice.[69] Sir Walter Lawrence praised the devotion amongst the white exiles and paid particular tribute to the memsahibs whose courage filled him with pride and admiration.

The discomforts of India are always detailed in Anglo-Indian writing. Maud Diver reminded her readers of the disease, wasps and mosquitoes, of the terrible monotony of life in the plains between

---

* Dunsterville (1865–1946), who served intermittently with the Indian Army, was the original of Kipling's Stalky.

† Baden-Powell (1857–1941) served with the Indian Army from 1876 until 1884 when his regiment left India. His Indian experiences contributed to his ideas about the Boy Scout Movement and one of the chapters in his Indian memoirs is called 'How India Develops Character'.

May and October, of lonely stations where five or six Englishmen and women were thrown together in a domestic existence which afforded few pleasures apart from riding. In this situation, the English had to fight 'daily battles against heat, dust, cholera, and that insidious inertia of soul and body that is the moral microbe of the East'.[70] Writing of his time as political agent to the Principality of Gujerat in the 1930s, Sir Edward Wakefield remembered the boredom which he and his wife endured in their leisure hours: 'In the evenings, lacking anything better to do, we would sit indoors watching lizards stalking their prey. Lack of exercise, the enervating climate and the absence of any social life had a depressing effect on both of us.'[71]

Melancholy was one of the principal ingredients of Anglo-Indian memoirs. 'The frivolities of life were made all the more piquant by not infrequent minor tragedies,' was Dunsterville's recollection,[72] one which he shared with Baden-Powell: 'there was in reality a deep import underlying our merriment. We worked hard, almost desperately, at theatricals and the like, fighting against the ennui which is the breeding ground of sickness.'[73] Many Englishmen and women died young in India, usually of disease, and thoughts of death perturbed Anglo-Indians, contributing to conceptions of their self-sacrificial calling. This is how Alan Butterworth* remembered the depressed spirits of his fellow-officials:

As June drew nigh we all, civilians and military, gathered together . . . to undergo our annual season of mourning . . . only too many of my European acquaintances in India have died by their own hands, and I do not remember a single case where a motive could be assigned; always the deed was done in response to the muttered promptings of that *nescio quid doloris* which lurks in our souls. . . At the foot of the hills is one of those little graveyards, more than sufficiently abundant, in which the dreams of youth have ended. For they are dedicated mainly to the young; subalterns and corporals and privates; the prey of Battle and Disease; humble and forgotten workers upon the vast, frail edifice of Empire.[74]

* Butterworth (1864–1937) joined the I.C.S. in 1883 and served in the Madras Presidency until 1918. Chapters III and XV on District Administration in Madras, 1818–57 and 1858–1918, in *The Cambridge History of India*, Vol. VI: *The Indian Empire*, were written by him.

The Anglo-Indians held it an achievement to survive India and certainly they did put up with discomforts which they could have avoided in England. However, in producing a literature of bombastic self-advertisement and cloying self-pity in which they featured as supermen, as marvels of efficiency and endurance, probity and moral excellence, they were not simply reporting on their existence but manufacturing their own legend and demanding adulation from the British at home. Critical judgements of the British in India came from various sources in England. At the turn of the century Liberal anti-imperialists condemned British assumptions and behaviour in India: writing in the *Contemporary Review* in 1899,[75] Robert Wallace, a Member of Parliament, dismissed the grand talk of a mission, dissociated himself from Liberal imperialists and reminded his readers that the conquest of Empire had involved injustice, tyranny, cruelty and fraud. He feared the detrimental influence on English life of those who returned after exercising despotism over conquered peoples, and considered the behaviour of the average reactionary Anglo-Indian to be offensive to any man of democratic spirit. Britain's imperial servants, he insisted, were not imparting civilization to their subjects; the conquered peoples would become civilized only when they expelled their masters.

Another contributor to the same journal, writing in 1908, claimed that British rule had brought little improvement in the material conditions of the masses and that this, together with educated Indians' hunger for power, lay at the root of Indian discontent. India's rulers gratified their pride and displayed the kindness of their hearts in being fathers to the people, caring for them and condescending to them: 'But to be a brother, to acknowledge their equality, and to share instead of bestowing rights – that he finds far harder.'[76]

In the 1930s left-wing radicals attacked the prejudice and ignorance of the men on the spot; Reginald Reynolds compared the neurosis of racial hatred in Anglo-Indians to the anti-Semitic complex of Fascist Germany.[77] In his book *Subject India*, H. N. Brailsford conceded that the civil servants were conscientious and hard-working but pointed out that 'they have evolved a routine as dilatory as it is exasperating in its lack of sympathy and imagination'.[78] The positive contributions had been imposed from above, 'they were not the fulfilment of this people's will. The people looked on passive and unmoved.'[79] He warned that, in the end, 'this conviction of the *Herrenvolk* which won India will as certainly lose it'.[80]*

The attack which a visitor of very moderate political views made against the British community in the 1920s centred on their deviating from what she considered the best British standards. Barbara Wingfield-Stratford reported that she found Anglo-Indians philistine and smug:

When one thinks of the unlimited possibilities life in India gives to those whose lot is cast there, the opportunities for artistic appreciation of some of nature's and man's most marvellous effects, for the study of one of the world's oldest civilizations, and for the better understanding of a very wonderful people, one is lost in astonishment at the apathy and unimaginativeness of the average Anglo-Indian, his insularity and supercilious contempt for all things Indian.[81]

British rule she considered undeniably just and tolerant, and the people of India prosperous and happy, but the rulers were lacking in sympathy for their wards. Nine out of ten Anglo-Indians, she had found, were obsessed with fanatical hatred and sneering contempt for Indians. Certainly the I.C.S. were a fine body of men; their integrity and ability were beyond question and they were just and fair in their official capacities. But they were saturated with prejudice against Indians, 'befogged by vague theories of prestige, secure in the certainty of their own superiority'.[82]

If we look back on how Anglo-Indians had traditionally depicted themselves, Barbara Wingfield-Stratford's protest that writers had been over-indulgent towards them becomes clear.

It is a true saying – one that should never be far from the minds of Englishwomen in India – that for the upholding of British prestige in the East, 'far more credit is due to the individual men and women who have carried out in their lives the loftiest conceptions of English truth and virtue, than to the collective wisdom of the office in Downing Street'.[83]

Thus Maud Diver quoting an unacknowledged source. Some years

* The analyses made by the Communist Party were principally concerned with Britain's imperialist exploitation of India and the development of social forces within Indian society, and paid little attention to Britain's imperial servants in India. See, for example, R. Palme Dutt, *India Today* (1940).

earlier Sir William Wilson Hunter in a signed review of Kipling's *Departmental Ditties* had written:

Besides the silly little world that disports itself throughout most of these ditties, there is another Anglo-Indian world which, for high aim and a certain steadfastness in effort after the personal interest in effort is well-nigh dead, has never had an equal in history. Some day a writer will arise – perhaps this young poet is the destined man – who will make that noble Anglo-Indian world known as it really is. It will then be seen by what a hard discipline of endurance our countrymen and countrywomen in India are trained to do England's greatest work on earth. Heat, solitude, anxiety, ill-health, the never-ending pain of separation from wife and child – these are the stern teachers who have schooled one generation of Anglo-Indian administrators after another to go on resolutely, if not hopefully, with their appointed task.[84]

The dissenters within Anglo-India were up against a powerful tradition and their criticisms are a measure of the breach between the rhetoric and the reality. Lieutenant-Colonel R. D. Osborn,[*] who as early as the 1880s favoured representative government for India, accused the Anglo-Indian administrators of perpetuating comforting legends on the mental incapacity of Indians and the excellence of the British government:

In the British Civilians whom we annually export to that country, we have (at least so our Anglo-Indian administrators assure us) struck upon a vein of human character, the like of which has never been witnessed in the world... It fits in with our indolence and our insular vanity to believe that we are conferring 'incalculable blessings' upon India when we appoint a certain number of quite commonplace Englishmen to be irresponsible despots over her... In India, no more than in England, is it possible for either rulers or subjects to flourish in the unhealthy and relaxing atmosphere of despotism.[85]

Henry Beveridge[†] was unhappy at his position as an alien ruler

---

[*] Osborn (1835–89) served for some twenty years in the Indian Army and fought during 1857. After retiring in 1877, he frequently contributed to journals on Indian affairs.

[†] Beveridge (1837–1929) served in the I.C.S. in Bengal from 1857 until 1893. He wrote a number of works on Indian history and was a frequent contributor to journals in India and England. His son and biographer suggests that his independent spirit antagonized his superiors and hindered his advancement in the service.

over people whom he felt hated British rule: 'every European in India is more or less in a false position. . . The longer you stay in the country, the more you will feel that at heart the natives fear and dislike us and that they look with suspicion on all our schemes, even when they are really for their benefit.'[86] He was sceptical of the British version of their motives in coming to India and though himself an agnostic respected the missionaries as 'the only Europeans who came to India for other purposes than to make a fortune or earn a livelihood'.[87] A letter to his wife written in 1884 complains of 'the vapidity of Anglo-Indian life' and 'the stupid talk of clubmen'.[88] Signing himself 'A Heretic', an anonymous Anglo-Indian made a biting attack on the official confession of faith of the English community in India, one of the articles being the belief that long residence in India qualified one for infallibly correct opinions relating to India and Indians.[89] In the same journal as this article appeared, the Reverend W. Bonnar, who had spent twenty-five years in India, criticized both the civil and military officers for being out of touch and out of sympathy with Indians.[90]

J. Chartres Molony,* who served in India between 1900 and 1925, was impatient of what he called Anglo-Indian cant:

As between English officials and educated Indians, relations were embittered by a widely read school of 'imperialist' fiction writers, whose method was to depict the Indian as *necessarily* incapable, and as *necessarily* inferior to the Englishman in qualities of energy, decision, and straightforwardness. Such writers were wont to join to a general depreciation of Indians a tactless exaltation of the 'fighting' at the expense of the 'educated' classes. Moreover, the 'martyr' attitude of the European was overdone. I have little patience with the pretence that the Englishman saves India every morning from plague, pestilence, battle and anarchy; or that immolated on the altar of humanitarianism, he spends body and soul in a thankless and ill-requited service.[91]

A kinder but equally detached appraisal of his colleagues was made by Sir Malcolm Darling:

I never felt completely at home with Anglo-Indians in general. With

* It has not been possible to find information about Molony other than what he provides in his memoir. He was Collector of a district in Madras and President of the Madras Municipal Corporation.

individuals it was different, and even in this early critical stage I realised what sterling qualities they had at their best. A letter of June 1906 describes them as robust, always practical, free and easy with each other, typically English in their love of activity and common sense, with a keen interest in the visible but with little or no imagination for what lay outside their surroundings. Independent, resourceful and capable of great endurance, they developed the qualities which the exacting daily Indian round required. But, says the letter, 'the softer virtues are needed too – now more than ever', by which I meant the qualities which, to quote Delphi's tribute to the Athenians, 'made gentle the life of the world'. Indeed they recalled Sparta rather than Athens.[92]

Sir Henry Cotton's* unusually frank autobiography,[93] in which he details damaging facts about himself, suggests the equivocal dispositions of Anglo-Indian officialdom and casts doubt on the unswerving probity of the administrators. As a young civilian, Cotton had been in charge of a district in Lower Bengal where he and his colleagues in the Services made friends with the indigo planters. Relations between planters and magistrates were delicate because of the way in which *ryots* working under contract on the plantations were treated, and the absolute impartiality which it was the first duty of the judicial officers to maintain was, Cotton stated, inevitably impaired through the social intimacy existing between planters and officials. At the height of his career in Assam Cotton's relations with the tea planters were cordial, even though he knew of the indentured labourers' plight; 'the coolie was bound down, not only by penalties under the law but by physical subjection to his employer, who, on a labourer attempting to run away, was empowered to seize him and bring him back to work'.[94] As his service was drawing to a close Cotton admitted that it was his 'inclination and interest to say nothing to disturb the existing harmony'.[95] However, the then Viceroy, Lord Curzon, asked him to examine relations between labourer and planter and was dissatisfied with Cotton's evasive replies. Encouraged by private letters from Curzon, Cotton

* Cotton (1845–1915) joined the I.C.S. in 1867. In 1896 he was appointed Chief Commissioner of Assam, a post he occupied until his retirement in 1902. He was President of the Indian National Congress in 1904 and Liberal M.P. in the British Parliament from 1906 until 1910.

proceeded to investigate the matter thoroughly, aware that he would not have dared to take action without Curzon's support because he was hobnobbing with the very men he was exposing. When the report was published the Anglo-Indian press launched a virulent attack on Cotton which, according to him, led Curzon to desert the cause. Realizing that the government would welcome his departure, Cotton resigned from the Service.

Despite these instances of self-criticism, the overwhelming tendency of Anglo-Indians was to believe absolutely in their own excellence and in that of their society's codes and customs and it was therefore inevitable that they would condemn Indians for deviating from these. Sir Robert Baden-Powell disapproved of Indians being treated as equals until they were fit to govern themselves, a skill they clearly lacked: 'In the training of the average Indian boy there is not as yet any discipline nor any attempt to inculcate in him a sense of honour, of fair play, of honesty, truth and self-discipline, and other attributes which go to make a reliable man of character.'[96] Less explicit in his account of Indian deficiencies, Sir Evan Maconochie, while denying any question of race superiority, explained that the difference between British and Indian was due to climate, environment and tradition and 'that is why the Empire grew up and we are still in India'.[97] In his speech to the Convocation of Calcutta University in 1905 Lord Curzon, who could conceive of Indians only as permanent wards of Britain because they lacked what he regarded as the basic attributes for self-rule, criticized the 'moral weakness' of Orientals:

I hope I am making no false or arrogant claim when I say that the highest ideal of truth is to a large extent a Western conception. I do not thereby claim that Europeans are universally or even generally truthful, still less do I mean that Asiatics deliberately or habitually deviate from truth. The one proposition would be absurd, and the other insulting. But undoubtedly truth took a higher place in the moral codes of the West before it had been similarly honoured in the East, where craftiness and diplomatic wile have always been held in much repute.[98]

It is interesting that even those who respected Indian norms followed the definitions of concepts laid down by the West, emphasizing the validity of other priorities but not examining the nature of

45

the idea itself. Henry Beveridge's comment, 'Truth and straight-for-wardness are not Oriental virtues and I fancy there will always be a secret preference in the Bengali mind for the milder virtues such as patience and charity',[99] is an instance of this tendency. Just how fundamental the evolution of Western attitudes has been in recent decades can be seen in the approach of a present-day psycho-analyst who involved himself with trying to understand India, for what Erik H. Erikson allows is that the basic notion of truth is con-ceived differently in the West and India.* Still the large-mindedness of some Anglo-Indians who had been schooled in their own tradi-tions should be acknowledged. J. Chartres Molony, who was doubtful of satisfactory social intercourse between persons 'whose opinions differ on almost every detail of social propriety ... until some genuine reconciliation of viewpoints can be effected', refused to sit in judgement on Indians and their beliefs. He was struck by the shallow and supercilious intolerance of a Christian hymn about the heathen in his blindness bowing down to wood and stone, and the large, wise tolerance of a line from Hindu scripture: 'Whosoever comes to Me, through whatsoever way I reach him; all men are struggling through paths which in the end lead to Me.'[100]

The physical and emotional separation of Anglo-India from Indians is a recurrent theme in Anglo-Indian writing. Basing his observations on notes supplied by his mother, Dennis Kincaid de-scribed the atmosphere at the end of a party in Poona in the early years of the century: 'A faint and murky glow came from the direc-tion of the teeming city, the Native Quarter, but that stirred little

---

* See *Gandhi's Truth: On the Origins of Militant Non-Violence* (1969): 'West-erners have "principles". Truth, for us, is the sum of what can be isolated and counted. It is what can be logically accounted for, what can be proved to have happened, or what you really mean at the moment when you say it, while keeping it somehow consistent with what you meant earlier or expect to say later. Devia-tion from such truth makes you a liar; and I have heard it said often enough that Indians, because truth means something different to them, are habitual liars. . . It is, therefore, important to note the baseline of truthfulness in India and to realize that such "principles" as *dharma*, *Artha*, *kama* and *Moksha* cannot be compared with Western principles in the sense that they provide categorical permissions or prohibitions. Rather they are forms of *immersion* in different orders of self-abandonment' (pp. 41–2).

interest in the departing guests. Few of them had ever driven through the streets of the city.'[101] Many were regretful of their ignorance: 'Nowhere in the world, so far as I am aware, certainly nowhere in the Western world, is it so possible and easy as in India for the stranger to dwell in a strange country, and yet so entirely apart from it,' wrote Molony,[102] and John Morris,* who served in a Gurkha Regiment from 1915 until 1930, admits that he left India having learned little about the people. During his time in India he acquired the habit of despising Indians, 'and as for the country, that marvellous kaleidoscope of ever-changing colours, it was merely a backdrop against which we existed in a manner that was made to resemble as closely as possible the life of an English country gentle-man in early Victorian England'.[103]

In some Anglo-Indians, arrogance forbade even the admission of ignorance. Condemning the Montagu–Chelmsford Reforms, Sir Michael O'Dwyer evoked the magic formula of knowing the true India:

They went astray because they did not understand the *real India* and what it wants – authority, justice and the power necessary to enforce them. They legislated only for the English-educated India, a minority of less than one per cent... Meantime the *real India* is steadily drifting away from the justice and authority to which it was so securely moored.[104]

Others who knew that their understanding of India and Indians was small were led to venture explanations in vague generalities:

Some Indians are curiously inconsequent and strangely influenced by trifles, or what seem to us trifles. Their ideas are often unrelated and in every brain there is a spacious religious compartment. This is reflected in their words and actions, and it is vain to expect that Indians will be impelled by the same motives as govern our conduct... No one can boast that he really knows and understands the Indians... As long as I shall live it will be the same contradiction, puzzle and paradox. Progress in

---

* Morris (b. 1895) joined the army in 1915 and served on the North-West Frontier. He travelled widely in the Far East and Africa. In 1934 he went to Cambridge and after taking his degree was for some years professor of English Literature in Tokyo. In 1966–7 he returned to India for six months; his impressions and responses helped him to assess his earlier years there.

one most unlikely quarter: reaction and confusion in another, where all seemed so hopeful. But the only conclusion I can arrive at is that, though there may be an outward and superficial change in the binding, the contents of the dark book, India, will remain the same.[105]

Lawrence believed that British bafflement about India could be solved by the loafers who knew things hidden from the administrators and 'could at times tell stories of the life of the bazaars and the views of villagers which were new and startling',[106] an idea advanced by Kipling and eagerly followed by other writers of fiction.

The most usual escape from dismay was to concentrate on accumulating facts and figures, and an exemplar of the administrative mind ranging over India can be seen in the memoirs of R. Carstairs, who retired in 1929 after serving in the I.C.S. for twenty-nine years.* Earnest about his duties as District Officer, diligent in amassing information about his district and the habits of his wards, Carstairs did make some important discoveries, one of which was the 'fearful advantage our system of Law Courts gave to the rich man over the poor'.[107] But when he served on the bench he realized that the people wore masks and afforded him no more than a globe-trotter's view. 'It took me a long time to get used to there being so many things that we did not know and could not find out. . . We live in the midst of mystery. . . My horizon was limited. I felt like a man wandering about with a dim lantern in the dark.'[108]

Officials tended to put the blame for muscular demonstrations of racial superiority on Europeans of low breeding and no education,[109] but soldiers and the rougher elements in the commercial community were not alone in accepting that assaults were a suitable way of chastising disobedient and impertinent natives. Nor was physical violence the only way in which Anglo-Indians gave vent to the virulence of their feelings for Indians. An anonymous 'Civilian' execrated the Indians as liars, cheats and criminally irresponsible.[110] A. Claude Brown, speaking for the unofficial community, offered these insights into the Indian mentality: 'The Indian mind is in-

* *The Little World of an Indian District Officer* (1912). It has not been possible to find any biographical information on Carstairs other than that which he provides in the book. He published his observations on his district in *A Plea for the Better Local Government of Bengal.*

herently imitative; I have yet to hear of a single invention which had its inception in India and was the child of an Indian brain. . . The Indian never really grows up; he remains a child all his life.'[111] The chewing of pan, the bargaining methods of traders, the fouling of streets, the megaphone voice, the lack of proportion, the primitive sense of humour, these and other characteristics set A. Claude Brown on edge and convinced him of the Indians' inherent inferiority, making him contemptuous of their absurd pride in the antiquity of their civilization: 'Ancient it undoubtedly is, but moth-eaten; and about as much use in the cross-currents of everyday life as Noah's Ark would be in the Atlantic.'[112] Emotional coarseness was more deviously expressed by Sir Michael O'Dwyer in recounting how he had made a 'fanatical mullah' apologize for calling him a cursed Kafir by ordering him to eat his words and 'put his *pugri* at my feet as an Oriental mark of repentance',[113] a method of teaching good manners which O'Dwyer, who guarded and asserted his European identity, claimed he had learned from Eastern custom.

When J. R. Ackerley was employed for a short period in the 1930s as private secretary to the Maharajah of Chhatarpur he found the deportment and conversations of the Anglo-Indians whom he met remarkable. One woman related how she had to get rid of a servant who had saved her from stepping on a deadly snake because he had done so by a means 'absolutely without precedent in India – he touched me! – he put his hand on my shoulder and pulled me back'.[114] The attitudes of Sir Robert Baden-Powell, who wrote about India as if it were a training-ground for British excellence and a vast, extravagantly stocked hunting reserve, are equally dubious. His recollections contain as much about Indian wild-life as Indian people and indeed the comments on them are interchangeable: 'To me an interesting item in India was the study of the natives themselves, and their variety is unlimited.'[115]*

The different sections of the Indian people attracted varied responses from the British. Anglo-Indians tended to find Moslems,

---

* Baden-Powell's use of 'niggers' to describe Indians is very rare in Anglo-Indian writing during the period discussed, though the authors of *Hobson-Jobson* have this to say: 'It is an old brutality of the Englishman in India to apply this title to the natives' (p. 625).

Sikhs and Rajputs, the 'fighting races', more congenial than the 'passive, supine' Hindus, and they infinitely preferred villagers to literate Indians. Sir Michael O'Dwyer, who actively disliked the urbanized Hindus, announced his affection for the sturdy Moslem land-owners, and A. Butterworth was delighted at the mosques he saw in the north, finding in them 'a quality of grace and cleanliness which is a distinguishing feature . . . and becomes a place of prayer so much better than the gloom and oily dirtiness of the Hindu temple'.[116] The correspondence and diaries of Sir James Dunlop Smith, who according to his editor had no sense of superiority towards Indians, has a reference to the difference he had noted between Rajputs and the 'oleaginous Babus'.[117] In these diaries are also extracts from letters he had received from Indians written in English and in a style which Smith found funny. In itself this may appear an innocent source of amusement but the omnipresent Anglo-Indian habit of deriding the interim style which western-educated Indians were evolving was a racist instinct against manners which they saw as a travesty of their own national characteristics.*

Officials were inclined to boast of the close and intimate friendships they enjoyed with members of traditional India; but these associations should be treated circumspectly in the light of the total response to India expressed by the claimants. J. Campbell Oman,† who believed that racial antipathies accentuated by political inequalities and religious exclusiveness placed insurmountable diffi-

---

* The colonial administrator's preference for the unsophisticated 'native' was explained by the Hon. W. G. A. Ormsby-Gore, Parliamentary Under-Secretary of State for the Colonies, during a visit to West Africa in 1926: 'The Englishman has an instinctive dislike of "assimilation". We like to keep our life distinct from other races, whether European or not. The more other people acquire our culture, our outlook, our social habits, very often the wider the gulf between us. We frequently get on better with people different from us, and we appreciate the differences more than the points we have in common.' Cmd 2744 (1926), p. 23.

† John Campbell Oman (1841–1911) was born in Calcutta, the son of a planter. He served in the Indian Public Works Department, 1866–77, was a professor in Government College, Lahore, from 1877 to 1897 and principal of the Sikh College in Amritsar, 1898–9. Author of books on Indian creeds and customs.

culties in the way of social intercourse between British and Indian, has a cynical comment on such friendships:

When one hears Sir Civilian Administrator, K.C.I.E., or General Sir Indian Army, K.C.S.I., speaking of his dear friends the Rajah of Racepore or Sirdar Polo Singh, we need not take their expressions literally but discount them freely, as being evidently tainted with that official *insincerity* (become second nature) which is engendered by and inseparable from the high position he holds or has held in his day.[118]

Indeed, those who wrote candid and self-critical accounts of their Indian days are at pains to confess that close and continuous official contact with Indians was not matched by social communication and that the latter had to be artificially contrived. To this admission Sir Edward Wakefield adds that he was glad that Indians were excluded from the up-country clubs which he knew because they were spared the humiliation of being treated as social inferiors.

In his story of the men who ruled India, Philip Mason offers an explanation for the racial exclusiveness of the British officials: 'The English Guardians certainly believed there was something in their composition that distinguished them from the people they ruled.'[119] As long as they only met with Indians who were not Westernized, relations were easy:

Between people so different there could be courtesy, kindliness and liking, there could be affection, but no dealing on equal terms. The relationship was paternal, accepted on both sides. It was fixed and settled, like caste; the district officer and his family were one kind of human being, the people of his district another. There was no thought of equality.[120]

Into this placid situation stepped the educated and Westernized Indian claiming equality, a shock to which the British officials could not easily adjust. Mason repeats the time-honoured British defence against intimacy with Indians – the difficulty in sharing a meal with either Hindus or Moslems because of their respective food taboos, and the unbridgeable gulf that must exist with people who keep their women segregated.

Such explanations leave too much unexplained. Why, for example, did the British in Calcutta fail to acknowledge the existence of the

cultivated Bengali community who were integrating into their patterns of living some of the mores of the West? Why should it have
been necessary for Sir Malcolm Darling to complain that after
arriving in India it took him a full year before he even found the
opportunity of talking with an educated Indian who was not also an
official? Why were a few individuals able to form human relations
with Indians?

In the corpus of British writing about India two accounts stand
out for the humane and supple attitudes expressed. Both E. M.
Forster and J. R. Ackerley took service for short periods as private
secretaries to Indian princes, Forster with the Maharajah of Dewas
Senior,[121] Ackerley with the Maharajah of Chhatarpur. Each responded to his environment in the expectation of discovering other
minds, other norms, and both were able to establish easy relationships with the Indians amongst whom they were living. They did
not like everything they met, they were often irritated, sometimes in
despair, but the tone of moral condemnation is absent even when
they felt inclined to pass stern judgements. Perhaps because both
men were critics of their own society, they were able to submit
themselves to experiencing India as an enlargement of their perceptions and understanding. Almost alone amongst accounts of living in
India in the years before independence it is possible to laugh with
them at what they found amusing and to share in their delight.

Cultural Incompatibility

The nature and extent of West-East interaction in the past century
is still being assessed by scholars whose interpretations differ radically. D. F. Pocock has suggested that it is a misapprehension to
assume that England was the dominant partner in the British-Indian
encounter and refers to the Indian 'impact upon European philoso-
phers and poets and upon religious and ethical points of view'.[122]
C. S. Venkatacher, on the other hand, maintains that the 'immense
output of scholarship on the studies of the past and of the contemporary history and civilization of Asia did not contribute to a
better understanding in Europe of the mind of Asia. The West
failed to bring about an effective interchange or a fruitful integration

of ideas, let alone a new synthesis. No significant two-way traffic of ideas developed.'[123]

In retrospect, it seems inevitable that the British, represented as they were by Anglo-Indians, would assimilate little from India's rich and varied cultures,[124] and that the ideas and life-styles of India would be uncongenial to a civilization in the process of revolutionizing the material environment and with it the estimate of man's relationship with the universe. While ethnographers, antiquarians, historians and administrators acquired information about India and its peoples, either as a disinterested scholarly pursuit or as a means of facilitating British rule, the application of Indian mores to existing ways of thought and value-systems was negligible.* By the mid nineteenth century racial exclusiveness had become an Anglo-Indian imperative† and the community clung tenaciously to the corporate character it had evolved, closing its ranks and attempting to protect its mind against the encroachment of India. This inflexibility was approved by an anonymous reviewer in a British quarterly:

It is in the religious atmosphere above all of India that the Englishman feels himself to be moving in a mysterious, unrealised world, and this feeling is of the essence of romance. He does well to resist the seduction which this atmosphere exercises upon those too curious about it. . . The English in India are wise to surround themselves, as far as they can, with English atmosphere, and to defend themselves from the magic of the land by sport, games, clubs and the chatter of fresh-imported girls, and by fairly regular attendance at Church. They are probably following the instincts of self-preservation; and certainly unless they remained themselves, they would not keep their Indian Empire.[125]

What then were the situations and temperaments which made the

---

* Amongst Anglo-Indians even dabbling in yoga and mysticism was rare. An exception was Francis Yeats-Brown who wrote two best-selling accounts of his Indian years, *Bengal Lancer* and *Lancer at Large* (1930 and 1936). Born in 1886 and educated at Sandhurst, Yeats-Brown served in the Indian Army from 1907 until 1925, was assistant editor of the *Spectator*, 1926–8, author of *Yoga Explained* (1937); he died in 1944.

† The eighteenth-century 'Indianization' of the British was limited to the adoption of Indian dress, food, rest-hours and concubines, habits which made life more comfortable but which did not necessarily mean the acceptance of Indian ideas and values.

British immune from any positive reshaping by India and which led them to recoil from an environment which they felt threatened all that was coherent, rational and healthy?

As rulers, the British were actors and initiators involved with India in a complicated but circumscribed relationship which defined the kind of knowledge they sought about their subjects and their society.[126] The counterpart to official involvement was private withdrawal and the British awareness of India was essentially that of non-participants in a social order which they formally dominated. Certainly India was changed under the British impact but not always in the ways forecast, just as it adhered to its own identity and extended it in a manner which had not been predicted. India herself determined what she would accept or reject from the West, and the more India evaded their authority and understanding, the more firmly did the British pronounce upon her inexorable nature. Of course, there were those who did approach Indian thought, institutions and conventions as expressions of an authentic civilization: Sir Alfred Lyall's commentaries on Indian religion and metaphysics[127] show his regard for the Indian philosophical achievement and it was not uncommon for commentators to recognize how totally the religious systems of the East were integrated with the social structure and how completely these satisfied the spiritual needs of the people.*

* Consider, for example, a review in the *Calcutta Review* (1880) by Thomas Edwardes, 'Christian Effort in India', where he condemns the myopia to which many missionaries were prone: 'Neither Buddhism, Hinduism nor Mohammedanism – religions which have more or less completely satisfied the spiritual needs and aspirations of millions of human beings of all ranks and ages, and which have accumulated around them the wildest extravagances of imagination and the grossest error and yet retain their hold on such a large proportion of humanity, – can be expected to fall asunder and evaporate at the touch of the Ithuriel spear of Christianity. These religions are part of the race characteristics of the peoples who possess them, and are worked into the very tissue of their lives, and interwoven with their traditions and history and all that a people hold dear, and, until events arise that shall materially alter the conditions of their existence, these historic faiths will retain their supremacy as living powers in the lives of their adherents' (pp. 766–7). Missionaries in their more sanguine moods prophesied that Hinduism was crumbling and were outraged when those whom they had supposed to be successful converts slipped off to watch 'the worst and vilest of all the Hindu festivals'. See *Report of Friends' Foreign Mission*

But it was more usual for the Anglo-Indians to join execration to their explanations of Indian beliefs and habits; even J. Campbell Oman, who was capable of ironic detachment from supercilious Western postures, so intruded his own opinions and moral preferences when interpreting India to the British public that denigration is indistinguishable from exegesis.

Oman was distressed by the 'primitive barbarism'[128] he saw in the burial practices of the Hindus and offended by the imagery and ideas of Hindu legends:

The total absence of beauty, either sentimental or artistic, from the legends and the ritual of Kali-ism, is not compensated by anything ennobling in the religion of the dread goddess in whom robbers and cutthroats recognise a congenial patroness. . . As for the battles these warrior goddesses fought with their giant opponents, they are such as only the wildest imagination could possibly have conceived. In Hindu legends one looks in vain for ordinary men and women. Only gods, superhuman monsters, and perhaps ascetic saints as fierce, unscrupulous, and powerful as the others, figure in the troubled pictures and dark creations of the mythmakers of India.[129]

The hazards of a gloss informed by the Western sensibility can best be seen if Oman's judgements are compared with Heinrich Zimmer's interpretation of Kali:

To us of the West – brought up under the shadow of the Gothic Cathedral, where the benign figure of the Blessed Mother, immaculate, is uncontaminated by the darker principle, the poison-brood of the serpent whose head she has come to crush, the hell-brood and the gargoyle-brood that swarms over the outer walls and up the spires – India's Mother, eternal India's horrific-beautiful, caressing-murdering symbolization of the totality of the worldcreating-destroying eating-eaten one, seems more than difficult to love. Nevertheless, we may learn from her Tantric philosophy and art, which unfold the rich Hegelian implications of her dialectic. Through these utterly disillusioned and yet world-affirming, profoundly living productions of the last great period of Indian creative

Association (1904). For accounts of missionary activities in India see Norman Goodall, *A History of the London Missionary Society, 1895–1945* (1954), and H. P. Thompson, *Into All Lands: A History of the Society for the Propagation of the Gospel in Foreign Parts, 1701–1950* (1951).

THE BRITISH–INDIAN ENCOUNTER

thought, the Goddess, in the fullness of her terrible beauty stands revealed to us. In the illuminations supplementary to the texts ... we too may discover – if we will pause – something that will speak to us of a wonder beyond beauty-and-ugliness, a peace balancing the terms of birth and death.[130]

When Anglo-Indians commented on the antithesis between West and East, praise of British norms and censure of the Indian system was implicit. That they thought Indian society irrational and corrupt without recognizing that the structures of that society were organic wholes containing contradictions and still providing social meanings, is a sign of the difficulty which faces those who are rooted in one culture when they encounter another.* It is a modern precaution to admit the handicap of cultural subjectivity when studying the traditions, institutions and sensibilities of foreign peoples and past epochs and it is this hazard which is specifically acknowledged by a contemporary scholar of Indian society:

It is widely recognized that the anthropologist describes a foreign society *with implicit reference to his own*: he 'translates' what he has observed and experienced, etc. It is clear that this process and the very rendering of any native concept involve a confrontation at least on the level of the personal *Erlebnis* and reflection. This double aspect, conceptual and empirical, makes the confrontation transcend the limitations of the two existing kinds of formal comparison. It would then seem that the problem of comparison could be solved in principle if only this confrontation were made articulate and explicit. What would this amount to? Nothing more and nothing less than expressing what is generally taken for granted, i.e. the social framework from which the anthropologist starts – his own.[131]

This formulation of the problem has central relevance to the mainstream of British commentary about India and Indians where

* In this connexion, the thoughts of the principal character in Hermann Hesse's *Steppenwolf* on the horrors of past ages are interesting: 'These horrors were really non-existent. A man of the Middle Ages would detest the whole mode of our present day life as something far more horrible and cruel, far more barbarous. Every age, every culture, every custom and tradition has its own character, its own weakness and strength, its beauties and cruelties; it accepts certain sufferings as matters of course, puts up patiently with certain evils.' (English translation, 1965, p. 28. First published 1927.)

the commentators did not recognize that their view was that of outsiders reacting to entities they did not fully understand and which
were often repugnant to their own tastes. This restriction was in part
due to the state of sociological knowledge and therefore of educated
awareness, but as important was the acceptance by the British in
India of the West as the highest form of life.* It was this pride of
race which stunted the receptivity of the British to thought and
behaviour which deviated from their own.

Yet, given the inhibitions of a community convinced of its own
superiority, real difficulties in identifying with the values and codes
of traditional India must exist for those nurtured in Western cultures
and accepting the Western outlook. When a present-day journalist
and writer describes his meeting with a naked adorer of the God
Vishnu, he does so with an added insight into his reactions but nonetheless in the archetypal Western fashion:

> I stood and stared at the sleeping man and did my best to make real
> the fact that we were of one species. Uneasily I assured myself that the
> difference between us was simply one of horse-power; I had commanded
> more of mechanical energy. The man opened his eyes and for a time
> which seemed very long we stared at each other: there was nothing I
> recognised in his eyes, not even curiosity or resentment and I suppose
> nothing he knew in mine. Had I known Tamil or he English it would
> have been the same. I knew from my morning in the temple among the
> hundred million gods of the Hindus that he could not have made me
> understand about the mark on his forehead, or I him about the pride in
> denial called humanism or stoicism.[132]

What are the sources of the estrangement known by relatively
tolerant men who were not Anglo-Indians?

The analysis of Goldsworthy Lowes Dickinson, don and writer,
who visited India in 1912–13 as holder of the Albert Kahn Travelling

---

* B. Cohn, *op. cit.*, observes that in the colonial society established by the
British in Benares, officials who made up the dominant class had gone out to
India when young and with an idealized view of their own society and culture,
an adolescent view which was arrested in India. 'It was to this idealized culture
that the British officials compared those segments of Indian culture with which
they came in contact. This comparison heightened the officials' sense of "moral
exile" and contributed to the separation of the British and the Indians' (p. 19).

Fellowship, attributed this to a deep chasm in fundamental pre-suppositions and goals, and his report, reprinted as *An Essay on the Civilisations of India, China and Japan*, measures his distance from the mind and sensibility of India:

> Hindu sculpture and architecture – I have examined it from North to South, and from East to West – is disquieting and terrible to the Western mind. It expresses the inexhaustible fertility, the ruthlessness, the irrationality of nature, never her beauty, her harmony, her adaptability to human needs. Man, in the Indian version, is a plaything and slave of natural forces, and only by ceasing to be man does he gain freedom and deliverance.[133]*

He found a real point of distinction between the Western belief that all effort ought to centre upon the process of living in real and significant time, and the Indian ideal, uncontaminated by Western culture, of the man who withdraws from the world to meditate and come into contact with the Universal. In India he saw 'a peculiar civilisation antithetical to that of the West . . . a religious consciousness which negates what is really the religious postulate of the West, that life in time is the real and important life'.[134] His attitude is summed up in his suggestion that 'the real antithesis is not between East and West, but between India and the rest of the world'.[135] Commenting on the clash and conflict between Anglo-Indians and Indians in a letter quoted by his biographer, E. M. Forster, Dickinson remarked:

> The barrier on both sides of incomprehension is almost impassable. I feel this incomprehension very strongly myself. Indian art, Indian religion, Indian society, is alien and unsympathetic to me. I have no sense of superiority about it, but one of estrangement. What indeed is there or can there be in common with the tradition of Greece and that of India?†

---

* cf. Zimmer's reading of a Shiva sculpture: 'Shiva contains and enacts all possible aspects of life, and his dance is a marvelous blending of opposites. The dance, like life itself, is a mixture of the terrific and the auspicious, a juxtaposition and unification of destruction, death and vital triumph. . . It is understood as expressive of the Divine, which in its totality comprises all the goods and evils, beauties and horrors, joys and agonies, of our phenomenal life' (*Myths and Symbols*, p. 174).

† *Goldsworthy Lowes Dickinson* (1934), p. 137. In defining the opposition

It would seem that the members of a culture which places man at the apex of the universe, which regards the evolution of the material environment as a valid goal and values evidence and discipline in thought, will tend to be repelled by the proliferation of styles, the casual disorder and the blurring of distinctions which seem to be the essence of India's nature, and Westernized Indians themselves have told of their alienation from India – consider the autobiographical writings of V. S. Naipaul,[136] Sasthi Brata[137] and Dom Moraes.[138] Perhaps the most explicit and severe explanation of Western hostility has been made by a Hindu writer, Nirad C. Chaudhuri, who until his middle years had not travelled outside his native land but had absorbed a great deal of the West's learning and some of its attitudes:

Intellectually, the European mind was outraged by the Hindu precisely in those three principles which were fundamental to its approach to life, and which it had been applying with ever greater strictness since the Renaissance: that of reason, that of order, and that of measure... To these men everything about these people appeared to be irrational, inconsistent, unholy and extravagant, also lush, awry, and hypertrophied beyond conception.[139]

But the Anglo-Indian reaction to India was not so firmly rooted in reason and nor was it rationally expressed. Despite the variety of traditions in India and the evolving life-styles, the British image of India was limited to a finite number of characteristics. Indians who by Western standards were educated and cultured, were ignored by the British residents, and few Englishmen had bothered to explore the sophisticated literature being written in Bengal since the end of the nineteenth century,* preferring to scoff at the greasy Babus and

between the intellectual traditions of the West and India, a contemporary American sociologist has suggested this difference: 'The former is open, empirical, experimental, as well as metaphysical. It is more cognitive than the Indian intellectual tradition; it seeks to discover hitherto unknown principles which govern the universe while the Indian intellectual traditions seek to attain a condition of fusion with the principle, already known, which governs the universe.' Edward Shils, 'The Intellectual between Tradition and Modernity: The Indian Situation', *Comparative Studies in Society and History* (1961), p. 22.

* This milieu was depicted in the writings of Rabindranath Tagore and Bankim Chandra Chatterji.

their ludicrous English. Those facets of Indian life, on the other hand, which lent themselves to obloquy were emphasized as the true and shameful India. When the Anglo-Indians inveighed against caste this was not because of a commitment to egalitarianism but because the system offended their belief that society should offer ways for ambitious and able men to change and improve their status,* a disposition not shared by their precursors in the eighteenth and early nineteenth centuries who found nothing incongruous in caste.[140]

But it was when the British sense of propriety and decency was shocked that the full range of their invective was summoned. The abhorrence of child-marriage, polygamy, purdah, erotic art, festivals which appeared lascivious and sexuality in religious ritual emphasizes that sexual mores represent the area of greatest sensitivity in cultural encounters. Further, the British in India were products of a milieu which publicly condemned sensuality as debasing, and the huge interest which Anglo-Indians took in the sexual conduct of Indians suggests that they attributed to them the erotic fancies and fantasies forbidden by their own society.

Moral outrage at the Indian failure to keep the sublime and the sensual apart could coexist with an obsessive interest in such meretricious unions. Consider J. Campbell Oman's account of the Hindu festival of Holi which he witnessed in the course of his researches into Indian customs:

Immediately behind the musicians was a young fellow on horseback, dressed up as a bridegroom, attended by rowdy companions, who sang, or rather shouted lustily, rhymes of flagrant indecency. As they sang and gesticulated in corybantic style, they addressed themselves pointedly to the occupants of the windows and balconies, aiming at them their ribald shafts of buffoonery and coarse indecencies, too gross for reproduction or description. . . The crowd surged on in a sort of intoxicated fanaticism of licentiousness. As hundreds passed along, other hundreds followed, equally bent on diffusing the moral contagion. . . 'Did you observe,' I

---

* The British conceived of caste as a rigidly immobile system. See M. N. Srinivas, *Caste in Modern India* (1962), where he shows that while pre-British India was a stationary society, there was upward and downward mobility in the caste system.

said to my companion, 'how that girl at the window opposite was listening to the obscene songs, and beating time with her fingers?' He nodded assent. 'Did you also,' I went on, 'note how the lad carried upon the arms of his companions indulged in a deliberate and shameless exposure of his person as he looked eagerly towards her window?' 'I did,' said the Hindu with a bland approving smile. 'I think she is an educated woman, for I saw a book in her hand.' 'A moral reader, no doubt!' I ventured to suggest. 'Perhaps so,' assented my friend with Eastern imperturbability, and a mind so steeped since childhood in the atmosphere of the Holi and similar joyous nature-festivals, as to be able to regard with vague, undefined *religious* approval the words we had heard, and the sights we had that day witnessed together from the pretty balcony in which we were seated. . . It is difficult for a non-Hindu to enter into the feelings and ideas of a people who call all things by their real names without euphemistic disguises, who use naked words to describe natural processes and functions, who while dreaming warm dreams of sexual gratification, love to speculate about the soul and the All-soul, till steeped in the mysticism and occultism of pantheistic philosophy, they revel in the orgies of the Holi festival, and make their gods partakers of their happiness, dwelling, while the licence of the Holi is still in their ears, 'on the devotional purity the grand festival of spring awakens in Hindu hearts' [this last phrase a quotation from a Hindu newspaper, *The Tribune*].[141]

In *The Underworld of India* Lieutenant-General Sir George MacMunn* assures his readers that every crime, perversion and curiosity of Eastern life has a parallel which might be found in the strange corners of the West, and that he has no wish to cast aspersions on the sidewalks of life nor on the people of India. He then proceeds to do just that; his approach to 'perversions' is rigid and moralistic, his attitude to Indians that they are perverts. His explorations of India's underworlds take him beyond the depressed castes to 'those devious ways of morals and of religious excitements that folk of higher degrees break away to, those strange subjugations of mind and body connected with Indian philosophies, the begging friars, the dancer and the courtesan, the temple prostitute male and

---

* MacMunn (1869–1952) served for many years in the Indian Army which he joined in 1888. In addition to novels and a study of the women in Kipling's writings, he wrote a number of books on the peoples of India and on Indian history.

female, the sodomites and sodomitesses'.[142] Much of the underground life of a nation, he explains, has to do with sex, and India
offers him a plethora of evidence.

It has been said that the continuation of the world, the procreation of
a body so that a soul may work out its *Karma*, is the absorbing duty of
man and woman in Hindu life ... anything and everything that deals
with sex, procreation, union and human passion is worshipped and glorified, and to the purer minds this is nothing but allegory, and is devoid of
grossness. But men and women are not pure, and to the lesser spirits and
minds the cults can be very lascivious. So much is this so, that equal
reverence is given to every manifestation of human amative concupiscence
and the temples think nothing of reverencing and displaying scenes not
only of homo-sexuality and its opposite, but even of bestiality... When
we come to the obscenities of perversion and bestiality the ground is not
covered by the aphorism, that what is not wrong in itself may be depicted
and spoken of without wrong. It is one of the great accusations of Brahminism both in the past and in the present that such excesses and abominations are not only permitted but encouraged; and the world as a whole
does not accept the excuse of imagery, allegory and warning that Hindu
philosophy urges in excuse.[143]

Amongst the most famous of the Hindu indecencies, MacMunn
continues, is the phallic temple of Jaganath. To approach the shrine
worshippers pass through a temple decorated with atrociously seductive carvings, 'and if need be are ministered to, *en route*, and purged of
worldly desire, by *devadasis*, the sacred temple dancing-girls and
lights o' loves'.[144] Perversion in India is mixed up with the religious
question: 'The story of the sacrifice to Kali shows an unsuspected
light on some depths in Indian character, while the horrors of
Dravidian religion cannot be too fully execrated.'[145]

In many Indian cities, MacMunn explains, there is a street of
male courtesans or rather eunuch-courtesans, 'who dressed as
women and farded as such, ply a strange, perverse and demoniacal
profession'.[146] Homosexuality is very rife in India:

While in the West homo-sexuality or pederasty is the sign of the
degenerate or mentally unstable, and accompanies the disappearance of
manliness and self-respect, in Asia, it is often the vice of the most resolute
characters... Unfortunately, the most in other respects reputable of

Eastern friends and conferencers may be so inclined, and it is the one hidden cause which stood in the past athwart frank friendship between Eastern and Western men, till all chance of the failing is ruled out.[147]

Again MacMunn returns to the horrors of bestiality which the Indian sensibility accepts:

In the description of the astounding indecency which to Western eyes the temples of Conjeveram, of Jaganath and The Black Pagoda offer, mention has been made of the bestiality recorded: the mingling of humans and animals in intimate embrace. . . The ancient religions did permit such terrible abominations, and India has always apparently been more openly acquainted with such matters than the rest of the world.[148]*

The reaction which Katherine Mayo's book *Mother India*, published in 1927, incited in Anglo-Indians and Englishmen discloses how large a part sexuality played in the British imaginings about India. The thesis of Miss Mayo, an American journalist who had spent a few months touring India, was this:

The whole pyramid of Indians' woes, material and spiritual – poverty, sickness, ignorance, political minority, melancholy, ineffectiveness, not forgetting that subconscious conviction of inferiority which he forever bares and advertises by his gnawing and imaginative alertness for social affronts – rests upon a rockbottom physical base. The base is simply, his manner of getting into the world and his sex-life thenceforward.[149]

Racial degeneration, Miss Mayo concluded, had occurred, not as Indians claimed because of poverty and exploitation, but through

* Beverley Nichols's record of a visit to India, *Verdict on India* (1944), also devotes much attention to the astonishing obscenity of phallic scenes in temples, the prevalence of homosexuality, *devadasis*, etc. A corrective to such earnest moral disapproval is J. R. Ackerley's wry description of a visit to a Shiva temple, in the company of Anglo-Indians: 'On the way Major Pomby warned us that one of the temples – and he described its exact position in the group – had some highly indecent sculptures on its walls. We must therefore keep clear of it, he said, in case the ladies followed us . . . one of the temples enshrined a gigantic black stone *lingam*. . . There was so much sculpture that I should certainly have missed the indecencies if Major Pomby had not been considerate enough to mention them; as it was, it took me a long time to locate them, but I found them at last, a long file of soldiers marching gaily along, and another smaller, more elaborate design which was frequently repeated. They were both sodomitic.' *Hindoo Holiday*, pp. 16–17, 17–18.

sexual indulgence; as a result, Indians were not fit to rule themselves. The book caused a stir in both India and England where it was attacked for reasons ranging from the inadequacy of her statistics to her unwarranted political conclusions; in both countries her pornographic depiction of Indians as a nation of sexual perverts was condemned. But there were other responses which laid bare the cesspool of British feelings about India. A reviewer writing in the *New Statesman*, 16 July 1927, found *Mother India*

a tremendous frontal attack upon the whole social system of India in all its aspects and by implication one of the most powerful defences of the British Raj that has ever been written... All who know anything of India are aware, of course, of the prime evils of Hinduism, of the horrors of the child marriage system, of the universality of sexual vice in its most extravagant forms, of the monstrously absurd brutalities of the caste system, of the filthy personal habits of even the most highly educated classes – which like the degradation of Hindu women, are unequalled even amongst the most primitive African or Australian savages – of the universal cruelty to animals, and of the equally universal prevalence of laziness, untruthfulness, cowardice and personal corruption which in the code of 'Mother India' are not recognized as faults at all.*

In defence of their hostility Anglo-Indians pointed to particular

---

* The review was entitled 'India As It Is'. The correspondence which followed included a letter from a retired member of the I.C.S., H. J. Maynard, deploring the review because he knew 'the simple, affectionate, much enduring people of India' (23 July 1927). Another correspondent, BM/PWMS, praised *Mother India*, a book he had not yet read, as revealing the whole truth about these 'degenerate and vicious people' to whom 'filth and holiness are almost synonymous terms', and declared that the British withdrawal would lead to anarchy because of the Indian character (30 July 1927). Although he was critical of Miss Mayo's book, Professor L. F. Rushbrook in the *Asiatic Review*, October 1927, considered it important for its fearless exposure of dysgenic customs in Indian life, a point previously made by Edward Thompson reviewing the book in the *Nation and Athenaeum* (30 July 1927). Referring to *Mother India* in his memoirs, Sir Claude H. Hill, whose career in the I.C.S. lasted from 1887 until 1920, concurred with her judgements on the Indian: 'Katherine Mayo has ... torn aside the veil behind which we have all, perhaps too silently, been carrying on our day-to-day work ... she has courageously exposed some of the fatal consequences following from customs almost universally embraced by orthodox Hindus.' *India: Stepmother* (1929), pp. 270, 271.

habits and beliefs as evidence that Indian society deviated from some human norm which they assumed as universally applicable.* But while the British seem to have found Hinduism uniquely repugnant, similar cultural-colonial attitudes extended to all non-white peoples over whom they ruled. Bearing in mind the British imperial posture of aloof superiority in all colonial situations, it is still important to try and estimate which particular expressions of Indian thought and existence disturbed them. In 'vast, stupefying India', where they seemed always recalled to the 'uncertainty of all things',[150] they met with some indefinable quality which they spoke of as a spell, or the call of the East or that elusive something, and which led writers of romances and memoirs into excesses of lush and bemused prose in an effort to express the ineffable: 'For no pen – not even the magic pen of a Kipling or a Mrs Steel – can convey to a mind unacquainted with the East the subtle atmosphere of India, the awful lifelessness of her vast dun-coloured Plains, the smells and sounds of her swarming cities, the majesty of her incomparable mountains, and the mystery that hangs over the lives and thoughts of her many peoples.'[151] Maud Diver was mistress of such writing, into which she poured reverence, sentimentality and self-pity, ingredients that did not always blend. No woman of intellect, moral feeling and power of sympathy, she asserts, could live in India without taking an interest in the country: 'The mysterious, compelling fascination of the East must, sooner or later, creep into her heart and dominate her imagination.'[152] Then she would 'reach past its surface strangeness and mystery, its unlikeness to her own world of thought and feeling, down to that stratum of humanity which lies at the root of all lives, and makes the wide world one'.[153] But in order to justify Anglo-Indian aloofness from Indians, Maud Diver quickly dropped to earth from these fanciful flights: 'To minds unacquainted with the East in all its unlovely actuality – its dust, heat, dirt, disease,

---

* British attitudes towards Indian institutions were not necessarily of late-nineteenth-century origin; Percival Spear in *The Nabobs*, describing the eighteenth century, writes of 'separation and disapproval without contempt' (p. 129), and G. Bearce in *British Attitudes Towards India, 1784–1858* (1961) analyses the spectrum of attitudes which included condemnation and distinguishes between the Orientalist's appreciation of Indian civilization and his approval.

and its all-pervading atmosphere of inertia – this lack of a common fellow-feeling may well appear strange and even reprehensible.'[154] This coexistence of awe and repugnance is a feature of Anglo-Indian efforts to describe the effect which India had on them.

Conditioned by the intellectual climate in which they had been reared to expect that phenomena would reveal their meanings when put to Western scrutiny, India's intractable but 'sublime' mystery was quite as unnerving to the British as was her acceptance of sensuality. Even when they professed a desire to understand and empathize, India somehow evaded them. Some took refuge in observing India as they would a frieze:

The unfailing interest of strange races, in number and variety beyond all Western experience, the daily spectacle of great religions and ancient social systems in being, the wide horizons of the plains, the awful grandeur of the hills, the high adventure of the frontier, the peaceful joys of life in camp, the solemn beauty of the relics of a venerable and historic past, the turmoil of the great commercial cities, the pageant of the seasons, the birds, the beasts, the fruits of the earth.[155]

Others disclosed their discomposure:

Here – at the mingling of the desert and the sown, where the vast plain of Panipat stirred to the first soft caress of the sacred Jummna, I received my first impression of the forces of evil in this strangely alluring country. Oft-times I was to experience this feeling in later years – but never with the same intensity. Never again did I know so surely that the place whereon I stood was haunted ground.[156]

Sir Walter Lawrence wrote of 'the illusion which is in the very air of India'* and recalled an odd experience of meeting a lovely woman while he was on the shores of a lake and of later being assured by the local inhabitants that no such lake existed: 'Hallucination? I do not think so. I have seen so much in India of what we in England would call the supernatural, that I have an open mind.'[157]

It is interesting that a childhood in India could spare the British that overpowering sense of alienation and confusion; Kipling comes immediately to mind and his experiences are confirmed by the

* In a television programme, 'Twilight of the Raj', November 1964, Malcolm Muggeridge, recalling his experience of India in the 1920s as an official in the Education Service, spoke of the sense of illusion which had engulfed him in India.

recollections of two other English writers, Jon and Rumer Godden, who spent five impressionable years in East Bengal (now East Pakistan) from 1914 until 1919:

Walking through the bazaar could start a whole tale of imaginings: what would it be like to be a Hindu and go worship in that temple where the priest was waving a little tray of lights in front of the god doll figures? What would it be like to be that family, father and sons, sitting on a mat spread in front of their hut?

'To their elders Indian music was simply a monotonous noise, to the young girls the throbbing tom-toms became almost like our own heart-beats'.[158] Why were so very few Englishmen able to make the imaginative leap to comprehend India in its own terms, to respond to her unique pulse of existence, her particular imaginative and intellectual creativity?

When Nehru wrote of his discovery of India he was finding his way through that same labyrinth which confronted and confounded the receptive Westerner trying to understand India:

India was in my blood and there was much in her that instinctively thrilled me. And yet I appreciated her almost as an alien critic, full of dislike for the present as well as for many of the relics of the past that I saw... India with all her infinite charm and variety began to grow upon me more and more, and yet the more I saw of her, the more I realized how very difficult it was for me or for anyone else to grasp the ideas she embodied. It was not her wide spaces that eluded me, or even her diversity, but some depth of soul which I could not fathom, though I had occasional and tantalizing glimpses of it. She was like some ancient palimpsest on which layer upon layer of thought and reverie had been inscribed, and yet no succeeding layer had completely hidden or erased what had been written previously. All of these existed in our conscious or subconscious selves, though we may not have been aware of them, and they had gone to build up the complex and mysterious personality of India... India is a geographical and economic entity, a cultural unity amidst diversity, a bundle of contradictions held together by strong but invisible threads. Overwhelmed again and again, her spirit was never conquered, and today when she appears the plaything of a proud conqueror, she remains un-subdued and unconquered. About her there is the elusive quality of a legend long ago; some enchantment seems to hold her mind. She is a myth and an idea, a dream and a vision, and yet very real and present and pervasive. There are terrifying glimpses of dark corridors which seem to lead back to primeval night, but also there is the fulness and warmth of day about her. Shameful and repellent she is occasionally perverse and obstinate, sometimes even a little hysteric, this lady with a past.[159]

Nehru's journey into India signposts the obstacles to Western understanding and empathy. Few Anglo-Indians came to grips with either the fundamental philosophical propositions or the religious temperament of India, yet in her customs, institutions and manners they sensed a profound and troubling strangeness. Zimmer has drawn attention to the way in which Indian myth 'opens before us an unfamiliar spectacle of space and throbs with an alien pulse of time'. In an account of the deeds of the God Vishnu in his Boar incarnation occurs

a casual reference to the cyclic recurrence of the great moments of myth. The boar, carrying on his arm the goddess Earth whom he is in the act of rescuing from the depths of the sea, passingly remarks to her:

'Every time I carry you this way . . .'

For the Western mind, which believes in single epoch-making, historical events (such as, for instance, the coming of Christ, or the emergence of certain decisive sets of ideals, or the long development of invention during the course of man's mastery of nature) this casual comment of the ageless god has a gently minimizing, annihilating effect. It vetoes conceptions of value that are intrinsic to our estimation of man, his life, his destiny and task.[160]

The vision of cosmic cycles and the blending of opposites, so integral to the Indian mind, fashioned a unique sensibility, making Indians seem opaque and misguided to those who conformed to the standards and presuppositions of the West, a mental barrier fortified by the colonial situation in which the British–Indian relationship existed and by an era of the West's confidence in itself. The response of the writer refuting in the *Edinburgh Review* of April 1885 Max Müller's assertion that Indian thought could provide a moral and religious corrective to the West, speaks of an arrogance which European intellectuals no longer express quite so blandly, even if they retain it. The *Rig-Veda*, the writer claims, reflects the inner child-life of the human spirit, and it would be grotesque to transplant things Eastern to the West, for that which in a child is beautiful, true and full of lessons, becomes not only unnatural but repulsive when adults play at it and pretend to be in earnest. His conclusion is that 'as regards all that is highest, India has not anything to teach us that we cannot learn far better in a quite other direction'.[161]

In the more fluid intellectual climate of the present day, where monolithic conceptions and absolute antitheses are increasingly mistrusted, it is possible for the paradox which India embodies to attract where once it dismayed. Already Indian philosophy is being rediscovered as yet one more source of ideas and perceptions, as one more therapy to unravel confusions: 'the primary concern – in striking contrast to the interests of the modern philosophies of the West – has always been, not information but transformation: a radical changing of man's nature and, therewith, a renovation of his understanding both of the outer world and of his own existence'.[162] To those members of a generation who are acutely conscious of perplexity and sceptical of the answers which their own traditions have offered to the enigmas of man's condition, Indian thought will surely seem a cornucopia of insights into the experience they are making for themselves. The wearing of beads and bells, the practice of yogic postures, the recitation of half-understood mantras, are easy to deride; still, they do signify a new receptivity to the East – even though it is a responsiveness filtered through life-styles being evolved in the United States by those seeking alternatives to the ethics and goals of their society – and if the searches of experimental youth lead them to discover qualities in India which were obscured to the British in their age of imperial power, then it could yet provide a symmetrical irony to the British–Indian encounter.

CHAPTER 2

The Romancers: Five Lady Novelists

'The Negro, then, is the white man's fear of himself.'[1]

Inscrutable India : Fantasy and Nightmare

A VAST number of novelettes with an Indian setting were written
between the 1890s and the 1920s by women authors of light fiction
who also wrote prolifically about life and love in England. Their
romances set in India were produced for the British at home and
abroad and were reviewed in the Anglo-Indian and the British
press.* In many, India is little more than an exotic backdrop to
tales of love and improbable adventures; in some the disastrous consequences of inter-racial unions are exposed, while others are presented as portrayals of Anglo-Indian life and the Indian Problem.
The novels to be discussed here are representative of the genre and
affinities between the five authors are immediately obvious. Indeed,
it is difficult to distinguish concept, style and texture of language, and
if Maud Diver's prodigious output is easily recognizable this is because her tone of pride in the British as a master-race is so strident.

With the exception of Miss Wylie these writers had lived in India
and, while they deal in superficialities and received opinions, their
fiction innocently reveals the sensations which India could evoke in
impressionable British people. The themes they repeatedly use point
to the way Anglo-Indians were haunted by Indian sensuality and
spirituality. Confronting an India of inscrutable and unthinkable
possibilities is upright, uncomplicated Anglo-India, its members
doing a grand job and doing it well, and if, as the British would
readily admit, they know little of the hidden secrets of the land over
which they rule, this is as well for their mental health and spiritual
cleanliness.

What appeared as a meretricious interlocking of sex and worship

* Reviews appeared, for example, in *The Times, Athenaeum, Graphic, Morning
Post, Scotsman, Queen* and *Spectator.*

in legend and the rites of some Hindu sects always attracted the shocked attention of Anglo-Indian writers; with these novelists it stimulated a corresponding extravagance in their portrayal of moral and emotional anarchy. In *Caste and Creed* Mrs F. E. F. Penny* gives this account of a festival celebrated in a Vishnu temple during which the worshippers are excited to fanaticism and madness, presenting a picture of 'seething, vital idolatry'.[2] The evidence of faith and awe is overwhelming: 'Can it all be useless? Some of it, be it even so little, must reach the Supreme Being whom the Christians worship through their Saviour. Yet the whole is so saturated with profanity and immorality, that it is difficult to believe that there can be any good in it.'[3] There were educated Indians who tried to pretend that all men worshipped the same God and that the differences lay only in ceremonial details, but the Hindu's religious observances are 'full of gross superstition and immoral practices which no educated man can accept'.[4] Mrs Penny derides the attempts of an Indian, Rutnam, to explain Hinduism to his half-English cousin Zelma:

How should she know that when Rutnam and his fellow-countrymen called upon the Great Preserver of the Universe, they cried, like the heathen of old, to a low, sensual god, the creation of their own diseased minds, and they appealed to him through his sensual acts, which were themselves sins against the natural laws of humanity and the divine laws of God?[5]

So polluted is Hinduism, she concludes, that reform of it is impossible.

In a later novel, *The Swami's Curse*, the same writer's febrile imaginings are fixed on what she conceives to be the rites of the Tantrics.† An ascetic of this sect has wild matted hair and a snake-

* Fanny Emily Farr Penny (died 1939). The daughter of a Reverend, she married in 1877 the Rev. Frank Penny, a chaplain in Madras. They lived in south India from 1877 until 1901. Mrs Penny wrote some forty-five novels, many of them set in India, as well as the text to *Southern India*, with paintings by Lady Lawley, where her descriptions and expositions are as mindless as the stuff of her fiction.

† The Tantric sect was a favourite target of Anglo-Indian writers, who ignoring, or ignorant of, the texts known as the Tantras which, according to a modern exponent, emphasize the 'identity of the Absolute and the phenomenal world when filtered through the experience of *sadhana*, i.e. contemplative exer-

like hand, 'a human claw, dry, cold, leathery and bloodless'; in his
eyes and those of his disciple 'burned the fire of mystics bordering
on insanity'.[6] An exegesis on the varieties of asceticism in India then
follows:

The saddhu of north India professes to kill all carnal desire by a rigid
abstention from indulgence and by the exercise of a self-denial that is
almost suicidal in its character. The saddhu of the south, the follower of
the Tantric cult, professes no austerities. He seeks to kill desire by an
unlimited indulgence which brings satiety and extinction of emotion. The
indulgence is enjoined by his so-called religion; and his depravity is
commended as a great virtue. It is a meritorious act on the part of the
ordinary worshipper to lend his aid to the saddhu in carrying out his
excesses.[7]

---

cises' and whose thought should be regarded as 'psycho-experimental speculation' (Agehananda Bharati, *The Tantric Tradition* (1965), pp. 18 and 15), concentrated on rites which to the average Western sensibility could appear as
bizarre. In discussing the Tantric and Saktic sects, i.e. those sects worshipping
feminine divinities, A. L. Basham writes: 'The tantric rites involved the breaking of all the usual taboos of Hinduism. Small groups of initiates met at night,
often in a temple or private house, but also frequently in a burning-ground,
among the bones of the dead. The group formed a circle, seated around the cir-
cumference of a large circular diagram . . . drawn on the ground. Though the
members of the circle might include brahmans and outcastes, there was no class
distinction at the ceremony – all were equal, and no ritual pollution occurred
from their contact. After regular evening worship, the propitiation of ghosts, and
other rites, the group would indulge in the five Ms [the translation of which is
alcoholic drink, meat, fish, symbolic hand gestures sometimes concretized as
roasted grain, and sexual intercourse]. The rites concluded with the worship
of the five elements, to which the five Ms mysteriously corresponded. Among
some tantric groups the last of the five Ms involved promiscuous copulation,
while the members of others brought their wives to the circle. With yet other
groups those rites which were reprehensible to orthodoxy were performed only
symbolically. The remarkable "black mass" of the tantric sects, whether in
Buddhism or Hinduism, became very popular in Eastern India in the late medieval
period. It is still sometimes practised, but quite without publicity, and it is
probable that with the growth of puritanism and rationalism the number of
tantric groups in India is now comparatively small.' *The Wonder That Was India*
(1967), p. 340. Appalled by the practices, no Anglo-Indian writer understood
the essential principle of the Tantric idea, which is 'that man . . . must rise
through and by means of nature, not by rejection of nature'. Heinrich Zimmer,
Philosophies of India (1967), p. 576.

Once his carnal desires have been controlled, the ascetic is thought to possess supernatural powers, and if the votary assists him in gratifying the five requisites – alcohol, meat, fish, grain and women – then evil spirits may be propitiated. In her efforts to draw her English-educated husband away from his British associates and back to the orthodox fold, a Hindu wife, Thiara, seeks the *sadhu*'s intercession with the powers of darkness. The seance is performed at night in a cemetery: 'It was the place of the dead, the deserted region of unnamed graves where corpses lay mouldering only a little below the surface of the ground.'[8] Sensing the disciple's lust – the *sadhu* himself is so saturated with sexual indulgence as to be impotent – Thiara flees from the creature and escapes by wrapping her sari around the drunken fiend.

In contrast to the depraved practices of dark India, Mrs Penny explains, the white race will commune with spirits only through white magic. In a cool climate seances take place amidst civilized surroundings,

a well-furnished room fitted luxuriously; velvet curtains, easy chairs, thick pile carpets on which the tread falls noiselessly, polished tables and glimmering mirrors. The men and women assembled for the seance are more or less cultivated human beings, whether they are believers or inquirers, and they seek communion with a harmless spiritual world, not an avowedly evil world. Their object, moreover, is to a great extent guileless.[9]

In India, however, it is malignant forces which are invoked; Thiara's flight from the disciple's vile embraces results in the curse intended for her husband's corrupters redounding on her own family. Small wonder then that the English heroines of such novels were innocent about India:

Heather knew nothing of how the people of India lived. Like most English girls who go out to their parents in the East, her eyes and ears were, unknown to herself, carefully guarded. She saw and heard nothing of the private life of the Hindu. There was no opportunity of knowing it. Even if it would have been presented to her with all its topsy-turvy morality, the inner intimate life would have been veiled and censored. There is so much in that life that cannot be explained to European ears.[10]

An exposé of this private Indian life is then provided: Savalu, whom the Anglo-Indians accept as a successfully Westernized man, has two wives, Thiara, who had been selected by his parents, and a beautiful young girl of his own choice. The atmosphere of the women's quarters in his household, as always in an orthodox home, is stale and overpowering. At his evening meal Savalu, naked to the waist and with a fine muslin cloth bound about his loins, eats alone, served by his second wife; and, despite his English education, he assiduously performs the *shradda* rites for the repose of his ancestors' souls, rituals which 'viewed with the eyes of the modern student of religious faith, seemed inconsequent and childish'.[11] Mrs Penny has now prepared the ground for showing that a cultured man like Savalu must reject his past and convert to Christianity: 'I long to cut myself loose from the domination, the tyranny of the purohit [priest]; the performance of rites that I know to be unworthy of my intelligence,'[12] he announces when appealing to a missionary. 'For a long time past I have been convinced that your religion is the best, the highest in its moral as well as its spiritual teaching.'[13]*

India as a place of vast mysteries and immense horrors is the composite theme of *East of Suez*, a collection of stories by Mrs Alice Perrin,† which suggests an obsession with sudden, violent death and sinister disasters. A civil servant sees a corpse being eaten by a crocodile and later when delirious with fever he stumbles into a weir and meets a like fate; a large grey rat kills a baby; an overworked official commits suicide by inhaling chloroform at the precise moment that his wife, who is undergoing an operation in England, dies under the anaesthetic. The diet of a man-eating tiger is the subject of one tale, the haunting of an Englishman by a jackal who had eaten the corpse of a fakir whom the man had killed, the theme of another. There is an account of an expectant mother who dies in

* This approval of Christian conversions is understandable in the daughter of a Reverend and the wife of a chaplain; it was not shared by the other novelists discussed in this chapter who stress rather the impossibility of true conversion because of the fatal attraction which Eastern customs have for Indians. Indeed, Mrs Penny herself makes this point in *The Rajah* and *Caste and Creed*.

† Alice Perrin (1867–1934) was the daughter of General J. I. Robinson of the Bengal Cavalry and wife of Charles Perrin, M.I.C.E., whom she married in 1886. Mrs Perrin spent some years in India when her husband was with the Indian Public Works. She wrote about twenty-five novels and a few collections of short stories many of which were set in India.

childbirth after the shock of a snake dropping onto her from the ceiling; shortly afterwards the baby dies and the bereaved father kills a snake who had taken to living in the child's grave, after which he goes mad; the devoted Indian servant who believes that the baby's soul had entered the slaughtered snake, dies of grief.

There are also two or three ghost stories and the regulation tale of India's weird ascetics, The Fakir's Island. Here the knowledgeable Captain Roberts assures Mona, a 'fair, fresh English girl',[14] who is amazed and revolted at what she hears and sees of Indians, that they are a wonderfully interesting people, the inheritors of a great civilization, a judicious claim which is immediately denied by the events which follow. The wilful Mona insists on visiting the Fakir's Island, a place usually shunned by Anglo-Indians, where she sees appalling sights: 'a group of almost nude priests passed close by, on their way to the river to bathe, staring boldly at the girl with fierce, blood-shot eyes. One of them whose body was smeared with ashes and whose hair, matted with tow, hung down to his feet, walked backwards as he gazed at Mona, muttering to himself.'[15] An ancient, loathsome fakir, with one arm withered to a stick and with nails growing through the palm of his other hand and protruding at the back, has with him a small humped cow with an extra tail dangling from its forehead, and from whose shoulder grows an additional leg, 'a very sacred animal, rendered still more holy by the cruel deformities that had been practised on it'.[16] The hordes of professional beggars are squalid, diseased and half-naked, some huge with elephantiasis, others rotting with leprosy, all covered with sores and whining for alms. When Mona and Captain Roberts drive the cringing crowd away, the fakir curses the girl, decreeing that she will lose her beauty, and indeed she is soon after stricken with smallpox. Physically she had not been touched but the very demeanour of the priest was an assault and the malediction of the fakir a violation on this pure young Englishwoman.

Mrs B. M. Croker's* account of an encounter between an

* Bithia Mary Croker, who died in 1920, was the daughter of a Reverend and the wife of Lieutenant-Colonel John Croker of the Royal Scots and the Royal Munster Fusiliers. She spent fourteen years in India and Burma. Of her many romances, twenty are set in India.

Englishwoman and an Indian is especially interesting because there are so few Indian characters in her books. The heroine, Juliet, who is gathering sticks for a fire while on a hike, comes across a neglected temple surrounded by numerous shrines:

It was a weird and dreadfully lonely spot – funereal, secret, ghostly. Its dark frowning walls, its solemn stillness, seemed to weigh upon her senses; she would tarry no longer. As she raised her eyes, her heart seemed about to jump from her breast. Silently as a shadow, a man had come out of the interior of the temple – a tall, emaciated, loathsome fakir. His hair, plastered with dirt, stood stiffly erect, like horns; his face and chest were daubed with wood ashes and of a bluish-white colour. From his unearthly white face gleamed a pair of devilish eyes that glowed like carbuncles. He was partly clothed in a panther's skin. In one hand he held the dripping carcase of a headless kid, and in the other an enormous sacrificial knife.[17]

When she realizes that the menacing figure approaching her is the mad fakir of whom tales are told, of how 'he haunted far away desolate shrines, and there, to make atonement, offered up human sacrifices',[18] she is naturally terrified. On seeing Juliet, he bursts into a 'low peal of demonical laughter',[19] but his plan to use the girl as a sacrifice is frustrated by the timely intervention of the hero. The language is familiar – loathsome religious mendicants whose appearance and manner suggest that they are acquainted with a depraved underworld, confront young and innocent white women, defiling them by their very presence. The covert sexual imagery and the intimations of violence as the corrupt beasts lust to ravish the wholesome maidens, suggest how the stuff of pornography can be present in trite and respectable novelettes, though in these the fiends are always routed and the heroines would be incapable of perversely enjoying their degradation.

A complementary motif is the attraction between the races, and here a suspicion that the very differences between people might make for sexual curiosity and excitement is overlaid with protestations that it is abhorrent to nature, a perversion. On hearing an Indian prince declare his love for an Englishwoman, the hero of Mrs Perrin's *The Anglo-Indians*, Clive Sommerton, experiences an 'almost maniacal antagonism, for unconsciously he was in the grip of that primitive sense of race admixture with a dark-skinned people – a repulsion arising from nature's tendency to breed upwards, not downwards'.[20] In defending racial purity the writer finds it necessary to justify the irrational, i.e. the maniacal antagonism, the unconscious grip of a primitive sense, by appeals to natural laws. Furthermore, she surrounds her case with an aura of science by suggesting that white peoples had attained their elevated status in accordance with an ascending evolutionary tendency which had selected them for promotion. When nature's intentions are violated, as they are in another of her novels, *The Stronger Claim*, the outcome is catastrophic. Paul Vereker, the son of a well-born English father and a feckless Eurasian mother, is doomed by these disparate racial ingredients to disintegration as a person, despite a sound British upbringing by his aristocratic relations. As a well-informed Anglo-Indian lady explains: 'The half-caste generally has all the drawbacks of both nations, and the virtues of neither, though I must say I don't think they are often vicious; they don't seem to have enough character for downright wickedness, but they are shifty and unreliable and have no enterprise.'[21]

These truths are demonstrated through the behaviour of Paul Vereker. A member of the I.C.S., and accepted as a peer by his colleagues, he betrays his inadequacies during religious disturbances; while the other officials act with firmness and authority to quell the riots, Paul vacillates and is killed by the fanatical crowd. To reiterate her conviction that the races should remain in their separate pens, Mrs Perrin states that, from the moment of his return to India, the East had 'claimed' Paul, and he dies calling to 'his gods' in Hindustani while the religious festival is in progress and the bells clang and the conches sound: 'in the atmosphere of the faith that by heritage was in his veins, Paul Vereker's spirit answered to the call of the gods'.[22]*

After her happy remarriage to a pure-blooded Englishman, his wife would recall Paul's 'strange green eyes that had spoken dumbly of the soul torn and tortured by the mingling of East and West; that had held in their depths the tired emotions of an ancient people – the

* The nonsense here is excessive as Paul's mother was Eurasian, a community which had severed the links with Hinduism.

tragic "something" that had drawn Paul Vereker to his fate'.[23] This fate turned out to be a merciful one because when Selma, his English wife, had learned of his mixed blood, she had been gripped by 'a sinister creeping dismay. She had suddenly recognized the same sense of antipathy that she had experienced when Mrs Goring's ayah had tried to assist her, and she realised slowly, strickenly, that in her husband's veins ran the blood of these dark people from whom she recoiled with involuntary aversion.'[24] Here Mrs Perrin's theories on racial antipathy are made more interesting by the introduction of concepts such as 'sinister' and 'creeping' with their connotations of the 'dark peoples' advancing on the citadel of white purity with intent to ravish. A procession of religious enthusiasts intensifies Selma's instinctive retreat from Indians:

> The fakirs were a hideous sight, and it was difficult to believe that some of them could be human; on most of their heads the hair was piled in masses, caked with mud that had been applied wet and allowed to dry; the bodies of the others were enwrapped with long tresses that hung over their shoulders down to the ground; their eyes were either fierce and fanatical or else held the remote, ascetic expression of those who are raised, almost to stupefaction, above earthly considerations.[25]

From this wonderful amalgam of sensations it would seem that Mrs Perrin was confused by the suspicion that Indians knew the secrets of both the world of beasts and the realm of spirits.

That the superior race must remain inviolable from contamination by Indians is a theme clamorously expounded by these writers. The young Eurasian women in their books are irresistible and destructive sirens to the innocent Englishmen whom they lure and enslave with pleasures only they are able to offer. One such girl, Rosita Fontaine, is said to be a 'deadly combination of several races – the flower of the old French noblesse – the pure blood of a proud Brahminee woman diluted with the strain of the bazaar'.[26] Her unstable disposition and turpitude of character, concealed beneath a pretty exterior, prove the hazards of inter-racial breeding, and the entire Eurasian community, sensual, loose in morals, and without backbone, are a living warning against mixed unions. Only by fleeing from the corrupting influence of India can a half-breed hope to find happiness, is Mrs

Penny's conclusion in *Caste and Creed*. The misalliance between a Scottish merchant and a Hindu woman has a dire outcome; not only does the wife revert to Hinduism despite her Christian conversion, but the daughter, Zelma, though educated in Scotland, where she had lived since early childhood, feels the call of her Eastern blood once she has returned to India as an adult. The conflict between her sunny European half and her native half, which is filled with shadows, is resolved only when she marries a kinsman and returns to live in Scotland far away from the temptations of India with its sensual gods and bizarre rites to which her half-heathen self had responded.

In another novel Mrs Penny hints at a mutual attraction between the English heroine Heather and the educated Hindu Savalu but rejects any possibility for lasting intimacy:

For the past century Englishwomen in the East have shown themselves capable of taking a deep interest in certain educated men of Indian birth. They have accorded them their friendship, a gift highly valued and duly appreciated. When the time has come for the parting of the ways, which is inevitable between the oriental and the exile from the west, the farewells have been made with real and lasting regret; for they have been without any hope of reunion in this life.[27]

These pompous phrases reveal the writer's belief that friendship from an Englishwoman given to an Indian is an immense condescension, and conceal her suspicion that social restraints are necessary to suppress sexual attraction between the races. In *The Rajah* Mrs Penny actually describes a growing love between an English girl, Delphine, and a young rajah who is attending an English university; they are saved once she sees him in his natural Indian surroundings where his regression to Eastern tastes and habits repels her and kills her love.

The saga* by Maud Diver† of a mixed marriage and its offspring

---

* *Lilamani* (1910), *Far to Seek* (1921) and *The Singer Passes* (1931).

† Maud Diver (1867–1945) was born in India. The daughter of Colonel C. H. T. Marshall of the Indian Army and the granddaughter of Lord Chief Baron Frederick Pollock, she married Lieutenant-Colonel Diver when he was a subaltern in the Indian Army. After settling in England in 1896 she began writing her many novels of Anglo-India and India and her accounts of British heroism in India.

is exceptional in that the marriage is successful and the son born to the Indian mother and English father grows up to be a noble and well-integrated person. But the individuals involved are exceptional. Lilamani, whose father Sir Lakshman Singh is a cultured man by Eastern and Western standards, is the deeply spiritual daughter of an ancient Rajput family. Sir Nevil Sinclair is an aristocrat and an artist who conquers his instinctive racialism only in his relations with his wife. Both Mrs Diver and Miss Wylie intimate that when a white man of class and quality comes to love an Indian woman this is because her superiority in beauty, spirituality and nobility is such as to raise her above the taint and squalor attaching to her people as a race. The assumption is a persistent one – that the black man or the Oriental, in order to establish his humanity in the eyes of the white man, must prove himself to be exceptional and not merely equal.

Lilamani, which is set in the 1890s, describes the courtship and early years of marriage. Mrs Diver is haunted by the repugnant concept of a 'half-breed' and of the daring proposition she is making in portraying a marriage between an Indian and an Englishman as desirable. She therefore has Sir Lakshman explain the special circumstances attending this particular union: 'She is of old Rajput family, of good birth and lineage, like yourself. In fact if you had not been her equal in that, I would never give consent,'[28] he tells Nevil Sinclair. 'Yet there is one thing not to be escaped. In spite of good blood on both sides those children must suffer the stigma of half-breed, which Nature herself is said to abhor.'[29] This statement makes Nevil wince and he asks why the stigma should be greater than if he were to marry a well-born Spaniard or Italian. Sir Lakshman agrees that it is a puzzling fact, especially as Indians are of Aryan stock, and since ideally the combination of the Western masculine and the Eastern feminine souls should produce fine results. 'Yet look how unsatisfactory are the mixed races created in India by such crossing', at which Nevil interrupts to remind him that in most cases this had been 'the wrong kind of crossing'.[30]*

---

* In *Far to Seek*, Roy Sinclair, the son, is repelled by the Eurasians he sees while he is in India: 'All that lot – the poor devils you despise – are usually made from the wrong sort of both races – in point of breeding, I mean' (p. 355).

The uniqueness of the union and its isolation from any general advocacy of inter-racial mixture through marriage, is repeatedly emphasized. Nevil is deeply in love with his wife but the idea of an Indian father-in-law continues to disturb him and a visit to Egypt leaves him uneasy: 'Hitherto he had seen the East through Lilamani's eyes, veiled and glorified by her idealism. Now he saw it in the fierce unsparing glare of its own sunlight.'[31] The knowledge that Egypt as part of the East calls to Lilamani and excites her, repels him and later, when the doctors recommend a further visit for the sake of her health, he confides to a friend his fear of Egypt, 'of that nameless alienation, and the struggle to win free of its insidious taint'.[32] For him, a visit to India is quite unthinkable and he pleads with his father-in-law that he is unable to give an explanation for this refusal. Thus for Sir Nevil Sinclair his marriage to the sensitive, spiritual and beautiful Lilamani who personifies the Indian ideal of wifely devotion and addresses her husband in elaborately formal phrases, is a single act divorced from his continuing sense of estrangement from all things Oriental. Lilamani is quite preposterously idealized by Mrs Diver; submission to her husband's desires is her fulfilment and she is shown as possessing the delicacy, grace and hieratic manners of some legendary heroines in Indian myth.

As if appalled at her own audacity, Mrs Diver further qualifies her approval of this marriage in the sequel, *Far to Seek*. The son Roy is now grown up and after Oxford tells his mother of his desire to visit India. This alarms her as she fears that he might come to love and marry an Indian girl and she impresses on him how disastrous it would be if the Sinclairs, an old family with roots deep in the English soil, were to have a further mixture of race. When in India Roy is attracted to Arina, his Oxford-educated Indian cousin, but two Anglo-Indians, Lance and Thea Desmond, the hero and heroine in other novels by Mrs Diver, contrive to separate them and prevent their marriage, and the author applauds their intervention. The Eurasians, 'the pathetic half and halfs who seemed to inhabit a racial no-man's-land',[33] fill Roy with distaste and he can recognize no affinity between himself and such people: 'He saw himself, rather, as of double caste, a fusion of the best in both races.'[34] After many vicissitudes Roy returns to England and marries an English girl who has long loved him. Renouncing his Indian ancestry, Roy invests the 'best' of this heritage, that is, spirituality, in a sturdy British future.

The taint and threat of India is most vividly realized in *The Daughter of Brahma*, a phantasmagoric novel written by Miss I. A. R. Wylie.* Published in 1912, shortly after a wave of agitation against British rule had expressed itself in the revival of obsolescent religious practices, the novel is a maelstrom of descriptions and happenings, 'a hideous fantasy of the brain',[35] a phrase the author uses to describe her hero's sensations at a critical moment. To their religious exercises, Miss Wylie believes, the Indians bring the fullest range of human desires and proclivities, and these include the descent to perversions and the flight to mysticism. Significantly, her picture of India was derived entirely from second-hand sources and her lurid imaginings are some indication of the European dream of India as a weird and mysterious place, primeval and licentious, evil and spiritual.

The novel is set in the Deccan during the first decade of the twentieth century. Here, without the knowledge of the obtuse British, ancient Vedic worship has been revived in the ruined temples and only the German professor who is researching into Indian religions realizes the significance and the danger:

> Do your clever friends come at midnight or at daybreak to the Temple of the Unknown? No, no, they are too clever for that. They know that the old Sakti rites are no more, and that Kali has ceased to ask blood as offering. So they come in the cool hours of the afternoon, and talk grave

* I. A. R. Wylie was born in Melbourne, Australia, in 1885 and died in 1959. She travelled extensively in Europe but never visited India and the only references to India in her autobiography, *My Life With George* (1940), are to her eating Indian food and to her friendship with an Anglo-Indian girl whom she had met while they were both at Cheltenham Ladies' College. Miss Wylie induced her father to allow her to join this friend for a year at a small finishing school at Karlsrühe in Germany. 'At the end of my first year Esme rejoined her parents in India but she left behind her enough sahibs, memsahibs, Bo-trees, ayahs and compounds to furnish me with all the necessary ingredients for an Anglo-Indian novel which I wrote when I was twenty-one' (p. 129). This novel, she adds, was very successful. *The Daughter of Brahma* was written a few years later when she was twenty-seven.

nonsense about dead religion and old civilizations and the progress of Christianity, and the dear God knows what else, until the very shadows mock at them. A mystery? Yes, it is a mystery. An empty sanctuary which at midnight belches out its hundreds, and at daybreak lies dead and silent.[36]

He is contemptuous of the sanguine official belief that Indian religious fanaticism is dead, scornful of the missionary efforts to convert the Hindu, and in the revival of ancient rites he sees a powder-cask and forecasts an explosion.

On the night of the hero's birth, some twenty years before the main action of the story, his father, an officer, had been killed by the temple Brahmans after he had stumbled on and witnessed their secret rituals. Twelve years later the boy, David Hurst, in his turn had accidentally seen a similar procession and had been captivated by a beautiful young girl of his own age who was being worshipped as a goddess. He had saved a young boy, Rama Pal, from being offered as a sacrifice to the gods and had brought him to the Anglo-Indian community where he had been brought up as a Christian by the missionaries. After being educated in England, David returns to India where his mother, a member of an old Anglo-Indian family, lives. His lame leg and his temperamental inability to enter into the hearty and strenuous Anglo-Indian existence make him a misfit. As Professor Heilig's assistant, he becomes absorbed in studying and observing Hindu customs and practices. In this way he again witnesses the secret Vedic rituals and sees the same beautiful girl, Sarasvati, now a woman, kneeling before the altar. Heilig explains her seeming deadness: 'She hears and sees us not. . . But also she sleeps not. Her soul is with Brahman, where there is no thought, no passion, no desire, only an endless contemplation.'[37] Sarasvati, he continues, had been selected and groomed as a divine daughter of the gods; her life is dedicated to the temple and this is the only existence she has ever known.

In the course of educating David, Professor Heilig reprimands him for referring to the worship as a vile devil's religion: 'Who are you to criticise a faith that dates its birth centuries before Christ, and taught mercy and love and truth, whilst the Jews still clamoured for a tooth for a tooth . . . that worshipped one Almighty God whilst your ancestors worshipped wooden idols?'[38] He explains that the devilry is nothing but 'the excrescence which grows on every religion'.[39]

This gesture to tolerant understanding plays no further part in the novel; indeed, it is precisely the diabolical excrescences which excite and preoccupy Miss Wylie. Her accounts of the rituals and of the impact these have on David are laden with epithets. In the temple dancers 'there was a suppressed, terrible violence . . . which appalled and fascinated':

David Hurst shivered, but the fear which possessed him was a new thing. Though he trembled, his blood was set on fire. He would have turned and fled, but he was held powerless by a mysterious fascination. There was frenzy in the air. It had its fierce source on the expressionless women's faces and in the dark eyes raised to the heavens in sombre, unfathomable contemplation. . . It was the spirit of the Horrible, yet mingled with the Sublime, and no man in that moment could have told whether it were God or the devil who had inspired the fantastic scene before him. It was lovely and hideous, like the faces of the dancing girls, who were not beautiful but transfigured by that same sinister, smothered passion; it intoxicated the senses and benumbed the mind; the order of things, purity, truth, mercy, were swept into a wild, shoreless sea; all thought, all humanity were lost.[40]

Despite its indulgence, there is something powerful in this passage, mirroring the writer's anarchy of emotion as her fascination with the scene clashes with her sense of propriety, obliging her to condemn as unseemly and immoral that which stimulates and excites her. The coexistence of the sublime and the sensual recurs in the juxtaposition of Sarasvati, her face expressing perfect innocence and ineffable sweetness, alongside the loathsome idol in the temple, 'a living fiend' with 'hideous features, distorted and animated by the flickering light', in whom 'cruelty, frenzy, devilment had built themselves a monument to all eternity'.[41] The temple Brahmans match the image of the god in the evil of their expressions. 'Evil', 'vile', 'fiendish', 'hideous', 'loathsome', are repeatedly used in accounts of the worship, described as a 'devil's orgy',[42] while the participants are dubbed a 'demon's army'[43] and their religion a 'soulless devil-worship'.[44] Licentiousness darkens the rites when

84

Sarasvati is symbolically given as a bride to the god Shiva while 'the cunning, sensual faces of the priests'[45] augur a less abstract consummation of marriage. The temple itself is a terrible place, with 'the vile and hideous reliefs upon the temple-pillars',[46] the note of evil in the priestly song and the 'sultry, ugly breath of Oriental passion'[47] permeating the atmosphere.

From this central theme of grotesque Hindu rites there are two tributaries: one is the seduction which this exercises over David Hurst, a man estranged from his own society. When as an adult he again finds Sarasvati, he is spellbound and sees the objects in the temple 'unconsciously – as details in some dream'.[48] His meeting with her and their declaration of love has a dream-like quality because she takes him to be Shiva her husband come to claim her and he feels that he has known and loved her all his life. He steals her from the temple and marries her and between them there is a 'mysterious bond' as she tells him that he has brought her 'out of loneliness, out of a long sleep full of shapeless dreams'.[49]

David, the misfit, the failure by Anglo-Indian standards, has turned away from his own people and has instinctively answered the call of India. But once he and Sarasvati have settled in England, where he has inherited a title and a stately home, there is a change. He becomes involved in the real world of politics and power, new possibilities for expressing himself are presented and his wife recedes from his consciousness: 'The dreams remained – faded unreal flowers of fancy, whose fragrance had been destroyed in the heat of battle.'[50]

The conflict is resolved when Sarasvati, misplaced and miserable in England, leaves him and returns to India. David Hurst had responded to the temptations offered by India, described by a wise judge as 'a woman all over – inscrutable, fascinating, dangerous';[51] and in accepting the real and worthwhile things in life, he had regained his equilibrium, realizing that his disaffection from Sarasvati had been inevitable: 'Was it not . . . the awakening of his abilities, stunted by the discouragement and his own diffidence, the natural desire to enter the world's lists and leave the unreal world of dreams behind him? The dreams had been a temporary refuge – a phase of his development.'[52] And so when Sarasvati is dead and he is about to marry a wholesome and uncomplicated English girl, he can serenely recall her as 'the mirror of his soul'.[53]

The other aspect of Indian religious fanaticism which is developed is the use to which it is put by political agitators. Rama Pal, the boy whom David had rescued, had been regarded by the missionaries as a successful conversion. In fact, he is bitterly resentful of the British, as he tells a cunning Brahman priest who is anxious to involve him in seditious activities: 'They took my gods from me – they took me from my people. They gave me a faith which their lives belie, and a brotherhood of bitterest humiliation. They made me an outcast.'[54] The priest is quick to detect the possibility of inflaming Rama Pal's hatred: 'They shot our fathers from the cannon's mouth. . . They tore from us the power and the wealth that was ours by heritage and right of conquest. They forced upon us their faith that we might serve them, bound by their slave's code.'[55] Rama Pal, he promises, shall go to England, imbibe Western learning and then return to 'help our mother to throw off her dishonouring shackles'.[56]

When in London, Rama Pal joins the conspirators, prominent amongst whom are a number of Chitpaven Brahmans. Miss Wylie's account approximates so closely to that given by Sir Valentine Chirol in his influential work, *Indian Unrest*,* as to suggest that she had drawn on this rather than on any independent investigation; the presence of a group of conspirators in London, the cold eyes of the Chitpaven Brahmans, their rallying cry that under Brahman rule India could attain a golden age freed from the British who had drained India of her wealth and undermined her religious and social institutions, these descriptions have been taken straight from Chirol. It is in what Miss Wylie makes of this information that her originality lies. In arousing the people to turn on their oppressors, the conspirators plan to use Sarasvati, the Daughter of Brahma, as their symbolic figure for she is the

---

* Chirol pointed out that there was amongst the Chitpaven Brahmans a strong tradition of hatred towards British rule and that many had been prominent in the violent agitation of the first decade of the twentieth century. From this able and powerful community of Deccani Brahmans came leaders with widely different political positions, such as Mahadev Govind Ranade, the pro-British leader, and Lal Gangadhar Tilak, the uncompromising antagonist of British rule.

one goddess in whom all India believes today. Their generation has seen her with their own eyes; if she were to appear again in the temple and call our people to arms in her name, the miracle would spread over India like a flame over dry stubble. No hand that could hold a sword would hang idle. The Englishmen and the traitor princes would be blotted out.[57]

Rama Pal, who, it emerges, is Sarasvati's brother (both were children of a temple priest), plays on Sarasvati's disappointment in her marriage and in the insensitive English who have snubbed and humiliated her. The veneer of European culture imposed on her by David peels away and she sees again with Oriental eyes, suffers with the Oriental's intense sensitiveness, burns 'with the Oriental's inherited stealthy passions of hatred and revenge'.[58] She returns to India with her brother, but at the moment when her manipulators intend to reveal her presence in order to spark off violence, she realizes what is at stake and declares that no life shall be destroyed in her name. Her brother kills her but because the people are stunned by the sight of the dead goddess on the altar the threat of bloodshed is averted.

Miss Wylie chastises the British for their hypocrisy, insensitivity and stupidity about Indians, but nonetheless they represent civilization, and it is the Oriental who is condemned for his inherited vices of barbarity, fanaticism and cruelty. European directness is contrasted with Eastern cunning[59] and Miss Wylie lingers salaciously over the 'queer and ugly things'[60] which happen in India and which escape the healthy minds of the British. Her hero's crisis she formulates as a natural response to all the horrors and evils inherent in India: when the people call to Sarasvati, David, who has followed her after her flight from England, feels that 'Here in this hell the name became a curse, conveying nothing to him but the idea of a diabolical force directed against his race and against civilization. The dreaming woman amongst the lotus-flowers was the personification of a bloodthirsty heathenism – of a religion replete with hideous cruelty.'[61]

This then is the India imagined by Miss Wylie in Europe, a country of unfathomable people, 'those natives constantly moving in the dark',[62] whose natures and proclivities can be glimpsed by the white man only if, like Professor Heilig, he goes amongst them in secret. Between the dark world and the Europeans there can be no lasting intimacy.

The love affairs of the British are presented by the Anglo-Indian romancers with the aseptic sentimentality common to the novelettes of that era, and procreation mysteriously follows the clasped hands and chaste kisses of fully-clothed bodies. But when Indians love or lust after whites the lacunae are kaleidoscopically filled. What fantasies inform the ethereal yet sensual passions of Lilamani and Sarasvati, the siren seductions of half-caste women, the smouldering appetites of Indian men? Assailed by such tainted thoughts, the ladies retreated to the safety of the wholesome British world.

A Herrenvolk in Exile

Apart from Maud Diver, the writers discussed in this chapter announced the excellence of British rule without providing exegesis; she, however, breaks into her narrative to preach and proclaim, to assert the indispensability of the Raj and champion British valour. One of her devices is to pour such praise from the lips of her good Indian characters: 'In my belief – and I am sharing it with scores of men better than myself – no worse harm could befall to India than that Great Britain should cease to be paramount power. But only this – in order for being paramount she must be, in the best sense, a *power*,' declares Sir Lakshman Singh.[63] In her trilogy about the men of the Frontier Force* Mrs Diver celebrates those Anglo-Saxon virtues which she sees brought to their apogee in the British as rulers of India: 'A pitiless country. . . A country that straightens the back and strings up nerves and muscle; where men learn to endure hardness, and carry their lives in their hands with cheerful unconcern, expecting and receiving small credit for either from those whose safety they ensure.'[64] This sonorous tone alternates with one of placid self-glorification:

The very air of Peshawur vibrates with lawlessness and unrest. Raids, murders, robberies are too much a part of the programme even to form a topic of conversation; and through it all the concentrated handful of

* *Captain Desmond, V.C., The Great Amulet* and *Desmond's Daughter* (1907, 1908 and 1916); revised and republished as *The Men of the Frontier Force* (1930).

Englishmen and women dance, drive and disport themselves; unconcerned, and for the most part wholly indifferent to the vast and varied
panorama in the midst of which they are constrained to spend the best
years of their lives.[65]

The choice of words like 'constrained' and the 'best years of their
lives' implies a preordained sacrifice to some high cause and suggests that Mrs Diver's statements are comprehensible only if they
are related to the myth of a stern destiny directing Anglo-Saxons to
rule over lesser peoples.

In *Desmond's Daughter*, the mature Colonel Wyndham tells the
young Vincent Leigh, who is contemplating a military career,

When all's said, the military virtues are the bed-rock virtues. And if
you have the sense to give soldiering a fair trial, you will find that it makes
larger all-round demands on a man's life and character than it is supposed
to do by those who know precious little about it. If you've the luck to
come in for a taste of the real thing, so much the better for you![66]

Vincent is guided to choose the 'stony path of courage'[67] and the
Colonel helps 'to ensure for him the hard, priceless privilege of
Frontier service'[68] in which Vincent is one of those who contributes
to keeping the peace and retaining the allegiance of the border
peoples. When the Afridis cheered Sir Theo Desmond, the com-
mander of the regiment, 'they honoured equally the race that breeds
such men; confirmed afresh, in their own unique fashion, the un-
questioned fact that England holds her supremacy in the East as
much by the power of the individual character as by the power of
the sword'.[69] This essential quality of the race, the 'readiness to take
a risk and face the consequences: a quality that breeds great mistakes, and, by the same token, great achievements too',[70] reaches its
apotheosis in Anglo-India. In the midst of the *hartals* and disorders
convulsing India in 1919 Roy Sinclair is reassured by the knowledge
that 'there were usually men on the spot who could be relied on, in
an emergency, to think and act and dare in accordance with the high
tradition of their race'.[71]

Service in India garnered its own mystique and those families who
traditionally sent their sons to India could claim possession of a
precious heritage: 'My grandfather was one of the men who made

India. . . My father was born out here, and is buried in Lucknow. My son will be born and will die out here, as I shall do. It is in the blood.' This is the proud declaration of David Hurst's mother in *The Daughter of Brahma*.[72] Of her character Mrs Fleetwood, Alice Perrin writes:

She herself came of a well-known Anglo-Indian family, whose sons for four generations had governed and soldiered, and distinguished themselves in various branches of Indian service, whose daughters came out to marry in the country, sending their children again to be soldiers, and civilians, and wives in the land where most of them were born and had spent their early childhood. Surely they are to be acclaimed, these time-honoured Indian families, inheritors of history, true to tradition, doing their duty without question, almost unconsciously, towards their great foster-mother India, often at the expense of health and home, sometimes of life itself, giving her their children to do likewise in their turn. Normal, self-reliant people, hall-marked with the hereditary faculty for work in exile.[73]

Maud Diver is the principal exponent of this cult; not only does she explicitly and repeatedly commend those families who are dedicated to serving India, but her trilogy traces the fortunes of the sons and daughters who constitute this tradition. How inexplicable then that this magnificent dominion should be challenged by the very people who were benefiting materially and morally from it. Mrs Diver presents the discontent and agitation against British rule as dangerous folly opposed by all thinking and responsible Indians, and in *Far to Seek* she provides her version of the 1919 disturbances. Through appeals to ancient Vedic worship and the adoration of the goddess Kali, the political movement which is demanding Home Rule gains support. An agitator deformed with hatred for the British arouses the people with the insidious cry: 'Shall the sacred Motherland be inoculated with Western poison? . . . Who kills the body kills naught. Thy concern is with action alone, never with results.'[74] Her thoughts on the secrets of India are far less febrile than those of her sister-romancers* and her preoccupation is rather

* She does, however, on numerous occasions describe practices such as animal sacrifices: in *The Great Amulet* a buffalo is forced to drown as part of a ritual; in *Candles in the Wind* a goat is ritually slaughtered; in *Far to Seek* the priests of Kali offer the goddess the severed head of a goat.

with the secular wickedness of those who are defying British rule
and the need for firmness in suppressing their attempts at rebellion.
She praises the Rowlatt Acts* as a courageous move by the authorities and her heroic Lance Desmond when breaking up a meeting
recommends with hard-won military wisdom: 'bullets not buck-
shot. . . It's the only argument for crowds. . . It takes a soldier of the
right sort to know just *when* a dash of cruelty is kindness, and the
reverse, in dealing with backward peoples, and crowds, of any colour,
are the backwardest people going.'[75] To save India from her wilder
elements, all agitation must be forcibly crushed and in this way 'the
letting in of the Jungle'[76] will be averted and the superlative British
permitted to exercise their natural function as rulers.

With complete absence of self-irony these writers hold up Anglo-
India for approbation as a society incorporating the highest attainments of the British people, indeed of the human race, and it is with
melancholy and innocent honesty that they lament how the cos-
mopolitan environment of Britain robs Anglo-Indians of the automatic superiority they acquired by ruling over Indians. Mrs Perrin
mourns for her characters' loss of rank once they return Home. A
retired official sees in London a civilian who had once held high
office in the Indian administration:

Logan was on a state elephant last time he saw him, going to open some
show or other – now here he was in a 'bus, squeezed up in a row of very
ordinary people, looking very ordinary himself, paying a penny for his
fare! Mr Fleetwood walked on, and all the time his heart was heavy with
a vague restlessness which he did not recognise as a tinge of nostalgia for
his old life, for the power, the purpose, the sun and the space.[77]

Once the exiles have returned to England's leaden skies and
yellow fogs, the splendour of India is vividly recalled, and the fine
and upright Anglo-Indians are favourably contrasted with the
snobbish and trivial people who constitute good English society.
After thirty-eight years in India one of Mrs Croker's characters
declares that she longs to return to the land where her best and

* The Rowlatt Acts of 1919, though never implemented, proposed allowing
judges to try political cases without juries and extended to provincial governments the powers already allowed to the centre of internment without trial.

happiest years had been spent, and that her husband, a retired colonel, is discontented with his long-awaited leisure: 'Yes, it was a sharp change to sink suddenly from being a person of considerable social importance, with a full life of many friends, into the role of an old fogey, with few acquaintances and nothing to do.'[78] The returned Anglo-Indians find social life in middle-class England exclusive and ungenerous and are nostalgic for the lavish community spirit of which they once were a part; the

friendly Indian life ... the social uniformity, the bond of common amusements and topics of interest. None of those difficulties existed in India that made life so complicated in England for those who had not the advantage of recognised family claims, or an assured monetary position. In India no English official people were wealthy, and the same recreations, the same meeting places were open to one and all.[79]

In claiming for Anglo-India a superiority in guts, endurance and generosity, these writers offered a spirited defence against their critics in England who accused them of frivolity, idleness and isolation from the country they served. An acclimatized lady tells a newcomer who is amazed at the apparent extravagance and lightheartedness of the community that certain standards are essential because of 'custom and prestige'; as to amusements,

what else have we to fall back upon but each other's society? We are all cut off from home and our relations and intellectual advantages; and wholesome exercise, whether tennis, riding, dancing or sport, cannot be classed as self-indulgence when it is well within our reach financially. The men work hard for the greater part of the day – perhaps you have not yet realised how much your husband gets through before he is free to follow the recreations that suit him best?[80]

Those who presume to judge the community without probing to detect that 'under the surface of muteness and officialdom' there lie 'the sturdy self-control, the patient and persistent driving force that have made the country what it is to-day'[81] are chastised by Mrs Diver. Some criticism she is willing to allow; she reprimands those who are deliberately rude to the natives and careless of their sensibilities and of a certain female type she writes scathingly: 'Both women were consumedly Anglo-Indian. All their values were social

– pay, promotion, prestige. All their lamentations were pitched in the same key – everything dearer, servants impossible, hospitality extinct with everyone saving and scraping to get Home. Both were deeply versed in bazaar prices and the sins of native servants.'[82] But the predominant theme in her writing is a paean in honour of the community whom she salutes as

> the little concentrated band of British men and women, pursuing their own ends; magnificently unmindful of alien eyes watching, speculating, misunderstanding at every turn; the whole heterogeneous mass drawn and held together by the universal love of hazard and sport, the spirit of competition without strife that is the cornerstone of British character and the British Empire.[83]

The Alien and Alluring

> I am truly sorry my information appears to be meagre, but the truth is that India – real India – is to the European a closed book. . . I have been out in the East for seven years, and I know precious little of the natives, although I speak their language. I was born there, too, and sent home as a kid. My father was a judge in the Punjaub for thirty years. Shall I tell you what he said? . . . That we Europeans are drops of oil on a great ocean of water, and will never penetrate or mix!

Thus an Indian Army officer in Mrs Croker's *Her Own People*.[84] It takes the singular situation of an English gentleman who has dropped out of his own society through drug addiction, to penetrate the meaning and mystery of India and its peoples.

In *The Company Servant*, Gojar, once the Honourable Algernon Craven, now a resident of the bazaar and living as an Indian, reveals his knowledge to the hero, boasting of the tales he could impart to Kipling:

> Lord, what copy! What amazing mysteries, what splendid deeds and horrors unbelievable I have witnessed! . . . I have drifted over India like a derelict for twenty long years. . . I tell you again that I have seen strange sights, and I've seen India; not merely its cities, tombs, temples, that the globe-trotter flashes through; not the trim military cantonments and hill stations – I know India under the skin – I have learned the patience, the repose, the stubborn intractability of the East. . . Yes, I've been down in

93

the slime of the bazaars . . . and through the opium dens in Calcutta and Rangoon. I've seen devil worship; I've witnessed the most hideous sacrifices – especially in the South, where the old gods die hard. . . Sacrifices for fertility. . . Long ago, the offerings made were human beings, and today, sometimes, in certain districts, such sacrifices are not unknown . . . I myself have seen the dead body of a handsome youth, who had been sacrificed to Kali; bled at the wrists and ankles, and disembowelled after the fashion of the ancient augurs. . . Once disguised as a native, I was present at the great annual festival at Vezwada. It was after sundown; many baskets of rice were contributed by the citizens to the sacrificial pile. On this pile a drove of buffaloes was killed by the Poojaris; the animals' heads were hacked off, the carcases carried away for food – all but one foreleg, which was placed in the brutes' mouths. Then two enormous carts were loaded with the red rice, and stacked with gruesome trophies; at the four corners of each were high iron stakes, on which were impaled alternately four live pigs, and four live lambs. The carts were led through the bazaars, the rice distributed by the Poojaris to be scattered over the land, and set before the next sundown. The scene was horrible; I shall never forget the hideous procession, the maddening tom-toms, the blare of horns, the frantic crowds, and the flaring torches illuminating the red dripping carts, with their writhing, shrieking victims.[85]

If this is the real India excoriated, then the British are wise to follow their instinctive recoil from any form of intimacy with its peoples.

About the Anglo-Indians' determination to hold themselves aloof from India, Maud Diver expresses an ambivalent attitude, deploring the tendency of the British to leave Indians to 'live their unknown lives apart'[86] from their rulers and applauding those who make the effort to become well-informed: 'It is one of the first facts that strikes an outsider, or a newcomer, – this frank detachment of the average Anglo-Indian from the country and its peoples. That there are exceptions goes without saying; and it is always the exceptions that count. In India's case, they are the foundation stones of Empire.'[87] Yet while Mrs Diver expresses her admiration for the hardy warlike border tribesmen and for the proud and 'spiritual' Rajputs, the tenor of her writings – her emphasis on the master-race qualities of the British, and conversely on the ineptitude, which she calls the feminine nature, of the Indians – is to vindicate Anglo-Indian isolation from India. In *The Englishwoman in India* her defence of this self-imposed isolation is more aggressive when she explains why it is that only a small minority come into direct touch with the lives of their Aryan brethren: 'To minds unacquainted with the East in all its unlovely actuality – its dust, heat, dirt, disease, and its all-pervading atmosphere of inertia – this lack of a common fellow-feeling may well appear strange, and even reprehensible.'[88] The fault then lies in India, and when Mrs Diver regrets the blindness which her hero Roy Sinclair calls 'the strange detachment of Anglo-Indians in general, from a land full of such vast and varied interests, lying at the very door',[89] it is not unfettered involvement she is advocating but academic acquaintance. As the wise judge in Miss Wylie's *The Daughter of Brahma* says, 'Queer and ugly things happen in India – things we Europeans never get to see, although we pretend to see everything. As a matter of fact, we never have and never shall, get to the bottom of the country we govern, and so we can always expect to have our theories upset.'[90]

Because none of these writers was able to portray an Indian remotely recognizable as derived from a human being, it is the commentary which is more revealing than the cardboard figures they move across their pages. 'The disposition of the Hindus of the south is marked by cheerfulness and placidity of temperament. All they ask is to be left in peace to pursue their ways. At the same time they are capable of being stirred if the agitator is let loose among them,' declares Mrs Penny.[91] 'Orientals do not always conceal their feelings as is commonly supposed. Amusement they will hide politely, for their sense of humour is not strong enough to overcome their natural good manners; but disappointment, vexation, anger they will betray involuntarily in their expression,' Mrs Perrin explains.[92] Behind their bland pronouncements is the claim that they are interpreting the Indian psyche and implicit in them is a justification for rejecting Indians as companions. In *The Anglo-Indians*, Mrs Perrin tells of an Indian prince who believed that self-indulgence was the right and prerogative of princely rank: 'he regarded interference with his inclinations as an insult to the dignity of his calling. But in this he only thought and felt according to the immemorial preceptions of the East; it could scarcely be condemned as an individual failing.'[93] At the suggestion of the Resident, a British officer had been employed to 'inculcate British notions of manliness and self-control into a being whose tendencies had been fostered in an opposite direction'.[94] Fay Fleetwood, the heroine, has a benign effect on this young heir to the spirit of despotism. She extracts from him the promise that, when he becomes ruler, he will be kind, just and unselfish. But the British influences lead only to conflict as he is torn between what he has inherited and what he is being taught: 'Why was I not let alone! . . . Why was I shown a different side to everything, so making me unsatisfied with the ways and customs of my ancestors! Why should desires have been put into my heart, when at the same time I am forbidden to fulfil them?'[95]

India rather frightens me . . . and yet I get fits of fascination that make me feel as if the country has bewitched me. It all seems so old and cruel, and yet so alluring. I felt the spell of it this evening on the river, and still more strongly when we were waiting in the bazaar for the procession to pass. That big city, full of people we really know nothing about, with all sorts of weird things happening in it that we never hear of. I think the bazaar is quite wonderful.[96]

Fright, fascination, allure, cruelty, weird – the turmoil concealed beneath the confident deportment of the Anglo-Indian writers is striking. In this curious novel, *The Woman in the Bazaar*, the bazaar is a metaphor for pleasure and vice, the repository of India's corruptions drawing weak white men and women into its vile embrace. The climax of Mrs Perrin's revelations shows the hero's ex-wife, once the sheltered daughter of a vicar, 'in her native dress and tinselled veil' emerging from the 'worm-eaten door' of a house in the bazaar to enter a clumsy, scarlet-hooded vehicle belonging to Babu Chandra Das, the current buyer of her favours.*

What then is the content of the love which the characters in Anglo-Indian romances declare for India? Because the British could not come to terms with Indians as a human community they found solace in India as a place of glorious scenery, of bright colours,

* Mrs Croker, too, makes frequent references to the insidious lure of the bazaars, corrupting Europeans who sink to the level of natives and forget their own speech and people.

wonderful sounds and fascinating scents. 'She could have cried with this strange emotion that came to her always when, as she tried to express it to herself, she was "alone with India." It moved her when she watched the dawn rise over the hills; at evening in the plains when she saw the sun set red behind the palm stems.'[97] Such is Fay Fleetwood's passion for India in *The Anglo-Indians*. Once she has returned to England, 'the sights and sounds and perfumes of India were with her in her memory night and day'[98] and pictures of India crowd through her mind: 'A sun-soaked bazaar, humming with the deep, sonorous murmur of voices, full of lazy movements, of excess colour, and trivial happenings; a scene so alluring despite the dust and the dirt and the flies, pervaded with that strange admixture of odours – the indescribable smell of the East, revolting yet attractive.'[99]

In sonorous and obscure terms Maud Diver gropes towards the source of India's fascination: 'India may truly be said to rank with Italy as a woman-country, "loved of male lands" and exercising the same irresistible magnetism, the same dominion over the hearts of men ... India, even to her intimates, seems still a veiled mystery, aloof, yet alluring, like one of her own purdah princesses.'[100] When Miss Wylie's hero, David Hurst, returns from England, he declares, 'I seem to belong to it, somehow';[101] and he is immediately aware of India's strange magnetism: 'He felt himself a passive spectator in a scene in which he had as yet no part, but which was in some strange way part of himself. The noise, the vivid colours, the very heat and dust, belonged to his innermost treasure-house of dreams and memories.'[102] The English girl whom he ultimately marries and who like himself had been brought up in India, tells him of her feelings on returning: 'I have always wanted to come back... It is as though the East called to me, and never ceased to call, though I tried to stifle its voice in a wild round of English pleasures ... somehow you belong to all these old memories, which always seem to be so full of sunshine and bright, warm colours.'[103] These tourist responses to exotic places, greedy for undifferentiated sensations of novelty and excitement, and uninterested in exploring the depths and contours of the glimpsed marvels, are some measure of how Anglo-India protected itself against India.

Conclusions

In *Fiction and the Reading Public* Mrs Q. D. Leavis in discussing the relationship of author and reader considers the appeal of a romantic writer: 'The bestseller who has collected for her "Indian" novels an enthusiastic public of a quarter of a million who writes to tell her how "real" and "true to life" her Indian characters are, admits in some bewilderment: "I don't know how or why I am so successful in getting the Indian quality of my characters so true. I have really known very few Indians: one didn't know them in my day. It is some sort of sympathetic insight that guides me – and guides me right." '[104] One can discount the complacency of the anonymous lady; what is more interesting is that the fictional India compounded of banal guesses and clichés, of inaccuracies and half-truths which the romancers fashioned won them an avid readership. Their fantasies met with and satisfied the readers' needs, their distortions served as valid insights.

The approach of these writers to emotional expressions, marital relationships and social tendencies shows an unquestioning and unswerving adherence to the bourgeois style of life then current. Their world was one of moral simplicities in which villains are brought to justice, adulterers punished and non-conformists driven to their knees, a tidy ordered world in which chastity and success are the household gods, status and prestige the icons. As conforming members of a community which proclaimed the ethos of work, advocated self-control, insisted on a rigorous system of behaviour and believed love, marriage and procreation to be a divinely ordained sequence, their impressions of India told of indolence, self-gratification and instinctual freedom. The ladies were enchanted by the prettier manifestations of the mysterious East, they acknowledged the achievements of Indian art and architecture and gestures of respect in the direction of Indian civilization and spirituality are common enough. But essentially, India was for them a dislocating experience, leaving them the prey of troubled sensations they could not interpret. The disquiet of a character in one of Mrs Perrin's novels generalizes a corporate response to that immense and

ancient land where the proliferation of peoples, sects and monu-
ments, and the extremities of scenes and seasons, made it appear
grotesque: 'There was no moderation, no balance in India; everything
was so devastating, so extreme, on such a gigantic scale.'[105] To
isolate themselves within the physical ghetto of the compound, the
cantonment and the club seemed not only the most expedient course
but the correct moral choice.

But it was as if India pursued and overtook them. The repressed
thoughts of these irreproachable matrons were brought to the
surface by India and were projected onto Indians as proof of their
depravity. From their prurient fantasies, from their confusions on
the intricacies of Indian philosophy and society came a meretricious
account of the many-layered culture they could not comprehend.
The coexistence of 'lofty concepts with elemental practices'[106] which
they saw as pervading and poisoning Indian life and thought was an
outrage against their creed of the sacred and the sensual as antagon-
ists. They were repelled because they saw their society's taboos
violated and were involved in the betrayal, they were allured by the
forbidden on shameless display.

CHAPTER 3

Flora Annie Steel, 1847–1929

Introduction

WHEN Flora Annie Steel boasted that her understanding of Indians came from living amongst them, observing their customs and studying their mentality, she was echoing a claim commonly made by the British official class. In 1867, shortly after her marriage, she went to India with her husband, a member of the I.C.S. posted to the Punjab, and, apart from home leaves, lived there until 1889, making two subsequent visits in 1894 and 1898. The years in India entailed the usual series of postings, sometimes to remote districts where the Steels were the only white people, sometimes to larger stations where they joined in the social life of Anglo-India. Whenever possible she participated in her husband's duties, accompanying him on tours of the district in his charge, assisting in school-inspection, arranging English classes, learning the language of the villagers, giving them elementary medical attention and offering them advice. Mrs Steel set about cultivating the acquaintance of the people and maintained that she easily established close relations with Indians of all classes, though her preference was for Moslems and ultimately for Moslem peasants. She claimed that she was closest to the peasant women, laughing and crying with them in that comfortable relationship where the Indians accepted their subservient role.

Mrs Steel informed herself on Indian art and architecture, on legends and folk-lore, and she translated Punjabi folk-tales into English. On seeing that the local handicrafts were in decline, she encouraged and assisted their revival. Mrs Steel's day-to-day existence was vastly different from that of her countrywomen,* and as an

---

* In *The Englishwoman in India* (1909) Maud Diver expresses admiration for Mrs Steel, writing that she 'stands alone in this respect; for she has left behind her such a legacy of good works as has not been bequeathed to India by any other Englishwoman in her sphere of life' (p. 154).

energetic and managing sort of person she deplored the languors into which so many ladies subsided, insisting that after twenty-two years in India neither the heat nor the discomforts had undermined her energies and enthusiasms. Clearly her experience of India was less vicarious than that of most Anglo-Indian women.

But how different was the knowledge she gained through these activities? In order to manage Indians, she writes in her auto-biography, it is necessary to learn their language and study their habits and conventions, a homily she repeats in her fiction. Rulers can only control and guide their wards if they understand them, but the depth and extent of this knowledge must be defined and con-fined, for when white men delve into India they meet with proclivities and customs so primeval that their personal equanimity will be dis-turbed and their confidence as masters shaken. To know natives, then, is to collect and digest information useful for ruling a subject people. But Mrs Steel, who saw herself as story-teller and teacher, as interpreter of 'the first postulates in the problem of Eastern life',[1] was obliged to explore the dark and dangerous mind of India so that she could give warning of the bizarre and the corrupt, the unintelligible and unthinkable. For her, all Indians were tainted, except that when she inveighs against Moslem depravities she is attacking profligacies which are earthy and earthly while her revelations about Hindu India are excursions into the arcane.

Mrs Steel's recollections of the relationships she established with Indians must be approached with circumspection, for what kind of intimacy could an Englishwoman give and receive who emphasized the 'absolute necessity for high-handed dignity in dealing with those who for thousands of years have been accustomed to it',[2] and who insisted that all the Indians with whom she associated delighted in her autocracy? Perhaps they did; if so, this throws into relief some-thing of the texture of the British–Indian encounter, the deference of the weak and the insolence of the powerful, and confirms the limited and limiting kind of relations in which such as Mrs Steel could participate. Her busy and interfering concern with the natives coexisted with a joyful retreat to the society of her peers when this was available. On all cardinal matters, she identified with the orthodoxies of her natural community, believing British rule to be just, efficient and indispensable, and the British people to be exceptionally able. It is precisely from her own developed sense of race that she was able to fashion her vivid expositions on 'the innate repulsion of the alien'.[3]

Convinced that she had discerned the real India, Mrs Steel proceeded to nail this down in rigid and absolute proclamations: it is a land stubbornly immutable, the people are slaves of custom and authority, items in a frozen social structure, in terror of their gods, the playthings of fate; but these same cowed and passive people have as a crowd a terrifying propensity to savagery and can be aroused to violence through appeals to their superstitious religious beliefs. On the most superficial plane some of her images do reflect appearances, but she lacked caution, claiming for her impressions the status of truth, disguising her preferences as eternal verities, her antipathies as perversions. Even where she drew aloofly sympathetic sketches of traditional Indians, calmly and dutifully pursuing their preordained destinies, she would deface these with her obsessions about Indian sexuality and the pervasive weirdness of ordinary life in India.

A confident and opinionated voice permeates all that Mrs Steel wrote. She does not hesitate to declare in her autobiography that she was never in love and considered that the best way to deal with passion was to wait for it to pass. She gives a high estimate of her talents and winning ways, boasts that every venture she undertook met with success, and is confident that her presence in India had enhanced the prestige of the British Raj. If assured self-righteousness was the gift of a solidly middle-class upbringing and a family which traditionally sent its sons to serve in India* then Mrs Steel exploited this inheritance to the full, and if it made for immodesty, it also allowed for individuality and she would sometimes express unconventional views on taboo matters. As she delighted in being thought

---

* Though her parents had permanent financial difficulties, her mother's family was wealthy and owned plantations in the West Indies. Her father was at one time Scottish Parliamentary Agent. Two of her brothers went to India; her aunt married an Indian Army officer who became a general; one nephew was an officer in the Indian Army; her daughter, who was born in India, married a cousin who was a member of the I.C.S.

daring, her motives may in part have been mischievous. Still, she refused, for example, to be prim about Indian erotic art:

To our modern modesty some of these imaginings must seem obscene, indecent, but in the days when they were lovingly, reverently given shape from the rude stone, they were but common, everyday symbols of a great thought which the West has not, and which the East has almost forgotten. Whether they shock our sensibilities or not, it is as well to remember that those who carved them carved with the wholehearted reverence for mysterious truth which also guided the hands and tools of those who built our catacombs, our basilicas, our churches.[4]

Also she voiced her contempt of those missionary efforts which sought to thrust nineteenth-century Christian patterns onto a people whom she considered were in many ways more moral than the English.[5] But it is important to note that, though she would sometimes defend Indian manners and laud Indian spirituality, she was always aware of India as alien and the meat of her novels is precisely the conscious depiction of the traumatic effect India had on her compatriots and, more obliquely, on herself: 'In almost every direction infinite tact is required in attempting to reconcile the mutual differences in thought and manners. Doubtless much of what the Indian sees in our aims and amusements is grievous to him, but, on the other hand, does he quite allow for the shock some of his culture gives to us?'[6]

The word 'shock' often occurs in the context of her discourses on Indian mores and the choice is important for, where her intelligence led her to make formal assertions of tolerance, her instincts and the whole weight of conformity compelled her into portrayals which are suffocated with distaste. The structure she fashioned was one in which British and Indian existed as separate entities between whom intimacy as equals was certainly undesirable and probably impossible, and the meaning of her sententious pronouncements on the assimilation of East with West – 'perhaps the two great streams of thought, one surcharged with activities, the other with passivities, may meet, not in collision or absorption, but in an absolute welding together of all that is good or true in either'[7] – remains obscure.

Her faith in common-sense was tempered with aspirations after the occult and there was more to Mrs Steel than the efficient and forthright Victorian matron who strides through her writings. Yet this she most certainly was, and who else would conjure up so useful a phantom as Nathaniel James Cradock, a down-to-earth and co-operative ghost dressed in the white coat of a railway-guard who, she tells in her autobiography, manifested himself with the express purpose of dictating his experiences to her in a form so neat that she had material for three short stories? In her middle-age she became interested in what she calls philosophy and metaphysics and, haunted by the idea that the key to human problems lay in sex, she spent years reading every available book on the subject in the British Museum. This intensive concentration on material not usually described as metaphysical, strengthened her belief that the sexual function in man had been perverted and that, in the animal kingdom, man alone was the victim of sex.* In her autobiography she owned to an 'inborn dislike of the sensual side of life';[8] this recoil from sexuality suggests that she was temperamentally unable to tolerate the conceptual and practical interrelationship between sex and worship in Indian culture or the frank acceptance of sexual passion in social norms.

Such dabbling in philosophy exemplifies Mrs Steel's method, or lack of it, as bizarre and eccentric theories and laws, generalizations and assertions which are simultaneously vague and rigid, are thrust into her texts as *ex cathedra* pronouncements. Her writings betray an undistinguished mind and an indifferent imagination; the style is prolix, the characters without light and shade, and the plots, where they are not preposterous, are trivial. Yet her pretensions to interpreting the real India while providing accounts of both Indian and Anglo-Indian existence as well as action-packed, romantic yarns, won her a large and eager readership and enthusiastic acclaim in the British press. 'It will always be hazardous to forestall the judgement of the age to come on the writers of the age that is closed; but it is difficult to believe that Mrs Steel's masterpiece – *On the Face of the*

---

* Her last novel, *The Curse of Eve*, which was posthumously published, contained the fruits of her researches and purports to show that in human society the Genesis story is perpetually played out in the temptations which over-sexed womanhood offers to weak mankind.

Waters – will not remain a classic as long as the Indian Mutiny is remembered. By virtue of that book alone, the author is entitled to rank with the great women writers of the English language.'[9] Thus the *Morning Post* at the time of her death. Mrs Steel recounts that publication of this novel established her reputation and that she was fêted in London as a lioness, being much in demand at literary gatherings.

That she was also noted with approbation by critics purporting to analyse the nature and direction of Anglo-Indian literature is more surprising until the basis of such praise is examined. Writing in 1908, E. F. Oaten, who lamented the mediocrity of the great mass of such literature, pronounced Mrs Steel a major writer and the greatest novelist of Anglo-Indian fiction. What he apparently sought in such literature was a memorial to the imperial achievement of the British race rather than virtuosity of imagination and pioneering insights.

It is the work of the British Empire, among her many other tasks, to enable the backward races of the world to take one short step toward that final consummation. As a record of the thoughts, emotions, joys and sorrows of those who are guiding one fifth of the human race as it painfully, falteringly and yet, it is to be trusted, finally takes that single step, Anglo-Indian literature, its lesser names alike with its greater, can never entirely lack interest for students of humanity.[10]

Certainly the most interesting facet of Mrs Steel's fiction is her concrete account of what it felt like to be a British Victorian in the ambience of the Indian Empire.

In all but her last, and very odd, Indian novel, *The Law of the Threshold* (1924), it is the pedestrian exposition of beliefs, the baldly stated accounts of the characters' feelings and the detailed descriptions of scenes and situations which dominate. But to approach her writings simply as a naturalistic record is to miss the dense undergrowth where the complicated response to India and Indians is planted among protestations of affection and sympathetic understanding. Her gift for descriptive writing produced vivid sketches of how India and its peoples appeared to an Englishwoman who had looked at them and met them; it is an image refracted through a prism of cultural convictions which distorted the subjects in view, and because of this is a window into an area of the British imperial mind.

Mrs Steel's India : Apathy and Excess

When two of Mrs Steel's British characters return to a village after an absence of some years, one of them remarks that in the interval their lives had been radically altered while the Indian people have remained unchanged. To this her companion replies: 'You never read Megasthenes' account of his travels through India in the year B.C. 300 or you wouldn't be surprised. It might have been written today; for these people do not change except under pressure from without, and then they disintegrate suddenly.'[11] Although Mrs Steel is partial to extracting laws and first principles from her observations, her accounts do communicate something of the inexorable quality of peasant existence, especially in the short stories where she tells of slow and simple people whose horizons are bounded by family, village and the pressing need to coax subsistence from the soil. Individuality is obliterated by this total immersion in the environment: 'Many and many a silent peaceful hour he spent in the forked seat behind the oxen, half asleep, half awake; while the well-wheel circled round, he circled round the wheel, and the great world circled beyond him. Whether it span swift or slow he knew not and he cared not.'[12] As this man, Gunesh Chand, is dying, he gazes 'with dull contented eyes at the broad expanse of the newly-tilled soil, where the sun gleamed on the furrows... There was nothing here to puzzle his slow brain; nothing to disturb a nature welded, by long centuries of toil under the sunny skies, into perfect accord with the environment.'[13] In another story she shows how the involvement of the placid and resigned peasants with this circumscribed existence is so entire that they cannot comprehend changing conditions. When an old man, Jaimal, loses the ancestral piece of land to a usurer who had manipulated the new British laws to foreclose the mortgage, Jaimal kills him and calmly awaits arrest. What he had done seemed right and necessary, for the land must pass from father to son; but he is defeated by the new system and the usurer's son gains the land while Jaimal's family is uprooted and dispersed.[14]

Both these stories begin as compassionate accounts of peasant existence, and both are characteristically spoiled by the meretricious introduction of horror – a snake is attracted to the smell of the usurer's blood on Jaimal's hands and he dies of the bite; the corpse of Gunesh Chand's infant daughter is left for the jackals as a sacrifice to ensure the birth of sons – for the cruelty of fate and the perversions to which Indians stoop are integral to Mrs Steel's conceptions of the true India.

The British are naturally hostile towards India's inertia, and as one of her favourite characters travels across the vast landscapes, 'he sat in judgement in his thought on those dead levels and the people who lived in them. Stagnant! – featureless! – A dead sea! – A mere waste of waters without form or void.'[15]* Compare this spineless capitulation with the British determination to conquer their surroundings recounted in *The Hosts of the Lord*. In order to construct a canal 'western ingenuity ... had been digging defiance for months'[16] in the dry stretches of the desert, and in setting up their camp, 'so white, so straight, so disciplined',[17] the British have declared war on nullity. Roses now blossom 'where nothing but sand had shown since the primeval sea receded from the hills', and 'an avenue of palms, bordered by green grass and beds of flowers, and intersected by broad paths leading back to the solid white squares of the tents'[18] has been coaxed from the arid earth.

Not only has the improving presence of the British changed the face of the Indian earth, but it has also penetrated men's perceptions so that when pious pilgrims enter a sacred place they sense 'an atmosphere in which nothing seemed sure save that there was change', for the searchlight the British had raised to illuminate their new canal pries even 'into the Holiest of Holies! Had it not shot into Mother Kali's very temple, and shown the worshipper that two of her mighty arms were stuck on with sealing wax! What God would stand that? And how could the very gods themselves work miracles if everybody could see how they were done?'[19]

This modernizing influence does not mean that Indians can adapt to Western ways, for the chains of religion and custom, especially

* Mrs Steel's debt to Kipling is apparent in this passage as it is throughout large areas of her writing.

those encircling Hindus, are so powerful that even the educated who boast of their emancipation are trapped. When the wife of one such enlightened man is dying, he consults a yogi, for 'one goes back at such times',[20] he explains to an agnostic friend who understands perfectly. Western-educated Indians, Mrs Steel emphatically states, remain wedded to their ancestral past, and their inherited racial characteristics make it impossible for them to understand and absorb the foreign culture. She illustrates this with reference to a young student who is writing an essay on Patriotism and who in searching 'for other men's words to embody mental conceptions that were foreign to his nature . . . was typical of his class'.[21] He is a pathetic figure, his brain crammed with unfamiliar knowledge, his heart full of inherited ignorance; it needs only a line from Macaulay's on 'The Temple of his Gods' to send the lad scurrying to perform his Brahmanical prayers. So too for another character in the same novel, Western learning had meant only mental confusion and conflict between himself and his family. For the resulting disorientation, the Cambridge-educated Devi-ditta blames the British: 'What right have they to alter all our standards, to educate us to be like them – at any rate in some ways – and then to let us stew in our own juice? What right, I say it again, had they to beguile me from the good old ways?'[22]

For the woman he loves, Maya Day, an American education has brought anguish and unrest. Trained so that she might return and proselytize for the Tantric cult, she is appalled at the depraved customs and superstitions associated with the sect in India. She is a stranger in her native land and determines that, if she is to regain her true identity, she must renounce the West entirely, for she feels herself to be 'a house divided against herself, half and half'.[23] When her American comrade, Blennerhasset, pleads that she return with him to America and forget India, she cries, 'How can I forget? It is true that I am Eastern! I am Western! And even in me that they will not meet . . . warring that old never-to-be-ended strife.'[24] She withdraws from the active world, retreats into contemplation and offers herself as a voluntary sacrifice to appease and calm the people's dangerous fanaticism.

The British mission is to change India, but it is neither possible nor desirable to modernize the people who are temperamentally and practically incapable of releasing themselves from the embrace of the cunning, malignant and all-powerful Mother. This is the theme of 'On the Second Story' which tells of Ramanund, B.A., science teacher and active member of reform societies, one of that circle which is scornful of religious superstitions and calcified social customs. During a cholera outbreak, self-acclaimed free-thinkers allow their womenfolk to intercede with Kali on their behalf, but Ramanund and his associates plead that cleanliness and filtered water will be of greater efficacy than offerings at the Mother's shrine. To the people this is blasphemy: 'If She wishes blood, shall She not drink it? Our fathers messed not with filters.'[25]

Though intelligent and courageous, Ramanund the Brahman has not really grasped the ideas to which his education has exposed him, and an evil-looking *sannyasi* who warns him of Kali's power and whispers the secret prayer of the twice-born, has the power to disturb him: 'Despite logarithms, despite pure morality, something thrilled in him, half exultation, half fear.'[26] He recovers his poise and, decent and civilized in his Western-style white clothes, repeats his call for the purging of wicked religious practices, at which the holy man, naked and savage-looking, challenges him: 'Let it be Kali, the Eternal Woman, against thee, Ramanund the Scholar.'[27] Ramanund's beloved, a despised widow, is used by the unscrupulous priests of the Kali temple as a sacrifice, and his account of events (following his finding her dead body in the shrine) is dismissed as the delirium of the illness. When he recovers, he is too dispirited to rejoin his optimistic associates, as in dull dazed wonder he realizes that, with the widow's death, the epidemic has slackened. Indeed, as the holy man had predicted, Kali, symbol of old India, has triumphed against the futile challenge of the emancipated Ramanund.

This particular story, while underscoring the power of tradition, suggests another of Mrs Steel's feelings about India, that it is a mighty force of incalculable malignancy, using magic as one of its means. For she is convinced that the supernatural operates in India, that magical ointments of great power are known to mystics (see *The Law of the Threshold*), that living Indians who roam the Indian earth in humble human form embody the attributes of their gods, always present because they represent the verities appropriate to Indian existence: a river-diver bears a curious resemblance to the local deity which has the disconcerting habit of vanishing from its plinth,[28] the children Ram and Sita are incarnations of that excellent and devoted legendary couple whose names they bear.[29]

There are pleasing mysteries in India, but more prevalent is the ominous frequency and cruelty with which death strikes. Existence is uncertain and entails adjusting to a savage environment hostile to human endeavour, and the people's response takes the form of the horrible rites they have evolved to placate the relentless and predatory India they pictorialize in many terrible guises as Mother Kali.

When the British build dams and bridges, the people tremble lest Mai Gunga exact retribution from them for permitting this interference in the old ways.[30] But in appeasing this fearful goddess Hindus gratify something essential in their nature: a procession honouring Mother Durga, 'the great Death Mother, implacable, athirst for blood', lights up 'the sordid life of the bazaar with a savage fire of something unknown – horribly unknown – that lay beyond that life'.[31] As a knowledgeable professor* tells a naïve American in *The Law of the Threshold*, 'Your public has the "blood-lust" in its veins. You saw today how the very babes in arms crowed over what made you feel sick.'[32]

A shrine which houses a grotesque image of the goddess 'in her most malevolent and crimson mood' bears witness to this perverted obsession with blood. 'A splash of red on the stone plinth showed that here also blood had been spilt.'[33] The corridor courtyard of the temple has

a floor black and fetid by centuries of foul human use; a floor still damp enough to keep the heaps of spent jasmin and marigold chaplets flung aside in the corners, after worship, from shrinking to dust; so they lay slowly rotting and sending out a scent of mingled decay and flowerfulness. The air was heavy with this, with the smell of stale incense, and the fumes of the lamp filled with rancid oil which showed dimly, a packed crowd of strange, weird figures.[34]

This lust betokens the real India and while well-meaning liberal

* This artless deference to the authority of the 'professors' is also made by Miss Wylie when she is enlarging on the depravities of Indians; see Chapter 2.

Englishmen are hosts at a mixed gathering, a festival of blood is in progress at the Mother's shrine: 'Humanity shouting, yelling obscene songs, and still calling on Mai Kali for help. How many thousands there were against the hundreds at the garden party is held, nowadays, to be of small account; but together they made up India.'[35] To the Indian multitudes the mystery of sex is symbolized in Kali and here another essential Indian proclivity finds expression, for Kali's shrines reek of the 'mingled perfume of love and worship, of sex and religion'.[36]

The desire for blood and the pursuit of promiscuous sex coalesce in the Tantric rites. Maharaj, a Kulin Brahman who exults in his ritualized role as bridegroom to the penniless daughters of high caste, is a 'figure of magnificent build, naked as the day it was born. Its statuesque yet fleshy limbs were bespattered with blood, and the beggar's bowl formed of a human skull which it carried, swayed like a pendulum as the figure moved with a lilt, evidently under the influence of some drug.'[37] This depraved creature – the pronoun 'it' is fitting – claims the lovely Maya Day as yet another bride:

A perfectly fiendish chuckle here broke in on the speaker as the tall, burly figure of the Maharaj rose to its feet with a horrible leer. 'Yea! Hand her over to me, and I'll warrant I'll teach her what women were made for! Hand her over – I can kill her when I've done with her.'[38]

In one of her later short stories Mrs Steel associates sensual and cruel religious practices with terrorist political activities, all of which, she suggests, spring from the same impulse for violence satiated through sacrifice. In 'A Maiden's Prayer', Parbutti, the daughter of Kulin Brahmans, is about to be married to a student of suitable caste. While the marriage preparations are being made, the female members of the family vicariously enjoy the sensuous pleasure of bridedom, the suggestive ceremonies, whisperings of secret delights – all this typical of a high-class Bengali marriage. 'The whole atmosphere was enervating, depraving.'[39] A goat is sacrificed, 'a jet of red, red bubbling blood spurting into the dim light. . . Graven by age-long iteration in their limited minds and lives was the dogma that the Blood is the Life thereof.'[40] Parbutti's father withdraws from such festivities, being both a sensible man and a prominent member of the

Nationalist Party, for 'the ceremonials of a Sakta wedding do not go well with talk of political rights and wrongs, of education, and equality, and exotic tyranny'.[41] When Parbutti goes to perform her devotions at the household shrine to Kali – where she daily chants an unbelievably silly prayer* of Flora Annie Steel's composition – she sees four lads, one of whom is her brother and another the student whom she feels sure is her bridegroom. While unobserved, she hears their discussions on liberty, equality, fraternity and on force being the one principle whereby men could rule. She sees them hide explosives in the image of Kali while hailing anarchism and the Motherland. 'It was a sad farrago of nonsense; Western individual-ism dished up skilfully by professional agitators in a garb of Eastern mysticism.'[42] On the wedding day comes the news that the brother and the bridegroom have been arrested, and soon after the brother dies in prison and the bridegroom kills himself. At first Parbutti is paralysed with disappointment but later, dressed in her bridal clothes, she goes to the shrine determined to offer the Great Goddess that for which She craves, and by igniting the explosives she sacri-fices herself.

Mrs Steel's basic conceptions about India did not change over the years; but, perhaps because the more immediate images were dimmed by long absence, the later writings show a greater surrender to wild fantasies and more closely resemble the romances discussed in Chapter 2. However, all her fiction carries the conviction that Indians are the slaves of sexual passion. The hero of *On the Face of the Waters*, who had taken an Indian mistress, finds that he cannot respond to the desires of Indian womanhood: 'Their eternal cult of purely physical passion, their eternal struggle for perfect purity and constancy, not of the soul but the body, their worship alike of Sex and He who made it, seemed incomprehensible.'[43] In *The Law of the Threshold* the pure and lovely Maya Day, after admitting that she loves a British officer, denounces her feelings in a speech of monu-mental banality, condemning her inherited Eastern passion as a love which 'sears and burns . . . scorches and shrivels' and which will 'smirch' the recipient.

* 'In Thy Heaven Kali Mai – Thou who lovest the flesh of man – By this blood I pray thee ban – Aliens in Hindustan' etc.

Nor is this particular depravity limited to Hindus. *The Hosts of the Lord* tells of a Begum's grandchild who though only part Indian and raised as a European, is temperamentally imprisoned in lawless passion and is the mistress of every feminine guile. Indeed, Mrs Steel is most concerned with Moslem depravity, seeing in the sexual excesses and addiction to drugs and alcohol of the upper stratum symptoms of the decay into which their once-great Empire had fallen. This is her account of a mid-nineteenth-century Delhi bazaar:

Abool-Burk meanwhile was already in a house with a wooden balcony. There were many such in the Thunbi bazaar, giving it an airiness, a cleanliness, a neatness it would otherwise have lacked. But Gul-anari's was the biggest, the most patronised; not only for the tired heads which looked out unblushingly from it, but for the news and gossip always to be had there. The lounging crowds looked up and asked for it, as they drifted backwards and forwards aimlessly, indifferently, among the fighting quails in their hooded cages, the dogs snarling in the filth of the gutters, while a mingled scent of musk and drains and humanity steamed through the hot sunshine. Sometimes a corpse lay in the very roadway awaiting burial, but it provoked no more notice than a passing remark that Nargeeza or Yasmeena had been a good one while she lasted; for there was a hideous, horrible lack of humanity about the Thunbi bazaar, even in the very women themselves, with their foreheads narrowed by plastered hair to a mere wedge above a bar of continuous eyebrow, their lips crimsoned in unnatural curves, their teeth reddened with *pan* or studded with gold wire, their figures stiffened to artificial prominence. It was as if humanity, tired of its own beauty, sought the lack of it as a stimulant to jaded sensuality.[44]

In *The Potter's Thumb* the court of the Hodinugger Moghuls is shown as a hideously decadent and corrupt place: the palace is squalid, the retainers shabby in their tawdry clothes, the masonry in ruins, the carpets filthy. What survives of the old courtly dignity resides in the old men dreaming of chances to thwart their overlords. But the youthful heir to the state, Dalel-Beg, is immoral, weak, drunken, the prey of loose women, and an insolent bounder who forces his unwelcome amiability on the British. He is, in short, a nasty compound of 'occidental follies, grafted on to a sound stock of ancestral vices'.[45] The bazaar contains 'a specimen of all the vices

which in past times had made the Moghuls of Hodinugger in-
famous':[46]

A couple of young men with uncovered heads were dicing on a string
bed thrust under a patched, dyed awning stretched from balcony to
balcony. A group of half-a-dozen more were quarrelling vilely over a quail
fight beside the liquor-seller's booth, gay in its coloured bottles. Two or
three of various ages, heavy with drugs, were sprawling and nodding in
the gutters. Just across the street a sutara-player was twanging away, and
above him a girl, powdered and painted, bent over the wooden balcony
flinging snatches of hideous song on the passers-by, and shrieking with
coarse laughter at a naked monstrosity who, as he begged, made capital
of his misfortunes. On this girl with grease-smirched hair and Brum-
magem jewellery, Chandni [a courtesan] from her shadows, cast glances
of scorn which she transferred after a time to Dalel Beg, who sat crouched
up against a plinth smoking a rank hookah and sipping a rajah's peg of
brandy and champagne. He had discarded European dress entirely, and
the few clothes he wore smelt horribly of musk.[47]

However contemptuous Mrs Steel is of Moslem sensuality and
decadence, this is disapproval of a people who seem to her to have
fallen from more civilized and moral ways, and is crucially different
from her attitude to Hindu India. This has its fullest expression in
the most curious piece of writing she produced, the account of
Professor Anderson's quest for arcane India in *The Law of the
Threshold*. An American convert to the Tantrics, Nigel Blennerhasset, accompanied by a lovely Indian girl, Maya Day, who has
grown up and been educated in the United States, arrives in India on
a mission to convert Indians to the sect. Neither Blennerhasset nor
Maya Day, who initially believe in the purity and spirituality of the
cult, realizes that their efforts are being exploited by two Bolshevist–
Jewish agents who are working with Indian nationalists to overthrow
British rule. The plotters know that the only appeal to the people is
through their religious psyche, their superstitious fanaticism, and by
using Tantricism they aim to arouse them to violence. So it is that
Markovitch, a Russian Jew who passes as Mr Markham, and Weissberg,* who prefers to be known as Mr Whitehall, repeat the famous

* Jews were high on Mrs Steel's list of evils. A minor character in an earlier
novel, *Miss Stuart's Legacy*, is John Raby whose greed and financial acumen

toast of the arch-Bolshevist, Bakumin [*sic*]: 'To the destruction of
Law and Order, and the unchaining of Evil Passions.'[48] It is the
good sense and wisdom of Anderson, a surgeon and a scholar, which
helps the British to outwit the agitators and restore peace, and his
wisdom has been gained through an intrepid exploration of darkest
India.

Towards India's 'perfectly amazing stability' Mrs Steel has two
contradictory attitudes: one that an abstract power of great malignancy intervenes to arrest change, the other that this immutability
implies adherence to a profound and benign philosophy. Both these
possibilities are combined in the professor's discoveries. What, asks
this wise man at the outset, is basic to India? Although he modestly
checks an admirer's gushing praise of his knowledge – 'I understand
sufficient to understand that I know nothing, my dear lady. . . I
have a skin-deep acquaintance with facts – motives are beyond me'[49]
– he discerns more than he will admit: 'Understand as he did, better
than most Englishmen, the mentality of India, he knew its incalculable possibilities: behind all the modernities, he saw the ancient rule,
fixed, firm as ever.'[50]

In his search for comprehension, he consults the Pandit Akas
Ram, a learned man loyal to the British, who proclaims: 'India is an
old land, a very old land! Was there not thirty centuries of lives,
thirty centuries of civilization before the West began to count? And
do not old trees send out strange growths? yea! even poisonous
ones?[51] He tells Anderson about the Valley of the Thousand
Trees, the meeting-place of the Aghorapanthis,* that sect which
holds the Godhead to be the Self, and the Self the Godhead which
permeates all, and since all things are One, they subsist upon themselves, eating the flesh and the blood as a sacrament. Increasingly
preoccupied with the need to unravel India's mystery and knowing
that he is obsessed with wanting to confront that monstrosity who

---

stem from his carefully concealed Jewish ancestry. Red Jews such as Markovitch
and Weissberg are, of course, for her the most pernicious of the breed.

  * The Aghori cult is an extreme Tantric group; Aghora is one of the five
faces of Shiva and in folk etymology the term means 'not-terrible'. The Aghori-
tantra is a tantra (scriptural text) defining the philosophy and practices of the
cult. See Agehananda Bharati, *The Tantric Tradition* (1965), p. 305.

seeks the Absolute within the Self through eating human flesh, Anderson asks Akas Ram to lead him to the valley. Here he meets a saint of the sect and suffers an attack of what seems to be malaria, to counteract which he is given a dose of opium. On awakening he is greeted by the chant of the Most-Learned One: 'Thou art That. All that can be seen when we perceive all in one and one in all; when self is cast aside and found anew in all things.'[52] To the professor the Eastern formula seems the clue for which he had been searching. 'Thou art That. Yes! There lay the secret of all true healing both of the Body and the Mind';[53] this was the fundamental teaching of the East, 'the unassailable ground in which the "pathetic content" of the millions of India found root'.[54]

In the valley Anderson sees Maya Day's dead head, her expression calm and composed, and he is assured by Akas Ram that her sacrifice was voluntary, that she had taken her life so that the people could see her repudiation of the evil plotters. Anderson returns to his hospital having understood India and is able to advise the British on how to deal with the unrest. The agitators are exposed; life returns to its normal pathetic contentment.

The doctrine of the individual Self, the Atman, as identical with the Absolute Brahman,* which Mrs Steel reports with such approbation, is central to one of Hinduism's most influential philosophies as expounded in *The Upanishads*. Why then does Mrs Steel introduce

---

* See William Theodore de Bary (ed.), *Sources of Indian Tradition* (1958). Also K. M. Sen, *Hinduism* (1961): 'By Brahman is meant the all pervading God. . . . The other term, Atman, means Self. The Upanishads point out that the Brahman and the Atman are the same. The Supreme has manifested Himself in every soul, and the student of religion is dramatically told in the Upanishads "Thou art That" (Tat tvam asi)' (p. 19). See Introduction to Penguin edition of *The Upanishads* (1965) by Juan Mascaró; 'Brahman in the Universe, God in his transcendence and immanence is also the Spirit of Man, the Self in every one and in all, Atman. Thus the momentous statement is made in the Upanishads that God must be sought as something far away, separate from us but rather as the most inmost of us, as the higher Self in us above the limitations of our little self. . . Thus when the sage of the Upanishads is pressed for a definition of God, he remains silent, meaning that God is silence. When asked again to express God in words, he says "Neti, Neti", "Not this, Not this", but when pressed for a positive explanation he utters the sublimely simple words "Tat Tvam Asi", "Thou art That".' (p. 12.)

a small and extreme sect* whose doctrines do not derive from *The Upanishads* and which practises ritual cannibalism in striving after a complete harnessing of the senses, as exemplars of the doctrine? In bringing to the fore a taboo rite particularly hideous to the Western sensibility as the pinnacle of Hindu thought, she paints the heart of secret India as a place of darkness. Indeed, the immense muddle of inaccuracies, impressions, half-formulated ideas and diffuse descriptions which make up this account, suggests that in the dim dark valley of a thousand trees where the uninitiated lose their way, Mrs Steel had her most complete imaginative experience of India.

Mindless Violence

From this murky source Mrs Steel traces the natural pattern of Indian existence: 'Those who decried content forgot that for thirty centuries the whole genius of India had been for this same placidity.'[55] Yet 'that curious resignation, that impassive acquiescence, which does more to separate East from West than all the seas which lie between England and India'[56] can be transformed and abandoned when the underlying savagery of these slow-brained and superstitious people is provoked by appeals to what is deepest in their psyche – their thraldom to the creator, the destroyer. Then a fury is unleashed which matches in intensity and mindlessness the assaults of elemental forces, of India's great rains and sweeping floods. In *The Hosts of the Lord*, fanatical yogis who fear that British innovations will undermine their hold on their followers incite the people to riot; they are joined by Moslem troops led by Roshan Khan, a descendant of the dispossessed Moghul Nawab. Although he had hitherto been an able and loyal officer, his racial instinct for lawlessness and ferocious passions had been called forth by jealousy over his cousin Laila Bonaventura, and when he sees her with her British lover, he kills her and runs amuck, 'that curious phase of the Oriental

* The frequency with which novelists introduce the Aghori cult is significant as it was always small and references to its existence in works on Indian philosophy, religion and cults barely give it passing reference. Even in *The Tantric Tradition* Agehananda Bharati only mentions its existence and classifies it as 'an extremist tantric group'.

mind when once it oversteps the hard and fast lines of custom in which it breathes and has its being'.[57] In his unbalanced state he bitterly resents the British who had humiliated his ancestors and made men like him 'a prey both to ignorance and wisdom, savagery and culture'.[58] Once the riot is quelled and the night of madness with its lack of 'reasonable explanation'[59] is over, the town returns to its sun-saturated calm and uneventful existence: 'The bazaar was full as ever with drifting humanity, busy in the details of everyday life. There was no hint anywhere of the past storm.'[60]

Outbreaks of Indian violence, Mrs Steel insists, have no political content, and her best-known novel, *On the Face of the Waters*, embodies her notions on the irrational sources of Indian rebellion. Modern historians have seen the rebellion as the culmination of resentment against British incursions into traditional India, in spheres ranging from the changes in agrarian relationships which disrupted village communities, to interference with religious customs.[61] If the rebellion began as a fight for the preservation of religion which both Hindus and Moslems saw as threatened by the British zeal to westernize India, it developed into a political struggle. It was the rebels' aim to oust an alien government and restore the Moghul king of Delhi, who in the north commanded the allegiance of both Moslems and Hindus.

Mrs Steel based her account on the official sources then available which viewed the rebellion as a mutiny against lawfully constituted authority, and she does set out to describe the course and interpret the causes of events. The British were culpable in their ignorance of Indians; the complacency of many political and military officers was such that they dismissed reported signs of discontent as bazaar rumours. The British should have been more sensitive to the humiliation felt by the dispossessed Moghuls. They should have realized that permitting the preaching of Christianity to native regiments was dangerous folly. They should have appreciated sepoy fears that greased cartridges contained cow's fat; instead of which they punished them for refusing to handle the cartridges: 'And you know what forcible injustice means to children – and these are really children – simple, ignorant, obstinate',[62] as her hero Jim Douglas explains.

But having suggested reasons for the outbreak, she abandons these and treats the rebellion as an aimless and meaningless explosion, a reversion to barbarism, a contest between forces of light and powers of darkness. When Edward Thompson in the 1920s wrote his book on the rebellion, *The Other Side of the Medal*, he attacked British histories of the events for detailing the excesses of the infuriated mutineers while veiling the excesses of the infuriated British forces. As a modern Indian historian has written, there were no moral issues involved in the war which was not 'a conflict between barbarism and civilization, for neither side observed a single restriction which humanity had imposed and which oriental and occidental nations had tacitly agreed to honour'.[63] If the contemporary British view tended to apportion good and evil, justice and infamy between themselves and the rebels, Mrs Steel's presentation, which claimed wide sympathies and objectivity, came within the conventional framework.*

In her version it is the whores who give the word encouraging the sepoys to storm the jail, and the battle is on between 'aimless, invertebrate discontent'[64] and 'law and order',[65] as savagery challenges civilization. The first sepoys to rebel act on a wave of confused and purposeless cruelty, arousing 'mad exultation'[66] in a crowd 'powerless for good or ill, sheep without a shepherd'.[67] Though 'intriguers, fanatics, the better class of patriots'[68] do participate, the majority are 'of different mettle, longing for loot and licence'.[69] And so the troopers, 'a procession of shouting black devils',[70] followed by 'refuse and rabble' race through the town, killing the helpless Christian women and children, 'poor, frightened, terror-struck'.[71] The mutineers are 'drunk with *bhang*' but a greater intoxication comes from the lust for blood which the fighting has called forth in them. Reasserting themselves against this vileness are 'the real Masters',[72] men imbued with 'personal courage',[73] with 'perseverance and pluck',[74] with 'courage and determination'.[75] To these 3,000 Englishmen marching on Delhi, there were 'but two things to be

* Sir John Marriott in *The English in India* (1932) writes: 'In striking contrast to the poverty of leadership among the mutineers was the plethora of talent, still more the remarkable demonstration of character, on the British side' (p. 176).

reckoned with in the wide world. Themselves – Men. Those others – Murderers.'[76]

In sonorous tones, she records the British desire for revenge, in which even the kindly heroine Mrs Erlton becomes involved. Witnessing an officer's unbridled hatred when he finds the murdered body of an Englishwoman,

her own gentler nature was conscious of a pride, almost a pleasure in the thought of the revenge which would surely be taken sooner or later, by such as he, for every woman, every child killed, wounded or even touched. She was conscious of it, even though she stood aghast before a vision of the years stretching away into an aeon of division and mutual hate.[77]

In conceiving of the rebellion as a moral conflict between good and evil, Mrs Steel is able to glory in the overpowering satisfaction of British retribution and in her version the revolt, like all Indian convulsions, is without conscious intention. Afterwards, no one could explain what had happened: 'Truly the whole thing was a mystery from beginning to end. I asked a native yesterday if he could explain it but he only shook his head and said the Lord had sent a "breath into the land." '[78]

In her most lurid novel, *The Law of the Threshold*, where she attempts to account for the terrorism in the early twentieth-century political movements of India, she dismisses the possibility of political grievances, nationalist aspirations or revolutionary theory as irrelevant to an Indian psyche dominated by inborn blood-lust and religious fanaticism.* It is these that agitators exploit in order to stir the people to unrest and violence.

So with the most appalling readiness of the East to swift intrigue,

* Mrs Steel's version of fanatical sects exploiting political movements is an inversion of what contemporary commentators and later historians saw in the situation. Valentine Chirol, by no means a sympathetic reporter, in his *Indian Unrest* (1910) shows how nationalist leaders invested the boycott movement against British goods, which was an outcome of the partition of Bengal, with a religious character, and in Bengal the movement became associated with Kali-worship. It does not fit in with Mrs Steel's ideas on Indian character and mentality that they should be motivated by political considerations, and she selects from the many expressions of nationalism the one which was regarded with caution and even distaste by many secular-minded nationalists. For her, Kali-worship represents, even constitutes, the nationalist movement.

plotters calmly set to work for they knew that they had at their command the finest secret association in the world; an association knit together, as it was, by sacred ties, by ancient traditions, such as the West knows not. For these were no political conspirators. Their care for freedom, for self-government, for all the shibboleths of the Young India party was as naught to their care for the honour and glory of their cult.[79]

This is how the natural passivity of Indians is transformed into resistance. From here Mrs Steel leads us through her nightmare world of Palaces of Dead Kings with secret entrances and exits where stones move on unseen axes, to the grotesque Kali temple in which fanatical votaries drunk with blood and aflame with sensuality are incited to riot. Only once does she allow a human rather than a devil-inspired content to the hostility Indians feel for their masters, and this is in *On the Face of the Waters* when she describes the behaviour of the Lucknow crowd. Angered at the deposition of the King of Oudh, they boldly express their disaffection in the streets as they re-enact a 'vile travesty' of the English at their pleasures:

Two white-masked figures, clasped waist to waist, were waltzing about tipsily. One had a curled flaxen wig, a muslin dress distended by an all too visible crinoline giving full play to a pair of prancing black legs. The other wore an old staff uniform, cocked hat and feather complete. The flaxen curls rested on the tarnished epaulet, the embracing arms flourished brandy bottles.[80]

Anglo-India in an Alien World

If the essence of Indian existence is inertia and fanaticism, passivity and violence, how can the British be expected to treat Indians as fellow human beings? A new set of responses must be fashioned for a people so different from themselves, and motivated by such incomprehensible wants and impulses. A young official newly arrived in India is upset at seeing a mother holding a sick baby covered with a rag, but finds that 'curiosity and repulsion froze the surface of pity'.[81] Later he is indifferent when his servant dies suddenly of cholera. His sense of superiority made him, like most of his race, 'inclined to consider the natives as automata, until personal experience in each case made them admit reluctantly that they were not'.[82] But this instinctive racialism is valuable in checking the spontaneous attraction he feels for a lovely young Indian girl, Azizan, as he responds to the look of surrender in her sun-coloured face:

but it was brown also! Truth is truth. It was not a sense of duty, it was a sense of colour which prevented him from kissing it then and there. So much may be said for him and his morality, but the difference between a brown and a white skin was the outward sign of the vast difference between sentiment and sheer passion. The transition was too abrupt; for a time it shocked his culture.[83]

The temptation is quickly conquered and, on finding a memsahib awaiting him in his bungalow, he is brought back 'with a round to civilization'.[84] Race feelings also check consummated relations between white and brown, and although Jim Douglas, the hero of *On the Face of the Waters*, loves his mistress, whom he had gallantly rescued from being sold into prostitution, his action had been prompted by 'romance' rather than 'passion'. Unlike other men who had contracted illicit liaisons, Douglas is not content 'to think half-caste thoughts, to rear up a tribe of half-caste children',[85] and he is relieved when their baby dies for he had thought of the child with a 'vague revulsion'.[86] Later, when he is hiding in Delhi in the company of an Englishwoman and her son, he realizes that it is the boy's white skin which makes him think of him as something to be proud of possessing, 'a boy who would go to school and be fagged and flogged and inherit familiar virtues and vices instead of strange ones'.[87]

Though Mrs Steel set herself apart from Anglo-India as one who *could* discern and interpret Indian thought and feeling, her most striking achievement is in communicating the antipathy and fear possessing the British and their consciousness of an abyss separating them from their human environment. When, before the rebellion, the heroine of *On the Face of the Waters* finds herself surrounded by a crowd of supplicating natives, she draws back to the farthest corner of her carriage,

as if to escape from what she did not understand and therefore did not like. That, indeed, was her attitude toward all things native; though at times, as now, she felt dim regret at her own ignorance... What were they thinking of, those dark incomprehensible faces closing closer and closer round her? What could they be thinking of? Uncivilized, heathen as they were – tied to hateful, horrible beliefs and customs, unmentionable thoughts! So the innate repulsion of the alien overpowered her dim desire to be kind.[88]

The *apartheid* which the British have observed in constructing their stations and cantonments announces that they see themselves as a people under arms inhabiting another country from that of the people over whom they rule. These are the first impressions of a young and innocent Englishwoman on returning to India after being brought up in England:

Belle, standing in the middle of the glaring white high-way, instinctively turned to where, in the distance, a slender church-spire rose above the bank of trees on the horizon. *That* was familiar! *that* she understood. Born in India, and therefore a daughter of the soil, she could not have been further removed in taste and feeling from the toiling self-centred cosmogony of the Indian village in which she stood, had she dropped into it from another planet. So, alien in heart, she passed through the tide of life which sets every morning towards a great cantonment, looking on it as on some strange, new picture. Beyond all this, among people who eat with forks and spoons and went to church on Sundays, lay the life of which she had dreamed for years. The rest was a picturesque background; that was all.[89]

She returns to this stark view of two communities coexisting without inter-communication:

Outside the parallelograms of white roads centred by brown stretches of stubbly grass, and bordered by red and blue houses wherein the European residents of Faisapore dwelt after their kind, and our poor Belle lay dreaming, a very different world had been going on its way placidly indifferent, not to her only, but to the whole colony of strangers within its gates. The great plains, sweeping like a sea to the horizon, had been ploughed, sown, watered and harvested: children had been born, strong men had died, crimes had been committed, noble acts done; and of all this not one word had reached the alien ear.[90]

Across this yawning gulf is the slender bridge of official relations between the people and their masters, between district officer and peasant, army officer and troops; and this is the only possible or desirable context for an encounter since a greater intimacy would subvert the sobriety and order of the British. Specifically, susceptible white men are liable to be seduced from the natural course of their lives by India's women – the innocent Azizan is as dangerous as the tinsel-clad, silver-belled and jasmine-perfumed Chandni, an experienced courtesan. So pervasive is the sense of risk that even Grace Boynton, a weak, self-indulgent and amoral Englishwoman who has accepted bribes from the Moghul house, blames India for her failings. After a fire in the Anglo-Indian camp she and her companions had taken shelter in the palace, living on the roof as did the Indians. But once she has returned to the security of her natural surroundings, she deplores the experience: 'I don't think civilized people ought to go to these wild places and live in uncivilized ways. . . It is demoralising living on the roof without doors and windows. . . Civilized people should eschew barbaric environments. They are not safe.'[91]

Mrs Steel clearly disapproves of Mrs Boynton's lack of moral fibre. However, the articulation of discomposure is not part of her criticism but a general expression of Anglo-Indian unease: 'Hodinugger civilized! I can't imagine it. . . When I think of the old potter, and that mirrored room on the roof . . . it seems like some old dream of life into which we nineteenth century folk have strayed by mistake.'[92] This is the remark of Rose Tweedie, a young girl who knows nothing at all about India, 'an ignorance not altogether to be deprecated'.[93] It is not only timid and cosseted women who flee from close contact with India: 'Understand! Of course you don't. I don't though I've been here two years. And what's more, I don't want to. . . So long as we don't understand them . . . and they don't understand us, we jog along the same path amicably. . . NO! It is when we begin to have glimmerings that the deuce and all comes in.'[94] This is the outburst of an English official, a balanced and temperate man who, after his community have lived through a riot and other strange happenings, repeats his judgement: 'We shouldn't understand. And that's our position now. You can't in fact. It's better you shouldn't; in India at any rate.'[95]

A rebellion of Indians appears to the British as an assault on something more than their physical safety: 'the delicacy, the culture, the civilization, the society, the security belonging to them, had been invaded'.[96] Indeed, they are always aware of an incipient encroachment and that is why they raise barricades in their consciousness:

'The fact is . . . that in an old civilization like this in India, there is such a confounded amount of dregs down below that the less they are disturbed, the better. Heaps of things one doesn't understand are best left alone.'[97] This is the advice of a Chief Secretary who has made a deliberate decision to restrict his knowledge to what is required for his official duties. In the same novel the weak and silly American convert to the Tantric cult, who before coming to India had believed that the sect adhered to the Vedas, learns after a short experience of India that it is a land where everything is upside down, where 'things terrible, unbelievable'[98] are the norm. On finding that he has been a tool in Eastern intrigue, he turns on India with hatred: 'I've been made a fool of all through by these devilish people, and the sooner I get away the better. . . I shall be glad to leave this land of disappointment and regrets.'[99] His disgust is the inevitable result of taking India on trust, believing in her spirituality and entering freely into her underground existence.

Strangers and exiles, baffled by their surroundings, the British try to create a semblance of Home to still their yearnings. Kate Erlton tenderly raises heartsease and sweet-peas,

for she loved her poor clumps of English annuals more than all the scented and blossoming shrubs which, in these late March days, turned the garden into a wilderness of strange perfumed beauty. Her cult of Home was a religion with her; and if a visitor remarked that anything in her environment was reminiscent of the old country, she rejoiced to have given another exile what was to her as the shadow of a rock in a thirsty land.[100]

And yet how ludicrous it was to plant little pieces of England in a setting which possessed so determined a character of its own that it derided the intrusion. In the park-like grounds of the Delhi Residency, kept like an English garden with not a leaf out of place or a blade of grass untrimmed, with each flower and plant disciplined, 'the palms swept their long fringes above them boldly, and strange perfumed creepers leapt to the branches of the forest trees'.[101] As Kate Erlton admires a landscape spoilt for her by the presence of a Moslem tomb – 'it always reminds me of England but for that' – her companion, an army officer and less sentimental, is obliged to point out 'yet that is the original owner'.[102] Even in the murky *The Law of the Threshold* Mrs Steel finds an apt occasion to point up the incongruity of British ways in India when, during a christening ceremony at a 'stucco imitation of a font at St Mary Magdalene Church at Shadipur', a guest is struck by the unsympathetic surroundings, 'with even their hopeless lack of rudimentary comprehension of that ceremonial'.[103]

Mrs Steel's approach to Anglo-Indian homesickness is sympathetic but detached, sometimes even ironic. But when describing the hardships the community endured and the excellence of the services they rendered India, she writes with regulation floridity. Here she is describing a Viceregal garden-party:

> So, with that curiously light-hearted, almost reckless frivolity of Indian society – a not unnatural recoil, perhaps, from the perpetual presence of the greatest social problem the world has ever seen, or is likely to see, that is, the mutual assimilation of East and West without injury to either, the little company of Englishmen and women, empire makers and breakers, drifted out into the sunshine. . . So the pageant of power passed into a garden-party, and nothing remained to show the hand-grip which had made the garden out of a wilderness, to tell of the tireless effort to solve the problem, the ceaseless striving to be just.[104]

As late as 1924 she repeats that it rested with Britain to rule India on 'civilized lines',[105] for village meetings were still more concerned about the iniquities of cow killing and reminiscences about the good old days, than with genuine reform. Democracy for India is impossible as it is out of gear with caste, with Indian backwardness and with the Hindu mentality. What then is the alternative?

> Consider the question quite calmly. Someone must govern India, that vast category of races, creeds, customs. On the one hand we have, say, a quarter of a million of Europeans, frankly alien, and a quarter of a million of educated natives quite as alien to the mass of the people – more so in some ways. Now to govern India as it should be governed postulates a *force majeure* behind that government. Which of the two claimants – as they stand today, mark you, not as they may or ought to stand in the future – has this backing? Surely the frankly alien; a race accustomed to Government for centuries, a race with capital, prestige, personnel at its command. It must govern and what is more it must – it is bound by the very fact of its existence – govern strongly – almost relentlessly.[106]

Professor Anderson's explanation to Blennerhasset proves that British rule must continue permanently. What is more, it is a burden gloriously borne, a one-way process in which the British give all and receive nothing; to emphasize this claim, it is made to come from the tragic Maya Day, the disappointed girl who has come to know her Motherland too late to accept it. As she watches Professor Anderson at work in his hospital,

a sudden overwhelming grasp of reality came to her heart. Was all this nothing? This that was being enacted in thousands and thousands of places all over India, where the West was turning all its learning, all its skill to the task of alleviating the agony of the East? . . . And as she sat staring into the sunlight, watching intently yet seeing nothing in reality, all her perceptions busy making up the Record of Good and Evil, the ingratitude of her native land, of her native race came home to her with hitherto unknown force.[107]

Mrs Steel was steeped in British imperial pride, a powerful emotion to which she gave fullest expression in her account of the 1857 rebellion. In her autobiography she discusses the acclaim with which her novel *On the Face of the Waters* was greeted: 'And here let me say that the subject had more to do with the success of the work than any quality of mine. It was one to touch all hearts, to rouse every Britisher's pride and enthusiasm. The Indian Mutiny was then the epic of the race. It held all possible emotion, all possible triumph.'[108] Her account of British revenge empathizes with the racial loathing the British participants were experiencing; the reaction of her hero, Jim Douglas, on finding the corpse of an Englishman, is one of wild rage and insane hatred as to him it seems that the cold touch of steel from a dark hand was a desecration. The response of an officer who comes across the murdered body of his loved one is as intense:

So fought young Mainwaring. . . He had not tried to escape as the others had done; not from superior courage, but because he never even thought of it when he was free to choose, how could he think of leaving those devils unpunished, leaving them unchecked to touch her dead body, while he lived? He gave a little faint sob of sheer satisfaction as he felt the first soft resistance, which meant that his sword had cut sheer into flesh and blood, for all his vigorous young life made for death, nothing but death – was not she dead yonder?[109]

As the Tommies march on Delhi, they too are impatient for revenge – 'weapons were never gripped more tightly, more sternly than by those three thousand Englishmen marching to their long-deferred chance of revenge'.[110] 'There Arose a Man' is the title of the section in which an actual historical figure, John Nicholson, 'king-like' and 'heroic', makes his appearance.[111] He cuts through the red tape and the hesitations, announcing in his sonorous voice: 'If I had them [the mutineers] in my power today . . . and knew I was to die tomorrow, I would inflict the most excruciating tortures I could think of on them with an easy conscience.'[112]* In reply to a question on what course he would follow, the hero says: 'I would kill them, sir, as I would kill a mad dog.'[113] So the British drank deeply of revenge, for while the mutineers' cruelty sprang from disloyalty and savage desires, the British in retaliating were preserving civilization. For Mrs Steel this suppression of rebellion is the epic of the British race.

Conclusions

Many aspects of Mrs Steel's writings rightly place her with the romancers discussed in Chapter 2, yet there are significant differences. Instead of ruminating about India with curtains drawn, she did attempt to meet Indians although she was unable to enter anything but a paternalist relationship. If her view came so close to that of her sister-novelists, this is because of those emotional blindspots which prevented the British from considering India in its own terms. Mrs Steel's accounts of Indians in particular situations is sufficiently graphic to suggest that prejudice and social conformity shackled her imagination. Consider those remarkable lines where she

* After the rebellion, John Nicholson proposed a bill for 'the flaying alive, impalement, or burning of the murderers of the women and children at Delhi. The idea of simply hanging the perpetrators of such atrocities is maddening.' Quoted in Metcalf, *op. cit.*, p. 291. Michael Edwardes, in *Bound to Exile* (1969), describes Nicholson as 'a violent, manic figure, a homosexual bully, an extreme egoist who was pleased to affect a laconic indifference to danger' (p. 100).

shows disaffected Indians travestying the British as they act out their hatred in theatrical display. It is because her total structure of themes allowed no place for Indians experiencing such human contempt that insights of promise are lost in the morass of devilry and primitiveness which for her is the only source of Indian anger.

What are the processes through which pleas for understanding and advocacy of 'intimacy' are transformed into their opposites, into a defence of locking India out of the British consciousness and relegating Indians to a sub-human status? By defining culture and civilization in terms of Western material habits and modes of feeling, Indians are found to be inferior and their very presence a menace to the British. But Mrs Steel's argument is more convoluted: the British are chided for their ignorance about India, India is then unveiled to show the odd, the grotesque and gruesome, ignorance then becomes defensible and knowing India is redefined as essential and useful knowledge to facilitate permanent British rule. The separation between British and Indian is shown as a clear and necessary division and so minutely concerned is she with defining the differences that two distinct emotional scales are introduced – Eastern love is a scorching and all-consuming experience which involves only the body and is a surrender to man's baser instincts, whereas Western love is that sentiment that engages the finer feelings. So that even when white men are attracted to brown women (she does not contemplate the obverse) they are succumbing to emotions which fall outside the range of the true British mode of love. Yet even within this patent nonsense is a muddled apprehension of the gradations and confusions of racial feelings. It is these modulations in Mrs Steel's writings, and the provocative contradictions which place her apart from her sister-romancers. Some lines in her autobiography exemplify the complexities of which she was aware and which she was driven to obliterate in a schema which falsified what she had hoped to interpret:

India . . . as I looked back on Bombay from the deck of the ship that was bearing me away from all personal touch in the future of the country, appeared to me temple-crowned, mosque-crowned, a blue mist enveloping both, and hiding alike the factories, the hovels, the offices, palaces and the millionaire mansions. All things seemed to merge in that blue mist.

Even the distant hills were lost in it. So India looked homogeneous, and so looked a lie. For India is as multitudinous as the sands of the sea.[114]*

* As Mrs Steel's autobiography was written during the last years of her life – she died in 1929 – it is possible that she had read *A Passage to India* and been influenced by Mrs Moore's last view of India from the ship in Bombay.

CHAPTER 4

Edmund Candler, 1874–1926

Introduction

IT was not the hope of serving Indians which brought Edmund Candler to India in 1896. Referring to Joseph Conrad's description of Asia as 'the lands of the brown nations, where a stealthy Nemesis lies in wait, pursues, overtakes, so many of the conquering race', Candler writes:

It was just that Nemesis which attracted me. I believed that the contacts and collisions of East and West still provided adventures akin to the medieval. I wanted to be pursued stealthily with the risk of being attacked and overtaken. Chivalry could not attain full stature in a *milieu* of pavements and chimney-pots.[1]

In his memoir, an account complete with Latin tags, nicknames and droll anecdotes, Candler looks back on his experiences and crystallizes his ideas on life in general and the East in particular. This work has the flavour of a deeply conventional man to whom travel was an apprenticeship in developing character and exercising the imagination, and far-away places the school in which to learn about the delights of Home. Candler liked to think of himself as the untrammelled wanderer, but he was by disposition and conviction bound to his own age and culture, a restriction which he came to accept and justify: 'It was a garish romance I had been seeking in outlandish places,' he wrote, recalling his return to England after his first travels in the Orient.

I loved England for its physical and spiritual tranquillity, because it had no scented gardens, or Sheikh Nafzaus, or wandering fakirs, or terrorist lamas, none of the elements that create them – no goblins more malicious than Puck, a land where there is little cruelty and violence, and less unkindness than elsewhere, where all the trees open and shed their leaves at the same time, and the people are all of one colour, and have no bitterness in their hearts.[2]

The author of this deeply felt panegyric could be no more than a tourist in the lands of dark peoples and his view of the East is determinedly and sometimes aggressively that of a Western man who, having been impelled to explore the strange and the different, discovers that pleasure is to be found only in the familiar.

Teacher and journalist, globe-trotter and man of action, travel-writer and novelist, Candler was a man of many parts and together these varied roles suggest aspects of a well-integrated person who set out to gather experiences for conversion into literary form. There is often no essential difference between the media he chose; opinions voiced and sensations recorded in his travel books and autobiography also appear in his fiction, incidents are repeated, scenes revisited, and apart from one phantasmagoric short story where Candler's usually disciplined imagination riots, containment and neatness temper his romantic protestations. Above all, it is in his journalism that his gift for discerning the human meanings and social import in the concrete physical details and static scenes which he so graphically draws is given its fullest expression.

The son of a medical doctor, Candler was born in 1874 and educated at Repton and Cambridge. He wanted to be a writer and decided on teaching as a career hoping this would give him opportunities for travel and leisure for writing. In 1896 he took a post at a school in Darjeeling; during the vacations he travelled in Burma, Cambodia, Siam and Cochin-China, writing articles for *Macmillan's Magazine* and various Anglo-Indian journals* which were later collected as *A Vagabond in Asia*. Candler resigned after three years but, because he could not find congenial work in England, he returned to India in 1900 as professor of English Literature in a college in the Madras Presidency. During this time he married and with his wife he visited the Himalayas and Tibet. After leaving the college, Candler joined the Younghusband Mission to Tibet† as the *Daily Mail*'s special correspondent; during an affray he

---

* The *Pioneer*, the *Outlook* and the *Civil and Military Gazette*.
† The British Mission to Tibet was ordered by the then Viceroy, Curzon,

INTRODUCTION

received severe injuries which necessitated the amputation of his left hand. For a short time he was literary editor of the *Daily Mail* and after touring Europe he returned to India in 1905, this time as tutor to a young Bengali rajah. This was followed first by a temporary post as principal of a Bengali college and then by an appointment as principal of a college in the Punjabi state of Patiala, where he remained from 1906 until 1914. In this time he wrote numerous sketches of his travels, published as *The Mantle of the East* (1910), a collection of short stories, *The General Plan* (1911), and a novel, *Siri Ram: Revolutionist* (1912). He spent the war years as a correspondent with the Indian Expeditionary Forces in Mesopotamia and for a short period after this he travelled in the Middle East reporting for *The Times*. In 1919 he again returned to India, this time as Director of Publicity for the Punjab, a government appointment which he found unsatisfactory and relinquished in 1921. In the six months he spent in Kashmir he wrote *Abdication*, the sequel to *Siri Ram*, which was published in 1922. During his last years, while living in the Basses-Pyrénées for reasons of health, he wrote his autobiographical memoir.[3]

Candler's writings record a journey which took him from dreams of the Orient drawn from prose and poetry, from Rustum's view of Orgunje, Marlow's of the East 'perfumed like a flower, silent like death, dark like the grave', to the raw actuality of India. The passage from romantic expectations to a disappointed acceptance of the unease which English and Indian generated in each other measures the distance between a traveller's hopes about the fascinating East and a white resident's experience of British India. 'Personally I have come to look upon racial incompatibility as something chemical or psychological, apart from reason, which is only called up among the supports of our self-respect in a losing battle. Reason

who with his advisers feared that the Dalai Lama would invite Russian intervention as a means of freeing himself from China and that this would give Russia a foothold on India's borders. Because of this traditional fear of Russian expansionism, a mission headed by Colonel Francis Younghusband and ostensibly concerned with trade, went to Tibet in 1904. Armed clashes with Tibetans resulted, which a participating British officer described as 'massacres'; Candler's account of the expedition, *The Unveiling of Lhasa* (1905), is not concerned with the political nature of the mission.

and logic in these debates are generally the disciplined reinforcements of instincts.'⁴ The man who reached this conclusion had abdicated from his vocation as a vagabond.

The Hearth-loving Traveller

When Candler took up his first Indian appointment in Darjeeling he accepted as natural that he and his British colleagues at the school should have no intimate association with cultured Indians: 'My interest in the mysterious Indian was as yet barely awakened. The fascination of the East lay for me in its beasts and birds and flowers and scenery.'⁵ Candler here deprecates the promptings of his nomadic soul of which he was proud and which he was soon to obey. In the Preface to the collection of articles published as *A Vagabond in Asia* he modestly writes that 'these sketches are for the most part merely the expressions of moods inspired by new environments. In voyaging, the author has had no other purpose than to indulge the nomad's instinct of restlessness. He does not pretend to speak authoritatively on matters oriental.'⁶

Where a casual observer would see only the picturesque, Candler reveals and interprets the human tendencies. In the Himalayas he notes that the native peoples are in harmony with their surroundings, and an old Bhootia woman at prayer, her eyes turned to the snows, makes him feel that she 'had imbibed the true atmosphere of the place, she had embraced the skirts of a beautiful creed. In a kind of ecstatic *yoga* she had united herself with the universal spirit of Nature. She was part of a great system.'⁷ He watches his *syce* (groom) dreaming under a cherry tree in full bloom as the pony confidentially bends over him, sees a *bhistie* (water-carrier) bowed under the weight of his skin-full, a group of Paharia girls in silver jewellery and colourful head-gear laughing and jesting, a Lepcha carrying a basket of green oranges on his back, and thinks, 'All were part of the place, the mountains, the valleys and the snows were made for these, not for the man in the church, a member of the dominant race.'⁸

In a setting inviting contentment and repose Candler is apprehensive, not only because of the 'sense of minuteness that most of us feel sometimes, in the midst of majestic surroundings',[9] but because in those hills the British were intruders as in their frock-coats and top-hats they entered their church with their eyes fixed on their boots, blind to their surroundings, to the people and the spirit of the place. He had become aware of this insensitivity soon after arrival:

European residents in the East are justly famed for their hospitality; yet their attitude towards travellers is often unsympathetic. Nothing can be more commonplace or devoid of interest to them than the land in which they drag out an involuntary exile. Apart from their sport, their interests are generally centred in European affairs, the Home Mail and the few make-shift European distractions which their colony affords.[10]

Such persons who deliberately isolated themselves from their surroundings offended against Candler's enthusiasm to plunge into the East and experience its challenge. In *The Mantle of the East* he recalls watching a blonde American tourist, Mrs P., on a boat travelling along the Ganges; he sees her tilt her parasol to blot from view a pious and helpless old woman being carried on her son's shoulders to the sacred *ghat*: 'The angle of Mrs P.'s sunshade measured the antipathy of East and West. It was continually tilted.'[11] The separation between European and Indian is constantly noted and implicitly deplored by Candler; while Indians in Benares seek out their dark and malodorous shrines, 'in spacious clean houses detached from one another by walled compounds, live that other half of the Aryan stock whose practical evolution is symbolised by the Club, *The Spectator*, the bicycle, the galvanised iron bath, and the Bible'.[12]

In the minutiae of people's deportment and in the artefacts of the two cultures, Candler perceives a brooding estrangement between West and East. Benares is physically dominated by two alien objects, 'the great minarets of Aurungzeb's mosque and the massive girders of the Dufferin Bridge', but these obtrude incongruously as mere surface excrescences 'while underneath hidden old-world influences which have outlasted change and revolution course the body like sap in the bough'.[13] In a civilization which he had initially thought of as static and plastic, Candler discovers the massive strength of immobility:

We soar the Ganges for them with iron, and the faithful use our road to approach their gods without sparing any of their awe for the new miracle. To the devout we and railways are a passing accident, to be used or ignored as indifferently as stepping-stones across a brook. The city is too old in spirit to resent these iron girders, that stucco mission church; they are merely another wrinkle on her brow. The parable is repeated from Rameswaram to Peshawar – India is too old to resent us. Yet who can doubt that she will survive us? The secret of her permanence lies, I think, in her passivity and power to assimilate. The faith that will not fight cannot yield.[14]*

Candler had heard Benares, or Kashi, the Holy City of Hinduism, described as a morbid place but it strikes him differently:

The superstition, the obscenities, the insatiate and corrupt priesthood – that is to say the mechanism which has made popular Brahminism what it is – one knew to be there. The unexpected thing is, that in spite of all this there is still something stirring in the sight of these hordes of simple folk – husbandmen, mechanics, the backbone of the country – drawn there by the only light which is perceptible to their blurred vision and feeling themselves beatified.[15]

If Candler's understanding is tainted with condescension it none-theless suggests an effort to accept alien religious forms. But it also underscores his limitations, for only when he is observing Indian ways as frozen postures is he relaxed. Faced with the living Indian personality, he recoils. Significantly, it is when the unencumbered traveller who had widened his initial interest in flora and fauna to include people becomes a practising member of the Anglo-Indian community that sympathy gives way to stern judgements and that sweet tolerance turns sour.

In his autobiography Candler recalls his first acquaintance with an Indian student outside of England where he had known only the 'hybrid memetic product of the English University'.[16] It was during

* 'If you want to see India as it has been the last few thousand years go to Parlakimedi. It is true that there is a new college and a brand-new palace, but these toys look as if some meddler had introduced them just to see if they were any good, and as if the honest folk, finding they were not, had left them there looking as incongruous as a model of a Hottentot village stuck in a glass exhibi-tion house . . . they are so palpably incidental that they emphasise the inveterate Brahminism of Parlakimedi.' *The Mantle of the East*, pp. 238–9.

his initial voyage to India and he was disturbed that this mysterious and complex young man seemed unaware that the English passengers ostracized him as he moved amongst them 'detached and self-contained'.[17] To Candler, the behaviour of the white passengers 'implied a kink in human relations that needed straightening out' and he therefore suggested that the student be invited to participate in the ship's last concert, to which the young man agreed by reading the whole of 'Adonais', unmindful of the yawns and cat-calls from the audience. This was Candler's first contact with the racial problem: 'Here was a clean, self-respecting, unobtrusive young man, responsive to courtesy, who read Shelley and Herbert Spencer, and yet was shut out of the world we had educated him to admire by our own senseless barriers.'[18] Candler rejects as irrelevant the usual Anglo-Indian explanations of race-barriers, the inhibitions of high-caste Indians, their instinct for segregation and their attitudes towards women. But in time he came reluctantly to concede that the races cannot live together in harmony. Candler, who liked parading in the accoutrements of the vagabond, was quite comfortable in the xenophobic garb of his class and culture. The explanation of the passionate concern which Indian Moslems feel about Turkey given by his character Riley, a man very much after his own heart, reflects a sentiment easily fitted into Candler's own outlook: 'If Turkey goes they have nothing left to hang on to. Imagine the whole of Christendom overrun by Jews – synagogues, old clo' shops, Yiddish schools, one small peninsula left unsemitic. You'd fight for it like a Crusader, even though you happened to be an agnostic.'[19]

'I was old-fashioned enough to hope to instil into him – dare I confess it? – the ideals of an English gentleman, which are probably still quite the best, though it has become unfashionable to say so.'[20] Candler is here recalling his experiences as tutor to a young Bengali rajah: 'The lad was generous according to his lights, but the wrong signals were up; and no sermons or moralisings could substitute red for green.'[21] When reading *The Prisoner of Zenda* with his tutor, the rajah missed the moral implications of the confrontation between hero and villain, and when the upright Rassendyll had obliged the treacherous Rupert to lay down his revolver first as a prelude to a duel, the lad excitedly suggested that this was an opportune moment for Rassendyll to shoot his adversary. Candler's material here is ordered to involve the reader in his disappointment, for even those who are uncertain about the absolute excellence of an English gentleman's ideals are expected to find the rajah's response ignominious. The lad's difficulty in understanding the Western concept of honour and his evasive attitude to truth left Candler melancholy.

Throughout his many years and various educational appointments in India Candler held himself aloof from the social environment to which his search for adventure had brought him. For almost eight years he was in the service of the Maharajah of Patiala and, although the occasion for his resignation was the outbreak of the First World War, his time there was running out because he was becoming increasingly intolerant of the courtiers' subterfuges to involve him in paying obeisance to the ruler. Nothing would induce him to bow and adore: 'This was their custom, I argued, not ours.'[22]

There is a wealth of social attitude in this sentence which emphasizes how Candler clung to the standards of his own society when he lived amongst peoples with different customs, and this is a logical outcome of his explicit pronouncements on true values. Ultimately, as he seeks out the recognizable, his journeys into alien lands become self-negating: 'In the Himalayas it was generally the familiar English flowers that gave most pleasure. A homely bank of selfheal, wood sanicle and yellow agrimony was worth all the show of poppies and the imperial lilies of the valley,'[23] he writes in his autobiography.

Candler's sensations are reproduced in his novels when his hero Riley finds after years in the East that the 'flowers of Jemal Hamrin were delicious because they were home-like, the towers at Tauz Kharmati reminded him of St Michael's Mount'.[24] Always the traveller searches for Home; in a region where a Western-educated college professor is regarded as the living representative of British influence, Candler sees instead a Pariah woman and a caste Hindu who have defied custom and dared to marry as the most English-minded persons, for 'they once dared to take a risk and meet a responsibility'.[25] The chivalry, pride and absence of apathy in the Rajputs pleases him and on meeting a student while visiting Mayo

College in Rajputana, he is favourably impressed by the boy's Englishness:

I had never in ten years of the East come across anyone so refreshingly unoriental. The accuracy, the enthusiasm, the interest in wild things for their own sake, apart from any personal vanity in the destruction of them; the frank admission that he had never shot a tiger, but that he meant to, upset all my ideas of Hindu youth, derived from a fairly close acquaintance with them.[26]

He feels at ease amongst the Sikhs of the Punjab because their worship is less superstitious than that of the Hindus, their temples less disturbing: 'In the place of distorted images and emblems there is the holy book. One is struck most with the gentleness of it all – there is no other word for it. In the Anglo-Indian slang the place would be called "a Sahib's temple." '[27]

In recounting the origins of Sikhism, Candler praises the vision of the founder, Guru Govind, who inaugurated the sacrament of steel:

For of all material things which genius has inspired with spiritual significance steel is the truest and most uncompromising. Let humanitarians prate as they will, there never has been a race who have not been purged and refined by it. In some it is the only combatter of grossness and the monster of self. . . Compare as emblems the steel bracelet of the Sikhs and the Lingam Yoni of Siva, and you have a standard of ideals, a fair gauge of how Sikhism has tempered the Jat.[28]

Again, Islam is congenial to Candler's temperament: 'The Moslems do not approach their Maker darkly or in any timid or huckstering spirit. The mosque is designed for the expansion of the soul. . . There is nothing obscure or fantastic about it. It contains no image or tortuous designs.'[29]

On finding facets of his own being mirrored and confirmed in Rajputs, Sikhs and Moslems, Candler is reassured of his common humanity with them, while the mannerisms and predilections of those communities which violate his own inherited sense of fitness irritate and enrage, and because they betoken differences so profound as to suggest that mankind is not a unitary species, are deeply disturbing. Candler's striking account of inert, static Parlakimedi

(Devagiri in his autobiography) is a measure of how alien and anti-pathetic he found its ways. He is here describing how this princely state reacted to being run by Mason, an Englishman employed by the ruler as Prime Minister, Accountant-General and Home and Foreign Minister:

Devagiri's endurance of the benevolent alien despotism was character-istically Indian. The Raja was hypnotised; and Brahminarchy timid and supine. Courage was wanting even for covert resistance. Efficiency spreads a hard bed for the Hindu to lie on. Sanitation, progress, inspections, accounts, reports, are the very devil. When Mason died, Devagiri turned over in its half-sleep like a fat man too inert to shake off an accustomed incubus, yet when it slides off of itself, just sufficiently awake to avert another visitation.[30]

He writes memorably of his ward, the little Rajah of Devagiri, and of the assaults on his own personality delivered by the sheer power of the lad's passivity:

I think of him as vacant, but vacuity implies an emptiness which ought to be filled. And my ward was far from empty. He was static, rather. What he contained had been deposited in him. You must think of him as the precious guarded vessel containing the *ruh*, or essence, of some secular immemorial principle preserved in the family since the days of the Pandavas... My ward did not fidget. He sat upright on his chair ... quite motionless. The idol awaited the ministrations of the priest; and I, the constrained ministrant, wished I were in any other galley... For a whole hour I should be exposed to the X-ray of ennui. I, who am cursed with a sensitive cellular tissue, peculiarly penetrable to such rays, had to suffer this. I have often been bored, but never quite so perforated; and it was an unequal encounter, for I could not bore him.[31]

On big issues and small Candler is acutely aware of how foreign he finds Indians, a feeling which persists even when he is being sympathetic:

The Hindu does not love nature. He feels no kinship with the earth as Englishmen do. He does not wander in the jungle to meet wild creatures... The truth is, the Indians find nature a hard mother... The blistering heat that cows a race into patience dries up the springs of occasional gratitude... There is something hostile and alien for him in the march of the seasons. . . . The very birds chirp in monotones, and repeat a song as sad and void of hope as his philosophy. Earth is a sad nurse and he hears her stoically.[32]

In time he came to believe that social custom and tradition were as cruel a prison to the natural impulses, but this realization only came when he read modern Bengali literature years after he had left India. At the time his students had seemed unknowable and outside of official duties he avoided them. In retrospect he saw this as a mistake: 'For if one cannot feel at home with the Indian, the next best thing is to be interested in him; and if one can be neither one nor the other, it is better to stay in one's own country and leave India alone.'[33]

Candler was teaching in Bengal at the time of the 'Golden Bengal' movement. The partition of Bengal into two provinces, proposed by Curzon and carried out in 1905, became the focus for radical nationalism which drew on the traditional religious practices, the legends and folk-beliefs of the region; Kali-worship was reinvigorated and Bengal was spoken of as the Motherland. Political agitation was organized through secret societies in which students were particularly active and Candler, who knew such young people, for the first time tried to put himself inside an Indian's skin: 'If I were born in a subject country of an indigenous but "inferior" race, I should not love my foreign teachers or their text-books about liberty. . . My dreams would be of liberation, independence, sacrifice.'[34] But because he had been brought up to regard nationalism as a virtue amongst his own people and a disease in subject races, he was slow to see that there might be a generous side to the revolutionary movement. 'Yet I do not know how it was, but somehow these young dissidents failed to engage my sympathies.'[35] Liberty, he believed, was intended only for those who deserved it, 'and these people, subject to my people, did not deserve it'.[36] Without breast-beating and tortuous self-justification Candler faces his inability to feel at home with Indians and recognizes that he does not consider them the equals of the British. Into his fiction he absorbs the discomforting experience of being an unrepentant Englishman in India, a situation which became untenable in his later years when he had lost confidence in his nation's mission to India:

No doubt it is the privilege of the weak to be ruled by the strong, but the older and wiser one becomes, the more one lacks the courage to tell them so. I suppose this weakness is a reaction from the age of cant. One suspects one's motives when duty and interest and inclination march together; and when the spectre of altruism joins the band, and one is not quite sure that it is not funk, one suffers a kind of moral paralysis.[37]

The Short Stories: The Reek of India

In a letter which Candler wrote to his brother in 1909, he estimates his literary abilities:

I am afraid I take my work rather too seriously: my own great regret is that I can't give my life to it entirely but have to work by scraps in the middle of the most dulling and brain-cloying routine of teaching. My stuff depends on temperament and individuality, it is entirely subjective, and there is nothing so destructive of that as Education: there never was a schoolmaster, bar Plato, with an ounce of literary flavour in him. I often feel that my work is much better than people think, that the style is a living organism and at its best the thought is pulsing in it, and the yarns are never mere incident but there is always something underlying them or embodied in them. . . In fact I often feel that the book of Indian short stories would have a great vogue if ever the literary world took me at my own valuation, that my stuff reeks of India more than any stuff but Kipling's. Then I read cleverer work with much more grasp and insight and subtlety and technical perfection and I feel my stuff utter rot; but I feel that if I could give up everything to literature I would make stuff that would live, and that after all there is something individual in what I do turn out which deserves recognition.[38]

Of Candler's fiction the short stories are furthest removed from reportage and show his literary imagination released from his self-imposed restriction of providing 'transcripts from life'. Collected as *The General Plan*, the themes of the tales, some of which are in the Kipling tradition, range from accounts of Hindu and Moslem piety to the strange world into which the British are plunged in India, a world of secular confusions and supernatural happenings. 'Probationary' moves from the cool, honeysuckle-scented air of England to Kordinghee, an outstation in the Madras Presidency, the first posting for Dick, a recent recruit to the Indian Police. Dick finds himself in a 'country of fever, discomfort and isolation',[39] his exile mitigated only by the opportunities for hunting. Cut off from British companionship, his immediate superior is the assistant-magistrate, a young Bengali of the hybrid-Cambridge type, 'a prig, preternaturally fat and a bundle of touchiness'.[40] Juxtaposed to these unattractive physical features and unappealing personality traits is a contemptible character: 'he might be trusted never to undertake a responsibility'.[41] Despite this desolate spot where mildew attacks his books, insects eat his clothes, white ants swarm and snakes creep, Dick retains his equilibrium, kept buoyant by knowing that his beloved fiancée will join him as his wife when his salary increases; in similar circumstances less determined men had succumbed to despair and even suicide.

Dick is amazed at the new world in which he must participate and on which it is his duty to act.

For a whole week Dick had been absorbed in a criminal case that had baffled him, and that evening his inspector had unravelled the intrigue for him, discovering subtle motives that had been unintelligible, revealing a network of by-issues too sordid to be believed. Dick lived in perplexity; he could not understand the native mind – he lost himself in the tortuousness of it.[42]

An informer tells him that the ruler's relations and the court Brahmans were implicated in the plot to poison the rajah's wife. This rajah is a 'weak-minded debauchee, but not imbecile enough to be deposed',[43] and Dick realizes that if justice is to be done, it rests with him alone, for in that soil chivalry is an alien plant: 'Men might die to preserve their caste or for a point of ritual, but Dick knew there was not a man in Kordinghee who would sacrifice himself for a generous ideal.'[44] In this situation his moral courage comes to the fore; he stops the burial of the rani and orders a post-mortem, and when bribery has ensured a verdict of death from natural causes, he arranges that a sample of the stomach contents be taken for analysis in Madras. Ultimately, through his intervention, the dark and hidden corruption is exposed and the guilty men punished: 'The accident of Dick's presence alone had disturbed the black ooze of undredged wickedness and intrigue that had collected in the stagnant backwater of Kordinghee.'[45]

143

Here is Indian moral flabbiness challenged by British integrity, Indian corruption defeated by British probity. But Candler concedes that there are other aspects to India: it is also the home of faith. In 'Gunga Water', Candler tells of a simple Hindu's self-denying and single-minded religious devotion, and in 'Mecca' he recounts the importance to devout Moslems of this pilgrimage. To an Englishman travelling in the Himalayas it seems reasonable that this is where the gods reside: 'At Chini the far bank of the Sutlej became the flank of Galdang and the holy Kailas, where men say, quite credibly, that Siva dwells.'[46] In this ambience the Oriental concepts of aeons and kalpas, of compartments of time and space through which the soul passes in its purification, seem intelligible to him, as if they fitted in with a rational explanation of existence. After an interview with a Buddhist abbot, he is left with the feeling that modern psychologists were stumbling upon the occasional manifestations of some simple pervading law which had been known to the ancient Buddhists and Vedantists by revelation. In his autobiography, Candler writes that the atmosphere of Tibet infected him with the outlook of the inhabitants:

Transcendental is a word that is always associated in my mind with Tibet. . . What I mean is that Tibet is a peculiarly evocative background for spirits. . . One cannot escape these spirits. One must appease them. The stranger in Tibet must live alone in the solitary high places to understand how or why. . . I have known the loneliness, the cold, the creeping mists, the mirages which make everything seem unreal, the naked desolation. . . Man here is but a shrivelled and attenuated atom.[47]

So too in this tale, the young Englishman becomes 'the spiritual prey of these mists and solitudes'.[48]

Candler is scornful of those British who remain immune to Asia's seductions. When one such Englishman, Carpendale, sees an apparition he is momentarily puzzled but, as a practical man, he 'could explain the oddest things quite easily',[49] and his complaisant wife readily accepts her husband's deductions: 'They were the most matter-of-fact unimaginative couple. Romance dogged their steps and they were blind to it. They came through without a halt from Bombay Cathedral to Munera and spent their honeymoon in the sepulchre of a Mohammedan poet.'[50] In this tomb of a man who had lived before Aurungzeb, where there was 'a mosaic of copper and gilt on the bathroom ceiling, two brass-studded doors, and a little dada of flowers and birds curiously interwoven in purple terra-cotta and gold',[51] Carpendale had introduced all modern conveniences by erecting wooden partitions and adding a low veranda with a galvanized iron roof. 'He made the tomb very comfortable. When his bride arrived she found electric light and bells installed. A gramophone was introduced soon afterwards, and an ice and soda-water machine.'[52] The philistinism of this couple and their ludicrous encounters with ghosts are ironically recounted to show up the incongruity of the phlegmatic British in surroundings of romance and mystery.

A more poignant account of the white man's displacement in India is 'Père Ailland', the story of a French priest who for many years had remained uncowed by his empty little chapel 'and the sullen antagonism of all created things in his wilderness of Agni Hotrodu'.[53] A chance encounter with a visiting Cambridge-educated Moslem, a vain and brilliant cynic, troubles this saintly man, and while the Moslem's polemics on the rational flaws in Christian doctrine had not shaken his simple faith, the 'reiterated blasphemies of the day had sunk into his brain and engendered a new kind of phantasm'.[54] Following the death of a child on whom he was said to have cast the evil eye, the people stone the priest, and the hitherto militant Christian does not resist, taking this punishment as God's way of letting him expiate his sins, for ultimately the wilderness had caught up with him and demoralized him: 'I was lost. . . I cried out to Him and found a great emptiness.'[55] After his death the little chapel becomes a shrine where the people worship him after their fashion: 'The old altar-cloth from the chapel was spread at his feet, strewn with stalkless marigolds. A wick burned in the niche by the door, and on either side of the bearded clay giant [an image of the priest resembling the usual depictions of Krishna] the lingam and the cross were laid against the wall like supporters in a coat-of-arms.'[56]

Candler's most powerful piece of fictional writing is 'A Break in the Rains', a story which reeks of India as a place of ancient corruptions. Gerard, who is on leave in Gerkal, a hill-station, meets and falls in love with a fellow-officer's sister, Margaret. Their love grows and is declared in the outrageously Indian setting of hills and cliffs which house shrines to local godlings. Under a niche, Margaret finds five gross stone images, some placid and obese, others evil and satirical: 'They told an artless legend of haunted woods, brooding presences in the rain, the struggle between the tutelary and malignant.'[57] When Margaret says that she covets one of the gods, which seems to her destined to be their phylactery, Gerard, despite her reluctance, removes it from the shrine, confident that he can square the people for their loss.

But Gerard, whose knowledge of Indians is limited to the military Tiwanas and Derajats, misjudges the hill people. Neither he nor Margaret understands the pleas of a distraught herdswoman who follows them as they depart with the image; neither realizes that they have rifled a shrine of the Panchpiryas sect, a cult so vague that the census has classed them as animists, and whose members, rude herdsmen, rely on their deities for protection and increase. In despair, the herdswoman appeals to the Brahman anchorite who shelters in the shrine, begging him to punish the offenders by laying a curse on Gerard. This depraved *guru*, whose chant sounds like 'the plaint of a man who has shut his eyes to the brightness of the world and lives within dark walls',[58] is a terrifying contrast to the wholesome and innocent English couple who move 'like lovers treading air'.[59]

When they return to the hills on the following day, they take the paroxysms of the herdswoman and the demented cries of the anchorite to indicate some village tragedy in which they are not involved. As they approach the shrine to investigate the cause of the lamentation, they are confronted by the *guru*, a deformed figure who looked as if he had escaped from the tomb, a creature with a gross and unmanly hairless chest, nails inches long and a mouth which is 'a mere gibbous fissure showing no teeth but a grey palate'.[60] His eyes, the pupils of which are covered by a white film, appear to be smiling arrogantly, giving one 'the idea of a beast inspired by some devil's contract with the knowledge of something in the light of which man and the shadows he pursued were the vainest phenomena on earth. There seemed to be pride in its disillusionment and in the physical and spiritual corruption it breathed.'[61] This beast almost causes Margaret to faint when he approaches her, and as she and Gerard depart both are plunged into gloom. The mischief had been done, a curse is laid on Gerard who feels so uneasy that he determines to return the image at the first opportunity.

That night, when dining at the Club, he learns from a policeman that the 'beastly monstrosity'[62] he and Margaret had encountered was an Aghori: 'These Aghoris ... think themselves the most spiritual sect among the Hindus. They eat human corpses and worse. The idea is that they have overcome all fleshly weaknesses, and so are nearer to God. Nothing revolts them; they are not subject to ordinary diseases.'[63] The particular Aghori whom Gerard had seen claimed to live on babies and the sect was known to desecrate tombs.

Before Gerard can replace the image, he is called away to meet his colonel at a junction and though ill with fever he feels obliged to obey the summons. On his return journey to Gerkal he dismounts to make a purchase for Margaret and, on taking a short cut through narrow alleys, finds himself in the intricate maze of an old city. He hears someone calling to him for help and, as he follows the voice, is led to a temple of Vishnu, where the image of Ganesh, in the form of an elephant, leers at him, and Hanuman, in the shape of a monkey, seems to leap at him from the wall. He traces the sound to a cell and on entering is trapped as the door closes behind him. 'Soon he became conscious that he was not alone. His hand touched something cold on a charpoy, that sent a chill through his veins. But that was not all: there was something else in the cell equally still, though it was alive. Gerard felt that it inhaled and breathed corruption.'[64] As his eyes become accustomed to the dim light, he sees that his companion is the Aghori: 'Its white filmy eyes explored the darkness above Gerard's head. There was some maggot of desire behind them which it was Gerard's business to subdue, even if he had to crush it with rending of tissues, as the rats the cockroaches.'[65] When the Aghori rises to lift the sheet covering the corpse, Gerard strikes him with his riding whip: 'The lashes fell on its naked back, and the sound of them was dear to his soul. The whimperings of the beast woke the savage in him.'[66]

Gerard loses consciousness and awakes many hours later to find himself alone with the door open and the full moon filling the cell

with light. He retrieves his horse and on his way home is struck
down by cholera. As he lies on the point of death, Margaret, driven
by an impulse she does not understand, goes alone at night to return
the image to its shrine:

> The five saints were united. For Margaret their moonlit countenances
> were invested with a strong pathos. They symbolised so much of hope
> and fear, timid questionings, idle propitiation and vain commerce with
> the unseen. Somehow she felt less aloof from the folk who had raised
> them. Her sense of sisterhood with earth and living creatures had
> deepened. She sank down on the stones beside the goblins and wept.[67]

Soothed by her tears, Margaret feels that 'the inspiration which
had impelled her to the cairn was stirred by some current of circumstances which was carrying Gerard through the ordeal'.[68] She
returns to Gerkal in a rosy dawn to find that Gerard has survived the
crisis, and they talk of beech and bracken and pheasants, of Scotland
and Kent and of sweet home air. And so the story ends, on a note of
clean calm, as if to wipe away the foul horror of the India which the
lovers had glimpsed.

The phantasmagoric experiences which befell Margaret and
Gerard are pregnant with indications of the terror which India
aroused in so sane and sober an Englishman as Candler. The shrine
which they thoughtlessly and innocently desecrate reflects the
sculptor's 'timid groping intimacy with the unseen' and tells an artless legend of the struggle between the tutelary and the malignant.
But for revenge against the British, the adherents of a gentle cult,
people in thrall to the elements, call on over-sophisticated Brahmanical India in the shape of a depraved anchorite who deliberately
pursues evil. But it is not the Aghori sect alone which is implicated,
for Gerard is lured to a Vishnu temple, the holy place of the Vaish-
navas, who approach the Absolute through *bhakti*, devotion and
love. Perhaps this indicates no more than Candler's ignorance about
the tendencies within Hinduism, and indeed he seems to have taken
no great interest in Indian religious thought. What it does reveal is
his conception of Hindu India as a place which contains within itself
the linear history of man in vital form and the entire spectrum of
human experience. The Aghori, who breathes physical and spiritual

corruption, has overcome the flesh, knows everything through experience and has experienced everything, reminds Gerard of 'a beast inspired by some devil's contract with the knowledge of something in the light of which man and the shadows he pursued were the vainest of phenomena on earth',[69] a description in which the syntactic confusion mirrors the chaotic sensations assaulting the author.

The audacity of the Aghoris' goal kept them an extremely small sect within Hinduism and it is significant that Anglo-Indian writers introduce them in order to reveal India's dark heart. In this tale Candler's images are those of a nightmare, of the stalking of dark fears suppressed in the daylight. As in a frightened dream Gerard whips the Aghori, a response which is both a symbolic exorcizing of the devil and a terrified need to drive the unconscious back to its subterranean squalor. Freed from restraints by the fanciful theme of this tale, Candler recoils from an India which is hospitable to man's every experience and aspiration, from the primeval to the decadent, and which is personalized in holy men who seek unity with the Absolute through trafficking with demoniac powers.

The Novels as Transcripts of Indian Life

Siri Ram: Revolutionist is set in the Punjab at a time when 'sedition and revolution were in the air'.[70] As the sub-title, *A Transcript from Life, 1907–1910*, suggests, the overt concern is with the political events of the period when some militant elements within the nationalist movement were turning to terrorism as a means of winning their demands for independence.* Candler's interest is not directed to the political debates engaging the Indian Congress, the disputes between those Congressmen who still retained their faith that the British would gradually concede measures of self-determination, and the 'New Party', dubbed 'Extremists' by the loyalists, who

* Between 1907 and 1909 some acts of terrorism were committed: a train carrying the Lieutenant-Governor of Bengal was derailed, a former district magistrate of Dacca was shot and wounded, two Englishwomen were killed by a bomb thrown into their railway-carriage and Sir Curzon Wylie, an Indian official, was assassinated in London.

demanded 'the entire removal of foreign control in order to make way for perfect national liberty'.[71] Because the novel is essentially an attempt to explore and explain the Indian mind, Candler concentrates on the inspiration of the political upsurge, and this he sees in Hindu revival and reform movements, the one a stream inviting and absorbing 'the strains of superstition', the other 'the Reformed Church which was to purge the nation'.[72] Candler's paradigm of a revolutionary leader is Narasimha Swami, a Western-educated man of intellect who is associated with the Arya Samaj.* A dreamer and a mystic, he was also an anarchist without scruples who believed 'that his people could not become regenerate until they were free, a much more dangerous doctrine than that they could not be free until they became regenerate'.[73] His influence on Indian youth is insidious and the basis of his appeal, which is to arouse pride in his followers through reminding them of their glorious heritage, is repudiated by a cynical pundit who tells them that Indians had lost their country because they were not worthy of it.

> They had no character... They had no sense of duty, responsibility, discipline, organisation. And until they had developed these characteristics in the way Englishmen have done, they could not hope to do anything... In the meantime they must serve the British Government faithfully, and they must imitate the good qualities of Englishmen, and learn to speak the truth and depend on one another, and to do their duty for its own sake, wherever they are placed, apart from the selfish motives.[74]

But this stern creed rooted in high principles has no attraction for the nationalists.

While he concedes that the political movement attracted rationalists and visionaries, sincere and dedicated men, Indian nationalism emerges from Candler's account as the expression of a vain, verbose, flabby and sentimental people. The older conspirators are cowardly and unscrupulous; their propaganda machine spreads abusive and venomous misrepresentations about the crimes inflicted on the Motherland by the British. They use silly and patriotic young men

* Founded in 1875 by the Brahman ascetic Swami Dayanand, this was a movement which aimed at reforming the practices of Hinduism by seeking sanctions in the Vedas and at instilling pride in Indian traditions.

to do the dangerous work while safeguarding their own persons and property.

The central character is Siri Ram; this is how he is described in *Abdication*, the sequel to this novel: 'A weak youth, compact of vanity, yet not devoid of virtue, he had become the dupe and scapegoat of the revolutionists, who had dragooned every generous instinct in him and perverted it, and then led him blindfold to the sacrificial stone.'[75] This dreamy, inert village lad grows up to be an unstable youth, avid for glory and martyrdom, yet lacking the stern stuff of which heroes are made. He is exhilarated by nationalist propaganda and moved by the wrongs which he believes the British have done to his country, and he sees himself playing many vital roles as a revolutionary. Lacking in moral fibre and discipline, his thoughts permanently confused, his mind hermetically sealed against 'true values',[76] his aspirations for austerity thwarted by his inclination for flamboyance, Siri Ram is a pitiful creature, crippled by the handicaps his culture imposes. After he is expelled from college for his political activities, he drifts with the conspirators, alternately ignored by them and flattered into undertaking dangerous tasks. When he serves as prison-editor (i.e. the front editor who takes responsibility for an issue calculated to be regarded by the authorities as seditious), he is arrested and pathetically enjoys the attention of his trial. In prison, he wilts, demoralized by hard labour and solitary confinement relieved only by the companionship of casteless vagabonds, gipsies and eaters of snakes and crows. Prison numbs his spirit and he wonders 'why liberty was not sweet. The fruit he had pined for was insipid.'[77]

On his release, the conspirators select him to assassinate Merivale, the district judge, promising him that this act will be the spark to ignite a revolution, after which he will be freed from prison by his victorious comrades. When they fête him and incite his flagging loyalty with emotional talk, the weak lad cannot resist their entreaties. And so Siri Ram's fruitless little life reaches its climax. Even as he prepares for the act of assassination, he is chilled with misgivings at seeing an Englishman 'in a white dinner jacket, driving a dogcart and looking confident and unconcerned though he was alone amidst thousands of Asiatics'.[78] As Merivale enters the train he is overwhelmed by garlands and behind one of these is Siri Ram and the revolver which slays the kindly and responsible Protector of the poor. The horror of the killing is heightened by what precedes it, for Merivale was on his way Home and had been speaking of the smell of hot mint on a cub-hunting morning. Initially confident of being freed, Siri Ram behaves with composure in jail, but as this hope fades he takes his own life. The reactions of the college principal, Skene, are a verdict: 'Poor little devil . . . he never had a dog's chance',[79] and as he leaves the cell 'ineffectual thunder rumbled in the distance',[80] a fitting comment on Siri Ram's life.*

* Valentine Chirol in his influential *Indian Unrest* (1910) discusses the secret societies and rites associated with Hindu revivalism: 'wherever political agitation assumes the most virulent character, there the Hindu revival also assumes the most extravagant shapes' (p. 30). In December 1909, Jackson, the collector of Nasik, a scholarly man devoted to Indian studies, sympathetic to Indians and trustful of them, was murdered by a young Chitpaven Brahman, Ananta Luxman Kanhere, when entering an Indian theatre on the eve of his departure from the district. He was waylaid by his assassin and shot with a revolver. Of the band of young Brahmans who had conspired to murder Jackson, Chirol continues, their 'unnatural depravity' represented a 'form of erotomania which is certainly much more common amongst Hindu political fanatics than amongst Hindus in general' (p. 30). Chirol stresses that the assassins were Chitpaven Brahmans, the most powerful and able Deccani Brahmans, who were 'the strange products both of the Western education which we have imported into India and of the religious revivalism which underlies the political agitation' (p. 59). 'They were certainly moral, if not physical degenerates, and most of them notoriously depraved, none bearing in this respect a worse character than the actual murderer. . . His appearance was puny, undergrown and effeminate, and his small, narrow and elongated head markedly prognathous, but he exercised over some of his companions a passionate, if unnatural, fascination which, I have been told by one who was present at the trial, betrayed itself shamelessly in their attitude and the glances they exchanged with him during the proceedings. Distorted pride of race and of caste combined with neuroticism and eroticism appear to have cooperated here in producing as complete a type of moral perversion as the records of criminal pathology can well show' (p. 60). Chirol's account suggests a different view of the 'psychology' of youthful nationalists, as well as providing a period-piece of sexual information. In his memoir, *Among Rajahs and Ryots* (1911), Sir Andrew H. L. Fraser, who was Lieutenant-Governor of Bengal from 1903 until 1908, i.e. the period of Bengali unrest, writes of the movement as being manipulated by mischievous wire-pullers influencing weedy young men, some of whom have strains of insanity in their blood,

Candler's version of the nationalist struggle is rooted in his conception of the Indian character.* The belief he records in his autobiography that men are helpless against race prejudice is here spoken by Skene, whose outlook and concerns provide the focus of the novel: 'Talking about colour prejudice. Don't you think it is rather a misnomer? I mean the whole thing is chemical. You might as well talk of the prejudices of acids and alkaloids.'[81] And, indeed, Candler's portrayal of Indians in *Siri Ram* and its sequel is coloured by the instinctive unease which Indians generate in him. But although sensations and judgements are placed beyond the province of the rational, reason is all the same invoked in the shape of intellectually supported arguments: the Indian is devoid of imagination, logic, philosophy and ethics he can understand, but 'there is no film in his mind that is responsive to poetic fancy. Imagination means much the same to him as multiplication. It is a kind of magnifying glass through which he sees a swollen universe.'[82] Western education is incomprehensible to Indians, the books they study bear no conceivable relation to their lives, yet the hybrid product 'is a better man in the end than the untutored product of the burnt clay'.[83] When Skene laments his pupils' lack of backbone and the failure of education to charge their batteries, Merivale, the judge, adds, 'It can't give fibre you mean. . . That only comes from the soil.'[84] And the Indian soil instead of nurturing its sons robs them of full human stature:

others of whom are stirred by personal grievances and the desire for revenge: 'the wretched lads whom they have influenced are found to be of unstable character, unsuccessful in their prosecution of education, and liable to that form of moral weakness which makes in India the half-brained and fanatical fakir or sanyasi' (p. 298). Compared with such contemporary opinions, Candler's attempt at interpreting a young assassin made a greater effort at understanding his motives.

* In his Introductory Memoir to his brother's autobiograhpy, Henry Candler quotes a letter from Joseph Conrad to Candler praising *Siri Ram*: 'as to the humanity of it, I have been immensely struck by the lofty impartiality of your insight and the sincere sympathy of your treatment. I have read those pages with sustained interest, and I have left them with a distinct sense of enlightenment in the intricate matter of racial psychology' (p. xxxvii); letter dated 12 November 1918. This praise from a friend, if restrained, is all the same interesting, coming as it does from an author who had himself explored 'racial psychology'.

Mool Chand, you would say, is a dear old man, slow-moving, slow-speaking, patient, strong, enduring, unbent in adversity. He is like an old prophet, clear eyed, grizzled in the sun, the brow and beard of Abraham, the gestures of an apostle. He salaams with a submissive dignity, raising both hands... But he would leave his aunt, or his little girl, at a pinch, to die in her plague-ridden bed alone.[85]

This attractive image, so appealing to an innocent observer, conceals an ignominious reality and when the village is infected with plague, Mool Chand does indeed tie his stricken daughter to her bed, providently locks the door of the hut and abandons her to join the flight of the villagers.

The soil drains curiosity and initiative, it shrinks awareness. This is a description of Mograon, a typical Punjab village:

Every house is the same, built of mud inside and out... The crumpled leaves of the neem, the garbage heap, the plough, every utensil in the house or the street except the brass cooking things is the colour of dust or mud. The cow, the buffalo, the cat, the children, the pig, the sleeping pariah dog, all more or less prostrated by the sun, look as if they had been modelled out of the different strata of discoloured clay in the blistered, cracked hollow which has served for the village pond. 'Dust to dust' is easy to understand in Mograon.[86]

Such is the birthright of Siri Ram, a lad whose consciousness is limited to knowledge of 'one kind of man and woman, one kind of food, one kind of house, and one kind of thought born of physical urgency or the puzzle of being';[87] 'in Mograon mud doesn't stop at matter, it permeates mind'.[88] From this sludge impressionable youths are transplanted to schools in urban centres, there to be exposed to the perplexing and heady influence of Western ideas and nationalist propaganda, and humiliated by British confidence and competence. The sight of a smooth-faced civilian driving past in his trap, 'spotlessly accoutred, cool, complacent, superior, masterful, infinitely remote', incites hatred in the freshly recruited young conspirators, 'newly fledged in liberal principles and the equality of man and inflated with a diet of Mill'.[89] It is such assaults on their self-esteem which drive the youths into political extremism.

At the time of writing *Siri Ram*, in 1910–11, Candler still tended to support British rule in India as morally justifiable. In a short addendum to the novel he expresses some admiration for the Arya Samaj as representing a religious and national revival but warns that it had become associated with sedition and 'it is our business to see that it does not threaten the stability of British rule'.[90] But already Candler's attitudes are beginning to oscillate between defending British rule and doubting it as he shows Skene grown weary of whipping and wheedling the reluctant East. By the time *Abdication* was written, in the early 1920s, Candler was convinced that the Empire was doomed. The theme of disenchantment with empire and imperial tasks is played out through the principal character, Riley, a newspaper editor, who dissociates himself from his countrymen's position of 'subordinating the interests of the ward to the privileges or prestige of the guardian'.[91]

Despite this shift in viewpoint and despite overt expressions of respect for the Indian nationalist movement under the leadership of Gandhi, the main Indian character, Banarsi Das, is once again depicted as a pathetic compound of vacuous idealism, spinelessness and muddled ruminations. This weak and impressionable youth develops as a carbon-copy of Siri Ram when he allows his cravings for glory to be exploited by the unscrupulous extremists. In turn obsequious and arrogant – to Riley who offers him a humble job on his newspaper he pompously replies, 'No doubt I am accomplished clerk and proof-reader. But you may try me on editorial staff. I am staunch nationalist of course. I spurn Rowlatt Acts and Punjab atrocities. Nevertheless I can be moderate if, and when, benign Government showers blessings'[92] – Banarsi Das is shown as typifying the confusions of the nationalist youth. Like Siri Ram he is attracted to the more florid expressions of the political movement, in this case the Kali cult. A prey to diverse influences, he becomes involved with the Hindu group which favours close cooperation with Moslems, and despite vacillation and fear, he accompanies the Wahabis, the fiery enthusiasts of Islam, on a pilgrimage. In contrast to these hardy men, Banarsi Das is exposed as being lamentably effete, and when he is suspected of being a spy, his erstwhile comrades tie him to a raft and leave him to his fate. He is rescued by a British officer and kindly treated – which is a further humiliation.

For some months he manages to avoid the Wahabis, but during a demonstration they find him and, as his assailant approaches, 'the pariah of fortune was too terrified to move. . . Banarsi Das, seeing the lathi in his hand turned his face to the wall, and covered his head with his hands. He recognized in the Shinwari the appointed agent of that arbiter whom he had never understood.'[93] The blow causes him to lose his reason. The final words of the novel are those of Skene to Riley: 'The doctor says it is a lesion, and there is just a chance that he may recover, but what the poor little devil will do if restored to an unsympathetically sane world, God only knows. He is a more pathetic figure than Siri Ram.'[94] The want of mental and physical stamina, the windy idealism, the courting of failure and disaster, make Banarsi Das and Siri Ram pitiful and ignominious figures, the powerless tools of contingency.

If Candler's estimate of the ingrained deficiencies in Indian character remained constant, there is an important evolution in his conception of the British dilemma. In *Siri Ram* we are shown Skene watching his countrymen at play and smiling to think that 'two hundred thousand of these folk ruled over three hundred million of the others by virtue of the vitality that was in them'.[95] It had been Skene's habit to reprimand his students for political involvement, the burden of his speeches being that 'the British have been straight and honourable in their dealings with you. . . We are here because it is our country. Incidentally it happens to be our way to recognise our obligations to our tenants as no other rulers have done or are ever likely to do.'[96]

Even while he is preaching such certainties at his pupils, uneasiness is beginning to enter his private conversations with his peers: 'When all is said and done, the case resolves itself in the end to the privilege of the weak to be ruled by the strong, and this is a very difficult thing for an Englishman to say without suspicion of brutality or pride.'[97] Nonetheless, a decade later Skene is recorded in *Abdication* as still enlarging on the benefits of British rule when talking to his students, but now his arguments are demolished by Riley. Without confidence in the Indians' capacity for self-government, and unconcerned with questions of a people's right to self-determination, Riley has no faith in the British claim of a mission to

India. He feels that race hatred has made British rule a calamity, disastrous to both sides: 'We don't want India. It's nothing but a festering sore. I'm all for a White Empire.'[98] 'We are neither of us good for the other.'[99] Riley's despairing 'mood of abdication'[100] is the converse of the triumphant British assertion that white men fulfilled their potentialities as empire-builders and imperial masters, and that because of their dominion the peoples of Asia would be aided and elevated. Through Riley, Candler reiterates his own sensations: 'It was being slowly impressed on me that neither white men nor brown contribute to the tranquillity of the other. The white man in his turn, when he unshoulders what has been called his burden, is glad that he will never again have to hustle the East.'[101]

Writing to his brother about the reception of *Abdication* Candler complained about the appraisals: 'The reviews are stupid in their attempt to classify "Abdication." "Is it a novel?" "Does it conform to the standard?" "Lacking in plot, love-interest" & C. I had no intention of writing a novel to any rule or standard or in imitation of any other novel, or in conformity with any tradition: all I aimed at was to show the collision between East and West in the clash of certain ideals, interests, personalities, and I chose my own way of presenting it.'[102] In both novels Candler shows that collisions and clashes between British and Indian are inevitable. To contrive meeting-points between Anglo-India and India is to invite failure. In the Club the members discuss the insuperable difficulties of the Governor's hobby, an East and West Club: the Indians are reluctant to socialize, British and Indian bore each other, blackballing will inevitably become a racial issue. A general recalls an official garden-party at which two Indians 'asked me to secure promotion for their relatives. Another solicited a chit';[103] Skene sadly remembers the comments of an Indian who had been consulted on the project and who had remarked that any Indian joining such a Club would be boycotted by his fellow-Indians. So much for artificial contact, but what of the possibilities for friendship between British and Indian?

'Can there be any genuine fellowship or sympathy between my countrymen and the English as a race until your people show a change of heart?'[104] asks Chatterji, the editor of a responsible Indian newspaper, a fair and disinterested man whose ironic and restrained journalism arouses the Indians and discomforts the British. Riley, who is regarded by the Anglo-Indians as an eccentric, favours cultivating personal relationships with Indians and is intensely curious about how Indians see the world. Yet when playing chess with Chatterji, whom he likes and respects, he feels the distance between himself and his companion: 'He saw a frail little man in a dhoti; bareheaded with bare calves. The casual Englishman in the street would probably have looked first at the calves, the white socks, black shoes, and incongruous black suspenders, covering a portion of the nakedness beneath the garment which is responsible, more than anything else, for the stranger's lack of sympathy with the Bengali.'[105]

Because Indians generate unease, because their appearance, deportment and habits are uncongenial to the British, the Anglo-Indian need for things English is intensified. From thoughts of Home they derive spiritual sustenance, from memories of 'new books on the table, the bowls of daffodils or snowdrops, the hostess sitting by the fire ... the wet furrow and the heath and the pine-woods and the autumn coverts which shed their leaves all at once and at the proper time'.[106] When Skene listens to a 'sleepy youth with large calves, stockings with embroidered flowers and patent leather slippers' reading 'Ode to a Nightingale', he is carried away in a daydream 'to a copse festooned with dog-roses and traveller's joy, the murmurous haunt of flies on summer eves – in which the rasping voice of the unhappy young man who read became a subconscious menace'.[107]

The actuality of India also sends Riley, vagabond and individualist, to escape into fragrant dreams of England: 'He longed to be out of the hybrid muddle, in a land where people were all of one complexion and the trees shed their leaves at the same time, and one could enjoy the sweet unpolitical smell of meadows, cut hay, sheep's parsley and meadow-sweet by the river, thyme and marjoram on the downs.'[108] Memories of Home are an essential refreshment in the aridity of India:

The heat of the afternoon was overpowering. The metallic sky hung low and solid above their heads like a dome or an oven, of the same consistency as earth, and emitting the same hard, fiery particles that pricked and parched the skin and dried up the moisture in one's throat.

It was the kind of day on which one is reminded that the East has been the home of futility for the last thousand years.[109]

India in all its manifestations drives the British back to their own kind and it is not only Skene who is soothed by the presence of his countrymen even though their minds are fallow, their interests narrow and their conversation confined in cliché. Riley, too, turns with relief from the extremists in the Indian press to the old-world pieties of old-time civil servants 'who regarded the English as divinely-appointed to chasten and chastise the heathen'.[110] So comforting is the atmosphere of the Club and the Anglo-Indian community that Riley's verdict on Anglo-India, despite his reservations about the Raj, is generous: 'They had led clean lives, single-minded, consistent, sane. In all direct personal relations with Indians, their influence had been wholesome.'[111]

Still Riley is not one of the Anglo-Indian herd and Gandhi appears to him as a Christ-like figure, 'a visionary void of self-deception',[112] a man with 'the gentle obstinacy of the seer'.[113] When Chatterji recounts incidents of the humiliating treatment he had received from Englishmen, of a drunken corporal ordering him from his seat in a railway-carriage, Riley is enraged: 'Commiseration would be an insult. The scum of Empire could not be excused or explained away. There is no room in a country, he thought, for a dominant and subject race. Each is bad for the other. One of the reasons why he had so little sympathy with the Imperial idea, was that he believed Empires were the nurseries of cads.'[114]

This idea comes to dominate Riley's thinking and ultimately determines his actions; he feels unable to participate in policing the East: 'We are too practical and cocksure. The curse of the country has been our gospel of efficiency. We have done everything imaginable for the Indians in a very superior and disagreeable way.'[115] Convinced that the Indian intelligentsia do not want the cooperation he had been willing to offer, he retreats from British India and becomes an itinerant eye-doctor in Tibet. By abdicating the white man's burden Riley is primarily seeking to save his own soul without tampering with the souls of others:

He would like to wander through Asia as a healer of the blind – a friendly magician, accepted everywhere. He would carry with him a serum for xenophobia; that was the best passport for the East. No one could fear the gifts he brought. He would hunt deer on horseback with the Cambodian and play polo in the streets of Hunza, a pagan among pagans, offering no spiritual prescription or good advice.[116]

His is the pre-imperialist dream of those romantics who sought the pristine in the East, who hoped to find tranquillity in the ancient, static cultures and who did not wish to remake Asia on Western lines or to dominate her politically. Riley is attracted by the Eastern stance of detachment from worldly things but he remains a Westerner in his fundamental judgements, maintaining that all the seers and prophets came from Asia only because Asia offers fewer opportunities for attachment. Englishmen, he feels, have too interested a sense of proportion to develop detachment from the phenomenal universe and the greater materialism of the West 'only means that we are more vital, more dynamic. We are more everything. If it came to the measure of spirituality, you would probably find we are more spiritual too, certainly more moral,'[117] he writes to Skene from his retreat. In the remote places of Asia he longs for Home, knowing that England will again drive him to the East. *Abdication* is permeated with a voyager's restlessness and dissatisfactions, for the West brings discontent and the East disillusion. In an obituary notice of Candler, Francis Yeats-Brown, himself the author of books recording his Indian experiences, referred to *Abdication* as Candler's finest achievement:

... through it ran a vein of doubt in the destiny of England which seemed to speak of Candler's failing health. It was as if Siva, the terrible God of the Ganges plains, destroyer of names and forms, had claimed another victim: one more fine brain succumbed to that disillusion that so often seeps into the marrow of those who work under the fierce sun of India and Iraq.[118]

Conclusions

Narrow in range and often superficial in conception Candler's writings do nonetheless transmit the white man's dilemma *vis-à-vis* 'the lands of the brown nations'. Disturbed by the suspicion that non-white peoples constituted a separate species, thoughtful men schooled in the proposition that mankind is one were driven to interpret and justify the sensation. Candler's explanation of racial incompatibility as something chemical is a most disarming plea for absolving those imprisoned or even sporadically gripped by racism of all responsibility either for their state of mind and emotion or for their overt behaviour, and establishes the futility of combating prejudice. But his apologia does not stop at this statement of a regrettable but inescapable fact and he advances an analysis of the Indian, i.e. the Hindu, psychology, attributing the defects of Indian character to a decadent social system in its turn deformed by the cruel Indian soil. Coexisting with this condemnation of an earthly India is Candler's inchoate fear of Hinduism's spiritual suppuration and its command of black magic.*

'Staying at home, they say, makes one insular; but, generally speaking, the more one sees of other people the more one loves and esteems one's own.'[119] This might suggest a curious limitation in one who sought his destiny as a traveller; still Candler was angry at Western blindness and arrogance towards the East and he recognized as a restriction in the British that 'we are slow to accept strange ideals and to admit that there can be much in views that jar with our own'.[120] He conjectures on how Orientals might see the West and on examining a frieze in a Jain temple imagines

my race as it appeared to the artist – proud, cruel, insolent, overbearing . . . mercenary, Philistine, busy and fussy about little things of the world, with no sense of the brevity of life and the enveloping shadow of the Infinite, doing everything for self-aggrandisement, yet believing themselves all the while to be the sole inheritors of the three cardinal virtues, which they dub Christian, and in obedience to which they drill the weak to their needs and exploit them to their material advantage in the name of righteousness. The Jain artist had defeated me. I blushed for the West.[121]

* Candler was also impressed by Indians' powers of benign magic and in *Siri Ram* he writes of a Swami active in the nationalist cause whose practice of yoga asceticism had equipped him to communicate his thoughts to others hundreds of miles away.

And yet this devastating judgement is ironically reversed by Candler's insistence on assessing Indians by Western standards of honour, integrity and attainment, fundamental to which is his innocent conviction that the British middle classes possessed a code of ideals based on true values. Deriving from this proposition is his casuistic scrutiny of Indian customs and activity – though no supporter of egalitarianism as a doctrine he despised caste as a barrier to mobility, and while not opposed on principle to the use of force in settling political conflicts, he was outraged at the militant methods which the nationalists were prepared to use against the Raj.

Perhaps Candler's major attainment is his account of how uncomfortable an environment India was to the white man. His consciousness of the British as displaced persons in Asia was intensified with the development of political unrest when a people whom they had seen as docile, supine and incompetent were challenging their mission to India. When Riley is gladdened by the Indian part of the city because though squalid it is real, he is struck by how ludicrous the British-built Outpost of Progress is: 'The Curzon Café, the Minto Motor Works, the Hardinge Home all spoke of the casual and matter-of-fact way in which we dump our British institutions on an unresponsive and reluctant soil.'[122] Without hope in the possibility of human relationships between the races, Candler offers in Riley's flight from a degrading situation the solution to the British problem in India. Only the white man as itinerant medicine man or as a traveller passing through, and neither with any expectation of integrating with the East, can survive the Orient. Candler's adventure with India led him to despair of intimacy on the human plane and drove him back to the lines of his own people. As in his early travel writings, when he had gazed on an India remote enough to seem admirable in certain lights, peopled with still figures strikingly posed against their incredible landscapes, his fictional transformation of India is enhanced by a distant view. Spared the discomfort of interacting with Indians, Candler can with assurance show them as marvellously interesting, as abstract representations within some fantastic design:

He saw a camel-sowar with his bright belt and rifle, riding the largest and cleanest camel he had ever seen, with bells jingling on its knees and

chest, and a bridle studded with cowrie shells and favours. He passed
through the metal bazaar, a whole street of shops, where spectacled old
men sat in dark recesses hammering bowls and cauldrons of copper and
brass. He saw a young blood on horseback with a falcon on his wrist; and
in the square in front of the fort by the big cannon the cart had to pull
up to let a Maharajah's body-guard sweep by, forty straight-set men in
green who passed on their cream-white chargers like one wave. In the
street by Siva's temple Siri Ram saw more fakirs and holy men than he
had seen in his life, some in ashen nakedness, and some in salmon-
coloured shifts with bowls and staves and leopards' skins and matted hair.
A shock-haired madman lurched along the street beside the cart, slowly
revolving one arm and crying out with every revolution that he was the
father of a devil. Beggars with lopped limbs and features all awry, with
no eyes or one, and that often webbed or wounded, with twisted lips or
mouth like a fleshy ring into which the snout had fallen, squatted under
the walls crying aloud for alms and stretching out their bowls with their
hands in supplication.[123]

CHAPTER 5

Edward J. Thompson, 1886–1946

Introduction

THE will to effect a Christian reconciliation inspired the message on India which Edward Thompson addressed to the two nations. Thompson was dedicated to humanizing an inhuman situation, putting forward and working to implement a multitude of suggestions and schemes aimed at making the British Empire a more generous and moral institution and the British–Indian relationship a more compassionate one. Yet to present Thompson as the paradigm of a liberal missionary–educationalist would be to muffle the resonances of his singular involvement with India. The many sides to his personality, his catholic interests, his diffuse talents, are suggested in his prolific and wide-ranging writings* and in his active participation in publicizing the cause of increased Indian independence from British tutelage. The focus of this chapter is on Thompson's consciousness of India and on the reordering of his Indian experience of his fiction, and his achievements as historian or activist, his political opinions and his attitudes to Empire will be considered only briefly as threads in the composite fabric of this transmutation. Both in his expositions and in his novels Thompson appears as an impassioned, volatile and contradictory man; perhaps this is a distorted view of an obviously complex person but, as the concern here is with a specific group of writings and not a biographical sketch, trust is placed in the tale and the teller is discovered through what he reveals and buries in the text. And Thompson gave fully of himself to his writings which are

---

* Thompson wrote novels, poems, plays, histories, biographies, essays and polemics; his versatility may be gauged from this sample of his published works – he edited a volume of Shakespeare, wrote biographies of Lord Metcalfe, Walter Raleigh, Robert Bridges and Rabindranath Tagore, translated and edited traditional and contemporary Indian literature and wrote studies of Indian history, customs, religions and ethics.

saturated with his thoughts, hopes and feelings; his persona is not effaced, his aspirations, disappointments and confusions are laid bare. In a letter lamenting the failure of his work to have a greater impact he wrote: 'it leaves no room for autobiography for such life as I have lived has been in my dreams and ideas which have been sufficiently set down'.[1]

The son of Wesleyan missionaries who had lived in southern India, Thompson was educated at a Methodist theological college and later took a London B.A. in 1909. In the following year he was ordained and went to Bankura Wesleyan College in Bengal as an educational missionary. During the war, as chaplain to the 7th Division, he participated in the Mesopotamian and Palestinian campaigns, winning an M.C. After his marriage in 1919 he returned to Bankura as acting principal of the college. During his early years in India Thompson had taken little interest in politics but now he became concerned with mounting tensions between British and Indian and he joined a group of missionaries in publicly opposing the Anglo-Indian community's endorsement of General Dyer's action at Amritsar. Thompson left India in 1923 to settle in England and after resigning from the ministry was for ten years lecturer in Bengali at Oxford where he taught I.C.S. probationers. Between 1934 and 1936 he was Leverhulme Research Fellow at Oxford and from 1936 until his death in 1946 he was Research Fellow of Indian History at Oriel College.[2]

It was after leaving India and the ministry that Thompson's efforts on behalf of British–Indian relations were intensified and his engagement in Indian political affairs, his visits to India in 1932, 1937 and 1939, his correspondence and meetings with Indian leaders, his consultations with influential English politicians, his lectures, articles, pamphlets and books were directed at mediating between the contending forces. Thompson admired Gandhi and was a friend of Nehru, but during the 1930s his political sympathies lay rather with the Liberals or Moderates, men like Sapru, Jayakar and Sastri who held aloof from the Indian National Congress, and the ways in which he formulated his support of Indian nationalism reflected this preference. In 1929–30 he criticized the Congress call for political independence as absurd and immoral, predicting that such counsel would result in administrative chaos and bloodshed, and advancing dominion status within the Empire as the correct solution.* Even when he came to accept that more far-reaching measures were needed, he continued to regret the pace of change.

Within the spectrum of British thinking on India during the 1920s and 1930s Thompson was on the left, one of a small minority who opposed their government's perspectives and policies, attacked Anglo-Indian attitudes and conduct and attempted to explain Indian grievances to an indifferent British public. Temperamentally Thompson was a radical; ideas, principles and matters of conscience excited and engaged him, yet ideologically he was during these years a moderate and his interventions were always in the direction of caution, of independence as a necessary and desirable ultimate goal rather than as an immediate prospect.† In later years Thompson came to question and reject totally the fact and concept of Empire,‡ but during the time of his active involvement in British–Indian politics his analyses of British rule in India did not come to grips with a critique of its imperialist core. Moreover, while he was outraged at British arrogance and moved by the humiliations to which Indians were subjected, while he scorned British claims to be fulfilling a racial mission and respected Indian demands for self-determination, he retained a commitment to the British idea of Empire: 'Not a few Englishmen are reluctant to let India go, not because of the tribute foreigners believe us to draw from it, but for the entirely unpractical reason that it has fired our dreams, and the best of our manhood has gone into her service.'[3]

Thompson's writings suggest a superb rhetorician who drew on an extensive emotional range, on eloquence and virtuosity of style, to convince his audience that his cause was just and his solutions viable, by demonstrating the absence of bigotry in his attitudes, the flexi-

* See *The Reconstruction of India* (1930).

† For a more radical non-Communist left-wing view on the Indian situation expressed during the thirties see Reginald Reynolds, *The White Sahibs in India* (1937). At this time the British Communist Party was producing analytical and propagandist material to influence opinion in support of the Indian struggle for independence; see especially the writings of R. Palme Dutt.

‡ *You Have Lived Through All This* (1939).

bility of his sympathies and the independence of his judgements. His highly personal expositions were coloured by the occasions on which they were delivered or written down, but his varied Indian writings are united by distinctive preoccupations and intentions: Thompson called on the British to make atonement for the wrongs which their nation had done to India, to guide and assist India with love instead of bureaucratic disdain. He exhorted them to strive for reconciliation with Indians, for a coming together which would merge Western values with Indian spiritual creativity. And he pleaded with the Indians to forgive while chastising them for complacency, rigidity and vanity. Much of what Thompson wrote reads like the incantations of a principled Englishman to the spirit of racial and international harmony rather than as coherent political analyses; some of his postures suggest the paradox of moral conscience joined with ineradicable paternalist suppositions. It is these ironies which set his writings apart from the many dusty museum pieces which clutter Anglo-Indian literature and make them such a significant source for understanding the British experience of India.

Expository Writings : The Impulse to Mediate

The diaries and letters which Thompson wrote during his early years in India suggest a spontaneous pleasure in Indian scenes and a slow discovery of Indian people. His initial contact with Indian youths enraged him and he was hostile to the form of nationalism then being expressed through the Hindu revival.* Anger of a different kind was aroused by the timidity of the jungle people whom

* In a letter dated 19 November 1912, Thompson wrote: 'Zila schools are hotbeds of silly Hinduism. When our school played them at football recently and one of my own side accidentally tripped me and I fell on the stones, barking my shins, the zila school-boys not only cheered but clapped... This is the kind of thing Hinduism is everywhere doing. These boys fancy these ethics are Hindu. It feeds their already bursting complacency.' Written to William Canton (1845–1926), sometime editor of *Contemporary Review*, author of verse and prose, including children's books and popular expositions written for the Bible Society. Zila denotes an administrative district; zila schools were run by Indians.

he met during his explorations of the surrounding countryside.* Thompson never lost a sense of irritation at certain Indian manner-isms but his responses from the outset sprang from compassion as well as annoyance. When in 1911 he visited the Wesleyan Mission at Trichinopoly where his parents had lived, he was embarrassed at the servile devotion shown him by his father's old sweeper:

> My bathroom door suddenly opened, and in fell an old woman, who threw herself on the ground and passionately kissed both my very filthy boots. All through the interview she wept. I lifted up the poor old creature... She is a Roman Catholic ... but she is absolutely heathen, always says 'swami' and has never been known to mention the name of Christ. She worshipped me in correct Hindu fashion as she spoke. It made me feel *very* bad. I could have cried.[4]

In a situation where it was usual for the British to retreat behind the lines of their own society, Thompson went out to meet and know the people he meant to teach and save, and it was through the ancient literature of India and the contemporary writings of Bengal that he came to sympathize with the peoples of India.†

This enthusiasm for Indian literature persisted when Thompson settled in England, and in the face of Anglo-Indian and British ignorance and indifference Thompson translated and edited both

---

* 'These peasants, if you ask them the way, stare and then bolt. One man I managed to catch. He worshipped me with hands orthodoxly folded, but told me nothing. Only great grace kept me from biffing him... I reached Raipin and switched off into the village. I addressed a woman, asking her the way to Sarenga. She laid down her water-pot, ran into her house and barricaded it... I came upon a group of boys playing... They fled but I circumvented them and pressed them against the wall. They were too terrified to do anything but whimper and slink away.' Letter to Canton, dated 10 February 1913. As well as expressing the frustrations of an Englishman trying to communicate with frightened people living in remote places, Thompson's self-mocking letter shows the reactions of the 'real Indians' to the presence of their masters in a light which Anglo-Indians did not care to emphasize.

† Amongst Thompson's papers is an article in the *Indian Methodist Times* of November 1913 interpreting a folk-play, *A Ram-Lila*, and an article in manu-script, probably written for the college newspaper, in which he explains how he had come to understand the emotional patriotism of Bengal through listening to the songs of D. L. Rai.

traditional writings and modern Bengali novels.* In his introduction
to a modern novel, Thompson explains that the author's fiction deals
largely with social problems, with tyrannies 'that have obsessed the
modern Bengali life against reason and humanity' and he stresses its
value in 'showing the view taken of themselves by Bengalis, and in
bringing the foreign reader closer to Indian life than perhaps any
other work given to the outer world'.⁵

This concern with showing his countrymen how much they could
learn about Indians from their literature is also apparent in his
biography of Rabindranath Tagore where he is especially interested
in those areas of Tagore's thinking which matched his own developing
ideas on Britain's relationship with India: 'he realised the greatness
of the contribution the West has made in things of the spirit no less
than of mechanics, and never had any sympathy with the wish to
shut India out of the community of thought and progress. . . East
and West, Tagore says, again and again, need each other.'⁶ He invokes Tagore to condemn British obtuseness in their dealings with
India, quoting his statement that 'they are fully aware that they do
not know us, and yet they do not *care* to know us', and he associates
himself with Tagore's censure of the Indian people for weakness.

Thompson seems to have seen his task as the chastisement of both
sides in the conflict, and he was indignant at his own nation's short-
sightedness and insensitivity as rulers of India. He deplored the
British lack of imagination about India and his judgement of the
educational policies imposed on Indians was harsh and unequivocal:
'If I seem unwilling to go into the problems of Indian education, it is
because I wasted the best years of my life trying to work the system. . . I think it is a monument to Indian ability that so many
became genuinely educated despite the system.'⁷ Thompson's experiences as an educational missionary convinced him that the quality

---

* See, for example, *Bengali Religious Lyrics*, translated with Arthur Marshman
Spencer (1923). Thompson introduced two modern writers, Dinesh Chandra
Sen and Narayan Bhattachariya, to English readers and enthused over the novels
of Bibhutibhusan Bandopadhyaya Banerji whose books, *Pather Panchali* and
Aparajita, became known in the West when they were filmed by Satyajit Ray
in the mid 1950s. These novels were subsequently translated by T. W. Clark
and Tarapada Mukerji (1968).

of education in India was inferior, its content irrelevant to the people's lives and its social effects disastrous. In his novels his *alter ego*, Alden, also an educational missionary, eloquently laments a system which had been foisted on a people against their traditions and temperament and geared to rote-learning and not enlightenment. *An End of the Hours*, Thompson's most melancholy Indian novel, tells of Alden's pain at realizing that by his vigour he had fooled the young men whom he had educated into the delusion that they mattered and had a future, because, unlike an independent country, India offered no rewards to the educated and the majority of his students had been destined to be either petty clerks or unemployed.

Thompson was convinced that lacerated relations between British and Indian could be healed, and he put great faith in the power of knowledge to alter men's feelings, to make British behaviour towards Indians gentler and more loving, to convince Indians that there were Englishmen sincerely anxious to make amends. The Preface to the American edition of his work on the 1857 rebellion expresses this hope:

This book sets out matters which no Indian could, or perhaps should, set out, and I believe that it will change the attitude of every Englishman who reads it to the end ... our thought about Indians and the Indian problem cannot but be more patient, more humble, when we remember the past. I hope too that some Indian readers will feel less despairing of a change in attitude in Englishmen when they realise how much our minds have been abused by untruthful history and will feel that an outlet has been found for an expressed bitterness that has been corroding their own thoughts.[8]

The history of India, Thompson believed, needed to be rewritten 'as an act of free grace and love of truth'.[9] He was uncertain, and on some issues guilty, about the British record in India and he desired to salvage the good things towards which he felt the British Empire aspired: 'Many special virtues, as well as feelings, went to the building up of the British Empire and its retention by a minute force. A high sense of duty, incorruptibility, a passion for improving, a recognition of social responsibility.'[10] These convictions influenced the emphasis in his concrete recommendations such as those made to the Rhodes Trustees on whose behalf he visited India in 1932 to report on the possibility of cooperation between British and Indian writers:

> These writers are very sensitive to Western opinion and immense good would be done even politically if their self-respect could be helped by feeling that their intellectual effort was not an isolated and unknown thing but recognised as part of the Empire's life. . . We need to get into Indians' thought the fact that a nation's prestige does not depend on its political and military importance but on its intellectual standing. . . It seems to me pikestaff plain that relations that exist solely on the administrative and political plane . . . are far too narrow to be safe.[11]

Two currents of thought seem to be flowing here: Thompson's expression of respect for Indian creativity is certainly genuine, as is his opinion that there are national attainments as valuable as political power. But in accepting the boundaries of 'the Empire's life' as fixed and in conceding as valid such concepts as making relations 'safe', Thompson is thinking within the conceptual framework of Britain's dominion over India and is offering proposals calculated to ensure its continuation. Indeed, in referring, in *The Reconstruction of India*, with pride and approbation to the achievements of the British Empire in India, he advances the classical justification for British overlordship in defending the 'saheb is a saheb' Punjabi tradition for having pulled the area out of barbarism by bringing roads, canals, irrigation and order.* The way that he contrasts Indian muddle with British efficiency is just as conventional:

> There is much to say for autocracy in India. It is exasperating to work with committees or boards. The one vigorous Englishman can get the

---

* This book in its original version, *Reconstructing India*, was directed at the American public and Thompson may have been on the defensive about the British achievement in India, and if so, this would only confirm his fundamental identification with the British. There is in Mrs Thompson's possession a letter from Colonel, later Sir, Nan Kuar Haksar, who with K. M. Pannikar represented the Indian States at the first session of the Round Table Conference: 'I can only wonder that there are people in England who can still look upon you as a hostile critic of Imperial policies, and therefore, as a sort of Empire-wrecker. At any rate, how can such people as have taken the trouble to read this book [*The Reconstruction of India*] look upon you otherwise than as the greatest, because the most impartial, friend of England?' Letter dated 20 November 1934.

job done; served with Indian colleagues, he is held up and blocked. It is almost impossible to exaggerate the casualness, the lack of interest, the miscellaneous futility, that many Indians bring as their sole contribution to any business in which they assist.[12]

There was in Thompson's approach to Indians a strong inclination to the didactic and a most telling instance of this was his reception of Katherine Mayo's notorious 'exposure', *Mother India* (see pp. 63–4), a book which condemned the culture as depraved and the people as perverted. Reviewing the book in the *Nation and Athenaeum* (30 July 1927), Thompson pointed out that the Hindu social system had already been criticized by Hindu reformers, missionaries and government commissions, but he felt that Miss Mayo's work offered new and valuable information on such things as the sexual injuries sustained by child-wives: 'There is no place for squeamishness when we come to the Hindu doctrine of women. Hinduism is beneath contempt in its worship of the male and its sex obsession generally.'* On another occasion when discussing the book Thompson wrote:

Hindu social practice, Hindu social and religious thought, are all in the same absurd confusion that everything else Indian is. Miss Mayo did this service – a grand one; for the first time, we see Hindu civilization fighting not for praise, but for bare respect. This should have happened long ago; Europe and America were once as unhygienic in practice as India now is and child marriage was not unknown. But we hold nothing of ours exempt from criticism. India needs to take the same attitude.[13]

The tone of both these commentaries points to a curious insensitivity in a sensitive man. Indian civilizations, Hindu and Moslem,

---

* Thompson criticizes the author for her consistently ungenerous attitudes, her reliance on hearsay and the paucity of her facts, and considers that she lost her case when she wove into it 'a conviction that the white man's rule is so overwhelmingly good for inferior breeds that it is only wickedness that makes it dissatisfied'. Referring to *Mother India*, a modern commentator has succinctly summed up its approach: 'Written on a single plane of total revulsion and narrowly focused bias, it had no room for qualifications... The most salient point made by the book's more thoughtful Indian and Western critics was that while it did not lie in its main particulars, it lied monumentally as a whole.' Harold Isaacs, *Scratches on Our Minds: American Images of China and India* (1958), p. 268.

had been fighting for bare respect for the greater part of British rule in India, a fact which Thompson knew and deplored in his capacity as historian. Yet in discussing with some tolerance a book which Gandhi had aptly described as 'a drainpipe study', Thompson ignores the tendency of a people, or class, in a relationship of political and social subservience to their critics, to retreat into a total defence of their customs and mores when these are held up to scorn by their rulers. Moreover, Thompson seems unaware that foreign domination can intensify a people's rigorous adherence to custom as a means of defending their corporate identity against the calculated assaults of the masters to alter and 'reform' this, and that these same customs can be suddenly abandoned in the course of a people's struggle to free themselves from overlordship.* Thompson's homily seems arid, and when he advises Indians to show a sense of humour about the whole affair while using so dubious a base as *Mother India* to deliver his own obloquy on Indian society, he is revealing deep-seated confusions in his attitudes to India.

Although Thompson adopted the stance of a clear-visioned and objective man aloof from herd-emotions – 'I am determined to keep my sanity over this Indian business. I am not going to be swayed by Indian mob-psychology any more than I will be swayed by the mob-psychology of my own folk'[14] – his opinions derived as often from credulousness and whim as from research and reason. A case in

---

* Frantz Fanon's studies of the Algerian Revolution offer important insights into this process, especially his essay, 'Algeria Unveiled', in which he discusses the significance of the veiled woman in colonial society: 'What is in fact the assertion of a distinct identity, concerned with keeping intact a few shreds of national existence, is attributed by the occupier to religious, magical, fanatical behaviour... There is thus a historical dynamism of the veil that is very concretely perceptible in the development of colonization in Algeria. In the beginning, the veil was a mechanism of resistance, but its value for the social group remained very strong. The veil was worn because tradition demanded a rigid separation of the sexes, but also because the occupier *was bent on unveiling Algeria.* In the second phase, the mutation occurred in connection with the Revolution and under special circumstances. The veil was abandoned in the course of revolutionary action. What had been used to block the psychological or political offensives of the occupier became a means, an instrument... It is the necessities of combat that give rise in Algerian society to new attitudes, to new modes of action, to new ways.' *A Dying Colonialism* (1965), pp. 41, 63-4.

point is his approach to the Amritsar incident. In 1920 he had publicly dissociated himself from the Anglo-Indian endorsement of General Dyer's action; but when visiting India in 1932, a dinner-time conversation with public figures involved in the event convinced him that Dyer had ordered the shooting without realizing that there was no exit for the crowd, and that Dyer, who was not at all anti-Indian, had indeed saved the Punjab from rebellion. It was because his countrymen treated him as a martyr of officialdom which had instituted the Hunter Commission of Inquiry that he was transformed from conscience-stricken soldier doing his duty into insolent braggart.* The account of interested parties is presented by Thompson as the definitive version of events and contrary information which would upset his thesis is ignored although it was known to him – for example, Dyer's order whereby all Indians wishing to pass through a particular street in which a woman missionary had been beaten were made to crawl its length. Here Thompson's concern seems to be focused on what Anglo-India insisted had been a danger to the Raj rather than on the victims of a belligerent action. But some years later he abandoned an appraisal of events formed during a

---

* Reactions to Thompson's version are interesting: a review of the book in which it appeared, *A Letter from India* (1932), in *The Times Literary Supplement*, 25 August 1932, praises Thompson for recording in print that which had long been known to the residents of the Punjab, a reference, it is assumed, to the white residents. Nehru, in *An Autobiography* (1936), is unimpressed by Thompson's account: he doubts that anyone standing on the raised ground where Dyer had stood could not have known that there were no exits, and even if this had been so, 'that would hardly lessen his responsibility'. He goes on to recall a train journey which he made in 1919. On waking in his upper berth he could not help overhearing the loud conversation of his fellow-passengers who were military officers: 'One of them was holding forth in an aggressive and triumphant tone, and soon I discovered that he was Dyer, the hero of Jallianwala Bagh, who was describing his Amritsar experiences. He pointed out how he had the whole town at his mercy and he had felt like reducing the rebellious city to a heap of ashes, but he took pity on it and refrained. He was evidently coming back from Lahore after giving his evidence before the Hunter Committee of Inquiry. I was greatly shocked to hear his conversation and to observe his callous manner' (pp. 43–4). A letter from Humayum Kabir, the Moslem poet, comments that Thompson's explanation of Dyer's psychology makes no difference to his judgement of the man (letter in Mrs Thompson's possession).

convivial evening and in his joint work with Garratt an entirely different view on Amritsar is presented. By 1939 Thompson was writing of the Jallianwala Bagh massacre and accusing Dyer and his associates of physical brutality and emotional cruelty.*

Thompson contained multitudes and was bound to contradict himself and it is not the inconsistencies which flaw his interpretations – indeed, these inconsistencies are often a development in viewpoint – but rather his surrender to impulsive judgements at moments when deliberation is essential. It is because Thompson set himself up as a soothsayer that he draws attention to the incorrect predictions he made, and the deficiencies in his method of reasoning and argument are nowhere more evident than in his correspondence with Nehru during the 1930s. In a letter dated 31 October 1936 Nehru writes:

I am very much surprised at your statement that the nationalist movement is weaker today than it has been for the last twenty years or more, and that we are in a position of humiliating helplessness such as we have not been in for many years past... You judge, I imagine, from the individuals you have met, mostly liberals, communalists and the like... You lay great stress rightly on the poverty of India. But having done so you seem to forget it when you suggest a line of action for the future. That line of action has no reference at all to poverty or unemployment.

A further letter, dated 22 April 1937, takes issue with the assessments and prophecies made by Thompson in a series of articles in the *News Chronicle* written late in 1936, where Thompson had suggested that Congress was composed of excited crowds of callow youths and Nehru was accused of cursing Sastri instead of cooperating with him:

I have not ceased to wonder at the fact that all your stress, in discussing India, was laid on unimportant and irrelevant factors... Your analysis of the Congress, again, astonishes me. I may be partisan and prejudiced but I have been very intimately connected with the Congress for over twenty years and I have come into touch with millions of our people all over India. During the last year I addressed audiences, not callow youths but huge peasant and city audiences, totalling, it is moderately estimated, ten million persons. Big audiences may not mean much and yet there is

* *You Have Lived Through All This.*

significance in these figures. And I saw enormous crowds from the Himalayas to Cape Camorin; I mixed with them, I sensed some of the ferment that moved them. . . You talk of democracy and regret the failure of it in Europe, and yet fail to appreciate the only real democratic organisation in India, and you think in terms of handfuls of people at the top imposing their will on others. The Congress may act wrongly of course. But even when it does so it represents the failings of the Indian people, and being a dynamic moving thing, it has the capacity to right itself.

If Thompson is regarded principally as an expositor then his intellectual weaknesses, which undermine his reliability as a reporter and diminish the intrinsic value of his analyses, occupy too prominent a place and overshadow his Christian commitment to resolving political strife and social conflict. A letter to E. W. Thompson, a friend who was a missionary in south India, expresses his belief in the beneficent power of repentance. Thompson argues the need for a book exposing British barbarities during the 1857 uprising and it is evident that his correspondent disagreed with him, fearing that such revelations would stir up further hatred:

I cannot bring myself to believe that hanging of – say ten thousand, I believe it was nearer twenty thousand – blowing to pieces of hundreds, burning of hundreds of villages, and a war without quarter, has passed unremembered and unresolved. The Indian Government has suppressed all the evidence of resentment, remember . . . why does Andrews* keep havering about the necessity of our doing prayaschitta?† For what? . . . I'm afraid I feel too bitterly about it. I'd like as an individual Englishman, to do my bit of prayaschitta, if I could. . . I don't seem to have got home to you how deeply I feel about the matter. It's obsessed me of recent months. I've thought of very little else. . . You and I hitherto have both been very distinct moderates. . . But now I'm becoming a left-winger pretty fast, and I feel how patronising nearly all propaganda, political *and*

* The Rev. Charles Fuller Andrews (1871–1940), a Cambridge don, went to India in 1904; he was a member of the Cambridge Mission at Delhi, a supporter of the Indian independence movement, and author of numerous books on Indian life and aspirations. His ideas on Bengali culture, on education, and on the form which the assimilation of East and West should ideally take, may have influenced Thompson. Andrews was an active supporter of Gandhi, joined Tagore's ashram at Santiniketan and was intimately identified with Indian life.

† A Sanskrit term meaning a gesture.

religious, and education, must seem to an Indian. I can hardly imagine an Indian accepting Christianity – an educated and thinking Indian that is – as it comes to him to-day, from missionaries who've got *all* their knowledge of India from books written by British... I understand why my Tagore annoyed them, and I marvel that they bore with me in my Indian days. We *are* a gauche, crass lot.[15]

Not only did Thompson wish to bear witness to the sins his nation had committed during the 1857 rebellion, but he hoped to alter his readers' perception of events and their aftermath. In a letter to S. K. Ratcliffe,* written after publication, Thompson insists that he is a misunderstood moderate whose purpose had been to counteract inflammatory material being published by both sides:† 'it was time a cruel, lying legend, which has poisoned our minds for twenty years, was blown out of existence, and time that Indian history began to be treated in a spirit of scholarship... I wanted to help root out of the Indian mind some of its "inferiority complex" and sense of misrepresentation, as well as our own misunderstanding.'

The Other Side of the Medal brought the Indian case into focus, suggesting the causes of their grievances and pointing to the inroads which British rule was making into their lives, presenting a perspective which at that time had received scant attention from Englishmen. Informed by passion and written in pursuit of a cause, motives which need not have impaired the spirit of scholarship to which Thompson aspired, the work is in fact a powerfully presented polemic, neither wholly academic nor entirely propagandist, which in its combination of historical perspective and moral concern

---

* Letter dated 15 December 1925. Thompson writes that publication was a great risk as he was then teaching at Oxford: 'the Indian Government practically pays for my Delegacy, and my fellow-lecturers without exception are ex-I.C.S. officials of distinction. They think I have done a very shocking thing.'

† A reference to the republication of Vinayaka Damodara Savakar's work, *The Indian War of Independence of 1857*, initially published anonymously in 1909. Savakar, who died in 1966 aged eighty-three, was a prominent Hindu communalist and one-time President of the Hindu Mahasabha, and author of *Hindutva* (Hinduism). His work on the 1857 rebellion was banned in India until 1946. The other reference is to *Letters Written During the Indian Mutiny* by Lord Frederick Sleigh Roberts with a Preface by his daughter, Countess Roberts (1924).

makes it something of a classic amongst British writings on India.

Thompson presents a succinctly argued indictment of the dangerous myths kept alive by the British:

our histories and our novels* have proceeded on certain clearly marked lines. There is the Indian, 'half devil and half child', docile, patient, capable of a dog-like devotion, given to mysticism and brooding contemplation, and yet with all these good qualities liable to perversion into a treacherous seditionist or blood-thirsty fanatic; there is the Englishman, silent, efficient, inflexible, just, dispensing to each his deserts. It is not strange that Indians should be restive under such a portrayal, or even that Kipling's magnificent work should be read with feelings of pain and humiliation.[16]

Such legends, Thompson continues, have contributed to Indian antagonism towards the British, but at the core of their hatred are popular memories of the rebellion and the subsequent uncritical treatment by the British of historical evidence relating to the event. Questions as to how far it was a popular movement, how far a real war of independence, had not been sufficiently explored, and Thompson's own assessment is that it was 'another of the world's great servile revolts . . . with all its accompaniments of sickening terror and cruelty'[17] and, as in all such revolts, there was 'suffering and devilish cruelty on both sides'.[18] English historians, however, expose the rebels' barbarities while veiling British excesses.† Therefore, it is essential 'that we should look, once, clearly and finally, at the side which has been hidden from ourselves; then we shall understand in part what madness is working subtly in the Indian mind today'.[19]

Despite his receptiveness to fresh ideas, some areas of Thompson's beliefs seemed unexposed to empirical scrutiny and this drove him

* Thompson deplores the Anglo-Indian conception of Indian life which was derived from the writings of Ethel M. Dell or Maud Diver, and stresses that Anglo-Indian attitudes towards Indians tend to be second-hand, much of them based on 'Mr Kipling's brilliant and by no means wholly misleading caricatures of Indians' (p. 15).

† Thompson quotes *The Oxford Dictionary of India* (1964), p. 719, where the following phrase occurs: 'the justly infuriated troops took terrible revenge'.

to present his personal emotions as viable political perspectives and social analyses: 'It is not larger measures of self-government for which they are longing, it is the magnanimous gesture of a great nation, so great that it can afford to admit mistakes and wrong-doing, and is too proud to distort facts.'[20] Certainly Thompson wanted to identify with the pain and humiliation which he knew Indians experienced but this generous disposition was counterbalanced by an inclination to impose on others the sensations which he *wanted* them to have: 'There is no commoner word on Indian lips today than *atonement*. England, they say, has never made atonement; and she must do it before we can be friends. The word in their minds is the Sanskrit *prayaschitta*, usually translated *atonement*; but its meaning is rather *a gesture*.'[21] But this exhortation to a bountiful act from the British was Thompson's cry and not that of articulate Indians who by this time were longing for larger measures of self-government. His conception of Indians as wounded and helpless, supplicating for the human touch, the gracious gesture from the ruling race, is one of the subtlest expressions of Christian-inspired liberalism in British writing about India; that which is offered as the cure for British guilt is made to serve also as the fulfilment of Indian desires and the implication of such an approach is to deny Indians the opportunity for discovering themselves through making their own experiences. At the heart of Thompson's litany of penance is the impulse to usurp the Indians' will to action and to colonize their capacity for feeling.

Neither his sincerity nor his passion for justice is in question and Thompson's hope that British repentance might lead to reconciliation is given its most explicit expression in a play, *Atonement*, which he wrote at the same time as *The Other Side of the Medal*. A dramatized debate between representatives of the British and Indians, uneasy officials and missionaries on the one hand, militant and pacifist nationalists on the other, the focal point of this play is a statement of the wrongs committed by both sides, the British throughout their years as rulers of India, the Indians recently and in retaliation. Thorp, a missionary, who has identified himself with Gandhi's cause, claims that at the root of Indian discontent is the failure of the British to make atonement: 'England has got to repent for all her injustice. Then there will be peace.'[22] This sentiment is echoed by Ranade, a Gandhi-like figure who, after a violent incident in which both Englishmen and Indians are killed, declares: 'Murder's audit is never settled. *This* is atonement – when an Indian – or an Englishman – says: "I will *not*. Blood is due to me, but I will not exact it. I will pay the price myself." God is listening for that voice.'[23] A healing resolution is recommended in the actions of the English who, shamed but ennobled by hearing the record of their wrongs from Indian lips, allow the Indians responsible for the riot to flee, and the gesture of penitence is cemented by Thorp who leaves his own community to live amongst Indians: 'You remember what we said about the spirit of hatred that was walking through India. But there is another spirit, that seeks reconciliation. . . It's taken possession of me.'[24]

It is the Indian characters who, while protesting at the injustices of British rule, also defend the British aspiration to revitalize and improve India, and both the attacks and the apologias appear as symptoms of Thompson tormenting himself with solving the conundrum of right motives entangled with cruelty and aggression, all of which he saw as inextricably involved in the British experience of India. The play, which is a succession of statements rather than a dramatic unfolding of latent possibilities – appeals are presented as solutions, the self-realization of the characters is facile and patently manipulated for didactic purposes – expresses the strength of Thompson's Christian belief that penance can redeem those who have sinned and expiate the wrongs which have been done, and the play is itself an act of exorcism. His novels, too, are permeated with hopes presented as actualities, but because his conscious concern with harmony is eroded by doubts and antipathies which run counter to his formulated ideas, they provide an altogether richer insight into how Thompson experienced India.

The Search for Meaning in the British–Indian Encounter

Amongst Thompson's numerous novels are three which constitute an Indian trilogy. These are loosely structured around his lament for warped relations between the races and his search for a value inhering in the British–Indian encounter. His estimate of these novels –

An Indian Day (1927), *A Farewell to India* (1931) and *An End of the Hours* (1938) – is suggested in a letter written to a friend:

An Indian Day, an unbelievably crude and grotesque book, nevertheless managed to give the best picture we have of the last generation of Anglo-Indian thought and existence, just as *An End of the Hours*, a very slight and unambitious and deliberately swift-moving book, no novel, yet not quite reminiscence except for its thinking aloud, showed prophetically the collapse and showed also in prediction, which was quite definite, that India was about to side-step us, making of the old controversies, about Dominion Status and the rest, an irrelevance.

Returning to *An Indian Day* in the same letter he comments: 'it struck just sufficiently athwart the strong and popular Kipling tradition to ensure that the student of Indian social life will sometimes glance at it'.[25]

At the time of publication, Thompson's novels were greeted as expositions of social attitudes and political opinions rather than as literary creations,* but however valuable they are as a record and

---

* The review of *An Indian Day* in the *New Statesman*, 4 June 1927, pp. 253–4, finds it heavily written, sentimental, filled with soliloquy and awkward and unreal social conversations, but displaying a larger, more intimate and exact knowledge of life in India than *A Passage to India*, to which book Thompson's novel had been offered as a 'counterblast' by the publishers for reasons not clear to the reviewer. The novel is praised for providing a concrete picture of India under the British and for revealing the fundamental dilemma – how impossible it is for the British either to remain or leave because of the intrinsically insoluble problem of Indian self-government. Like Forster, Thompson is concerned with the complex nature of the British problem in India, and he succeeds in showing the difference between Eastern and Western ethics. The reviewer in *The Times Literary Supplement*, 9 June 1927, describes the novel as a thoughtful work, an anatomy of Indian melancholy, and the author's delight in Indian scenery is noted. *The Times Literary Supplement* review of *A Farewell to India*, 15 January 1931, suggests that, although cast in the form of a novel, it is a political dissertation, the subject rather than the aesthetic appropriateness of what is said being of interest. The book, this review continues, is a monologue on Indian problems and the opinions of the main character, Alden, are worth attention although these take the form of unsatisfying antinomies. The English are portrayed as lacking in grace, the Indians as not desirous of making positive, practical use of freedom, and it is not clear on what Alden bases his hopes that reason will ultimately triumph. *An End of the Hours* was described in *The Times*

interpretation of an actual situation, their real significance is as distillations of a receptive and multiplex man's total experience of India. The tension between ideas formally stated and sensations actually known by the characters gives dimension to Thompson's account as does the interplay of divergent manners, beliefs and aspirations which survive as fluid and unresolved entities despite the author's imposition of syntheses.

An Indian Day is set in Vishnugram, a Bengali station near Darjeeling; the time is 1925–6. Thompson, whose voice pervades the novels, expresses his exasperation with both the Anglo-Indian and the Indian communities, although condemnation is tempered by an exegesis on the sources of estrangement between the races. The plea is that hostility be wiped out by love. These concepts and processes are communicated through the speech and actions of one-dimensional characters whose function it is to articulate viewpoints and state problems and who exist only to act out the conflict and its solution. The Indian characters declare their reactions to the presence and impact of the British and model those facets which Thompson considers are essential to the Indian personality. Government clerks, inefficient and dignified, are shown to tolerate their masters without in any way adjusting their dispositions, and the fury of the new judge at finding his office in disorder elicits only calm disapproval from the record-keeper: ' "Why do you vex an old man with these vanities?" his manner asked. "Saheb, saheb, let the wheels of justice start revolving, but do not seek to know too much about them. We shall be gone tomorrow – what does it matter who or what an accused person is?" '[26]

British rule, however, has made deep inroads into Kamalakanta Neogyi, magistrate and collector of Vishnugram, an Oxford-educated and painfully displaced person 'without a country or an ethos'.[27] Unlike his father, who had been an English-worshipping

---

Literary Supplement, 22 October 1938, as a 'ruminative epilogue that looks back upon and in some relations summarizes not the Rev. Robin Alden's physical but his spiritual adventure', as well as being a conspectus of certain aspects of contemporary life in India. Thompson is said to be concerned with what he sees as the loss of physical and mental vitality of the British race and their loss of power.

member of the Brahmo Samaj in the days when this reform movement within Hinduism was oriented to the West, Neogyi is serving
the Raj 'at a time when such service seemed to most of his countrymen unprincipled selfishness and lack of courage and patriotism'.[28]
Contemptuous and abrupt towards minor rajahs who assume that he
will connive at their corrupt practices, and outraged at the appointment of an unprincipled Indian Commissioner over him, this model
of Indian Civil Service probity knows that he remains a stranger to
his British friends who giggle and sneer at his flowery manner of
speech. Sadhu Jayananda, once a member of the I.C.S., who has
renounced worldly concerns to live as an anchorite in the jungle,
incarnates Thompson's conception of Indian spiritual attainments.
The Sadhu had been an active opponent of the government over the
partition of Bengal and, although he is still known to associate with
political agitators, 'he was dreaming of infinity, withdrawing from
existence into union with the *Paramatma*, the Absolute, that un-
conditioned pulseless Silence over whose surface our brief lives flit
and twitter for their imaginary hour'.[29]

The Anglo-Indians are less abstractly conceived and have more
substance as naturalistic portraits. If Thompson was repelled by the
philistinism of his peers, their herd-behaviour and circumscribed
outlook, he still retained his emotional membership of the empire-
building family and this becomes apparent in his treatment of
British motives and behaviour in India. A major who 'spoke of
Indians and of everything Indian as if their presence on the planet
distressed him physically' and who believed every Indian nationalist
to be venal, had 'read largely about Indian history, customs, religion,
even literature'[30] and, despite these enormous gaps in his awareness,
is said to be a fundamentally decent, generous and sympathetic man.
If the Anglo-Indian community was intellectually third-rate there
were reasons for this: 'Everyone had to get on with his job.'[31] When
Anglo-Indians returned to England they appeared as mouths and
pens of folly and prejudice, reduced by the 'uneasy new environment of the West, where men thought and where they were contra-
dicted by their peers, and not eternally deferred to and employed in
action only'.[32] But in India, Thompson continues, the Englishman
was a giant:

administering the affairs of myriads evenly and firmly – administering
them with an utter lack of perception of what was in the minds of a subject
populace and with an unshakeable conviction that he was in the place of
God and could not err – if you like doing his magnificent work like a
damned fool – but has the world ever seen such glorious damned fools?
Has it ever seen such stupidity yoked with such patience, watchfulness,
courage, boundless capacity for work, indifference to pain and discomfort?
Oh, not in officials only; in the men who controlled vast businesses, in
the missionaries who ran colleges, leper asylums, Christian villages and
communities.[33]*

This generosity did not extend to his portrayal of those Anglo-
Indian women who behaved with that particular brand of brutality
which flourished amongst British females replanted in the colonies.
Such women he shows as cruel to Indians, whom they simply did
not see as human, as emotionally coarsened by their unearned
privilege. Mrs Nixon, the wife of the police superintendent, recounts
how she hit her cook with a catapult intended to deter squirrels from
eating the horse-feed: 'The recollection seemed to please Mrs
Nixon. "He was carrying a dish of absolutely *boiling* stew when the
pellet touched him up. He smashed the dish, of course! You should
have heard him howl! I thought I must have hit a jackal." '[34] This
same lady sniffs discontentedly at hearing the missionaries discuss
estimates for the new laboratory being built in the college: 'Haven't
you spent enough money on these natives... No wonder they get
uppish.'[35] When Alden, the principal of the college and a missionary,
reminds her that it is *their* money, she retorts, 'Not if it's our
country.'[36]

The certainties to which Anglo-Indians have been accustomed
are now being disturbed by Indian nationalism and those few who
understand the inevitability of aspirations to political independence,
are theoretically sympathetic. Nixon, the police superintendent,
accepts his official responsibility for smashing the agitators but

* cf. 'No part of the Empire has been served by so many men in commerce
and missions as well as in military and civil ranks, of striking and individual
ability. If you form part of the after-tennis circle in any "station" in India, you
can look around on the motley activities represented there, from collector to
"coolie-catcher", from policeman to educationalist, and reflect that every one
"is a good man at his job".' *The Reconstruction of India*, p. 17.

admits that, were he an Indian, he would 'want to take a hand in the movement' and fool the sahibs 'because they *don't* know things, don't know what the folk think or feel, don't know *anything*'.[37] Hamar, the judge, who is with Nixon when they come across a hoard of ammunition secreted in some caves, feels 'the pulse of wild excitement and hatred, the excitement greater than the hatred ... that was knitting the educated classes together... Hindus and Mussalmans would quarrel after we were gone, and they quarrelled now. But what did we know of systems in whose interaction we bore no part?'[38] The majority of Anglo-Indians, however, are simply exasperated and bewildered by what they cannot comprehend, and Indian political discontent intensifies the divisions between the two communities.

While Thompson does not glorify the missionaries in India – he is scathing about the diplomatic Christian's deference to the Foreign and Colonial Offices and to Anglo-Indian public opinion, and he is despairing of an earnest young man who is distressed by the minds of the heathens and is always ready to acclaim Christianity's superiority over all other creeds – the men in the novel who care about having human relationships with Indians, who are said to be motivated by love and who demonstrate the possibility of British empathy with India, are both missionaries. Through Alden, Thompson acts out a significant area of his confusions and in Findlay he presents his ideal of the spiritual Englishman. Between them these two characters suggest Thompson's powerful need to identify with India and his failure. Alden is angry at the Anglo-Indian whine for gratitude, pointing out that service in India was both a means through which Englishmen fulfilled themselves and a source of self-aggrandizement, whether by wealth or honours. He accepts the claim that the British had contributed to India's well-being but is severe on proper actions performed without love for the recipients. When Vincent Hamar dismissed a political case against Indians on the grounds of insufficient evidence, he is said to have acted out of 'an almost savage sense of fairness',[39] 'a passion for absolute abstract justice'[40] and not because of any sympathy for Indians, towards whom his feelings are coldly impersonal and his behaviour boorish: 'outside his duties he was merely the ordinary official, anxious for relaxation and to forget the country he served'.[41] In a subsequent judgement, again guided solely by evidence, he sentences two Indians to five years' transportation, and this passionless equity prompts Alden's reprimand: 'You, Hamar, have chosen to be just, when the circumstances gave you abundant loophole to be kind.'[42]

Alden and Findlay feel intensely about India: 'daily their lives were striking deeper roots in this arid land, were drawing enrichment, in knowledge, interest, emotion'.[43] Boyishly ready to laugh at a local rajah resplendent in orange shoes and scarlet stockings, a turban of gold and purple, and a blue seaman's jersey, or at Neogyi's prolixity in official speeches, Alden has a real regard for Indians and respects their cultural mores. He tries intellectually to identify with them and his statement of the difficulties is explicit:

> You get to see with their eyes... I know how vexing they are, in ways enough. But we never shake free from our herd-morality, any more than they do; and we go on judging them because they're not first-rate Englishmen in dark skins. I suppose it's a question of different ethics. They *hate* many of the virtues that we praise; and we hate many that *they* are keen on. We seem to them incredibly rough and rasping; and they seem to us worms. We're both right – by our standards... We think first, second and last, of doing our job; our favourite virtues are justice, firmness, integrity. To us mere kindness, as such, is weak sentimentality. But Indians don't give a damn for *our* cardinal virtues. To them any sort of harshness seems infinitely worse than the worst lapse from absolute justice. Oh, I know they often *seem* to assent to our code, and to accept it. But they never do... They would rather tell a lie than give pain; we would rather give the pain. We worship Themis, they Charis. Hang it all, the world wants a shrine where both statues have a place.[44]

For all the passion and intelligence of Alden's appeal, the artificiality of counterposing two value-systems and showing them both to be valid is exposed when Alden, especially in the later novels, experiences the very barriers against which he rages. It is doubtful if this was Thompson's intention, but what is revealed is that irrational emotions can be more powerful than intellectual honesty, even when this is supported by the earnest wish to sympathize with the alien. What he does set out to depict is the conquest of estrangement by goodwill. When the demoniac and hysterical cries of the *kokil*, a bird

beloved of Indian poets, madden the English, Alden suggests:
' "Next time we hear the beastly bird . . . let's try and hear it as
Indians." They had done so; putting himself where Indian minds
were, withdrawing for a moment from his own herd-psychology,
with cool, sweet unprejudiced mind each had listened to the *kokil*'s
shouts at dawn, and had admitted their exhilarating quality.'[45]

This is a significant passage: through the exercise of imagination
hostility is momentarily transformed into sympathy. But this re-
freshing escape from the prison of automatic responses and judgements does not ease the sense of alienation which overwhelms the
British as they are confronted by an India of intangibles:

It was a characteristic enough hill, one of many thousands, of every
height from twenty feet to several thousand, that are scattered over India.
You may see them from the train, as you go through Central India or the
jungles of Chota Nagpur or Orissa. They stud the Mysore plateau, they
sprinkle the Madras plain; they rise everywhere from the thorn-pampas
of Rajputana. When the volcanoes were lighting vast sheets of shallow
ocean or the huge rivers were silting those sheets up with soil filched
from Himalayan peaks and gullies, these rocks were there, blazing and
smouldering. The geologist finds fossils in them. The temples of post-
Aryan India seem alien, an annoying excrescence of yesterday.[46]

This passage is, of course, derivative, drawing heavily on Forster's
remarkable account of the Marabar Hills and caves.* For Forster,
these are multi-symbolic, expressing the Indian time-consciousness
and the scale by which man is to be measured, telling of an impersonal universe and spirit, auguring a return to the unconscious
and to an ancient sensibility, and as such they are integrated into the
larger structure of image and idea within the novel. Here the hills
have a more circumscribed function, announcing the unrelenting
presence of an India immensely old, remote from the British and the
modern world, and contemptuous of its works. This theme is
developed when Alden's sister-in-law, Hilda Mannering, is drawn
to the dead city outside Vishnugram where she sees the past 'in
vivid procession'[47] and dreams of people who thought and did things

* Of *A Passage to India* Thompson wrote that it was a work which he had
initially resented but later on re-reading had come to admire greatly. See *The
Reconstruction of India.*

inexplicable to her race and epoch. The effect of contemplating an Indian scene emptied of men is intensely disquieting: 'The noises which the generations raise seemed to be nothing – the struggles of insects flung into a sea which is drowning them. The rustle was the eternal voice of the sea itself, the sound which was before man and will be after man has perished. All was unreal, nothing mattered.'[48] Again, the influence of *A Passage to India* is obvious, but from this image of India Thompson goes on to pursue his own concerns as two themes are developed: one, that modern nationalism is the reawakening of elemental India, a possibility which especially grips the British characters in the sequel to this novel but here is already noted when the activists use the decaying temples of their gods as secret meeting-places and storehouses for ammunition. The other is the possibilities for spiritual self-discovery which Indian mysticism might offer to the Christian.

Thompson's insistence on *rapprochement* between East and West is both the most contrived and the most interesting facet of his writing, representing as it does a momentous battle against instinct and for the fusing of British and Indian ethics. His belief that this process has commenced is suggested in the Sadhu telling Findlay not to measure his success or failure in the number of conversions but to gauge the extent to which the life and spirit of the people has changed under his influence, even though they remain Hindu:

the general movement of the age happened to reach us incarnate in an Englishman. Vishnu has had many avatars [manifestations] – but some of us are expecting his next one to be as a football-playing, famine-relief-organizing person in shorts, with a hockey-stick for discus and a bicycle for *vahan* [vehicle]. That's the way you have corrupted our good old Hinduism. And we've made a difference to you too. Confess, missionary. You're half Vedantist. Tat tvam asi [Thou art That] – isn't *that* where you're finding the Kingdom of Heaven?[49]

But how are the profound differences between the creeds to be annihilated? In contrasting Eastern and Western attitudes on the priority of thought and action and on the nature of the physical world and its material problems, Thompson is attempting to make a general statement about man's existence. The Hindu philosophy of contemplation is weighed against the British creed of doing when Findlay and Alden question the Sadhu on his search for peace in the midst of the world's sickness, poverty, cruelty and misery. They are dissatisfied with his periphrastic answers about the conquest of desire and the revelation that 'this life was but a wave flung up from the quiescent Life'.[50] After many discussions the Sadhu concedes that were he to be shown men whose lives combined 'our peace and your energy' and transcended both, then he would be forced to review his withdrawal from the world.

> I will tell you, Alden the *padre* saheb, what it is that we have not seen. Through these three centuries countless Englishmen have shown us courage, honour, justice. We are not forgetful of this, though we will not acknowledge it now. But hardly one, whether missionary or official, has shown . . . the grace of the Lord Jesus Christ. And until you can show us your peace, we will not believe in your victory. It is not energy that proves holiness.[51]

It is the saintly Findlay who attains this victory but only after a crisis which takes him on a perilous journey through the heart of India. He is said to love India 'with a passion that was very near worship',[52] to accept the presence of God in all things, to perceive the world as the creation of God in his phase as the active Lord and to recognize the manifold universe as but a form of the Absolute. But despite his assimilation of Indian modes of apprehension, his mind breaks in the grove of the jungle goddess where he had gone to seek comfort after the death of his wife and child. Here he feels that God has deserted him and that he is being sought by a malignant deity. Sanity returns but he is left spiritually depleted and when he goes back to his mission he does so automatically in obedience to the religion of the British and to Christianity. Once more he enters the jungle alone and now he experiences a revelation of love for all things and all men, and that which in his madness had seemed to him malevolent, he sees as the beneficent work of God. Having understood good-and-evil as facets of God and factors in the phenomenal universe, he translates this deeply Indian experience into the acceptance of Western activity and Eastern contemplation as complementary rather than opposite forms of behaviour and aspiration, to be integrated into a richer unity by rejecting both heartless efficiency and total renunciation of the world:

he, John Findlay, was the servant of all, and his body should be the dust of every road along which man goes in lonely pilgrimage. He would lighten everyone's burdens. . . Hitherto his service had been vile, hateful, unworthy – he had given it grudgingly, given it because he was a Christian man, was a missionary . . . to be one with every leaf and bird and human creature, to have a heart as free and infinite as the sky that was his friend, this earth that was his mother.[53]

In the subsequent novel of the trilogy Findlay takes to living as an Indian, giving service to the people as an itinerant ascetic, the inevitable sequel to his new understanding. But already at this point of his spiritual development, Findlay's chains had been broken.

He no longer felt that he must produce a knowledge of God at all hours . . . that he must preach and pray as the time-table dictated. . . He was free to wait till God came; and if He came not, still – He was there. He was free to walk the roads and the jungles, and where he found himself, there he slept. . . And always, always, there was the mind's inner glow, composing the body and its cravings, so that all discomfort fell away, unheeded and unnoted.[54]

As he rests in the jungle after gaining enlightenment, he meets with the Sadhu who recognizes his victory: 'I need no other witness than the same the ascetics found who came to the Lord Buddha. Henceforward thy home is in the universe, and thou and I are one. I serve the Lord of the Ascetics, Siva the Naked'; to which Findlay replies, 'I follow my friend and master . . . who walked the shores of a lake and whose days and nights were spent at His Father's side.'[55] The Sadhu has found in Findlay that combination of Indian peace and English energy which he had been seeking; Hinduism and Christianity are shown to be not two alternative ways to truth and right living but as essentially the same path.

The disharmony between overt message and intrinsic emotional tone grows with the progression of the trilogy. In *An Indian Day* it emerges through the deliberate announcement of the pleasures which India offers – 'The air was a lavish wine, spilt and sprinkled by the winds. Hilda, walking through the morning's splendour to her famine-relief station, marvelled that men and women of her race should have lived and worked in this despised Bengal, year after year, and yet have carried away nothing but a bitter and disdainful memory'[56] – and the pervading note of hysteria which drowns the affirmations voiced by the author through his characters. The high spirits of Alden, his peals of delight, his suppressed enjoyment,[57] his insane guffawing and struggling with internal jollity,[58] are as uneasy as his shrill denunciations, passionate avowals and frenzied thrusting of logical expositions against the recalcitrance of a complex and emotionally charged situation.

A Farewell to India further examines the strains which a changing India imposes on the British. It is 1929. In the struggle between the moderates who set their sights at dominion status and the militants whose goal was complete independence, the Congress militants had won. The Sadhu warns Findlay and Alden that they are all three of them out of date: 'You have a new India on the stage, one that has seen wealth and power and arrogance, and wants to have a hand in the game.'[59] The situation is becoming intolerable for Alden, imprisoned as he is in outworn attitudes. When he and Findlay meet a fiery nationalist, Dinabandhu, Alden argues 'infatuated, as was his wont, with his own thesis. . . You can steer India into peaceful partnership with the rest of Empire, or you can enter on the path which you think has always led to independence and glory before – that of assassination and guerrilla warfare.'[60] This incenses Dinabandhu: 'Your condescension is your worst insolence of all!'[61] and leads Findlay to remark, 'He jawed to Dinabandhu as if we were still in 1925, instead of 1929.'[62]

This is Thompson at his most paradoxical, for in deflating the windy pronouncements made by Alden within the novel he is also devaluing those he himself made in his expository writings. A modern Indian historian has written of the political issues of the period:

In attacking the ideal of Dominion Status, Jawaharlal Nehru in fact attacked the reformist psychology of the Liberals and of moderate Congressmen. He accused them of having no vision of a new India. Those who thought in terms of Dominion Status, he said, wanted only an Indianization of the administration. . . Independence stood, he claimed, for a new state and a new society – democratic and socialist... The Dominion Status-versus-Independence controversy in 1928-9 was but a symptom of the deeper schism within the Congress. It was the conflict between palsied age and fiery youth, between an upper-middle-class leadership and a lower-middle-class following within the organization. A wave of leftist ideas was rolling forward in India.[63]

The times threatened Thompson–Alden; they knew that they were being rejected by the new India and were unable to accommodate to the knowledge.

Alden's discomposure intensifies; he is assailed by India as an intangible entity invading and evading the Western mind: 'At its most stable, the Indian scene had appeared, to those minds most deeply immersed in it, the merest illusion. It was now, even to Alden the Englishman, a mockery of windy voices and swaying, elvish shadows and distortions.'[64] But still he insists on his right to be in India as he pleads with the Sadhu: 'These skies and spaces have gone into my blood, as they have gone into the blood of many an old colonial or district officer who you folk think is hanging on to India for the sake of what you are pleased to call exploitation. You haven't begun to realise the way our brains move; we simply don't look on India as alien.'[65] While claiming to understand Indian bitterness at British arrogance, he continues to demand *his* rights as God's emissary in India, rights which are an outrage to Indian sensibilities and pride:

I used to try and cut out everything but God. But now I know that I am merely a man who has found his roots and home in this India he came – God forgive him, no! it was God who sent him – to save... I care about my fellows. And that's the only thing, after twenty years of missionary work, that entitles me to call myself God's servant.[66]

To him the manifestations of an 'angry and insolent nationalism'[67] are evidence of a whole nation gone mad and he longs for the old days when Indian protest broke frailly against the granite of the Raj. He admits that he cannot accept the new attitudes towards white men: 'There was an unregenerate self of memory within him that lived on from those first days when the saheb was still a god.'[68]

When Findlay's response to his disconsolate complaint that the British no longer had a place in India is to ask whether this is 'because a missionary daren't swipe the misguided heathen any more',[69] he concedes that this is so. Despite these honest admissions, his fundamental stance remains, as the Sadhu reminds him, that of a paternalist, 'graciously interested in the folk and their ways, touched by their poetry'.[70] And even here there is a rub: though he is acquainted with the Bengalis' literature and appreciative of their culture, he reacts to 'babuisms' with as much venom as does the most philistine and bigoted Anglo-Indian. For his students, whom he sees as flabby and cringing, perpetually whining about the 'insultations' they consider they have received from the authorities, he has the greatest contempt. And he is infuriated by his Indian colleagues on the District Board whose silly and flowery expressions of nationalist sentiments interfere with getting useful things done. When his sister-in-law Hilda protests, 'If anything could show up the folly – the criminal folly of the whole business out here, it is that men like you should be wasting their lives being harassed and lied about by those perfectly imbecile babies'[71] (a reference to his politically active students), Alden does not dissent and it stands as the author's judgement on the situation.

For Alden, service in India had been the means through which he had sought to satisfy his creative urges and religious impulses, and he had believed in his capacity to perform right actions with the requisite love needed to justify such works. Now Indians are denying his life's work and while he continues to protest his love for the country and its peoples, what he actually expresses is a raging hostility. Under these pressures he collapses, possessed by the fear that it is India's nameless and insidious threat which is disintegrating him and driving him out. Again we see the paradox within Thompson, for Alden's dilemma and breakdown, which are handled with honesty and critical insight, reproduce the conflict in Thompson's Indian writings. Just as Alden is possessed by the need to love and the sensation of dislike, by concern for others and an appetite for self-indulgence, by humility and arrogance, perceptiveness and obtuseness, so is Thompson in articulating his Indian experience. Both author and character evince a manic temperament, both protest their love for the abstract India while betraying an emotional aloofness from the actualities, and neither can admit the possibility that their dreams of a mission to India have ended. As Alden prepares to leave India he says, 'I've done nothing. . . I've achieved nothing. . . I'm sure of nothing at all. But don't let anyone tell you I've given the fight over. I'm not out of it.'[72] In similar vein is Thompson's quotation of a conversation he had had with Gandhi and which pleased him sufficiently to reproduce on the title-page of *A Letter from India*: ' "They tell me, Mr Thompson, that you have published a book entitled *A Farewell to India*." "That is so, Mahatmaji." "Well, it seems to me that you have been wasting your time again. How do you think that you are ever going to say farewell to India? You are India's prisoner." '

In *An Indian Day* Thompson introduced the theme of an ancient India rising up against the just and efficient masterdom of the British, and now this perception comes to the fore through Alden's sense of a rebellion transcending politics:

The Ancient Gods were rising from their slumber of decades, the stirring abroad in their own land had blown upon even their drowsy lids . . . I'm beginning to think that there's something elemental in this land, that's in revolt against us. . . I think the age, from time to time, in one land or another, gets sick of a certain people, and gets rid of them. It isn't reason, it isn't even the sword that kicks them out. It's the bhuts [demons]. . . The age is tired of us and wants a change. . . There's something stirring that's getting on our nerves. You can't use guns against it, as you could once. . . I'm beginning to believe in bhuts – in something dull, stupid, brute, malignant, invulnerable, with feet that take hold of the very soil.[73]

Here again Thompson has drawn on the powerfully suggestive language used by Forster to communicate Mrs Moore's sensations of the caves, but Thompson's purpose is to convey a very specific threat: 'these serried forces of earth and air', welling up against British domination as the past, 'sitting here, waiting for us to go',[74] prepares to reassert itself. The English are helpless against this upsurge of demons who spurn human conciliation and have worked madness in men's minds, and Alden visualizes the *bhuts* in conclave, a parliament of 'Padalsini, Mother Ganges, Mother Indus, the thakurs of the forest trees, the bhuts of the wayside, the devatas of the upper and lower air'.[75]*

Alden's mixture of bitter grief at the present and obscure hope in the future is not shared by the pragmatic Hamar, who is ready to concede defeat: 'They're not our race, they don't think our thoughts. Why the devil were we ever tied up with them and sent revolving on the same wheel of destiny?'[76] As before, the victor is Findlay and when the Sadhu and Alden despair of India's present and future it is he who reassures them that India will return to 'her old high road'.[77] On a deeper level, he symbolizes the entry of Britain into India's soul, a unification realized through serving the people by humble participation in their lives and a surrender to the liberating power of mysticism: 'I've learned things I would never have dreamed possible, since I began to live this way. Once you've finished worrying about what happens in the world, every voice in the world seems to drift up to you. I listen to nothing now, but I seem to hear everything. I've begun to think the intellect is Satan himself.'[78] When he joins a religious procession, 'Outward circumstances fell away... His heart filled with infinite pity; and in that moment he knew the mystic's experience of oneness with the pity and passion of God. He *loved* that crowd ... all were children of the one Love... In that moment Findlay felt that his heart would break with unbearable happiness, if in some way, in any way, it might be given to him to die and bring some good to that multitude.'[79] Findlay's triumphant integration of the Christian and the Indian spiritual heritages permits him to satisfy the Sadhu's demands that he be shown the marriage of Western activity and Indian tranquillity. Despite this announcement of Love victorious, the novel is made discordant by the shrill voice of Alden, the self-pitying colonial whom the ungrateful natives have rejected, a siren sound which persists even when Alden the sober and optimistic servant of a great cause is talking. The British–Indian relationship, he insists, is not one between brutal, overbearing alien and passive subjugated native but one of 'close comradeship, in which the partners despite themselves have learned something of each other's psychology, and have in thousands

* This image is reminiscent of that fashioned by Kipling in *The Bridge-Builders*; see Chapter 6 below.

of cases found it impossible not to like each other'.[80] Ultimately the contrivances in the novel are swept aside by its real dynamic, which is the expression of frustration and anger, and the synthesis so hopefully offered through Findlay reverts to the fission which is the true state of the British–Indian relationship.

In the final novel of the trilogy, *An End of the Hours*, Alden visits India after an absence of five years to report for a Commission on changing conditions and their effect on Christian missions; it is 1936. In the Preface Thompson writes that, although the book is not autobiographical and the opinions expressed are not necessarily his own, into the novel have passed 'some of the things seen and heard and thought in a thirty years experience of the matters with which it deals',* and it is certainly the most shapeless and ruminative of the three novels. Alden's distress at the ludicrous forms which the Hollywood influence on India are taking, the cloak of pseudo-modernity over squalor, is part of his despair at the malaise of contemporary civilization which he feels to be 'daft in all its values'.[81] He is disturbed and perplexed by the new mood in political India where moderates are damned as traitors and bitterness dominates relations between British and Indian. He is impressed by the sight of a large crowd in Calcutta welcoming Nehru and thinks regretfully of how British rule had affected this intelligent and cultivated person: 'if this man is a bigot then he ought not to have been made one'.[82] He is aware of the wrongs done to the Indians by the imperial race in treating them as inferiors but his real sorrow lies in having to acknowledge his own failure as one of the Empire's servants. He dwells on the passing of an Empire which poets had hymned as eternal:

Our own British–Indian system, so carefully, tightly wrapped about with 'safe-guards' and 'regulations', and equilibrium of check and counter-check, this also was dying out from the land. What was once passion and wrath and misery and pride was becoming an historian's tale. It was all platitude, and so well known and so little worth remembrance, even by oneself. Yet so appalling when you felt it in this remote Central Indian silence and tangle. Enough to make the heart stand still at the futility and tenuity of this life which you symbolised and shared. Alden's

* Thompson visited India in 1937.

Indian days were all but over, and he knew well that not even in history would there be a tiny plot left for his name . . .[83]

This then is one aspect of the British dilemma as Alden sees it – melancholy at the passing of an institution in which men had believed and with it a recognition of personal defeat.

Although Findlay has found peace in India he, too, has had to face some disappointment. But he remains serene as he calmly contemplates the end of an era: 'the days of our pride are nearly finished and our race is about to come to judgement'; the generous-minded would have to seek 'extenuating circumstances and to find out the ways in which our pride had – well, *some* justification'.[84] Yet there is sorrow as he looks back at his years in India: 'We had thought of a calm, steady, process which would make India Christian and England understanding and pitiful, and both of us wise and great.'[85]

The mood of bereavement, of failure and pierced dreams pervades the book. The British are behaving as if they had already relinquished their rule, as if they conceded the battle as lost. Alden defines the now obsolete aspiration of a mission to India as a

widening of the bounds of peace, beginning with an Empire which was at rest within herself, and a source of confidence to every other decent purposed nation, and, last of all, the whole world awake to its common humanity and all nations at peace at last! Each following meekly a Westminster model and precedent and Great Britain leading them all into the millennium.[86]

Just how unattainable such aspirations are is emphasized when matched against the view which Alden has of the confused contemporary world. He laments the changes but is critical of unchanging, stagnant Anglo-India where narrow and complacent prejudices are substituted for thought; compared with the doubt and scepticism dominating British attitudes, the British in India suffice with 'primal simplicities, on which the Empire is built'.[87] But despite this sober judgement Alden indulges in orgies of nostalgia for the old days, rebuking God for unkindness: 'When a man has known a landscape as I have the one to which I am going, and has taken it into his blood and brain, God should allow him to abide in it for eternity.'[88] He searches for that India which he had known in his far-off youth, an

India now refined and sweetened by memory, where in the good old days before the war relations between the races were more amicable, when the British were high-handed but compassionate and India was 'better-tempered, less sophisticated, and still bemused with a belief in the white man's superiority and even his generosity and good intentions'.[89] He realizes that he still expects deference from Indians and that an 'affable, unthinking acceptance of suzerainty still clung to him'.[90]

Alden's malaise is exacerbated by his finding contemporary life sordid, and in searching for meaning in his Indian experiences he is seeking a cure for the sickness of his soul. Alden is a product of Western values, energetic and capable, interested in social and political matters, a Christian activist. But his longing for spiritual explorations draws him to Eastern religion and thought, and when he visits Buddh Gaya he is made happy by thoughts of Buddha and by reminding himself that his lot had been cast in India: 'And it seemed to him as if he had been pleading humbly that he had a right to be here, in this silence and peace... Perhaps it is the Englishman who ends as the true *sannyasi*, having run through so many forms of action and learnt the vanity of them all.'[91] During his journeys through India he finds himself drawing closer 'to a dim vision that was India, and not conventional India at all, but an India which had endured and known thought and feeling, whose spiritual values were not all bogus'.[92] In these values he sees an offer of hope to all the world and he leaves India spiritually revitalized, confident of the future despite the immediate gloom of the political situation.

As in the previous two novels, it is the eternal, essential India which is shown to be asserting itself against British domination. 'Do you imagine then that *Indian* India has been pushed out by the flitting hybrid India, half here, half gone even while here, which you people have imposed on it?'[93] asks the Sadhu. He predicts that the world made by the British will pass away and be forgotten, but if the time has come for Britain as an imperial power to die, nonetheless the British entry into India had been of great value. Holding out his hands to Findlay and Alden in a symbolic gesture, the Sadhu pays tribute to the gift they had given India: 'But you know well, you two ... how deeply your own dreams have gone into this Indian brain, that has all these years been trying to dream otherwise, in places where no English foot has ever come but yours.'[94] This affirmation cancels out Alden's fears that the British influence had been irrelevant and that East and West could never meet. Findlay's religious beliefs have been profoundly reshaped by Eastern concepts and Alden's idea of Christianity which he formulates as 'God's effort . . . age after age to draw out from all the ages and all the nations a race of spirits whose whole existence and self is one with His',[95] is sufficiently general to include some aspects of the Indian aspiration. Both men know that Christianity has ostensibly failed to take root in India and agree that this is because Christianity is not a merciful religion whereas Hinduism is theoretically pitiful. Both fear the Western obsession with personality and when Findlay is dying he feels certain that, for Buddha and St Paul, on whose similarity he had earlier remarked, the true self was hidden in God and that by Nirvana Buddha had meant the extinction of the shadow self. Both men need to be reassured that their efforts have touched India: 'The systems we have placed upon her are every day becoming like leaves whose sap is dying out in the twig that joins them to the tree. It used to trouble me, until I saw that a new life was forming within.'[96] The Sadhu confirms Findlay's verdict telling him that people such as he and Alden are not aliens but men bound up as he was 'in the same queer half-Indian, half-British business that has now nearly finished'.[97]

Between the formal affirmations of empathy, love and unity and the actual expressions of distance, hostility and division, lies the cardinal area of Thompson's Indian experience. Alden suggests to Findlay that Christianity has failed to appeal to Indians because it cannot cover the whole of life for them, but when confronted by the particular ways in which Hinduism does in fact accommodate its adherents' varied needs and activities, Alden is scornful. He mocks at the recollection of a *zemindar* who asked him to establish a football cup in memory of his baby daughter, the final to be played on the anniversary of her death which fell during a religious festival when it was customary to sing smutty songs. The professor of science who bathes in the filthy Ganges on the appointed holy midnights, the merchant who combines a pilgrimage with the purchasing of a new motor-lorry, these instances offend Alden's deep-seated mechanistic conviction that science will rout superstition and sully his Christian-Protestant sensibility that the secular and the divine *are* distinct. About the less ascetic aspects of Hinduism, Alden voices scathing contempt, declaring that the sight of the holy temples at Madura in southern India could restore the Englishman's imperial faith: 'Incredible that any animal which could think (let alone the people who are so often extolled as the crown of the world's spiritual effort!) could have produced anything so vast, so imbecile, and so variously repulsive!'[98] This hostility is intensified when a guide with a highly developed interest in sex points out the tawdry and roguish figures of Brahma, Shiva and Vishnu.

Thompson's effort to communicate an eternal, quintessential India, spiritual and containing multitudes, is the struggle of an outsider to empathize. What he does graphically reveal is that sensitive and concerned Englishmen found in a distantly seen India the source of their doubts about their own civilization and their hopes for its spiritual resurgence, while the India of real people with political aspirations, cultural idiosyncrasies and bodily and emotional needs, discomposed and sometimes even repelled them.

Conclusions

During the 1930s Thompson had a considerable reputation as an expert on Indian affairs. Through his writings, lectures, discussions and correspondence with influential Indian and British politicians,* he contributed to the state of knowledge in Britain about India and to the climate of concerned opinion. Thompson had an alert and inquiring mind but he was not a profound and original thinker; the combination of fixed suppositions and loose thinking and a tendency

---

* Amongst Thompson's papers are letters from many Indian political figures as well as from British politicians. See also a letter from Thompson written in 1939 to Nehru in *A Bunch of Old Letters: Mostly Written to Jawaharlal Nehru and Some Written by Him* (1960): 'Everyone wants to know the truth about India. My 'phone and mail bring invitations all the time, from the Manchester Chamber of Commerce and Cambridge University to the House of Commons and diehard learned societies. . . I am talking to two groups of M.P.s this Wednesday' (p. 412).

to convert his own emotional dispositions into moral imperatives and concrete facts detract from the significance of his commentaries as analyses. But assessments of Thompson should focus on qualities other than his stature as a man of ideas. His determination to inform his audiences about the dilemmas of the British–Indian relationship coexisted with the zeal to transform his nation's perceptions of India, to move their conscience and to persuade the Indian peoples that the British were capable of compassion, magnanimity and penance.

A vision of Christian reconciliation and spiritual re-birth informs Thompson's Indian writings; consider the Preface to his joint work with G. T. Garratt:

We have both had long and close connections with India, and friendships that have given us a feeling of a second nationality; but inevitably our first loyalty is to our own country, one of the last in which free and unregimented thinking is still possible. Yet love of England cannot blind us to the dangers which beset Western civilization, and we are convinced of the immense influence that India, called to a reinvigorated existence, could exert in solving these problems which now oppress the mind of man. We send out this book hoping that it will work for that understanding between the two countries which fate has linked so strongly together.[99]

Where most Anglo-Indian writers pronounced that friendships between British and Indians as equals were neither possible nor desirable and recoiled from intimacy with Indians, Thompson insisted that the separation of the races was a violation of mankind's oneness and he shaped his writings to serve the cause of *rapprochement*.

Thompson's Indian novels are about ideas rather than novels of ideas and their discursive form allows for debates on conflicting viewpoints amongst Anglo-Indians and between British and Indian. The trilogy was not conceived as an entity and when the first was written, events and their effects on the characters in the second and third could not have been foreseen. But if they are artistically arbitrary, lacking the long view in which the incipient and potential can be seen unfolding, they are truthful as an instant record of crisis and change.

The most elusive aspect in Thompson's version of his Indian experience is also the central one – his relationship to the inclinations and dilemmas of the British which he depicts sometimes with critical insight but often as a participant incapable of detachment. For Thompson does not so much explore paradox as embody it. It is as if his moral intelligence informed him that certain dispositions were reprehensible while his ineradicable commitment to what the British as human beings had invested in India implicated him in the very attitudes of which he disapproved. This would explain the coincidence of his own thoughts and feelings with those of Alden, a man he shows as emotionally self-indulgent and self-flagellating. Indeed, Thompson's moral confusions reveal with a devastating honesty how painful and costly the British involvement with India was to a sensitive and emotional man. 'I wish we could chuck this governing trade. Why is it you can't stay a gentleman, if once you start standing over other people?'[100]

Thompson's was one of the clearest and most frequently heard voices of the British conscience. But he also offered himself as the spokesman of Indian protest, imposing on Indians the forms of suffering and redemption which he thought appropriate, and here he gave expressions to paternalist predilections shared by those who were in the governing trade. Thompson's ambition was to aid the healing of political strife through moral persuasion and personal witness; his attainments as a writer lay elsewhere. The will to reconciliation coexists with strong currents of hostility towards India, the urge to atone with insistent self-justifications. Finally the inchoate tendencies are more powerful than the conscious design. The words of his character Gregory, the principal of a missionary college, as he appeals to an Indian member of staff, are perhaps a commentary on Thompson's agonized and frustrated hope of knowing India:

Sarat Babu, help me. I'm frankly puzzled. All these years I've been trying to get at what you people really do think and feel. I've read your literature, I've studied your religion... You said I didn't understand – that I couldn't understand... I really *have* thought sometimes that I've got through to what Indians were thinking – and then I've pushed hard, and it's been like going through a curtain and finding a solid wall behind.[101]

CHAPTER 6

Rudyard Kipling, 1865–1936

Introduction

THE history of Kipling criticism reproduces the history of Western attitudes to the modern imperial experience. His contemporaries at the turn of the century reacted very immediately to his writings, finding in them political beliefs and social ideals which some admired and others deplored: in 1899, W. T. Stead, an outspoken imperialist, praised Kipling as the interpreter of the popular consciousness and the inspiration for the popular imagination, while Herbert Spencer attacked him for abetting the recrudescence of barbaric ambitions and sentiments.[1] Kipling's imagination was daring, his themes diversified, his tales always more than pegs on which to hang ideas, and textual analysis of his prose can proceed without reference to his imperialist postures. Yet few critics have chosen this approach[2] and even in a study wholly concerned with Kipling's craftsmanship and one which avoids a consideration of social and political matters, Professor J. M. S. Tompkins offers a revealing prefatory remark: 'I was a child of the British Empire as I am a subject of the British commonwealth and I have never found either position embarrassing. I regret that I shall not live long enough to see our humanly imperfect but undeniably great achievement of Empire fairly assessed in the long view of history.'[3]

Other modern scholars, arguing that Kipling be recognized as a great artist and a profound thinker, have accepted his imperialism as a politically viable and ethically justifiable stance. J. I. M. Stewart, for example, defends Kipling's views on the Indians' unfitness for self-rule by extrapolating the political realities of the period from Kipling's fictional reconstruction of the situation.*

* *Rudyard Kipling* (1966), see pp. 64–5. Consider also the curiously sneering tone in Bonamy Dobrée's *Rudyard Kipling: Realist and Fabulist* (1967) where he refers to Kipling's being dubbed a reactionary: 'How far he may have been right, especially in the creation of democracies in Africa, only time will show, as it will as regards the new "advances" in education' (p. 122).

More analytical is the method of those critics who interpret Kipling's imperialism as a metaphor for an existential situation rather than as a political creed. Already in 1929, Bonamy Dobrée was suggesting that for Kipling the Empire 'is to be cherished not so much because it is in itself an achievement, but because, like old Rome, it is the most superb instrument to cause man to out-face the universe, assert himself against vacancy'.[4] It is this interpretation which has recently been extended by Alan Sandison: 'Anglo-India and the fabric of Empire served Kipling as a paradigm for the structure of his moral universe. . . Kipling is not writing in order to express the idea of empire. Given the idea, he reacted in the way any artist would – by finding in it a means through which to express his own artistic vision.'[5] Yet despite the abstract nature of Sandison's thesis he also praises Kipling's realism in his treatment of imperial themes, offering Anglo-Indian memoirs as the test of veracity, sources which to a significant extent were devices for image-building.

It was during the 1960s that scholars advocating Kipling's admission to the pantheon of Great Writers redirected the trend of criticism.[6] Before this, Kipling's reputation as a serious artist remained negligible, although he had been the subject of assessment by major critics.[7] Certainly this shift points not only to changing standards of literary excellence but to the discovery of latent meanings which for a variety of reasons were obscured from previous critics. Still, the extension of tolerance to postures and assumptions which earlier generations found obnoxious, suggests that for an adequate explanation of this evolution we must look to extra-literary considerations.* Here we are concerned with one area of Kipling's vision and it is pertinent to ask why his literal and figurative deployment of imperialism has become acceptable and even congenial to so many Western scholars. Alan Sandison sees Kipling as a man and writer who deliberately chose the material world as his field of action and values, scorning politics based on abstract theories when millions of people were dying through lack of planned agriculture

* A leader-writer in *The Times Literary Supplement*, 3 February 1966, in discussing recent historical revisions of imperialism pointed out that it had ceased to be a dirty word and suggested that the Kipling revival was 'not an exclusively literary phenomenon' (pp. 73–4).

and medical treatment and through what one of his characters in talking about India describes as 'an all-round entanglement of physical, social and moral evils and corruptions'.[8]

Even though the notion of a mission to backward peoples now seems a conceit and the concept of guardianship over the under-developed world the white man's vanity, it is still possible for scholars holding liberal values to give an affirmative judgement on imperialism's role by invoking utility, by arguing that poverty, economic retardation and social immobility are more relevant and worthy priorities than abstractions and ideals about rights to self-determination and a people's need to develop and extend their unique cultural traditions.* Within this essentially Western-centred conceptual framework the problem is approached as one to be over-come by social engineering; practical considerations take precedence over the emotional needs of the subject or 'under-developed' peoples, pragmatic criteria displace ethical judgements and the arrogance of the white world persists in its abrogation of the right to determine what is desirable for a society, what constitutes progress and how this is to be effected. If we follow the implications of this defence further we find it meeting with the ideas which informed Kipling's

---

* Two statements, one by an American political scientist, the other by an Indian historian and political theorist, offer an interesting contrast. Speculating about a verdict on colonialism, Professor Rupert Emerson writes: 'I am not contending that colonialism offered any ideal means of access to the modern world. Indeed, I am not at all sure that any ideal means of access exists, although I am sure that colonial regimes do not provide it. But when I play the game of ruling out colonialism, leaving other conditions realistically as they were, I find myself inexorably driven to the conclusion that, as an interim and transitional measure, colonialism is likely to be the lesser of the evils in a predatory world. It has in fact been the agency of diffusion through which hundreds of millions of people have begun the long and painful transition from their traditional societies into the modern world created by the West and now available in the alternative packaging of communism.' 'Colonialism', *Journal of Contemporary History*, Vol. 4, No. 1, 1969, entitled 'Colonialism and Decolonisation', p. 12. In discussing the ideas of Gandhi, Professor Raghavan Iyer writes: 'no material benefits, no cultural influences could outweigh the wrong of a relationship that lamed a people's will, insulted its self-respect and doomed it to passivity and political slavery'. 'Utilitarianism and All That: The Political Theory of Imperialism in India', *St Antony's Papers*, No. 8, 1960, p. 71.

fiction. The new critics are right in emphasizing that he saw in imperialism a means through which men could win their moral integrity by self-abnegation, commitment to a task and the exercise of responsibility. But imperialism was an encounter between peoples, a relationship involving other men, the underdeveloped world, the helpless millions, the 'new caught, sullen peoples, half devil and half child', and what of their selfhoods, what of the moral integrity of those men on whom Europe was carrying out its great experiment in affirming the exhilaration of existentialism? The ideological foundation of modern imperialism was and remains racialism and only through preempting rights to the white world on the basis that their civilizations are the only sources of norms, can imperialism and its achievements ultimately be justified. 'The White Man's Burden' is Kipling's starkest artistic statement of his imperialist ethic and the association of duties with the rights he asserts does nothing to diminish the superb insolence of the claim, its blind ethnocentrism and its total egocentricity:

> Take up the White Man's burden
> Send forth the best ye breed –
> Go bind your sons to exile
> To serve your captives' need;
> To wait in heavy harness
> On fluttered folk and wild –
> Your new caught, sullen peoples,
> Half devil and half child.

> Take up the White Man's burden –
> Have done with childish days –
> The lightly proffered laurel,
> The easy, ungrudged praise.
> Comes now, to search your manhood
> Through all the thankless years,
> Cold-edged with dear-bought wisdom,
> The judgement of your peers!*

* Written in 1899 to celebrate the victory of the United States against Spain which had resulted in the acquisition of Cuba and the Philippine Islands, the verses called on the United States to play its part in the imperialist task.

INTRODUCTION

When Kipling makes the colonial situation serve as a model of the hostile universe, daring men to remake it, the colonial peoples feature as a facet of the larger challenge and the human content is conceived entirely in terms of the white world's self-realization. The complex of national and individual incentives which propelled empire-building and sustained empires is excised from this model and the tension and conflict between masters and the subjugated peoples is obliterated.

To categorize Kipling as the bard of Empire is a grotesque over-simplification, but the instincts and ideas of imperialism did seep into his art.[9] Vocal as he was about the austere traditions of imperial service and the stoicism manifest in imperialism's servants, he accepted the entire range of proclivities and aspirations expressed by the builders and defenders of Empire. When Kipling was asked by Cecil Rhodes about his dream he answered 'that he [Rhodes] was part of it'.[10] If imperialism as a historical actuality was not the compass of Kipling's artistic vision, nonetheless the man who shared Rhodes's extravagant and predatory idea of Empire built into his writings those suppositions thought up to justify Western rule over Asia, Africa and the South Americas and those sentiments which spurred white men to participate in this dominion. And it was in Kipling's fiction and verse that these assumptions and feelings took on a further growth to become part of imperialism's mythology for, more than any other single author, Kipling articulated the pride which a segment of the British people took in seeing themselves as a nation of law-givers. It was he who gave a spurious grandeur to their posturing and endowed the discomforts of their job as imperial rulers with the glory of suffering and sacrifice.

In one of his verses Kipling thanks Allah for giving him two separate sides to his head. Always concrete in the vividness of detail, Kipling was often as concrete in deriving the moral content of a situation from the specific context without reference to. a larger system of beliefs and values. Thus in one tale India is valued as an authentic civilization, in another it is a villainous enemy to the white man; in one instance Kipling's understanding of Indians leads him to deride the efforts of reformers and especially of missionaries to impose Western mores and manners on Indians, while in another

207

situation this same consciousness emerges as contempt for Indian customs. To read Kipling's Indian writings is to plunge into conflicting emotions, to confront in one story a blind racial rage, to be charmed in another by the delight which the author took in things characteristically Indian. The interpreter of the white man's view of Empire was also able to saturate his writings with the ambience of India as he had experienced it, moving beyond a sensuous awareness of its landscapes to perceptions of its unique secular life and the continuous flow from its traditions to the people's psyche and sensibility. His profoundest explorations of India in its diversity of meanings are those where the conflict with the white world is submerged or at least peripheral to the central structure of themes. But where Indians challenged the white man's image of himself and questioned his status as ruler, it was the other side of Kipling's head which was thrust forward, sometimes with a very ugly expression on his face. Where there was competition in rights between West and East, Kipling presented the intentions and actions of the white world as part of a moral order from which the dark peoples were excluded. It was this commitment to the prior rights of the white man in his relations with the rest of humanity which shaped Kipling's vision of imperialism as the triumphant expressions of an Anglo-Saxon manifest destiny.

Kipling's ambivalent attitudes towards India, its peoples and cultures, was in part due to his being a 'country-born' Anglo-Indian. His parents had come to India shortly before his birth when his father took up an appointment as professor of architectural sculpture at an art school in Bombay. Until he was six Kipling lived in India, thinking and dreaming, as he recalls in his autobiography, in the vernacular, accompanying his Hindu bearer to the temples where he would gaze at the 'dimly-seen, friendly gods'.[11] This early and natural exposure to Indian life was crucial to Kipling's adult emotional relationship with India and, although he joined his peers in heaping obloquy on Indian norms and practices, he was free of the Anglo-Indian obsession with what they saw as Hinduism's sensual and bloodstained gods and the uninhibited expressions of sexuality in Asian cultures. A relaxed intimacy with India was exactly what the Anglo-Indians feared and, as was customary, the young

Kipling and his sister were sent to England when they were aged respectively six and three, and until Kipling went to a minor public school, the United Services College, he endured five unhappy years with an insensitive and cruel foster-mother. His literary talent was already obvious during his school days and when he returned to India in 1882 he became assistant editor of the *Civil and Military Gazette* in Lahore where his parents were then living. After five years he moved to the *Pioneer* in Allahabad and here he remained until he left India in 1889. During these seven years he learned to identify with Anglo-India. His vivacious mother, talented father and attractive sister were luminaries in the Anglo-Indian society of Lahore and Simla and for Kipling the centre of his world was the 'family square'. This and the Punjab Club,

where bachelors, for the most part, gathered to eat meals of no merit among men whose merits they knew well. . . And in that Club and elsewhere I met none except picked men at their definite work . . . my world was filled with boys, but a few years older than I, who lived utterly alone, and died from typhoid mostly at the regulation age of twenty-two. . . Death was always our near companion.[12]

So authentic was Kipling's rendering of the Voice of Anglo-India that it continued to be heard in the land until the end of the Raj and to be echoed in recollections long after its passing.

The Voice of Anglo-India

As Anglo-India's chronicler, Kipling showed how 'conditions of life in India were constantly testing the physical and emotional stamina of Europeans'[13] and his droll stories of adultery in hill-stations and nepotism in high places play a relatively insignificant part in the essentially compassionate portrayal of his countrymen. The British impulse to place Indians outside their consciousness and to deny them status as fellow-humans stemmed from the fear of a social and physical environment which disturbed and discomposed because it seemed to threaten their identity and values. Although Kipling's own experiences and intuitions had liberated him from this acute

sense of alienness, he interpreted their displacement and need
for flight into the closed circle of their own community. White men
posted to stations isolated from the cantonments and towns are
described as being quite alone and the population of one such outstation is said to number five people. In 'At the End of the Passage'
the four civilians who meet each week regard the rest of their days as
being spent in utter isolation, although they are surrounded by the
Indians on whom their dedicated service is being expended, and
what is more they feel that they are condemned to cling together:
'they were not conscious of any special regard for each other. They
squabbled whenever they met; but they ardently desired to meet, as
men without water desire to drink. They were lonely folk who understood the dread meaning of loneliness.'[14]

When Kipling wrote from within the mind of Anglo-India he
could identify with their version of Indians as a separate species, as
objects to be manipulated rather than as individuals with whom
relationships could be formed. Even Kipling's wit could be sufficiently disagreeable to call his dispositions into question:

'Very Young' Gayerson's papa held a Division, or a Collectorate or
something administrative, in a particularly unpleasant part of Bengal –
full of Babus who edited newspapers proving that 'Young' Gayerson was
a 'Nero' and a 'Scylla' and a 'Charybdis'; and in addition to the Babus,
there was a good deal of dysentery and cholera abroad for nine months of
the year.[15]

Something other than compassion for man's helplessness against
nature's assaults and the crushing weight of Indian poverty informs
language such as this: 'Life was cheap. . . The soil spawned humanity as it bred frogs in the Rains, and the gap of the sickness of one
season was filled to overflowing by the fecundity of the next.'[16]
There is a similar diminution of Indians' humanity in 'William the
Conqueror', an account of famine-relief work where concern for the
victims is subordinated to the celebration of Anglo-Indian heroism:
'for the famine was sore in the land and white men were needed'.[17]

For Anglo-Indians, 'knowing natives' was not thought of as
human intercourse. Kipling knew that this circumscribed view was
debilitating to a sense of life, and he knew also that it was a bid for

security: 'This is the story of a man who wilfully stepped beyond the safe limits of decent everyday society, and paid for it heavily. He knew too much in the first instance; and he saw too much in the second. He took too deep an interest in native life; but he will never do so again.'[18] Despite his ironic and detached awareness, Kipling reproduced the Anglo-Indian idea of the path to understanding Indians and its purpose: Strickland of the police 'knows as much of the natives of India as is good for any man' and 'hates being mystified by natives, because his business in life is to overmatch them with their own weapons',[19] and when after an absence 'the streets and the bazaars, and the sounds in them . . . called him to come back and take up his wandering and his discoveries',[20] this was the call of his job.

The explorations of McIntosh Jellaludin, however, were of a different order for his learning had been paid for in years of damnation, a descent into the inferno of drunkenness, a sinking to the degradation of native life. Scholar, gentleman and loafer, 'he knew enough about the natives, among whom seven years of his life had been spent, to make his acquaintance worth having'. His boast that he 'had his hand on the pulse of native life' was true, and 'he used actually to laugh at Strickland as an ignorant man – "ignorant West and East" '.[21] Salvaged, indeed gleaned from his degradation, was a mass of unsorted writings about his life and that of Mother Maturin, whom he called a great woman; this 'Book' he hands to the narrator as he is dying, pronouncing it the definitive revelation of native life. After McIntosh Jellaludin's death, Strickland and the narrator read through the papers and it is Strickland's opinion 'that the writer was either an extreme liar or a most wonderful person. He thought the former.'[22]

At the time of writing this tale Kipling was working on a novel to be entitled *Mother Maturin* which was completed but never published and of which no manuscript appears to exist. His reference to the novel in a letter indicates that it dealt with the submerged life of India: 'It's not one bit nice or proper but it carries a grim sort of moral with it and tries to deal with the unutterable horrors of lower class Eurasian and native life as they exist outside reports and reports and reports. . . Mother says it's nasty but powerful and I

know it to be in large measure true.'* Kipling's biographer suggests
that when he came to write *Kim* he ransacked this youthful romance
for notions,[23] but by this time Kipling's insight into India had left
Anglo-Indian conceptions far behind.

Kipling's journalism is as fecund and diversified in mood and
tone as is his fiction[24] and amongst his many styles was one which
drew on the fund of clichés and complaints which were the common
property of Anglo-India. In an article, 'A Real Life City', Kipling,
in what he calls a genial diatribe, inveighs against the Big Calcutta
Stink and attacks the English residents of the city for allowing, even
encouraging, natives to look after the place:

> The damp, drainage-soaked soil is sick with the teeming life of a
> hundred years, and the Municipal Board list is choked with the names of
> natives – men of the breed born in and raised off this surfeited muck-
> heap! They own property, these amiable Aryans on the Municipal and
> Bengal Legislative Council. Launch a proposal to tax them on that
> property, and they naturally howl... Why, asks a savage, let them vote
> at all? They can put up with this filthiness. They *cannot* have feelings
> worth caring a rush for. Let them live quietly and hide away their money
> under our protection, while we tax them till they know through their
> purses the measure of their neglect in the past... They are fenced and
> protected and made inviolate. Surely they might be content with all those
> things without entering into matters which they cannot, by the nature of
> their birth, understand.[25]

The issue here is not the aptitude or ineptitude of Bengalis as city
councillors but Kipling's choice of language which is calculated to
intensify the contempt in which his readers already held the

* Quoted in Carrington, *op. cit.*, p. 66. Carrington writes that no one now
living had read *Mother Maturin*; however, Mrs Edmonia Hill, the American
wife of a meteorologist in government service, whom Kipling had known intimately during his Indian years, had given the following account: '*Mother
Maturin* I have read, which was never published because John Lockwood
Kipling was not satisfied with it. It is the story of an old Irishwoman who kept
an opium den in Lahore but sent her daughter to be educated in England. She
married a Civilian and came to live in Lahore – hence a story how Government
secrets came to be known in the Bazaar and *vice versa*.' Quoted *ibid.*, p. 358, from
Catalogue of English and American Authors, issued by the American Art Association, 30 April 1921.

Indians.[26] It is interesting to compare Kipling's terminology with an article in the *Planter's Gazette*, one of the organs of the unofficial European community, where the writer condemns the extension of power to Indians and recalls an earlier and more desirable situation 'before the lives of the dwellers in our towns had become the play-things for the sanitary ideas of men whose early youth was spent by a cesspool and where moral and physical development took place under the malarious influences which pervade every Bengal village'.*

Again, consider Kipling's article, 'The Council of the Gods', where he reports on a meeting of the Bengal Legislative Council and observes the dress and address of the members:

The little man in the black dressing-gown revels in his subject. He is great on principles and precedents, and the necessity of 'popularising our system.' He fears that under certain circumstances 'the status of the candidates will decline.' He riots in 'self-adjusting majorities' and 'the healthy influence of the educated middle-classes.'[27]

Reporting a similar occasion, the writer of the *Indian Planter's Gazette* describes 'The gentleman with ladies' stockings and shiny shoes, whose lisping, infantile accents prattled of mukadama's in his native village.'[28]

In this persona Kipling was a fully paid-up member of Anglo-India. The emotive words signifying repugnance and contempt are unmistakable signs of a racial rage which reaches a crescendo in the pun on the title, 'The Head of the District'. This story weighs 'racial' characteristics so that the probity of the British Civilian is balanced against the venality of the Western-educated Bengali aspiring to replace him, so that British courage is counterposed to Bengali cowardice. Befuddled by theories and principles, the Viceroy had with criminal irresponsibility appointed Mr Grish Chunder Dè, M.A., as head of a district peopled by fighting Afghans, Sikhs and Pathans, tribesmen who loathe Bengalis, and with whom the British

---

* 5 October 1886, pp. 357–8. According to Flora V. Livingston's *Bibliography of the Works of Rudyard Kipling* (1927), he did publish in the *Indian Planter's Gazette*, but she does not specify particular pieces. It is not being suggested that the pieces with which Kipling's articles are being compared are in fact his; but the possibility should be noted.

officials had established good relations. When rebellion against his appointment appears imminent, Chunder Dè flees by train and escapes the people's wrath, but his brother, for whom he had found a sine-cure in his new district, departs on horseback and loses his head.* This is later delivered by the tribesmen to the new and worthy Head: 'Slowly rolled to Tallantire's feet the crop-haired head of a spectacled Bengali gentleman, open-eyed, open-mouthed, the head of Terror incarnate.'[29] The voice in this tale is that of a man whose contempt for a people[†] has turned to hatred when they dare to enter the lists where only white men are fit to compete. But Kipling's extravagant condemnation of Indians was not restricted to the Western-educated middle classes of Bengal; 'The Enlightenments of Pagett M.P.' is an unrestrained attack on the totality of Indian norms and customs. The naïve visiting Member of the British Parliament who favours political reform for India is told by an American woman doctor who works amongst Indians that 'the foundations of their life are rotten – utterly and bestially rotten', a judgement in which Orde, a civil servant, concurs: 'In effect, native habits and beliefs are an organised conspiracy against the laws of healthy and happy life.'[30] That a recent critic has found in this story 'a reasoned and responsible defence of the Anglo-Indian point of view'[‡] suggests how analysis conducted at a high level of abstraction can lose touch with the tone and intention of the text.

---

* Kipling had a highly developed lack of taste: 'Now originality is fatal to the Bengali. Debendra Nath should have stayed with his brother' (p. 138).

† Apart from Hurree Babu in *Kim*, Kipling wrote of Bengalis as supine and contemptible. He was apparently content with the Anglo-Indian stereotype and there is no evidence that he knew of contemporary Bengali novelists like Rabindranath Tagore and Bankim Chandra Chatterjee whose works were sympathetically and ironically interpreting the dilemmas of Bengalis, in particu-lar the educated ones.

‡ Alan Sandison, 'Kipling: The Artist and the Empire', p. 148. Consider, too, this assessment: 'Thus, if in his notorious story "The Head of the District" Kipling can be seen, on one level, as launching perhaps his most savage and bitter attack on the educated native who presumed to do the Sahib's job, the second level must, at the same time, be kept in mind, for what Grish Chunder Dè threatened was to introduce an entirely different code, and one that would utterly profane the Stoic ideal in which Kipling's vision emerged' (*ibid.*, p. 154).

'The Man Who Would Be King' : An Ambiguous Myth of Empire*

Few men have seen as much as Kipling; few have experienced so little in the true sense of experience.[31]

In 'Recessional', written during the Jubilee Year of 1897, Kipling rebuked the British people for their immoderate toasting of Empire:

> If drunk with sight of power we loose
> Wild tongues that have not Thee in awe,
> Such boastings as the Gentiles use
> Or lesser breeds without the Law –
> Lord God of Hosts, be with us yet
> Lest we forget, lest we forget.

When Kipling dons the robes of stern patriarch it is tempting to investigate what he is wearing underneath, and his saga of the two loafers who win a kingdom for their own shows him in motley. The narrator of this tale, a journalist on an Anglo-Indian newspaper, initially introduces Daniel Dravot and Peachey Carnehan as hollow and cruel men who, when more mundane methods of employment were wanting, lied, cheated and blackmailed their way across India.

---

* Since writing this I have read Jeffrey Myers's excellent analysis of the tale, 'The Idea of Moral Authority in "The Man Who Would be King"', *Studies in English Literature*, Vol. VIII, No. 4, Autumn 1968, pp. 711–23. Since there is some coincidence of treatment, the Synopsis of Mr Myers's essay is quoted in full: 'Though Kipling's theme is the need for moral authority represented by the law of the British Empire and the dangers and horrors that would result if the organized governments of civilized powers refused the task of colonialism, he fails to maintain a consistent moral perspective in the story. Kipling's portrayal of Dan's bravery and Peachey's martyrdom shows his sympathy for the roguish and daring aspects of their personalities. This obscures the moral issue of their past behaviour as kings – their greed, exploitation, despotism and murder – which he is trying to criticise, in the story. Their terrible deaths, which should have been a just punishment for their crimes, becomes instead an attempt to vindicate their character. The serious flaw of this story is that Kipling is essentially sympathetic to their imperialistic ambitions (that is, the need to replace native anarchy with British order), so that his criticism of their failure to establish progressive beneficent rule and their lack of fidelity to the Law is never forcefully established.'

Through their own words they emerge as archetypes of those adventurers whose greed, grandiose dreams and psychological need for licence made them dangerous men in ordered society:

We have been all over India, mostly on foot. We have been boiler-fitters, engine-drivers, petty contractors, and all that, and we have decided that India isn't big enough for such as us. . . The country isn't half worked out because they that governs it won't let you touch it. They spend all their blessed time in governing it and you can't lift a spade, nor chip a rock, nor look for oil, nor anything like that, without all the Government saying – 'Leave it alone and let us govern.' Therefore such *as* it is, we will let it alone, and go away to some other place where a man isn't crowded and can come to his own. We are not little men and there is nothing that we are afraid of except Drink, and we have signed a Contrack on that. *Therefore* we are going away to be Kings.[32]

Carnehan's account of their frustrations and extravagant hopes is affirmed by Dravot: 'We have slept over the notion half a year . . . and we have decided that there is only one place now in the world that two strong men can Sar-a-*whack*. They call it Kafiristan. . . They have two and thirty heathen idols there, and we'll be the thirty-third and fourth.'[33] They recognize that even in British India, which they had thought preferable to the metropolitan homeland, they remain superfluous men: 'we *are* loafers, Dan, until we get out of India'.[34] The spur to their ambitions is the achievement of Rajah Brooke, the Englishman who in 1841 was rewarded with the principality of Sarawak as his own kingdom for aiding the Sultan of Brunei in suppressing a Dyak rebellion.* Brooke was following in a tradition begun in the eighteenth century, before the consolidation of Western rule in the East, when Europeans of many nations, and often men of obscure origins, moved through Asia and especially India, a few in pursuit of ethnographical and antiquarian information, but most seeking their fortunes through private trading or in the service of independent rulers. Accounts of such exploits had been chronicled by Tod, the historian of Rajasthan, with whose *Annals and Antiquities of Rajasthan*, published between 1829 and 1832,

---

* James Brooke (1803–68), son of an East India Company servant; entered the Indian Army, 1819. Brooke and his family successors ruled Sarawak for more than a century as benevolent despots.

Kipling was familiar.[35] One extraordinary career described by Tod was that of George Thomas (1756–1802), an Irishman of humble origins who, while employed by Indian princes in a military capacity, conceived the plan of ruling an independent kingdom and fulfilled this ambition when he conquered the vast area of Hurrianah, or Huriana, ninety miles to the north-west of Delhi.[36]

Like their historical antecedents, Dravot and Carnehan are the antithesis of those disciplined and sacrificial Anglo-Indian administrators, soldiers and technicians on whom Kipling lavishes such heroic qualities in his Indian writings and who give some credence to theories about his Stoic vision of imperialism. When the men visit the narrator to plan the final details of their venture, the extravagance of their ambitions is shown to be matched by the prominence of their physical features, so that in the small newspaper-office 'Dravot's beard seemed to fill half the room and Carnehan's shoulders the other half, as they sat on the big table'.[37] The angle from which they are viewed has changed and they come to fill the story as big men with big dreams and capable of big achievements. When some two years later the crippled and demented Carnehan returns to tell of their triumph and ordeal, the evolution is complete: the greedy loafers who had intensified their initial dispositions and acted out their ambitions are offered as fully fledged heroes.

In winning their kingdom the men had demonstrated those attributes which characterize colonizers, pioneers and freebooters – the readiness to take risks, to act promptly and without scruple, to utilize every propitious occasion in pursuit of their ends. In disguise and by deception, they had made their way through Afghanistan, eating their camels and then their mules when faced with hunger and killing those who threatened to impede their progress. On reaching their destination in Kafiristan, a region they knew to be peopled by warring tribes and as yet beyond the influence of white men, they sided with the weaker of the groups, defeating their enemies, and through this elementary display of military skill – they had both served with Roberts's army in India – laying the basis for their dominion. This rule they cemented by associating the priests and village chieftains with their regime, and they then developed into able administrators, Dravot mediating between the villages and settling disputes, Carnehan training an army to maintain internal peace and protect their borders against their belligerent Afghan and Mohammedan neighbours. Their kingdom grew as it came to embrace more distant villages; where the soil was poor the people were resettled on fertile land, and the tribes were taught efficient agricultural methods by Carnehan who also supervised the spanning of ravines with rope-bridges, set up powder shops and established factories for producing essential commodities. By deploying their nascent talents in a situation which yielded to their pragmatic and promiscuous methods, the redundant men of the West became kings. The state of lawless violence was replaced by law maintained through force; a benighted people were led out of their native darkness towards civilization.*

During one of his expeditions into the valleys Dravot found precious stones and metals, the wealth which he and Carnehan had coveted and which seemed to be awaiting their arrival. Their good fortune indeed appeared providential and when Dravot through a happy accident learned that the tribes knew something of Free-masonry,[38] he proposed that they bolster their rule by setting themselves up as Masters of the Craft, a scheme to which his partner hesitantly agreed after expediency had conquered scruple. At the ceremonies and levees loosely derived from Masonic ritual Dravot pronounced that he and Carnehan were gods and sons of Alexander: 'Dravot he was the King, and a handsome man he looked with the gold crown on his head and all . . . and every morning Dravot sat by the side of old Imbra† and the people came and worshipped. That was Dravot's order.'[39] Dravot then announced his intention of ex-

* Francklin, *op. cit.*, writes that George Thomas ruled his kingdom autocratically and benevolently, selecting the town of Hansi as his capital. Quoting from Thomas's own account, he records: 'Here I established my capital, rebuilt the walls of the city long since fallen into decay, and repaired the fortifications. As it had long been deserted, at first I found difficulty in procuring inhabitants, but by degrees and gentle treatment, I selected between five and six thousand persons, to whom I allowed every lawful indulgence' (p. 93). Thomas drew up a code of civil administration and law, organized the revenue allocations, built court-houses, established arsenals and munitions factories and set up a mint where he coined his own rupees.

† Imbra was the tribal god.

tending their kingdom to become an empire, thus logically following the sequence implied in their initial ambitions; but here he erred when, in defiance of Carnehan's pleas and the priests' warnings, and in violation of the 'Contrack'* which the men had drawn up before embarking on the adventure, he insisted on taking a bride to comfort him in the winter months and to found a dynasty. The terrified girl selected by the tribes bit him to test his divinity, and when he bled like a man the irate and demoralized people cast their rulers out.† Dravot was flung to his death from a rope-bridge which had been the men's gift to the people, and Carnehan was crucified. When he survived this torture the tribesmen allowed him to leave, and so he dragged himself back to British India to tell his tale before dying.

The story mimics historical occurrences from whose ethical assumptions Kipling did not dissent, forming as these did an integral part of the white man's imperialist experience.

I won't make a Nation... I'll make an Empire... There must be a fair two million of 'em in these hills... Two hundred and fifty thousand fighting men, ready to cut in on Russia's right flank when she tries for India! Peachey man... we shall be Emperors – Emperors of the Earth! ... I'll treat with the Viceroy on equal terms... When everything was ship-shape, I'd hand over the crown – this crown I'm wearing now – to Queen Victoria on my knees, and she'd say: 'Rise up, Sir Daniel Dravot!' Oh, it's big! It's big, I tell you.[40]

Dravot is here expressing an outsider's dream of gaining admission to the established society which had rejected him but, more important, his is a *lumpen* version of that aspiration which moved men of higher social standing to acquire territorial possessions for their own

---

* 'That you and me will not, while this matter is being settled, look at any Liquor, nor any Woman black, white or brown, so as to get mixed up with one or the other harmful' (p. 217).

† Mannoni, *Prospero and Caliban: The Psychology of Colonization* (1956), writes: '*a colonial situation* is created so to speak the very instant a white man, even if he is alone, appears in the midst of a tribe, even if it is independent, so long as he is thought to be rich or powerful or merely immune to the local forces of magic, and so long as he derives from his position, even though only in his most secret self, a feeling of his own superiority. The man-in-the-street will say instinctively and without experience that if the white man who goes amongst the Negroes avoids being eaten, he will become King' (p. 18).

and Britain's glory. Kipling's hero, Rhodes, comes immediately to mind,* as does the declaration of Sir George Goldie, the creator of British Nigeria: 'All achievement begins with a dream. My dream as a young child was to colour the map red. In 1877 I left England ... to explore the interior of Nigeria... On the journey back I conceived the ambition of adding the region of the Niger to the British Empire.'†

Because Kipling believed that the spirit of enterprise, resolution and courage was expressed in imperial conquest and dominion, he tended to telescope the motivations of those who went to the colonies as administrators, soldiers and entrepreneurs in such a way that dubious impulses were obscured. What makes 'The Man Who Would Be King' so germane to understanding Kipling's intellectual and emotional relationship with imperialism is that in this story he does bring into marginal view those facets of imperial ventures which he elsewhere ignored – avarice, the thirst for personal glory, the satisfactions of feeding on the homage of dependent peoples – and then by focusing attention on other matters, subverts the significance of his own suggestions. Two moral universes are assumed, that of the

* Consider Rhodes's will of 1877 leaving his wealth to form a secret society with the purpose of extending British rule across the earth, the British settlers to occupy the continent of Africa, as well as Palestine, South America, the Pacific Islands, the Malay Archipelago, the seaboard of China and Japan. See Richard Faber, *The Vision and the Need: Late Victorian Imperialist Aims* (1966), p. 125.

† Quoted in Margery Perham, *Lugard: The Years of Adventure, 1858–1898* (1956), p. 482. Consider also the less successful empire-builder, George Thomas, who on being shown a map of India by Lord Wellesley, asked the meaning of the red shading. 'On being told, he sorrowfully placed his hand over the whole of the Punjab and said, "Had I been left alone I would have made all this red with this hand." ' Quoted in Grey and Garrett, *op. cit.*, pp. 57–8. Francklin, *op. cit.*, records that it had been Thomas's ambition to conquer the Punjab, and having perceived his inability to do so because of the paucity of his forces, he in 1801 made an offer of service to the British government. 'Having offered to advance, and take possession of the Punjaub, and give up his army to the direction and control of the English; To take the country and in short, to become an active partisan in *their* cause; He thus in a patriotic and truly loyal strain, concludes his remarks on the interesting subject; "By this plan (says he) I have nothing in view but the welfare of my King and country" ' (pp. 247–8).

white men and that of the tribesmen of Kafiristan. Within the white world we see the paradox of loafers escaping the restrictions of their own society and developing their frustrated gifts to become princes and law-givers.* 'Brother to a Prince and fellow to a beggar if he be found worthy' is the caption at the beginning of the tale, and it is indeed this concept which determines the fashion in which the men's experiences are mediated through the narrator. Although he sees them for what they are, loafers avid for loot, once his ironic disbelief in their scheme turns to admiration, he refrains from judging their aims and methods. But this neutrality is only apparent and he in fact contributes to casting the black world in the role of villains; for him the native states are 'the dark places of the earth'[41] and it is he who warns the men that the natives across the borders of British India are 'utter brutes'.[42] Through the men's eyes, this view of the tribesmen is developed so that they are seen indeed as sub-human, and this, ironically, despite their being as fair-skinned as the English, a fact on which the men repeatedly comment. When conquering their king-dom Carnehan recalls how he 'sights for the brown of the men half a mile across the snow and wings one of them'.[43] So thin is their apprehension of the tribesmen as individuals that the men give the loyal chiefs names 'according as they was like men we had known in India – Billy Fish, Holy Dilworth, Pikky Kergan'.[44] When their subjects rebel, Carnehan remembers the valley as 'full of howling creatures' who, after he had fired his last cartridge into 'the brown of 'em', silently advanced to capture their kings. 'Not a single solitary sound did those swines make. They just closed up tight, and I tell you their furs stunk.'[45] This concrete remembrance of a silent horde clothed in reeking animal furs, speaks of something sullen, menacing and inhuman overtaking the men. And so compassion is invited for the fallen kings, overwhelmed by forces they might have controlled, the tragic victims of their own errors.

Because the people of Kafiristan are sealed off from the white universe, the possibility that Dravot and Carnehan behaved towards them in a corrupt and unscrupulous way simply does not arise. Kipling knew that under certain conditions primitive peoples would

* Paul Fussell, *op. cit.*, finds the primary theme of the story to be 'the ironic and paradoxical quality of kingship or nobility' (p. 217).

pay obeisance to the white man as god, and he approves of this – consider his account of the Bhils who believe young Chinn to be a 'demi-god twice-born, tutelary deity of their land and people',[46] a situation he finds admirable. But it is not necessary to interpolate evidence from other stories, for within the context of this tale the kingdom is destroyed not because the adventurers transgressed a moral law in deceiving the tribes or acted out of motives of greed and overweening ambition, but because Dravot undermined the mystery of their rule. For if white men in colonial situations are to retain their hegemony, they must remain remote from the people over whom they rule.* When Dravot insisted on taking a bride, an act which was to expose their human vulnerability and lose them their kingdom, Carnehan recalls him walking away through the pine-trees 'looking like a big red devil, the sun being on his crown and beard and all'.[47] Already Dravot had fallen from the plinth of the gods into the furnace of hell.

The portrayal of Dravot and Carnehan suggests Kipling's failure to discriminate between a sympathetic understanding of his characters and a sanctioning of their conduct. As avaricious, unscrupulous and brave adventurers, the talented outcastes of respectable societies who have no use for their gifts, they are marvellously realized; but as heroic figures they exist only through the author's legerdemain.† Kipling's complicity in treating meretricious aspirations and their consummation as the stuff of nobility illuminates, as no other tale does, his involvement with the presumptions of imperialism.

---

* ' "For a century," wrote a former Cabinet minister in 1892, "the Englishman has behaved in India as a demi-god ... any weakening of this confidence in the minds of the English or of the Indians would be dangerous." ' Sir C. W. Dilke and S. Wilkinson, *Imperial Defence* (1897), p. 80, cited in V. G. Kiernan, *The Lords of Human Kind: European Attitudes Towards the Outside World in the Imperial Age* (1969), p. 55.

† cf. Myers, *op. cit.* For a different estimate consider Louis L. Cornell, *op. cit.*: 'Dravot and Carnehan are tragic figures, conquerors who like Tamburlaine, conceive the ambition of becoming Emperors. They are above the common run of mankind... With courage and luck they pile success upon success until they become gods in the eyes of their primitive subjects. But in the end they violate the conditions of their own success' (p. 162). Edmund Wilson, *op. cit.*, has

A Montage of India

I

If Kipling is compared with those novelists who wrote about India concurrently and immediately after him, it can be seen that his work contained the obvious which was easy to imitate as well as the subtle which escaped the counterfeiters. The magic of India, its dark secrets, mystery, romantic splendours, rarefied delights and majestic decay are all there in Kipling, as are the stenches, sapping heat and *ennui*, the disease and immobility. But where lesser writers could not go beyond an amazed commentary on a static and passive people, Kipling showed India in the perpetual process of absorbing and consuming new influences. Where other writers were intoxicated at the extremes of asceticism and sensual saturation, self-denial and promiscuity, Kipling saw a mundane and diversified secular life with which spiritual concerns were integrated.

India played many concrete and ideal roles in Kipling's art. He was capable of depicting with approval pasteboard figures of quaint and childlike Indians genuflecting before the West – consider those mechanical little tales collected as *The Eyes of Asia* in which Indian soldiers serving abroad during the Great War send letters home expressing fulsome admiration for the ways and marvels of Europe. Nor did he avoid the most obvious recipe for concocting the flavour of India; phrases such as 'proud-stomached city' and 'Healer of Sick Pearls', which may or may not be accurate renderings of the vernacular, are facile ways of evoking atmosphere. At its simplest level India was a presence which he knew through his senses, as in the sketch 'The City of Dreadful Night' where he records his midnight wanderings in Lahore, watching, smelling, listening, aware of the sleeping people and their lives, conscious of being a stranger, yet

---

described the story as 'a parable of what might happen to the English if they should forfeit their moral authority . . . the man who has made himself King is destroyed by the natives that have adored him the instant they come to realise that he is not a god, as they had supposed, but a man. The Wesleyan preacher in Kipling knows that the valiant dust of man can build only on dust if it builds not in the name of God' (p. 55).

responding to the muezzin's call from the mosque. In 'The Mark of the Beast', India is the place of happenings which are 'beyond any human and rational explanation'. When the drunken Fleete, a planter ignorant of native customs, desecrates the shrine of Hanuman the monkey-god, he is bitten by a leper and transformed into a beast. Only through the application of hot irons to the leper's person by the planter's associates is the spell lifted and Fleete restored to his humanity. 'East of Suez, some hold, the direct control of Providence ceases; Man being there handed over to the power of the Gods and Devils of Asia.'[48]

Sometimes India is explored as an authentic world with a uniquely structured society, with aesthetic standards, moral principles, spiritual aspirations and pulses of existence very different from the West. But whether this world is accepted at its own value or judged in relationship to Western institutions and habits and found to be wanting, depends on the particular concern Kipling is pursuing in the tale. He recognized that white men experienced India as a menace, showed how the British reacted to the threat, interpreted their sense of strangeness, and ironically revealed the inadequacies of that serenity won by shunning India. 'Beyond the Pale' begins with this bland advice: 'A man should, whatever happens, keep to his own caste, race and breed. Let the White go to the White and the Black to the Black. Then whatever trouble falls is in the ordinary course of things – neither sudden, alien nor unexpected.' But this injunction is negated by the 'Hindu Proverb', 'Love heeds not caste nor sleep a broken bed. I went in search of love and lost myself',[49] and by the emotional content of the story for, while the unfortunate Englishman and his tragic Mohammedan mistress pay dearly for their brief and secret union, it was because they met in defiance of caste, race and breed that their love was so affirmative. When Kipling saw India with the eyes of a white man he knew that the view was partial, even deceptive. When he looked on India through Indian lenses he still retained his psychological detachment as a Westerner. From these various angles he received the images which formed his montage of India.

II

Even in *The Naulahka*,* which Kipling wrote in collaboration with the American author, Wolcott Balestier, and where East is weighed against West on loaded scales, there is in the ironic verses at the chapter-heads an implied commentary on the restricted awareness and aspirations of the white characters. Though the India of this novel is obviously Kipling's contribution, it is less multi-dimensional than in his independent writings for it is portrayed largely through the eyes of Tarvin, real-estate man and go-getter from the American mid-West and hence it stands as the strange, apathetic, supine land, the 'abyss of oblivion',[50] an obstacle to the creative dynamism of American capitalist enterprise. The Westerner can have no sympathy with this India, where its people's 'passionless regard' seems to be 'borrowed from the purple hills'[51] of their desolate landscape; the only conceivable relationship is one in which the white man rules, exploits or attempts to improve her. From the mid-Western American town of Topaz two people with different aims go to India: Kate Sheriff, inspired by a sense of duty to work as a medical missionary among *zenana* women, and Tarvin, who wishes to marry her, in pursuit of a priceless necklace, the Naulahka. For if he can acquire the gems for a jewel-obsessed woman, she will persuade her railway-tycoon husband to bring his railroad to Topaz with whose future Tarvin is totally involved. Through the eyes of two such people, India takes shape.

To Kate, the fresh-faced all-American girl, the *zenanas* seem a twilight world: 'Monstrous and obscene pictures glared at her from the walls of the little rooms, and the images of shameless gods mocked her from their greasy niches above the doorways.'[52] Her

---

* Written in 1892. There are obvious difficulties in discussing a work of joint authorship, but from the internal evidence it appears that the India of the novel is largely Kipling's, although its function is defined by Balestier's determined view of the West's superiority. A letter of Balestier's to some extent confirms this conjecture: 'Kipling and I have been wading deep in our story lately, and have written rather more than two thirds of it. It begins in the West where I have a free hand for several chapters. Then we lock arms and march upon India. The process of collaboration is much easier than one could have supposed.' Quoted in Carrington, *op. cit.*, p. 181.

encounters with 'a sudden land of poison and death'⁵³ and the defeat of her high hopes by India's stubborn adherence to custom, make her experience seem like a 'plunge into the world's evil'⁵⁴ from which she is glad to escape into Tarvin's arms and the certainties of Topaz.

For Tarvin India is a series of negatives; its physical and social expressions affront his work-and-progress ethic, the inertia threatens the energy of white men. His search for the necklace takes him to holy places where he gazes on the dried blood of the sacrifices in a Hindu temple and measures his distance from India: 'Standing there, he recognized with fresh force how entirely the life, habits and traditions of this strange people alienated them from all that seemed good and right to him, and he was vaguely angered to know that it was the servants of these horrors who possessed a necklace which had the power to change the destiny of a Christian and civilized town like Topaz.'⁵⁵* Tarvin's dispositions are fixed, his priorities determined and neither the bizarre sight of Gunnaur's ruins – 'Tall-built, sharp-domed palaces, flushing to the colour of blood, revealed the horror of their emptiness, and glared at the day that pierced them through and through'⁵⁶ – nor the 'malignant chuckle' of a jet of water spurting fitfully through the rudely carved cow's head in the sacred shrine, checks his search for the treasure. Although the 'silence of the place and the insolent nakedness of the empty ways lay on him like a dead weight',⁵⁷ he asserts his authority by defiantly ordering the offending sound to 'dry up', and proceeds in his descent to the disused quarry. Here there is a tank as old as time with water so stagnant 'that it had corrupted past corruption',⁵⁸ and now he is uneasy, acutely desiring the blessed sunshine.

After stepping on a human skull and seeing himself observed by an alligator with pale emerald eyes and 'horny eyelids, heavy with slime', he flees having tasted 'all the agonies of pure physical terror'.⁵⁹ It is the recollection of the green eyes and the intolerable smell of musk which decides Tarvin that he can never again set foot in the Cow's Mouth. When he had descended 'to the darkness and horror below', he had confronted the symbol of an interminably

* It would have been impossible for Kipling to attach 'Christian' to 'civilized' in any of his independent writings.

ancient India in the alligator, a sacred animal who, although he did not know it, was 'waiting for his morning meal, as he had waited in the days when Gunnaur was peopled'.[60]* Tarvin flees from actual objects which have induced physical terror, but his personality and outlook do not change. Instead, the experience reinforces his outrage at the purposelessness and emptiness of India, typified by a shrine in a dead city, and confirms his contempt for India as a denial of all he conceives of as important.†

It is the verses which bring some dimension and chiaroscuro to the novel and give to Tarvin's encounter with India a perspective hidden from him: ''Twas a white man from the West came expressly to invest-/igate the natural wealth of Hindustan.'[61] While Tarvin blandly pronounces his faith in activity and progress and aggressively condemns the passive and immobile East as an 'infernal land', India emerges as infinitely stronger and subtler than the West, evading the intruders, continuing with its own existence, and so defeating Tarvin's attempts to exploit her and Kate's eagerness to serve and save her:

> We be the Gods of the East –
> Older than all –
> Masters of mourning and feast,
> How shall we fall?

* Though this alligator is apparently male, it is worth noting that the creature is one of the forms assumed by Mother Kali, the female deity, and is referred to by Kipling in 'The Bridge-Builders'; see p. 231.

† Stanley Cooperman's analysis, 'The Imperial Posture and the Shrine of Darkness: Kipling's *The Naulahka* and E. M. Forster's *A Passage to India*', *English Literature in Transition*, Vol. VI, No. 1, 1963, pp. 9–13, salvages the novel from critical neglect, but overdraws the area of similarity between the two novels and attributes greater import to Kipling's book than the text can support. His thesis is that both novels focus upon identical crises, 'those of total negation', and that 'Kipling's hero – man of action though he is – confronts the same ultimate *nada* in the Shrine at the "Cow's Mouth" as Forster's Mrs Moore and Miss Quested do in the Marabar Caves' (p. 9). But Tarvin in fact experiences no crisis and no radical alteration in his perceptions, nor is there any evidence of his gaining 'a new and shattering perspective' (p. 11); in fact he continues his pursuits as before. Whatever the significance of the confrontation between Tarvin and India, this emerges obliquely in the verses.

Will they gape to the husks that ye proffer,
    Or yearn to your song,
And we, have we nothing to offer
    Who ruled them so long
In the fume of the incense, the clash of the cymbal, the blare
    of the conch and the gong?

Over the strife of the schools,
    Low the day burns –
Back with the kine from the pools,
    Each one returns,
To the life that he knows where the altar-flame glows
    And the *tulsi* is trimmed in the urns.[62]

III

The East–West antithesis determines the representation of India in *The Naulahka* and the Western-centric view dominates. On the other hand, in 'The Bridge-Builders' the differences of precepts, aspirations and temperaments are absorbed into the context of two equally authentic cultures. Through this allegory Kipling achieves his most consummate evocation of India's unique identity as it was imaginatively conceived in myth and legend, where daring experiments with thought were expressed as poetry and the guidance of the gods sought in mundane concerns.

The Kashi Bridge is a triumph of technical ingenuity, a massive structure of stone and iron spanning the Ganges, erected by the British to foster trade and travel and to facilitate their rule. The work has been supervised by Findlayson and his assistant, two Englishmen whose pioneering spirit and determination to leave their imprint on the material world drives them to battle against the intimidating obstacles which India's physical environment and social structure place in the way of progress. Findlayson's reverie of the preceding three years 'covered storm, sudden freshets, death in every manner and shape ... drought, sanitation, finance; birth, wedding, burial and riot in the village of twenty warring castes'.[63] Now he surveys with satisfaction 'the face of the country that he had changed for seven miles around', at the heart of which is his bridge, 'raw, ugly as original sin, but *pukka* – permanent – to endure when all memory of the builder ... had perished'.[64] Initially what dominates is the British version of man's most meaningful relationship with the universe. Findlayson the engineer is a creature of his social milieu, a man immersed in his work and shaped by a discipline which, while essential for professional excellence, inhibits the instincts. If there are perceptions beyond the boundaries of his culturally determined awareness, these are not normally available to him and nor is he interested. When he recovers from the opium which had expanded his consciousness and permitted him an astonishing vision of India, he instantly rejects the experience: 'in that clear light there was no room for a man to think dreams of the dark.'[65]

As the story proceeds, the metaphoric implications of the bridge unfold. On the most apparent level it is the material manifestation of the British impact on India. The Indian foreman, Peroo, one-time lascar (sailor), is the personification of East meeting West and is in this sense the true bridge-builder. His experiences in the West have taught him technical skills and knowledge about societies radically different from his own and have made him sufficiently sophisticated to free himself from enslavement to religious prohibitions and rigorous customs. But what he has acquired has been assimilated into his essentially Indian personality and this, while extended, has remained integral. 'I like sus-sus-pen-sheen bridges that fly from bank to bank, with one big step, like a gang-plank',[66] he comments, suggesting that men from technically retarded societies can with one big step appreciate and absorb the most radical technical innovations. But 'port missions or those creeds which are thrust upon sailors by agencies along Thames' bank'[67] had left him, as they had his fellow sea-rovers, unaffected. Peroo is a religious relativist, even a cautious agnostic who favours widespread insurance with many gods, whose potency he suspects may be limited to their particular locales: 'London is London Sahib, Sydney is Sydney and Port Darwin is Port Darwin. Also Mother Gunga is Mother Gunga, and when I come back to her banks I know this and worship.'[68]

He has accepted the science of the West but not its ethics, nor its aggressive confidence in the omnipotence of reason, and as the work nears completion he has a premonition of disaster: 'We have bitted and bridled her. She is not like the sea, that can beat against a soft beach. She is Mother Gunga – in irons.'[69] Because his belief in the efficacy of science is tempered by the speculation that there is a residue which science cannot penetrate, Peroo, who knows and respects nature's incalculable moods, takes the precaution of propitiating his gods. Two months before they were due, the floods threaten the still incomplete bridge. As the waters rush in, Findlayson rages against the elements' capricious disruption of his plans to impose change according to schedule, and he affirms his dependence on reasoning when he checks and rechecks the calculations which went to make the plates, spans, bricks and piers.* The more flexible Peroo keeps his powder dry and trusts in the gods; against the threat to the bridge he vigorously assists in taking all possible precautions, but once these are done and he is keeping watch with Findlayson, he chides the Englishman for his obstinate refusal to recognize fate: 'Wilt thou hold it up with thy hands then? . . . I was troubled for my boats and sheers *before* the flood came. Now we are in the hands of the Gods.'[70]

To guard against fever Peroo and Findlayson swallow opium pellets and through Findlayson's hallucinatory scheme to rescue some loosened boats they are cast onto a small and deserted island. Here the story opens out to reveal the many faces of India, for the drug is a bridge to a lucid vision of India as it exists in its phenomenal form and as it is conceived in metaphysical speculation and given form in legend and myth. When they see beasts in conclave Findlayson accepts Peroo's explanation that they are witnessing a *punchayet* [assembly] of the gods: 'After the flood, who should be alive in the land except the Gods who made it, the Gods to whom his village prayed nightly – the Gods who were in all men's mouths and about all men's ways?'[71] Now it seems to him that 'Somewhere in the night of time he had built a bridge – a bridge that spanned illimitable levels of shining seas',[72] and indeed in the presence of the gods, the Kashi Bridge, a solid achievement in the empirical world, is transformed into yet another abstract quality of their divine cosmos.

The discussion of the gods reflects not only the hierarchy of

* Kipling's fondness for technical inventories is here directed towards showing a frame of mind and an outlook.

deities within the Hindu pantheon, which embraces both priestly and popular divinities inherited from the Aryan and pre-Aryan traditions, but also the diverse social realities here manifest in their mythological expressions. What is recreated is the Indian religious experience as understood by ordinary people in its devotional, practical aspect, and the esoteric cosmology of the epics and sacred books as studied by the priestly caste.* Because Hinduism is the accretion of a multitude of cults and traditions, the gods represent the many preoccupations and temperaments of their followers, but all are manifestations of One Universal Spirit. As Ganesh, who has the form of an elephant, announces: 'We be here . . . the Great Ones. One only and very many.'† The purpose of the gathering is to decide what is to be done about the bridge and what emerges is a spectrum of responses amongst Indian people to the presence and influence of the West. Here the Mother Goddess appears in her grim aspects:‡ it was Kali the Tiger, the Mother of Death, and Sitala the Ass, the bringer of smallpox, who had harried the work, spreading disease and death amongst the labourers, and now it is Mother Gunga, the crocodile, the goddess of the sacred river, who calls for

* To those neither immersed in Hinduism nor acquainted through scholarship with the Hindu sacred texts and the practices and beliefs of the cults and sects, the different manifestations and concepts of the divinities in the scriptures, myths and legends, is extraordinarily difficult to grasp. In *A Passage to India*, E. M. Forster perfectly captures the confusion which most Westerners experience: 'The fissures in the Indian soil are infinite: Hinduism, so solid from a distance, is riven into sects and clans, which radiate and join and change their names according to the aspect from which they are approached.'

† A. L. Basham, *The Wonder That Was India* (1967), writes, 'The more devout Hindus, even when illiterate and ignorant, have always been fundamentally monotheist' (p. 312). K. M. Sen, *Hinduism* (1961), points out that the West has mistakenly understood Hinduism to be a polytheistic religion because God is worshipped in different forms. 'Depending on the social traditions of particular sections of the people, Hindus show a particular attachment to a particular figure in Hindu mythology and worship God in that form. The Nameless and the Formless is called by different names, and the different forms are attributed to Him, but it is not forgotten that He is One' (pp. 20–21).

‡ 'The chief form of the Mother goddess was that of the wife of Siva, called in her benevolent aspect, Parvati, ... Mahadevi, ... Sati, ... Gauri, ... Annapurna ... or simply "the Mother".' Basham, *op. cit.*, p. 314.

vengeance against the bridge-builders. These deities who see the gods mocked by the bridge-builders speak for the social traditions which militate against change and the conservative forces hostile to new ways.

A different outlook is voiced by Ganesh who knows that the fire-carriages now threaded through the land have stimulated economic changes and profited the money-lenders who worship him especially. Hanuman the ape, himself a legendary bridge-builder,* also sees the British intervention as propitious and finds their cult of toil congenial. When he boasts of his continued prowess, 'I am the builder of bridges indeed – bridges between this and that, and each bridge leads surely to us in the end',[73] he is claiming responsibility for bringing the people of other faiths to the gods, and he numbers amongst his conquests the British themselves, 'the men who believe their God is toil'.[74] His concern is not with converting men to Hinduism and his boast is simply a statement of Hinduism's ability to absorb new influences, of India's enormous assimilative powers and of the people's devotion to tradition. When Krishna, an avatar of Vishnu, warns the gods that the people *are* changing, Hanuman replies, 'They will only change a little the names of their Gods. . . Beloved, they will do no more than change the names, and that we have seen a thousand times.'[75]

Aloof from the secular concerns of Ganesh and Hanuman, who are confident that the British are the servants and not the masters of India, are the gods of the higher pantheon: Indra, the war-god in the sacred book the *Vedas*, and here manifest as a buck, reproaches the female deities for their myopia: 'Does Mother Gunga die, then, in a year, that she is so anxious to see vengeance now? The deep sea was where she runs but yesterday, and tomorrow the sea shall cover her again as the Gods count that which men call time. Can any say that

---

* The feat of Hanuman the monkey-god as recorded in the *Ramayana* was to build a bridge with his monkey-army from India to Ceylon, across which Rama led his troops, the monkeys, to defeat the demon-king Ravana and regain his kidnapped Queen Sita. In Kipling's tale Hanuman says: 'For my own part . . . it pleases me well to watch these men, remembering that I also builded no small bridge in the world's youth. . . They toil as my armies toiled in Lanka [Ceylon], and they believe that their toil endures' (p. 29).

this their bridge endures till tomorrow?'[76] In the cosmic mythology
of Hinduism the cosmos eternally passes through cycles within
cycles: the Universe emanates from Vishnu, or Visnu, the Preserver
who causes the birth of Brahma the demiurge-creator from whom
stems the world, to be dissolved by Shiv, or Siva or Shiva, only to be
recreated again in an endless cycle. All three are functions of
Ishwara, God considered with attributes and as aspects of Brahman
or Brahm the All-Pervading Godhead who is immanent and transcendent, and who is the indwelling spirit in man, the Self or Atman.*
Here in 'The Bridge-Builders' Shiv, in the form of a bull, reminds
the lesser gods of their lowly stature and asserts his power to move
the minds of men to worship particular divinities. As the patron
deity of ascetics and scholars, Shiv 'hears the talk of the schools and
the dreams of holy men',[77] and in his total aspect as the Dissolver
he receives all men: 'Men go to and fro, making words and talking
talk of strange Gods, and I listen. Faith follows faith among my
people in the schools, and I have no anger; for when the words
are said, and the new talk is ended, to Shiv all men return at the
last.'[78]

With the arrival of Krishna, a human and humane element is
introduced, for unlike the deities who represent sectarian interests
and the gods who are the attributes of Brahm, Krishna identifies
with mankind in the totality of their concerns. 'There came up from
the water a snatch of a love-song such as the boys sing when they
watch their cattle in the moon-heats of the late spring . . . in a patch

* 'Brahman is that which is immutable, and independent of any cause but
Itself. When we consider Brahman as lodged within the individual being, we
call Him the Atman. The creative energy of Brahman is that which causes all
existence to come into being.' *Bhagavad Gita* (*The Song of God*), Part VIII, 'The
Way to Eternal Brahman', translation by Swami Prabhavananda and Christopher
Isherwood (1954), p. 74. Heinrich Zimmer in *Myths and Symbols* (1962) explains: 'The noun *Brahman* is neuter. The Absolute is beyond the differentiating
qualifications of sex, beyond all limiting, individualizing characteristics whatsoever. It is the all-containing transcendent source of every possible virtue and
form. Out of Brahman, the Absolute, proceed the energies of Nature, to produce our world of individuated forms, the swarming world of our empirical
experience, which is characterized by limitations, antagonisms, cooperation'
(p. 123).

of clear moonlight stood revealed the young herd, the darling of the Gopis,* the idol of dreaming maids and of mothers ere their children are born.'[79] He pleads for his people who are dying in the floods, courteously reminding Mother Gunga that there is no need to slay them now for life is brief: 'Have pity, mother, for a little – and it is only for a little.'[80] Krishna spans the phenomenal and the absolute, the ephemeral and the continuous, bridging indifference to material actualities and short-sighted preoccupation with the manifest universe. Though he is divine, his incarnation as a man embraces the transient and the infinite, the relative and the absolute. He warns the lesser gods that as society becomes more complex and centralized they will be rejected by their followers and will revert to 'rag-Gods, pot-Godlings of the tree and the village-mark, as ye were at the beginning'.[81] To the great gods he says, 'Wise are ye, but ye live far off, forgetting whence ye came',[82] and he entreats them to take notice of the changes taking place because of the bridge-builders: 'Now my people see their work, and go away thinking. They do not think of the Heavenly Ones altogether',[83] and when Hanuman boasts of how he had transformed the gods of the bridge-builders, Krishna replies, 'This is no question of their Gods – one or three, man or woman. The matter is with the people. *They* move and not the Gods of the bridge-builders.'[84] By men's calculations the end of the gods is far, 'but as we who know reckon it is today'.[85] When Indra is called upon to pronounce on these dire prophecies, he answers with the riddle of the gods: 'When Brahm ceases to dream the Heavens and the Hells and Earth disappear. Be content. Brahm dreams still. The dreams come and go, and the nature of the dream changes, but still Brahm dreams. Krishna has walked too long upon earth, and yet I love him the more for the tale he has told. The Gods change, beloved – all save One. . . Brahm dreams – and till He wakes the Gods die not.'[86]†

---

* Wives and daughters of cowherds. In his pastoral and erotic aspect Krishna was the inspiration for much romantic literature. But it is Krishna as god-hero who features in the traditions of the *Mahabharata* and the *Bhagavad Gita*. See Basham, *op. cit.*, pp. 306–9.

† 'From the human standpoint the lifetime of a Brahma seems to be very lengthy; nevertheless it is limited. It endures for only one hundred Brahma years of Brahma days and nights, and concludes with a great, or universal

Thus is Krishna's humane plea reabsorbed into the eternal cycles of the cosmic processes in which the phenomenal universe is subject to permanent alteration while the world-spirit, who is immanent and transcendent, persists as the unvarying reality, indissoluble and immutable.*

When day breaks and the gods have disappeared, Findlayson quickly returns to the world of his confined perceptions: 'the work of the opium was over, and, as he sluiced his forehead in a pool, the Chief Engineer of the Kashi Bridge was wondering how he had managed to fall upon the island, what chances the day offered of return, and, above all, how his work stood.'[87] But for Peroo what he had seen is a profound experience, and here it is difficult to interpret the text: has he in fact realized his Atman, the identity of his individual soul with Brahman, which is for Hinduism the aim of human existence? Or has he merely understood the implications of the metaphysical proposition that Brahman or Brahm is immanent, transcendent and imperishable while the deities with which men commune are themselves transient? ' "When Brahm ceases to

---

dissolution. Then vanish not only the visible spheres of the three worlds (earth, heaven and the space between), but all spheres of being whatsoever, even those of the highest worlds. All become resolved into the divine, primeval Substance. A state of total reabsorption then prevails for another Brahma century, after which the entire cycle of 311,040,000,000,000 human years begins anew.' Zimmer, *op. cit.*, p. 19. See also Appendix on the Cosmology of the *Gita* in the translation cited: 'Since it is subject to the eternal power of Brahman, the universe is part of a beginningless and endless process, which alternates between the two phases of potentiality and expression. When at the beginning of a time-cycle, or kalpa, the universe is dissolved, it passes into a phase of potentiality, a seed-state, and thus awaits its next creation. In Chapter VIII of the Gita, this process is described. The phase of expression is called by Sri Krishna "the day of Brahma", and the phase of potentiality "the night of Brahma". The creatures inhabiting the worlds subject to these cycles are perpetually being reborn and redissolved, with each cosmic day and night' (pp. 132–3).

* In his Introduction to *Vedanta for the Western World* (1960), Christopher Isherwood writes: 'The universe is other than its outward aspect. Moreover, this outward aspect is subject to perpetual change... Vedanta goes on to assert that, beneath this appearance, this flux, there is an essential unchanging Reality, which it calls Brahman, the Godhead. Brahman is Existence itself, Consciousness itself' (p. 2).

dream, the Gods die." Now I know, indeed, what he meant. Once, too, the *guru* said as much to me, but then I did not understand. Now I am wise.'[88] Peroo ponders on the gods' words as he remembers his doubts on the efficacy and durability of the deities when he had called on them during a typhoon and his life was in danger: ' "How shall I be sure," I said, "that the Gods to whom I pray will abide at all" . . . but I did not die and I have seen the Gods. They are good for live men, but for the dead – They have spoken Themselves. . . When Brahm ceases to dream, the Gods go.'[89] Though Peroo's words do in an earthy way reproduce the text of hymns in the *Upanishads* – 'Knowing this Atman, wise and ageless yet ever young, one has no fear of death. . . This my self within the heart is that Brahman. When I depart from hence I shall merge into it'* – the second conjecture is the more likely because it conforms with the dispositions of Peroo the action-loving eclectic who believes that living is to be fully enjoyed within the transient phase permitted to men.†

Through ideas and images drawn from the Indian experience, Kipling evokes an Indian apprehension of life which confirms the universal apprehension of tension between permanence and fluidity, between matter and essence. Diffused in the tale is the belief that the phenomenal world is but a momentary expression of the ultimate and enduring reality but that this does not deprive the empirical

* Cited in R. C. Zaehner, *Hinduism* (1966), p. 50. See also Basham, *op. cit.*: 'The great and saving knowledge which the *Upanishads* claim to impart lies not in the mere recognition of the existence of Brahman, but in continual consciousness of it. For Brahman resides in the human soul – indeed Brahman *is* the human soul, is *Atman*, the Self. When a man realizes this fact fully he is wholly freed from transmigration. His soul becomes one with Brahman, and he transcends joy and sorrow, life and death' (p. 252). In his Introduction to his translation of the *Bhagavad Gita*, Juan Mascaró writes: 'In the *Katha Upanishad* the question is asked by the boy Nachiketas when he meets the Spirit of Death: "When a man dies, this doubt arises: some say 'he is' and some say 'he is not'. Teach me the truth." The answer is the same as that of the *Bhagavad Gita*: "The Atman, the Self, is never born and never dies" ' (p. 14).

† Peroo did not follow any of the disciplines which, it is postulated, enable men to supersede the limitations of their personalities and apprehend God, but as Kipling interpreted Hindu thought loosely, this would not in itself exclude the possibility that Peroo comes to know his Self.

world of meaning or life of value.* A choice of priorities is offered in
'The Bridge-Builders': the British stance is personified in Findlayson who is wholly absorbed in a purposeful refashioning of the
material environment and whose ethic of work, responsibility and
personal honour through achievement, matches this concern. The
Indian attitude is suggested in a conceptualization of the gods as the
aspiration towards an Absolute transcending the individual ego.
Between these two poles is Krishna, who bridges the separation
between the specific and the universal, and Peroo, the humble lascar
whose instincts have not been atrophied by practical knowledge and
who is aware of larger matters while participating fully in the
material world.

Just as the story suggests a gradation of realities and planes of
being, so does it exist on various levels. The bridge symbolizes that
area across which ideas and influences have passed from the British
to affect the lives and thoughts of the Indian people, and it is also a
metaphor for the passage connecting the finite to the infinite.† There

* Both Tompkins, *op. cit.*, and Alan Sandison, in 'Kipling: The Artist and the
Empire', suggest that the vision emerging in this tale points to the transcendent
reducing the world to illusion. The dichotomy in Kipling conforms rather to
that accepted by Hindu thought – of the material world not as illusion but as a
form of the ultimate. S. Radhakrishnan in *Eastern Religions and Western Thought*
(1958), in referring to the familiar criticism that for Hindu thought the world is
illusion, points out: 'The manifold world is not an illusion; it is being, though
of a lower order, subject to change, waxing and waning, growing and shrinking...
For the Hindu thinkers the objective world exists. It is not an illusion. It is real
not in being ultimate, but in being a form, an expression of the ultimate. To
regard the world as ultimately real is delusion (*moha*)' (pp. 30–31). Zaehner,
op. cit., explains: 'It has too often been said that Hinduism as such regards the
world as illusion. This has never been true of Hinduism as a whole but only of
one (though at present predominant) school of Vedanta philosophy which is
itself only one among six philosophical schools: it has never been true of the
sacred writings themselves nor of popular religion' (p. 7).

† There are, in addition, tributary meanings to the bridge – e.g. when
Hanuman recalls his legendary feat. Also there is in Indian thought another
bridge-image from Moslem sources which also evokes the gap between the
immediate and the eternal: 'The world is a bridge: pass over it, but build no
house upon it. Who hopes for an hour, hopes for Eternity. The world is an
hour: spend it in prayer, for what follows is unseen.' Quoted in H. G. Rawlinson,
India: A Short Cultural History (1965), p. 305. After conquering the Deccan in

is further a dual meaning to the bridge-builders who are Englishmen precipitating change and Indians adapting to new ways. The importance of this last implication is underscored by the brief but pointed appearance of the local maharajah, who is a walking perversion of what the West can offer to the East. In 'tweed shooting-suit and seven-hued turban'[90] he lends his steam-launch and his presence to rescue Findlayson and Peroo from the island, and while he speaks disparagingly of his gods in babu-English and confesses that he cannot handle his boat, 'Peroo, well known to the crew, had possessed himself of the wheel, and was taking the launch craftily up-stream'.[91]

Those Indians who were seduced into imitating the superficialities of the West, and because of this blasphemed against their own inheritance, earned Kipling's contempt as much as did the educated stratum who aspired to integrate East and West within their persons. On the other hand, Peroo, the uneducated and technically proficient Indian willing to work under the supervision of the British, serves Kipling as the perfect exemplar of the East's modernization, a process in which participants would be unconcerned with matters of political independence and would reject the adoption of European manners. Other ethnocentric presumptions intrude when Kipling is writing about Findlayson and from his point of view – consider the bland statement about his appointment as a magistrate of the third class 'with whipping powers, for the better government of the community'[92] or the stentorian announcement of the function which the Kashi Bridge will serve: 'At either end rose towers of red brick, loop-holed for musketry and pierced for big guns.'[93] But seldom are Kipling's political alignments and racial prejudices so little in evidence. Although the Kashi Bridge withstands the floods and soldiers will indeed march over it, by the end of the story it is overtowered by more fundamental and far-reaching images of a bridge. What finally dominates is a vision of India as an authentic world; Kipling has seen beyond the bewildering variety and apparent inflexibility to an India which, like Brahm, is Many but One and which, like Peroo, endures even while it changes.

1601, Akbar inscribed these words on the triumphal arch in Fathpur Sikri, the City of Victory.

IV

Because 'On the City Wall' is both a political prognosis and an affectionate acknowledgement of India's charms, its internal contradictions provide an interesting insight into Kipling's emotional involvement with India. Wali Dad, 'a young Muhammadan who was suffering acutely from education of the English variety and knew it',[94] and Lalun, the graceful and witty courtesan, are regarded with warmth and admiration by the young Englishman who tells the tale. Wali Dad's dalliance with Lalun, exchanging Persian couplets and singing love-songs, seems a most civilized way to pass the time:

Lalun has not yet been described. She would need, so Wali Dad says, a thousand pens of gold and ink scented with musk. She has been variously compared to the Moon, the Dil Sagar Lake, a spotted quail, a gazelle, the Sun on the Desert of Kutch, the Dawn, the Stars, and the young bamboo. These comparisons imply that she is beautiful exceedingly according to the native standards, which are practically the same as those of the West. Her eyes are black and her hair is black, and her eyebrows are black as leeches; her mouth is tiny and says witty things; her hands are tiny and have saved much money; her feet are tiny and have trodden on the naked hearts of many men. But, as Wali Dad sings; 'Lalun *is* Lalun, and when you have said that, you have only come to the Beginnings of Knowledge.'[95]

But both characters portend more than careless love. Lalun, as a member of the world's oldest profession, sang 'all the songs that have ever been sung, from the war-songs of the South, that make the old men angry with the young men and the young men angry with the State, to the love-songs of the North'[96] and the battle-songs of the Mahrattas celebrating the prowess of the warrior Sivaji.* This catholic repertoire is fitting for a lady of all India in whose little house on the city wall congregate

Shiahs of the grimmest and most uncompromising persuasion; Sufis who had lost all belief in the Prophet and retained but little in God; wandering Hindu priests passing southward on their way to the Central India fairs and other affairs; Pundits in black gowns, with spectacles on their noses and undigested wisdom in their insides; bearded headmen of

* Mahratta chief in the Deccan who in 1670 rebelled against the Moghul Empire.

the wards; Sikhs with all the details of the latest ecclesiastical scandal in
the Golden Temple; red-eyed priests from beyond the Border, looking
like trapped wolves and talking like ravens; M.A.s of the University, very
superior and very voluble.[97]

Within sight of 'the line of guns that could pound the City to
powder in half an hour',[98] these subtle and argumentative visionaries
dream of a future. The man they have chosen to raise the standard of
revolt is a relic of the past, the old rebel Khem Singh who had consistently fought against the British and is now imprisoned in the fort
by the city wall. Lalun succeeds in implementing his escape but the
old man finds himself without a following in the new world and,
though his enmity towards the British is unquenched, he voluntarily
returns to prison.

Kipling perceived that Indians would call on their traditions and
past heroes when building a new political organization and that such
a movement would attract an eclectic following. What he traduced
was the possibility that the modern Westernized Indian could provide a viable leadership, and this is the significance of Wali Dad's
development within the tale. Initially he is marvellously drawn as a
romantic, cultivated, witty and cynical young man, the prototype of
a culturally displaced person. When the narrator advises him to give
up dreaming and take his place in the world, he replies: 'I might
wear an English coat and trousers. I might be a leading Muhammadan pleader. I might be received even at the Commissioner's
tennis-parties where the English stand on one side and the natives on
the other, in order to promote social intercourse throughout the
Empire.'[99]* Then, during Mohurram, when Moslems mourn the
martyrs of their faith and there is the usual riot between them and
the Hindus, Wali Dad reverts to a passionate participation in the
procession, beating his breast and chanting, and in the heat of
religious passion forgetting the part he was to have played in freeing
Khem Singh. As Kipling presents it, his is not a dignified return to

* Significantly, Kipling does not oblige Wali Dad to speak in babu-English
as is the case even with Hurree Babu in *Kim*, the only other educated Indian he
did not treat with contempt. But whereas Hurree Babu is 'good' because he is
working for the British, Wali Dad is initially portrayed with affection simply
because of his intrinsic charm.

the gods and the ways which he had betrayed, but an ignominious reversion to primitive mob passion, proof of the inevitable atavism which in Kipling's eyes makes Westernization of Orientals such a futile process.* His contempt for the educated young Indian collapsing into the past contrasts with his admiration for Khem Singh, who belongs to the past: 'He went to the young men, but the glamour of his name had passed away, and they were entering native regiments or Government offices and Khem Singh could give them neither pension, decorations, nor influence – nothing but a glorious death with their back to the mouth of a gun.'[100]

Wali Dad's retreat to orthodoxy during the Mohurram riots emphasizes India's obstinate adherence to custom and traditional hostilities, forces which proved for Kipling that India would be permanently dependent on Western rule: 'Year by year England sends out fresh drafts for the first fighting line, which is officially called the Indian Civil Service. They die, or kill themselves by overwork, or are worried to death, or broken in health and hope in order that the land may be protected from death and sickness, famine and war and may eventually become capable of standing alone. It will never stand alone.'[101] Indeed, when the Moslems and Hindus are fighting, it is the British who lead the quelling of the riot and greatly enjoy the chance of 'a little fun'.[102]† What is so striking in 'On The City Wall'

---

* Francis G. Hutchins in *The Illusion of Permanence: British Imperialism in India* (1967) offers an interesting explanation of the apparent tolerance in that attitude which advocated leaving Indian culture intact: 'The Victorians pictured the decadence and disarray of Indian society as a reflection of Indian racial character rather than the primary deterrent to its true expression. The decline of enthusiasm for remaking Indian society and replacing Indian religion led to a more general acceptance of the notion that Indian society and religion were only what Indians deserved. If it were assumed that the condition of Indian society was not the result of a chain of unfortunate historical accidents but, instead, an expression of the peculiar genius of the Indian people, it followed that attempts at social or religious reform were futile. Conceiving of Indian society in this fashion became a sufficient explanation of leaving it as it was. Indians were thought incapable of appreciating or adopting successfully superior British habits and institutions' (pp. 72–3).

† 'I am sorry to say that they were all pleased, unholily pleased, at the chance of what they called "a little fun." ' In his manner of describing how the riot was ended, Kipling certainly joins in the fun.

is the range and deliberate shrinking of Kipling's perceptions. Having shown both the deep traditional divisions between Hindu and Moslem, he also indicated the incipient nationalism striving to supersede these; knowing the pull of the past, he understood too the magnet of change. But he would not leave these diverse forces in their natural state of dialogue and imposed instead a final solution which conformed with his political preferences. Yet, despite the rhetoric, what lingers is the mood of unease portending change which is so perfectly captured in the voice of Wali Dad, the Westernized Indian weary of West and East, poised between eras.

V

It is in *Kim* that many critics have found Kipling's most triumphant mastery of his Indian material.* Certainly human India is shown as vigorous and various and the people's sensitivity to intangibles is portrayed with sympathetic feeling. Yet ultimately and ironically the novel is debased by the very complexity of its thematic structure. Concealed in a boy's adventure story of prophecies fulfilled, of amulets and secret signs and prescribed cadences of speech, of men who listen at doors, do their deeds under cover of darkness and are masters of disguise and white magic, is a dialogue on the content of human existence and its purpose. Conducted in terms of Indian thought, this debate may be said to revolve around the 'double

* See, in particular, Nirad C. Chaudhuri, 'The Finest Story About India in English', *Encounter*, VIII, April 1957, pp. 47–53: 'the book is specially important in this that through it Kipling projects not only his vision of the basic India he knew so well, but also his feelings for the core and the most significant part of this basic India. . . As regards the human material the best choice in India is always the simplest choice, namely the people and their religion. . . A Hindu's existence in the temporal order is isolated from his aspirations in the spiritual . . . worldly existence hangs in the air like the Indo-Gangetic plain, robbed of all significance unless it can be given anchorage in true spirituality, which the Hindu imagination has always placed in the Himalayas, the abode of beatitude and salvation. The result is an articulation between worldly life and religion, and the affiliation of this articulation to the geographical articulation between the mountains and the plain, and all four are fused to make up the highest unity in India. Kipling took over this unity, with its fourfold articulation, as the foundation of *Kim*' (pp. 49, 50, 51–2).

tension within the Hindu religion – the striving after liberation from this world which all admit to be the final goal of man on the one hand and man's obligation to do what is right *in* this world on the other'.[103]

The journey through the plains and hills of India made by Kim the Irish orphan reared in the bazaars, and the Lama, a Buddhist monk from Tibet, the one pursuing the life of action, the other the path of meditation, is a spiritual pilgrimage along routes drawn from scriptural sources in the Indian tradition. Common to all Indian religious philosophies is the concept that men can know the Divine Absolute through their own exertions, and the *Bhagavad Gita*,* which infuses the novel, postulates three ways for the man seeking realization of the Atman, the eternal dimension within himself: *jnana*, the way of knowledge; *karma*, the way of action; and *bhakti*, the way of devotion. The Lama's aspiration to be free from bondage to the Wheel of Life, to annihilate his individual personality in union with the Absolute, is not distinct from Indian spiritual ambitions. In origin an Indian religion, Buddhism began as a heresy and developed the Hindu ideals of renunciation, love and harmlessness (*ahimsa*) to all creatures. It is in India that the Lama who had come to seek his faith in its pristine purity, suffers spiritual anguish and gains enlightenment, acting out in his person both the experiences of the Buddha and the reabsorption of Buddhist values into Hinduism. Aspects of Kim's personality also model Indian versions of human aspirations, and here Kipling freely borrowed concepts from within Hinduism and outside of it to create a character who mimics and transcends his symbolic roles. This eclecticism is ingenious craftsmanship but, because Kim travesties the ethical propositions he is representing, the theme of man's essential purpose is finally trivialized. Both the casuistry in the treatment of concepts and the manipulation of characters in the service of priorities Kipling

* *The Song of God, Bhagavad Gita*, is part of the gigantic epic, the *Mahabharata*. The *Gita* is placed by scholars as having probably been composed between the fifth and the second centuries B.C. It is regarded by Hindus as the teaching of divine incarnations, saints or prophets who elucidate and elaborate on the scriptural teachings as revealed by God to man. See Isherwood, Zaehner, Basham and Mascaró, *op. cit.*

espouses, create an imbalance between the portent of the novel and its final achievement.*

When Kim attaches himself to the Lama as his *chela* (disciple) it is so that he can leave the bazaars in search of his fate which, from his Eurasian foster-mother's garbled accounts of his father's drunken prophecies, he believes to be connected with a Red Bull on a Green Field, the standard of his father's regiment, and the symbol of a destiny to be realized in the material world. From this beginning, a relationship of mutual dependence and love grows between the wily and worldly boy and the gentle childlike monk. The Lama's search is for the river of Buddhist legend, 'whose nature . . . is that whosoever bathes in it washes away all trace and speckle of sin',[104] and for him sin is that which feeds the senses, sustains the personality and hinders men from knowing the Absolute and realizing themselves as an expression of the One. As they move along the Grand Trunk Road, Kim is brought

to the seventh heaven of joy. . . It was beautiful to behold the many-yoked grain and cotton wagons crawling over the country-roads. . . It was equally beautiful to watch the people. . . This was seeing the world in real truth; this was life as he would have it – bustling and shouting, the buckling of belts, the beating of bullocks and creaking of wheels, lighting of fires and cooking of food, and new sights at every turn of the approving eye.[105]

The road is a 'river of life',[106] 'a broad smiling river of life',[107] and through Kim's wholehearted responses which affirm the richness and worth of empirical objects to be known through the senses, the river for which the Lama longs is etiolated. To the Lama the people of the road 'are all bound upon the Wheel . . . bound from life to life' and as Kim drinks in his surroundings, 'the Lama never raised his eyes'.[108]

On their journeys Kim meets his friend from the bazaar days, Mahbub Ali, horse-dealer and British agent, who entrusts him with a message for a fellow-agent, Colonel Creighton, and this brings Kim to the regiment of the Red Bull. Creighton observes Kim's 'stalki-

* Cf. Chaudhuri, 'The Finest Story', who maintains that 'once a writer has grasped the fundamental unity [of India] he is free to put anything on it' in terms of adventitious themes (p. 52).

ness', sees him as a valuable recruit to the Great Game, the Secret Service, and when the chaplains of the regiment virtually kidnap the white boy from his beggar's life and send him to a boarding-school, he maintains communication with Kim. During the vacations Kim is permitted to be reunited with his Lama on the road, and here he serves his apprenticeship as a spy, his assignments admirably executed under cover of his being *chela* to a holy man. For the Lama the seasons of parting are painful and he continues his search alone, striving always to escape human involvement. He interprets his suffering as a punishment for the pleasure he had begun to take in the world through loving Kim: 'those who follow the Way must permit not the fire of any desire or attachment for that is all illusion.'[109]

Kim completes his schooling and rejoins the Lama and when it becomes necessary for him to assist Hurree Babu, a Bengali agent whose task it is to harry a Russian agent and his French companion known to be operating in the Himalayas, Kim gently guides his *guru* (teacher) to direct their search towards the hills, knowing that as a hill-man he longs for the mountains. Here the obtuse Russian, who sees only insolence in his monumental calm, assaults the Lama provoking in him rage and desire to retaliate: 'In fighting that lust, my soul was torn and wrenched beyond a thousand blows.'[110] His task completed, Kim leads the Lama back to the plains, which is his wish, and here the Lama, sick in body and agonized in his mind at his failure to abstract his mind when he had been dealt the physical blow, meditates for two days and nights and then attains freedom: 'the Soul had passed beyond the illusion of Time and Space and Things. . . Then my Soul was all alone, and I saw nothing, for I was all things, having reached the Great Soul. And I meditated a thousand, thousand years, passionless, well aware of the Causes of All Things.'[111] And having approached the threshold of that blissful state of Nirvana* the Lama renounces it for love of Kim: 'Then a voice cried: "What shall come to the boy if thou art dead?" and I

---

* 'The process of rebirth can only be stopped by achieving Nirvana, first by adopting right views about the nature of existence, then by a carefully controlled system of moral conduct, and finally by concentration and meditation. The state of Nirvana cannot be described, but it can be hinted at or suggested metaphorically. The word literally means "blowing out", as of a lamp. In

was shaken back and forth in myself with pity for thee, and I said: "I will return to my *chela*, lest he miss the Way." Upon this my Soul, which is the Soul of Teshoo Lama, withdrew itself from the Great Soul with strivings and yearnings and retchings and agonies not to be told.'[112] In becoming a *bodhisattva*,* one who with Nirvana within his grasp postpones entrance into it until, partly through his intervention, all living things have been saved, the River he had been seeking breaks at his feet, the same little stream he had seen previously on his journeys but had not recognized, and now because of his renunciation for compassion's sake, the waters free him from sin.

The Lama grows in the passage of the tale. At the outset his simplicity seems often to be mere silliness, his search for a mythical

---

Nirvana all idea of an individual personality or ego ceases to exist and there is nothing to be reborn – as far as the individual is concerned Nirvana is annihilation. But it was certainly not thought of by the early Buddhists in such negative terms. It was rather conceived of as a transcendent state, beyond the possibility of full comprehension by the ordinary being enmeshed in the illusion of selfhood, but not fundamentally different from the state of supreme bliss as described in other non-theistic Indian systems.' A. L. Basham in Wm. Theodore de Bary (ed.), *Sources of Indian Tradition* (1958), pp. 97–8. The Brahman–Atman identification of Hinduism may be compared with the attainment of Nirvana; see Basham, *ibid.*: 'Brahman resides in the human soul – indeed Brahman *is* the human soul, is Atman, the Self. When a man realizes this fact fully he is wholly freed from transmigration. His soul becomes one with Brahman, and he transcends joy and sorrow, life and death. . . When he reaches Brahman, man is free' (p. 252). However, the difference between the Hindu and Buddhist conception should be noted: Basham considers that despite the interpretation of some modern authorities who claim that Buddha 'merely taught the abandonment of selfhood and individualism on the lower plane of everyday life, but maintained the existence of an eternal soul', the orthodox teaching is the doctrine that the source of man's sorrow and suffering is the thirst for personal satisfaction caused by 'the innate but mistaken conviction of individuality – that there is in each living being a permanent core, an ego or soul'. It is this, Basham argues, which characterizes the knowledge Buddha is said to have gained under the Tree of Wisdom and distinguishes it from the lore of the Upanisadic sages (*ibid.*, p. 270).

* 'This term, literally meaning "Being of Wisdom", was first used in the sense of a previous incarnation of the Buddha. For many years before his final birth as Siddhartha Gautama the Bodhisattva did mighty deeds of compassion and self-sacrifice, as he gradually perfected himself in wisdom and virtue' (*ibid.*, p. 155).

river hardly the pursuit of a wise and learned man seeped in metaphysical speculation and his erudition little more than the repetition
of formulae and fantastic happenings, and on this level he matches
the sustained note of immaturity sounded throughout the novel. But
as the book draws to a close, his stature both as a mystic and as a
complete man is confirmed when he renounces Nirvana out of concern for others. The Middle Way of which he had so often spoken is
now truly his: in the 'Sermon of the Wheel of the Law' which it is
traditionally believed Buddha preached to his first disciples at
Benares, he taught that the desire for individual satisfaction caused
the sorrow which is inherent in ordinary life and that this craving
can be suppressed only by following 'a middle course between self-
indulgence and extreme asceticism and leading a moral and well-
ordered life'.*

* 'The basic propositions of this great body of literature are not metaphysical
but psychological. Sorrow, suffering, dissatisfaction, and all the manifold un-
pleasantness which are referred to by the word *dukkha*, are inherent in life as
it is ordinarily lived; they can only be eliminated by giving up "thirst" (*tanha*,
often translated "craving") which includes personal ambition, desire, longing
and selfishness of all kinds. According to orthodox teaching the cause of this
"thirst" is the innate but mistaken conviction of individuality – that there is in
each living being a permanent core, an ego or soul' (*ibid.*, p. 270). The Lama's
aspiration to knowing Nirvana and his attainment of the Middle Way may be
compared with the Hindu concept of *maya*; see Radhakrishnan, *op. cit.* 'When
man apprehends the supreme being, returns to the concrete and controls his
life in the light of its truth, he is a complete man. He reaches an almost in-
conceivable universality. All his powers which have been hitherto bound up
with narrow pursuits are liberated to larger ends. The doctrine of *maya* tells
us that we fall away from our authentic being if we are lost in the world of
empirical objects and earthly desires, turning our back on the reality, which
gives them value. They are so alluring that they provoke ardent desires, but
they cannot satisfy the inner being, and in the world outside they break forth
into frantic disorder. This does not mean that we have to neglect worldly
welfare or despise body and mind. The body is necessary for the soul. . . Personal life is not to be repressed in order to gain the end of religion. It is recreated
and purified in the light of the higher truth. He in whom the spark of spirit
glows, grows into a new man, the man of God, the transfigured person. The
divine penetrates his self, wells up and flows through him, absorbing him
and enriching him within it. God is not for him another self, he is the real self
closer than his own ego' (pp. 31–2).

The Lama as *guru* and Kim as *chela* act out one of the problems posed and resolved in the *Bhagavad Gita*. Here Krishna as the incarnate God teaches Arjuna the warrior the ways of reaching the highest good which is the realization of man's true nature through union with Brahman: 'in this world, aspirants may find enlightenment by two different paths. For the contemplative is the path of knowledge: for the active is the path of selfless action.'[113] The context of the dialogue between Krishna and Arjuna is vital: it is the eve of a battle and Krishna in advising the heartsore Arjuna to fight against his friends and relatives is referring to his caste-duty as a warrior.* But because the content of Krishna's teaching operates on the level of the absolute as well as the immediate, the nature of action is defined in moral and metaphysical terms: only action which is performed without desire, which is unattached to rewards and indifferent to results, will lead man along the path to union with Brahman, when the aspirant will recognize his true nature and perceive the Reality which is beyond action. Kim's question, 'Then all Doing is Evil?' and the Lama's reply, 'To abstain from action is well – except to acquire merit'[114] resembles the exchange between Arjuna and Krishna when Arjuna asks: 'You speak so highly of the renunciation of action; yet you ask me to follow the yoga† of action. Now tell me definitely: which of these is better', and Krishna replies, 'Action rightly renounced brings freedom:/Action rightly performed brings freedom:/Both are better/Than mere shunning of action.'[115]

No action is in itself good or evil; no act of abstaining is in itself good or evil; neither has absolute value and in both cases the fundamental proposition is whether the action or the renunciation is

* 'The teaching of the *Bhagavad Gita* is summed up in the maxim "your business is with the deed, and not with the result." In an organized society each individual has his special part to play, and in every circumstance there are actions which are intrinsically right – from the point of view of the poet who wrote the *Gita* they are those laid down by the Sacred Law of the Aryans and the traditions of class and clan. The right course must be chosen according to the circumstances, without any consideration of personal interest or sentiment. Thus man serves God, and in so far as he lives up to this ideal, he draws nearer to God.' Basham, *op. cit.*, p. 344.

† Spiritual discipline.

performed in a spirit which will further man's discovery of his nature in union with the Absolute, and with that end in view. The mimicry of these propositions in *Kim* is, however, of surfaces only for Kim's participation in action is essentially different in content and direction from the recommended yoga. Kim does not seek to dissociate himself from the deeds he performs, nor are his senses unattached, and the Lama's instruction on the significance of the symbolic Wheel of Life escapes him: 'Obediently then, with bowed head and brown finger alert to follow the pointer, did the *chela* study; but when they came to the human world, busy and profitless ... his mind was distracted; for by the roadside trundled the very Wheel itself, eating, drinking, trading, marrying and quarrelling – all warmly alive.'[116] Indeed, it is in defiance of the Lama's concept of wisdom that Kim develops a creed of total involvement in the empirical universe, flinging himself again and again 'whole-heartedly upon the next turn of the wheel'.[117*]

The Indian religious experience is again invoked when Kim is cast in another role, this time as a votary of the 'game' who in imitating God expresses his *karma*, action, through *lila*, sport. The wisdom of some Saivite sects† within the devotional movements seeking union with the Absolute through *bhakti*, devotion or love, 'allows it to enter harmoniously into the great "game", lila, of life, to take part in

---

* Kim deviates absolutely from the ideal path of action as conceived in the *Gita*. Consider Zaehner's exposition: 'The perfect man is the one who has dutifully performed the duties of his caste (in Arjuna's case the ruthless prosecution of a just but senseless war) yet knowing all the time that these actions are in no sense "his."' Such a man's 'consciousness is wholly unattached, he has conquered self, desire has left him, and by renunciation he attains to that absolute perfection which consists in the disappearance of action (*karma*). And as he wins this perfection so does he win Brahman ... which is the final goal of knowledge. Integrated, his intellect made clean, resolute in his self-control, putting behind him the senses and their objects, love (*raga*) and hate, cultivating solitude, eating lightly, with body, speech and mind controlled, constantly engaged in meditation, wholly dispassionate, abandoning all thought of self (*ahamkara*), force, pride, desire, anger, and acquisitiveness, thinking nothing his own, at peace [the perfected man] is conformed to becoming Brahman. Having become Brahman, his soul assuaged, he knows neither grief nor desire.' *op. cit.*, p. 97.

† Devotees of Shiva.

it by dancing and singing with all one's heart and all one's joy'.* Kim's joyous participation in the bustling world of active people as he revels in the smells, tastes and sounds of the physical environment, exactly matches the affirmative note sounded by this sect, and Kipling uses the word 'game' as a metaphor for Kim's fashion of existence. As an urchin Kim had assisted in bazaar-intrigues as much for the pleasure as the reward: 'what he loved was the game for its own sake.'[118] As he grows up he continues to delight in 'the visible effect of action',[119] in double-talk and secret assignments: 'Kim warmed to the game, for it reminded him of experiences in the letter-carrying line, when, for the sake of a few pice, he pretended to know more than he knew. But he was now playing for larger things – the sheer excitement and the sense of power.'[120]

If the game signifies the delight of living in a wonderful world, then the Great Game is for Kim the summation of experience. Here he meets diverse men united in the common cause of the Secret Service – Colonel Creighton, Mahbub Ali, Lurgan, the Indian-born Englishman, Hurree Babu, the fearless Bengali, E25, the Mahratta.

Well is the game called great! I was four days a scullion at Quetta, waiting on the wife of the man whose book I stole. And that was a part of the Great Game! From the South – God knows how far – came the Mahratta, playing the Great Game in fear of his life. Now I shall go far and far into the North playing the Great Game. Truly it runs like a shuttle throughout Hind.[121]

The actual function of the Great Game, which is scotching the attempts of recalcitrant Indian rulers at rebellion and repulsing

* *Larousse Encyclopedia of Mythology* (1959, reference to 1965 edn, p. 384). Basham, *op. cit.*, in discussing Hindu cosmogony writes: 'The motive of creation was explained by the Vedanta school as the "sport" (lila) of the World Soul and the creation of the cosmos was thought of on the analogy of the production of a work of art from the mind of the artist' (p. 324), Zaehner, *op. cit.*, writes: 'As in the *Saiva Siddhanta* so in the *Gita* and *Ramanuja* God imprisons souls in matter only to release them and unite them with himself. This constitutes his adorable "game" (*krida*, *lila*). Moreover, just as the devotee longs for God and loves him, so does God long for the soul' (p. 99). In discussing the school which Rabindranath Tagore founded at Santiniketan, Zaehner states: 'He wished his pupils to be like God whose work is at the same time his play – his *karma* is his *lila* – effortless effort expended in joy' (p. 190).

Russian efforts at encroaching on the borders of the Raj, is casually
assumed within the context of the novel to be politically necessary
and morally good. It is an old and loyal Indian soldier who answers
the Lama's remark that there is no profit in killing with the retort,
'but if evil men were not now and then slain it would not be a good
world for weaponless dreamers'.[122] How has the theme evolved from
action in order to acquire merit, through action as a game imitating
God's joyous creation of the universe, to action aimed at ensuring
the permanence of the Raj? Because Kim concentrates on the deed
performed without regard for its fruits – the game for its own sake,
and in accordance with the duty required of his caste, for he is a
sahib – he *is* imitating the yoga of action. Thus, under cover of the
Gita, the Secret Service is introduced as a value-free commitment
exempt from moral scrutiny as a specific form of action. But the
ethics of the *Gita* are misrepresented because Kim's purpose in
action is not suppression of the ego on the path of union with the
Divine Ground but the completest development of his personality
through interacting with material realities. The resolution of his
crisis which has been precipitated by the need to comprehend his
own identity, affirms his passionate involvement with the phenomenal world:

'I am Kim, I am Kim. And what is Kim?' His soul repeated it again
and again. He did not want to cry, – and had never felt less like crying in
his life, – but of a sudden easy, stupid tears trickled down his nose, and
with an almost audible click he felt the wheels of his being locked up
anew on the world without. Things that rode meaningless on the eyeball
an instant before slid into proper proportion. Roads were meant to be
walked upon, houses to be lived in, cattle to be driven, fields to be tilled,
and men and women to be talked to. They were all real and true – solidly
planted upon the feet – perfectly comprehensible – clay of his clay,
neither more nor less.[123]

The game is vindicated through asserting the primacy of experience
which invokes the senses and involves personal commitment, and
when the Great Game as the apogee of experience is by inference
given value as a right form of behaviour, the concepts borrowed
from the Indian teachings have again been traduced, for *lila* is

recommended as a path to know God, to become God, that and only that is its end.*

The Great Game as the peak of action and as the summit of Kim's attainments adds a further dimension to the relationship between Kim and the Lama, for the innocent monk has been duped into an unwitting association with a cause alien to his pacific creed. He arranges for his wealthy monastery to finance Kim's education because he thinks Kim is acquiring wisdom at school when all he is receiving is the rudimentary learning considered necessary to a spy. As Kim's *guru* he provides the perfect cover for his Great Game assignations, and it is because of Kim's assignment that the Lama receives the humiliating and spiritually agonizing blow from the Russian agent. On one plane the Lama is approached by Kipling with sympathetic insight, on another he is treated as an object to be used in furthering the Great Game. In this Game Kim himself is no more than an actor playing a part, playing in fact many parts, and for this reason exempt from the charge of deceiving the Lama whom he loves.

Kipling's paradoxical involvement with India is reproduced through Kim; his pleasure in Indian scenes gives the book its colour and vivacity; his awe at the majesty of the Himalayas brings reverence for the Indian spiritual temperament. It is through the person of Kim that Kipling's conception of India's multiplicity takes shape – Kim not only dresses like an Indian, in fact like many different Indians, but feels like an Indian, with Indian prejudices and preferences in the marrow of his bones. At school he finds communal eating in public 'peculiarly revolting', preferring to turn his back on the world when at meals; to him it appears that most sahibs have 'dull, fat eyes'[124] and he regards himself as belonging to the people of this 'great and beautiful land'.[125] From the confines of his school he yearns for 'the caress of soft mud squishing up between his toes, as his mouth watered for mutton stewed with butter and cabbages, for rice speckled with strong-scented cardamoms, for the saffron-tinted rice, garlic and onions, for the forbidden greasy sweetmeats of

* Hannah Arendt, *Origins of Totalitarianism* (1951), finds a coinciding between life and the Great Game: 'Since life itself has to be lived and loved for its own sake, adventure and love of the game for its own sake appear to be a most intensely human symbol of life' (p. 217).

the bazaars'.[126] The smells of musk, sandalwood and jessamine-oil 'made him forget that he was to be a Sahib'.[127]* In one symbolic moment Kim becomes manifold India when 'forgetting his white blood; forgetting even the Great Game' he stoops 'Mohammedan fashion, to touch his master's feet in the dust of the Jain temple'.[128] It is as the personification of secular India that Kim has most substance as a character: 'India was awake, and Kim was in the middle of it . . . chewing on a twig that he would presently use as a tooth-brush; for he borrowed right- and left-handedly from all the customs of the country he knew and loved.'[129] When the white men take him in hand to make a sahib of him, he expresses his confusion in phrases a Mohammedan would use: *'Hai Mai!* I go from one place to another as it might be a kick-ball. It is my *Kismet.* No man can escape his *Kismet.* But I am to pray to Bibi Miriam and I am a Sahib. . . No, I am Kim.'[130] Later, he asks Mahbub Ali, 'What am I, Mussalman, Hindu, Jain or Buddhist?'[131] and the answer seems not to matter.

But if Kim is confused about his identity and ready to wear with equal enthusiasm all the masks offered him, Kipling is clear on his significance as the Janus-faced figure who can know India, and yet remain a white man. Throughout the novel, the sins of ignorance and prejudice are explicitly condemned, yet the same text which is so suffused with expressions of love for the people of the road, is defaced by references to 'babbling Asiatics'[132] and by derision for the sufferings which the educated Bengalis claim they endure. More significantly, Kim's notion that he has rank as a sahib is applauded, and soon it is only in the presence of his beloved Lama that he is willing and able to forget. Thus, ironically, the triumph of Kipling's quest to know natives is attained through Kim, the white orphan reared by the people of the bazaars, cared for by the people of the road, the boy who had thought of himself as an Indian until his race-peers taught him to be a sahib and showed him that his destiny was to assist in retaining the great and beautiful land of Hind in perpetuity as a possession of the British Empire.†

* Compare this abandonment to the senses with the austerity Kipling advocated as essential in those who would be leaders.

† The analysis of Edmund Wilson, *op. cit.*, which has in recent criticism

Kim is infinitely more than the sum of its themes, however these are interpreted,* and in its loveliness of language, compassion for living things and striving after the quality of the Infinite, surpasses all that Kipling ever wrote about India. So seductive is the world which he has conjured up that a conscious effort is needed to disengage from it. The justification of following the suggested threads along which the novel explores two divergent human goals is that these illuminate both Kipling's emotional involvement with India and his ideological commitment to the Raj. At the risk of over-

---

tended to be dismissed, contains pungent insights despite the unwarranted inferences: 'Now what the reader tends to expect is that Kim will come eventually to realise that he is delivering into bondage to the British invaders those whom he has always considered his own people, and that a struggle between allegiances will result. Kipling has established for the reader – and established with considerable dramatic effect – the contrast between East with its mysticism and its sensuality, its extremes of saintliness and roguery, and the English with their superior organisation, their confidence in modern method, their instinct to brush away like cobwebs the native myths and beliefs. We have been shown two entirely different worlds existing side by side, with neither really understanding the other, and we have watched the oscillation of Kim, as he passes to and fro between them. But the parallel lines never meet: the alternating attractions felt by Kim never give rise to a genuine stuggle. And the climax itself is double: the adventures of the Lama and of Kim simply arrive at different consummations, without any final victory or synthesis ever being allowed to take place' (p. 30).

* For an analysis of *Kim* see John Munro, 'Kipling's *Kim* and Co-existence', *English Literature in Transition*, Vol. VII, No. 4, 1964, pp. 222–7: 'It is . . . an apprenticeship novel in which the eponymous hero undergoes a series of trials which lead him to maturation; and not only does the novel deal with the education of Kim, it also has to do with the enlightenment of the Lama . . . the main deficiency in the Lama's attitude to life is that in spite of his saintliness, it is totally removed from actuality, and is ultimately self-centred' (pp. 223, 226). Mark Kincaid-Weekes, 'Vision in Kipling's Novels', in *Kipling's Mind and Art*, suggests that, '*Kim* is the answer to nine-tenths of the charges levelled against Kipling and the refutation of most of the generalizations about him. Yet it is not the result of a change in his personality or his thought. . . It is the product of a peculiar tension between different ways of seeing: the affectionate fascination with the kaleidoscope of external reality for its own sake; the negative capability of getting under the skin of attitudes different from one another and one's own; and finally, a product of the last, but at its most intense and creative, the triumphant achievement of an anti-self so powerful that it became a touchstone of everything else – the creation of the Lama' (p. 233).

simplification, one could suggest that the novel embraces the impulse to love India and the acceptance of whatever expedients are necessary to maintain the British Empire. Kipling's curious misquotation of Indian moral and metaphysical concepts in order to show as equally worthy the divergent routes taken by Kim and the Lama is brought to its final irony when Kim, through his own talents and exertions, becomes a competent and qualified spy, rendering a good account of himself in this world, while through the intercession of the Lama he is assured of paradise. ' "Son of my Soul, I have wrenched my Soul back from the Threshold of Freedom, to free thee from all sin – as I am free and sinless. Just is the Wheel. Certain is our deliverance. Come!" He crossed his hands on his lap and smiled, as a man may who has won Salvation for himself and his beloved.'[133] So ends the book and the Lama's love for Kim, his reverence for all living things and his innocence are mocked by the stealth and cynicism of the Great Game.

Conclusions

The case of Kipling is of great importance to the student of literature, for it raises in the plainest form the question: 'Can an immature person be a great writer?' The answer is 'Yes'. When he turns from his 'job' to his 'Daemon' as he calls it, he enters another world at once, the world of inspiration, and he moves with authority there.[134]

These remarks suggest a pathway through the labyrinth of Kipling's gifts and debilities: his inventiveness was no less fertile when he was intent on demonstrating the validity of some prejudice or belief. Still, it is when he is least committed to ideology that his writing is at its most inspired. This chapter has attempted an interpretation of what Kipling communicated in his Indian writings and has not been concerned with systematizing each mode of expression and every mood as a further elucidation of some postulated world-view,[135] but as some aspects of his vision have emerged these should be related to the larger structure of his general outlook.

Modern critics have discerned a timeless and universal insight into man's essential being in Kipling's work and have supported this claim with close and subtle analyses of the texts. Elliot L. Gilbert, for

example, has suggested that Kipling's vision embodied the existen-
tialist view of an absurd universe:

> In that universe, in which there are only two basic truths – man's desire
> for order and his absolute knowledge that he can never achieve it – the
> human being must learn to live with the absurdity of this enormous contra-
> diction without, on the one hand, accepting the easy answers he finds all
> about him, or, on the other, abandoning the search for meaning even when
> confronted with the certainty of failure in that search.[136]

The transmutations of a vision cannot be divorced from the myriad
apprehensions informing it nor from the form in which it is finally expressed, and a case can be made for finding many of Kipling's 'truths'
to be class-oriented and archaic. Too often, his translation of perceptions is circumscribed and diminished by its association with a finite
era, a temporary national self-image and an historically determined
creed to which he does not bring the focus of critical detachment.

One of the definitive expressions of Kipling's values is the poem
'If–'. Delivered as a general prescription for attaining maturity,
it is no more than a ritual to be followed by those who would lead,
rule and dominate others: belief in the divine rights of an *élite* must
be upheld; self-doubt and introspection annihilated; the emotions
must be curbed; the intellect regarded with suspicion; tolerance for
the multitudes, rooted in the conviction of superiority, must be
cultivated. On the route of this adventure the ego must be developed
and encased in an impenetrable shell; the goal is the triumph of the
will over the instincts. No more devastating commentary has been
made on the ethic which Kipling commends than Lindsay Anderson's surrealist film, *If. . .* Set in a public school, in the sort of
institution where traditionally the servants of empire and rulers of
men had been trained for their field-work in the colonies and at
home, it overthrows every precept which Kipling advocated in his
'If–'.* The film is a fantasy of liberation; the rebellious youths of

---

* In a review in *Sight and Sound*, Winter 1968–9, Gavin Millar connects the
bitter vision of Anderson's film with the legacy of Kipling: 'Anderson was born
in India, of Scottish extraction. The legend of service with honour is for him a
giant lie, since it is a life inevitably corrupted by the system of government it
upholds. However benevolent it is, Anderson will have no time for paternalism.
And Kipling would not recognise Mick, the hero of this new *If. . .*, as an English-

the school set free the desires Kipling would have young men restrain, they revel in the pleasures of the senses and the flesh which he would have them repress. Their ultimate resistance of 'Law, Orrder, Duty an' Restraint, Obedience, Discipline' (*McAndrew's Hymn*, 1893) is an armed assault on the school's authorities in defence of the priorities they believe to be alternatives.

The *Kipling Journal* is a voice which critics should hear attentively; published by the Kipling Society, which was founded during Kipling's lifetime, the journal has published both marginal information on Kipling's life and work as well as discerning critical articles. But the most interesting aspect to this publication is its reflection of extra-literary values, its reverence for Kipling as the sage of the Services and the ideologue of the middle-brow middle classes. It is a question of tone as much as of formulated statements, and this is nowhere more belligerent than when contributors are castigating scholars critical of Kipling, or comparing Kipling's work with the Indian writings of E. M. Forster and J. R. Ackerley, both of whom are firmly placed in the pinchbeck class. No artist can be blamed for the excesses of his admirers, but Kipling's appeal on the level indicated by some of his enthusiasts is surely significant. Perhaps his non-specialist following understand him better than do the experts, responding to him without the mediation of scholarship and theorizing. Indeed, the recollections of Sir Michael O'Dwyer, hero of Anglo-India for his support of Dyer's action at Amritsar,* are a necessary reminder of Kipling's political stance *vis-à-vis* the Indian national movement:

More than once in recent years I urged him to come forward and expose the dangers of the policy of surrender, arguing that his name and authority would compel people to think. His reply was to this effect: 'I have been forty years before my time in uttering the warning. For over thirty years I have been trying to hammer into the heads of certain British public men the elementary facts about India. I have had no success.' . . . He was sore

man at all. Anderson talks of him as "someone who arrives at his own beliefs, and who stands up for them, even against the world. . ." But then there must be many a colonial administrator, honourable men, long gone, who would have recognised themselves in that description' (p. 42).

* See Chapter 1 for information on O'Dwyer.

at heart in contemplating the surrender of so much that the British in India had stood for and that he had glorified in his writings. But a few years ago I persuaded him to join the Indian Defence League, and he was made one of the Vice-Presidents.[137]

Kipling's autobiography, though notoriously reticent and elliptical, tells a great deal about its author's personality, preferences and prejudices. This reminiscence, for example, of his family's sunny days in South Africa as the guests of Cecil Rhodes, suggests much more than just an absence of taste: 'The children's chaperon on their walks was a bulldog – Jumbo – of terrific aspect, to whom all Kaffirs gave right of way. There was a legend that he had once taken hold of a native and, when at last removed, came away with his mouth full of native.'[138]

Kipling's emotional coarseness fed on biases which were not personal eccentricities but the prejudices of his nation, class and age. His view of social and cultural developments in the United States during the early decades of the twentieth century was determined by racial presumptions. He decried the importation of the 'wreckage of Eastern Europe',[139] the 'hastily imported Continental supplanters'[140] of autochthonous Americans, lamenting the uplifting of 'the Semitic strain . . . in a too-much-at-ease Zion'.[141] In recounting an anecdote about a staff-member of *Punch* who was 'non-Aryan "and a German at that"', Kipling concludes 'Israel is a race to leave alone. It abets disorder.'[142] His autobiography was written during the 1930s when it was commonplace amongst certain circles of English society to flaunt their anti-semitism. Kipling is doing this and more, for he is voicing the tribesman's fear of cosmopolitanism, the disciplinarian's rage against anarchic explorations, the conformist's hostility to dissent. This is Kipling in mufti and in his persona as artist he revealed an Anglo-Saxon tribesman's view of imperialism, censoring it of its content as a confrontation between peoples. Embedded in his Indian fiction are ideas and feelings which are neither casual interpositions nor contingent representations of a moral vision merely symbolized by Empire, but which are an essential part of imperialism conceived as the triumphant expression of the white world's destiny. But his Indian writings are denser than his imperial beliefs and their diversity of theme and multiplicity of viewpoint make them the most vivid fictional transmutation of the sub-continent's many faces, of its moods and sensibility. This is the fruit not of Kipling the theorist but of an inspired artist who at a deep unconscious level accepted India as his native soil and who, when he looked at India through ethnocentric lenses, did so in full knowledge that the images he received were those of a white man of the West.

CHAPTER 7

E. M. Forster: A Passage to India

Introduction

WHEN *A Passage to India* was published in 1924 it was received by many readers as a work of social realism and praised or execrated for its critique of the British in India.* While some notices, such as the one in *The Times Literary Supplement*, saw it as a definite picture rather than a creative imagining,† there were reviewers who recognized it as the work of a major novelist. L. P. Hartley found it a disturbing, uncomfortable book and greeted it as the most considerable novel of the year: '*A Passage to India* is much more than a study of racial contrasts and disabilities. It is intensely personal and (if the phrase may be pardoned) intensely cosmic.'[1] In a review, 'Arch Beyond Arch', Leonard Woolf wrote: 'it marches firmly, triumphantly, even grimly and sadly – the adverbs can only be explained by reading the book – through the real life and politics of India, the intricacy of personal relations, the story itself, the muddle and mystery of life.'[2] Since then, and especially during the last decade,

---

* Reassessing the novel in 1966, Paul Scott recalled its initial reception when those who saw themselves caricatured as Anglo-Indians 'threw copies overboard from the P. & O. into the Red Sea'. Scott considers that *A Passage to India* was 'the right book about the right subject at the right time. It gave vivid dramatic evidence to justify the direction of a swing that had already begun. It helped the swing to gather momentum. A novel that has a marked effect on society takes a long time to rid itself of its reputation as a public utility and retire into its private, sometimes intenser, life as a work of art.' In series, 'How Well Have They Worn?', *The Times*, 6 January 1966, p. 15. Reviewing it in the *London Mercury*, July 1924, Vol. X, No. 57, J. B. Priestley wrote: 'Anglo-India is caught here, I imagine, as it has never been caught before, and its sharp divisions, its crushing institutionalism and officialism, its racial and herd thought and emotion, provide an excellent background for Mr Forster's somewhat elusive philosophy of personal relations' (p. 319).

† 12 June 1924, p. 370. The reviewer praised the novel for its subtle portraiture, its acute studies of the Moslem and Hindu mind, its irony and poetry.

the large body of critical literature on Forster's writings has been predominantly concerned with understanding his poetic vision by analysing thematic structure, deciphering symbolic patterns and probing psychological depths. Such appraisals have opened a vista crowded with complementary and competing insights into the novel's multiple levels of meaning, discrediting attempts at pedestrian socio-political interpretations.[3]

A Passage to India can be read as a novel of ideas which is deeply involved in the contemporary realities of the human situation, in racial conflict and political aggression, cultural faiths and rituals, social institutions, mores and relationships. But it is also a metaphysical drama whose action passes across man's dilemmas as a social and sentient being to the subdued energies of his hidden and silenced psyche, to 'the part of the mind that seldom speaks'.[4] When *A Passage to India* moves from the milieux of men interacting with their phenomenal environments to detached states of extraordinary intensity, it measures the distance between what men are conditioned and permitted by their social orders to experience and their existential capacities. The presentation of human existence as it is, defined and confined by society, enriched by satisfactions, impoverished by denials, coexists with a contradictory vision which overturns normality and brings into close view dimensions from the far horizons of experience. 'Inside its cocoon of work or social obligation, the human spirit slumbers for the most part, registering the distinction between pleasure and pain, but not nearly as alert as we pretend.'[5] The climactic areas of *A Passage to India* are those where man's social destiny is challenged by his unconscious mind and the somnolent spirit awakens to mystical illumination or is startled into a state of pathological fear. Through the enactment of irrational experiences in their opposite forms of ecstatic visions and demonic visitations, Forster speculates on the source and quality of insights which are unconnected to the sanctioned modes of cognition: do such perceptions come from buried strata of the mind; do they discern an order of reality which neither reason nor the senses can apprehend; do they liberate facets of man's nature repressed by civilization? 'Were there worlds beyond which they could never touch, or did all that is possible enter their consciousness?'[6]

E. M. FORSTER: 'A PASSAGE TO INDIA'

Although the doubts of Adela Quested and Fielding, who are
rationalists and sceptics, are never positively allayed by the triumphant revelation of a more extensive reality outside the phenomenal
universe, Forster does suggest that there exists in man a need for
'the unattainable friend . . . the eternal promise, the never-withdrawn
suggestion that haunts our consciousness',[7] an emotional and
spiritual appetite which religious mysticism may perhaps appease,
opening the way to significant areas of experience. In *The Hill of
Devi*, an account of his stay in Dewas Senior and his friendship with
the Maharajah of the state, Forster has written: 'His religion was the
deepest thing in him. It ought to be studied – neither by the
psychologist nor by the mythologist but by the individual who has
experienced similar promptings. He penetrated into rare regions and
he was always hoping that others would follow him there.'[8] When
Forster characterized the ideas about religion and metaphysics held
by his friend and mentor, Goldsworthy Lowes Dickinson, he was
also expressing something of his own position: 'He was not only
concerned with "this interesting world" but with whatever may be
outside its walls and he suspected that there is a key to our prison,
though we shall never hold it in hands of flesh and blood. Though
the intellect is our best friend, there are regions whither it cannot
guide us.'[9]*

* Forster's reflections as they are expressed here and in the novel are in the
spirit of William James's *The Varieties of Religious Experience: A Study in
Human Nature* (1902). Discussing his own experience of mystical consciousness
stimulated through nitrous oxide intoxication, James writes: 'One conclusion
was forced upon my mind at that time, and my impression of its truth has ever
since remained unshaken. It is that our normal waking consciousness, rational
consciousness as we call it, is but one special type of consciousness, whilst all
about it, parted from it by the filmiest of screens, there lie potential forms of
consciousness entirely different. We may go through life without suspecting
their existence; but apply the requisite stimulus, and at a touch they are there
in all their completeness, definite types of mentality which probably somewhere
have their field of application and adaptation. No account of the universe in its
totality can be final which leaves these other forms of consciousness quite disregarded. How to regard them is the question – for they are so discontinuous
with ordinary consciousness. Yet they may determine attitudes though they
cannot furnish formulas, and open a region though they fail to give a map. At
any rate, they forbid a premature closing of our accounts with reality . . . the

262

Forster has said that in *A Passage to India* he had tried 'to indicate the human predicament in a universe which is not, so far, comprehensible to our minds'.[10] As man pushes forward the boundaries of his knowledge, so does he discover the regions which are still unknown, and perhaps unknowable, to the intellect, and the possibility that the universe is ultimately inexplicable is one which he should absorb into his active awareness of reality. Forster approaches the beliefs and goals of communities as the context within which man can develop a version of his nature and as the cause of his alienation both from his fellows and from his own elemental being. The race has been splintered into categories, divided into classes so that man is confused at his membership of the species, his place amongst 'the incompatible multitudes of mankind'.[11] Modern civilization has dismembered his wholeness by cutting him off from his beginnings as yet another creature in the chain of creation, divorcing him from the animal kingdom, the monkeys, jackals and wasps, and separating him from his roots in the basic environment, the oranges, cactuses, crystals and mud. How then are men 'to initiate their own unity';[12] which social order re-connects man to his essential sources and permits the fullest unfolding of his potentialities; which form of society stills his confusions about his social and spiritual identity? Within civilizations there are tendencies which have directed men away from such elusive intricacies to that which can be seen, understood and controlled. Diametrically opposite life-styles, on the other hand, invoke men 'to ravish the unknown',[13] to realize through a harnessing of mind and feeling a state of hyperconsciousness surpassing intellectual cognition and sensory perceptions. Both traditions and goals are efforts at demystification, the one by systematically acquiring information about the universe, the other by recommending that the individual through a process of psychological self-experimentation integrate himself with the Absolute, thereby gaining transcendent knowledge.

---

existence of mystical states absolutely overthrows the pretension of non-mystical states to be the sole and ultimate dictators of what we may believe... It must always remain an open question whether mystical states may not possibly be ... superior points of view, windows through which the mind looks out upon a more extensive and inclusive world' (1968 edn) (pp. 374, 411, 412).

E. M. FORSTER: 'A PASSAGE TO INDIA'

Forster's view of the sickness of modern civilization which represses the instincts and puts taboos on experiences which transcend so-called norms, predisposed him to a sympathetic exploration of India's diverse patterns of civilization. He found that the Indian temperament gave love a place of honour denied it in the West, and while in *A Passage to India* it is the Moslems who follow the promptings of the heart in their daily relations, whereas the Hindus ritually celebrate the triumph of Infinite Love, he knew from his acquaintance with Indians that such a sensibility belonged to all India: 'Affection, all through his checkered life, was the only force to which Bapu Sahib [the Maharajah of Dewas] responded. It did not always work, but without it nothing worked. Affection and its attendants of human warmth and instinctive courtesy – when they were present his heart awoke and dictated his actions.'[14] Even at the time of his stay in Dewas, Forster was able to write, 'I love H.H. [His Highness] and he me, and I am glad to have had this extraordinary experience.'[15]

Forster saw Indian society, both Hindu and Moslem, not only as structured to connect the liberated passions with the sphere of intellect, but to accommodate in secular life man's hunger for the sacred: a Hindu *raga* implores Krishna to come, 'Multiply yourself into a hundred Krishnas, and let one go to each of my hundred companions, but one, O Lord of the Universe, come to me';[16] a poem by the Moslem Ghalib, though less explicit than the call to Krishna, voices 'our loneliness nevertheless, our isolation, our need for the Friend [a Persian expression for God] who never comes yet is not entirely disproved'.[17]

The Indian traditions teach that through yoga, a spiritual and mental discipline,* the conscious mind can be connected to the unconscious so that all the perceptions which the mind can receive and all the sensations which the body can know are joined and expressed; but the ultimate and true goal of man is to escape from the restraints

* See Heinrich Zimmer, *Myths and Symbols* (1962), footnote to p. 39: '*Yoga*, from the root *yuj*, "to yoke, join together, harness; to come into union or conjunction with; to concentrate or fix the mind; to bestow anything upon any one; to grant, confer". Yoga is a strict spiritual discipline, practised in order to gain control over the forces of one's own being, to gain occult powers, to dominate certain specific forces of nature, or finally (and chiefly) to attain union with the Deity or with the Universal Spirit.'

of egocentric consciousness in the attainment of a cosmic awareness.* Without accepting the revolutionary concepts of man's
nature postulated in Indian philosophies, or the radical forms of
psychological self-exploration recommended, Forster implies how
attenuated the approach of modern civilization is to the enigmas of
man's potential for experience.† *A Passage to India* treats the
British–Indian relationship in the historical context of the Raj during
the early decades of the century. But it is also shown as an encounter
between disparate temperaments and aspirations. The will to conceptual rigour and emotional restraint faces the surrender to 'sacred
bewilderment'[18] and the search for ecstasy. The impulse to define
and enclose the area which men inhabit against encroachment, conflicts with the desire to be absorbed with the totality of the cosmos.
For one, awareness of the mystery of the universe brings terror, for
the other, rapture.

It is as if India re-drew the contours of reality for Forster and in
A Passage to India appearances are proved to be unreliable and
empirical observation superficial; 'nothing in India is identifiable,
the mere asking of a question causes it to disappear or to merge in
something else'.[19]‡ Enfolded in the novel is a shapeless, arbitrary,

---

* Zimmer, in *Philosophies of India* (1967), interprets the chief aim of Indian
thought as the unveiling and integrating into consciousness of what lies beyond
nama-rupa which denotes 'on the one hand, man, the experiencing, thinking
individual, man as endowed with mind and senses, and on the other, all the
means and objects of thought and perception. Nama-rupa is the whole world,
subjective and objective, as observed and known. . . Indian philosophy insists
that the sphere of logical thought is far exceeded by the mind's possible experiences of reality' (pp. 24, 27).

† Reviewing Wilfred Stone's book, *op. cit.*, Stuart Hampshire suggests that
Forster's oft-quoted 'only connect' has a philosophical rather than a social
sense: 'The connection that needs to be made is between the upper and literate
reaches of the mind and the lower and unwashed, or proletarian, levels of consciousness, which can no longer be downtrodden and despised; for they are
ready to strike back, to withdraw their energies, if they are not accepted and set
free. . . The story of the national and social misunderstanding, fascinating in
itself, is a fitting sign of the meeting of the two philosophical attitudes.' *New
York Review of Books*, Vol. VI, No. 8, 12 May 1966, pp. 14–16.

‡ Indian epistemology draws a distinction between empirical and higher
knowledge. Bharati's definition of *maya*, the key word of Brahman and Vedantic

intricate and discordant India, a microcosm of 'the echoing contradictory world',[20] which opens out to reveal an intrinsic concord and
unity. For if 'nothing embraces the whole of India, nothing, nothing',[21] if 'no one is India'[22] and 'it's nobody's India',[23] nevertheless
it is possible that 'the hundred Indias which fuss and squabble so
tiresomely are one, and the universe they mirror is one'.[24] India
spans stages of man's development from the primitive to the over-
sophisticated; India is riven into sects and clans; but though there is
friction between the different branches of Indians, all are of one tree
and it is as a composite whole that India finally emerges in the novel,
as a complex of different but coexistent societies, temperaments and
outlooks. Not hostile polarization but the harmonious containment
of disparities, not antithesis but complexity, is suggested by these
many Indias.

India has few important towns. India is the country, fields, fields, then
hills, jungle, hills, and more fields. The branch line stops, the road is only
practicable for cars to a point, the bullock-carts lumber down the side-
tracks, paths fray out into the cultivation, and disappear near a splash of
red paint. How can the mind take hold of such a country? Generations of
invaders have tried but they remain in exile. The important towns they
build are only retreats, their quarrels the malaise of men who cannot find
their way home. India knows of their troubles. She knows of the whole
world's trouble, to its uttermost depth. She calls 'Come' through her
hundred mouths, through objects ridiculous and august. But come to
what? She has never defined. She is not a promise, only an appeal.[25]

India is the uncharted region of reality, inviting men to find their

---

thought, is that it is 'inaccurately rendered "illusion"; correctly it means the
totality of phenomenal experience and of relative existence, it denotes the
qualified universe as opposed to the absolute, the *brahman*. The classical analogy
showing the relationship of *brahman* and *maya*: a man sees a rope and thinks it
is a snake, and he is affected as though it were a snake, unless he realizes its
real character: the snake is *maya*, the "rope" is *brahman*.' *The Tantric Tradition*
(1965), p. 38n. Jainism, a non-Vedantic tradition, teaches the doctrine of many-
sidedness: 'Implicit in the epistemological relativity of *anekantavada* is a recognition that the world is more complex than it seems, that reality is more subtle
than we are inclined to believe.' A. L. Basham, 'Jainism and Buddhism' in
Wm. Theodore de Bary (ed.), *Sources of Indian Tradition* (1958), p. 75. Only
perfected beings can see whole truth; ordinary men can only discern partial
truths.

INTRODUCTION

way back to her beyond the world of objects and appearances, and
back to the innermost depths of their psyches beyond the intellect,
the emotions and the senses. Yet to suggest that India is the place of
the unconscious, a metaphor for apprehensions which cannot be
known through reasoning, is to overlook her paradox. If India is 'the
hopeless melancholy of the plain',[26] the abased and monotonous
town of Chandrapore whose outlines swell and shrink 'like some low
but indestructible form of life',[27] it is also the huge and noble
bastions of Asirgarh, it is Delhi and Agra, the Rajputana cities and
Kashmir and 'the obscurer marvels that had sometimes shone
through men's speech: the bilingual rock of Girnar, the statue of
Belgola, the ruins of Mandu and Hampi, temples of Khajraha,
gardens of Shalimar'.[28]

India is personified in both Das, the assistant magistrate of
Chandrapore, who is 'cultivated, self-conscious and conscientious',
and the punkah-wallah sitting opposite him in the court-room who
is 'none of these things; he scarcely knew that he existed'.[29] Indeed,
the punkah-wallah is the symbolic Indian figure in whom the conscious and the supraconscious participate:

Almost naked, and splendidly formed, he sat on a raised platform near
the back. . . He had the strength and beauty that sometimes comes to
flower in Indians of low birth. When that strange race nears the dust and
is condemned as untouchable, then nature remembers the physical perfection that she accomplished elsewhere, and throws out a god – not many,
but one here and there, to prove to society how little its categories impress
her. This man would have been notable anywhere; among the thin-
hammed, flat-chested mediocrities of Chandrapore he stood out as divine,
yet he was of the city, its garbage had nourished him, he would end on its
rubbish heaps. Pulling the rope towards him, relaxing it rhythmically,
sending swirls of air over others, receiving none himself, he seemed apart
from human destinies, a male fate, a winnower of souls.[30]

In 'Mosque', 'Caves' and 'Temple', a division which follows the
course of the Indian year, cool weather, heat and monsoons, and the
inexorable cycle of birth, destruction and fertilization, the novel visits
three temples fashioned by the Indian mind and expressing major
currents in man's spiritual and psychological history. Like a palimpsest, India records man's archaic responses to the mystery of his

267

being, over which are written subsequent and contradictory discoveries. The continuum as it is explored in *A Passage to India* forgoes the time sequence for a route which leads away from what the contemporary sensibility can recognize and accept to the extremes of ascetic world-rejection and rapturous world-acceptance which lie outside the standard Western modes of apprehension.

The journey into India begins with 'Mosque', a variation of the modern outlook, a compromise between commitment to the material world and devotion to spiritual fulfilment, accommodating both science and sensuality, flesh and soul, personal relationships and reverence for the unseen.

Then in 'Caves' there is a passing back to the forgotten life of the race buried in the unconscious of modern man but preserved in India's ascetic traditions which pessimistically reject the whole world of man and matter in the search for detachment, the pristine condition before the life-monad became entangled in matter.

Finally, in 'Temple', there is a transition forward to the possibilities of superconsciousness which the modern world has not yet explored, to an affirmation of the total universe, all spirit and all matter, as emanating from and participating in the One Divine. Together, 'Mosque', 'Caves' and 'Temple' tell of the important insights of the Indian mind exploring man's nature,* and if *A Passage to India* con-

---

* Zimmer, *Philosophies of India*, points to the coexistence in India of attitudes of negation with the vigorous affirmation of the world of flux and time. 'The Brahman mind . . . did not capitulate unconditionally to the principle of world-rejection. The psycho-physical problems posed by the Vedic monist philosophy that matured during the period of the Upanishads are as open to world-assertive as to negating replies. The more amply documented Indian philosophical tendency, and the one first encountered by the Western scholars, was that represented in the schools of the Vedanta and Hinayana, but in recent years the power and profundity of the Tantric system have begun to be appreciated, and therewith has been facilitated a new understanding of Indian life and art. Indeed, one could only have been amazed had it been found that in the most durable civilization known to history the sole intellectual response to such a dictum as "All is Brahman" had been that of a monistic renunciation of the manifest for the unmanifest aspect of the metaphysical equation. Had we not learned what we now know of the philosophy of the Tantric Agamas, we should have had to posit some such tradition; for as the Indian centuries open their secrets to us we become more and more aware of the power of something very

templates how personality and proclivities are varied by culture and historical situation, it also unifies the passages made by the human psyche as constituting one experience.

Before writing *A Passage to India* Forster had twice visited India. In 1912–13 he toured the country for some six months in the company of Goldsworthy Lowes Dickinson and R. C. Trevelyan,[31] and in 1921 he spent a similar period as private secretary to the Maharajah of Dewas Senior, an interlude of which he later wrote, 'It was the great opportunity of my life.'[32]* In his essays and reviews Forster acknowledges how friendship with Indians extended his outlook; in his tribute to Syed Ross Masood he wrote, 'My own debt to him is incalculable. He woke me up out of my suburban and academic life, showed me new horizons and a new civilization and helped me towards the understanding of a continent.'† While in India and participating in the social existence of his Indian friends and acquaintances Forster was often bewildered – 'Life here will be queer beyond description'; 'Everything that happens is said to be one thing and proves to be another', were comments he made during his months in Dewas.[33]

Forster's emotional relationships with Hinduism and Islam suggest a shifting viewpoint, the exercise of a sense of discrimination making for ambivalent attitudes and a critical appreciation of the value in both.‡ While living in Dewas Senior he was relieved to get

---

different from the sublimated melancholy of the monks, in the life-loving Hindu contemplation of the delicacies of the world of name and form' (p. 597).

* Dewas Senior was a princely state in Central India which lost its identity after independence.

† 'Syed Ross Masood' (1937), contributed to the Memorial Number of an Urdu journal and reprinted in *Two Cheers for Democracy* (1951), p. 229. Masood, who came from an eminent Moslem family and who was at one time Vice-Chancellor of the University of Aligarh, was Forster's friend from 1907 until his death in 1937.

‡ In *The Hill of Devi* Forster includes what he describes as 'a stern little entry' from his 1912–13 journal: 'Land of petty treacheries, of reptiles moving about too cautious to strike each other. No line between the insolent and the servile in social intercourse. In every remark and gesture, does not the Indian prince either decrease his own "izzat" or that of his interlocutor? Is there ever civility with manliness here? And is foreign conquest or national character to blame?' (p. 27). In a letter to Dickinson in 1921 he wrote that he had been

away from Hinduism and be amongst Moslems: 'I do like Islam, though I have had to come through Hinduism to discover it. After all the mess and profusion and confusion of Gokul Ashtami, where nothing ever stopped or need ever have begun, it was like standing on a mountain.'[34] Though he was to pass beyond this facile assessment of the festival, Forster's sympathy with the Emperor Babur's complaints of Hinduism comes through in an essay written in 1921: 'Witty and unphilosophic, definite and luxuriant as a Persian miniature, he had small patience with a race which has never found either moral or aesthetic excellence by focusing upon details.'[35] A similar preference is expressed in another essay: 'The serving of Pan is in itself a little art – and the arts of littleness are tragically lacking in India; there is scarcely anything in that tormented land which fills up the gulf between the illimitable and the inane, and society suffers in consequence.'[36] Yet an essay on Mohammed Iqbal, written in 1946, suggests that he finds the poet's orderly doctrines uncongenial:

Iqbal dislikes the pantheism which he saw all around him in India – for instance in Tagore – and he castigates those Moslem teachers who have infected Islam with it. It is weakening and wrong to seek unity with the divine. Vision – perhaps. Union – no. Such – if an outsider may sum-

---

'coming round a little to your view that the Indian or anyhow the Hindu character – that it is unaesthetic' (*ibid.*, p. 27). During the same year he wrote to a friend, 'Except in the direction of religion, where I allow them much, these people don't seem to move towards anything important; there is no intellectual interest, though His Highness at least has an excellent intellect. The music – some singers are good but most that I have heard are not, and all become bawdy at the least encouragement. It is a great misfortune for art to be associated with prostitution, not for moral reasons but because every flight of beauty or fancy is apt to be cut short' (pp. 121–2). Another letter written at the time tells of the New Palace which had been under construction for ten years, the original parts already falling into decay: 'You would weep at the destruction, expense and hideousness, and I do almost... I don't know what to do about it all, and scarcely what to feel. It's no good trying to make something different out of it, for it is as profoundly Indian as an Indian temple' (pp. 59, 60). In *Indian Entries* is the following note about his Moslem friend, Syed: 'Conversation with S. about debt depressed me. They yearn for political freedom and don't care about economic. Won't leave one fine impulse ungratified – must be well dressed, housed and served and lavish hospitality' (p. 27).

marise – is his philosophy. It is not a philosophy I like. . . Mohammed Iqbal is a genius and a commanding one, and though I often disagree with him and usually agree with Tagore, it is Iqbal I would rather read.[37]

Forster delicately but firmly treading his way through India, Moslem and Hindu, is a discerning guide into its complexities, its strengths and weaknesses: 'If one can judge from a translation, and if one can condone silliness and prolixity, the tenth book of the *Bhagavad Purana* must be a remarkable work. It has warmth and emotion and a sort of divine recklessness and a sort of crude human happiness.'[38] But perhaps the most memorable records of Forster's feelings for India are those where he remembers the pleasures he found in friendship with Indians and his readiness to join in their revelry:

The April Fools' Day arrived to reinforce the merriment of Holi. He [the Maharajah] sent me a message to my office asking me to go at once to a remote shed in the garden since something peculiar had been observed there. I excused myself. Nor, when bidden to refreshment, did I accept a cigarette of unusual shape. Nor was I asked to get an electric shock by sitting on a sofa. But I did drink some whisky-and-salt, to the court's uncategorical delight. Foolery, fun, practical jokes, bawdry – I was to be involved in them all as soon as I felt myself safe. He even made a pun on my name which eludes quotation: too indecent, too silly. But gay, gay.[39]

In *The Hill of Devi* Forster refers to the long gestation of *A Passage to India*:

I began this novel before my 1921 visit, and took out the opening chapters with me, with the intention of continuing them. But as soon as they were confronted with the country they purported to describe, they seemed to wilt and go dead and I could do nothing with them. I used to look at them of an evening in my room at Dewas, and felt only distaste and despair. The gap between India remembered and India experienced was too wide. When I got back to England the gap narrowed, and I was able to resume.[40]

Forster brought to India an understanding of the paradoxes in man's situation matured through contemplating other societies; from India he learned of aspects to the existential condition atrophied or stultified by modern civilization and in Indian thought and the symbolism of her myths, art and architecture, he discovered other dimensions to man's perpetual search for self-understanding.*

A special quality of Forster's philosophy is his double vision as a liberal humanist and, in the words of H. A. Smith, as a reverent agnostic. In his essay, 'Forster's Humanism and the Nineteenth Century',[41] Smith relates Forster's two voices – 'instinct and intelligence, Culture and Nature, reason and religious insight'[42] – to the forms which humanism has taken in the modern world:

There is a rational, sceptical humanism, which stems from the Enlightenment, and an imaginative (and often religious) humanism which draws its sustenance primarily from the Romantic Movement. Clearly something of both of these are to be found in Forster, but there can be no doubt as to where his sympathies essentially lie . . . his humanism is both romantic and, in a perfectly acceptable sense of the word, religious.[43]

In all Forster's novels there is a recognition of the two planes, the phenomenal and the metaphysical, on which the universe can be known, and a regret that the culturally conditioned severance of mind from the senses has fragmented man's power to experience. In

* George H. Thomson in 'A Forster Miscellany: Thoughts on the Uncollected Writings', in *Aspects of E. M. Forster* (1969), edited by Oliver Stallybrass, refers to two articles on the Indian temple which show Forster's intuitive grasp of its meaning: 'When we tire of being pleased and of being improved, and of the other gymnastics of the West, and care, or think we care, for Truth alone; then the Indian temple exerts its power, and beckons down absurd or detestable vistas to an exit unknown to the Parthenon' (p. 160), quoted from an article written in 1919. It was not until 1940 that Forster learned of the temple's symbolism from reading Herbert Read and Stella Kramrisch and from seeing a photographic exhibition at the Warburg Institute. Wilfred Stone, *op. cit.*, writes: 'He was taught to see the temple as the "World Mountain," a mountain "on whose exterior is displayed life in all its forms, life human and superhuman and subhuman and animal, life tragic and cheerful, cruel and kind, seemly and obscene, all crowned at the Mountain's summit by the sun." In the interior of the mountain, he continues, there is "a tiny cavity, a central cell, where in the heart of the world complexity, the individual could be alone with his god" ' (pp. 301–2); quotation from Forster's article, 'The World Mountain' in the *Listener*, XXXII, 1954, p. 978. Stone suggests that when Forster discovered the meaning of the Hindu temple, long after *A Passage to India* had been written, 'he did so with a delighted shock of recognition – as if the full meaning of his book were only now opening to his expanding vision' (p. 301).

Howard's End (1910), especially, there is the urge to connect the prose with the poetry so that man may be made whole.

As in the previous novels, Forster in *A Passage to India* commends the liberal value system for encouraging free intellectual inquiry and accommodating civilized personal relations. The negation of these values is institutionalized in Anglo-India. The British in India have suppressed their intellectual curiosity; their purpose is not to share the ideas and techniques of the West with Indians but to administer a subject people; official relationships take the place of human ones, social intimacy is taboo. In Fielding, the schoolmaster who stands apart from Anglo-India and represents culture, tolerance and kindness, Forster suggests the virtues of a rationalist and sceptical humanism. But it is a recommendation even more deeply qualified than before by an acknowledgement of its limitations. For Fielding is not only emotionally restrained, but spiritually atrophied. His creed is meaningful only in the seen world, in the prosaic existence.

The vision in *A Passage to India* is of arches beyond those arches through which the human imagination has passed, of distances further than those distances measured or estimated by science, of social orders other than those known in recorded history. In this sense the novel is a departure from Forster's earlier concerns. The dichotomy between intellect and instinct and the possibility of joining them is still posed but these insights are overshadowed by perceptions previously latent in Forster's writings. What he now contemplates is the nature of the sublime, the capacity for terror and joy imprisoned in the unconscious which the liberated human spirit alone can know. In speculating on the infinite dimensions of experience, Forster has not abandoned rationalism but he has subordinated it to a vision which also supersedes his romantic humanism.

If the emphasis in this chapter is on Forster's interpretation of Indian world-views as significant insights into man's nature and conjectures on his psyche, rather than on Anglo-Indian attitudes and images of India, this is because *A Passage to India* goes beyond a portrayal of how the British experienced India. Forster's Anglo-Indians are not only an arrogant and uncomfortable imperial presence; they are men and women burdened by massive social pressures and crippled by tight emotional restraints; they are the paradigm of modern one-dimensional man. Forster's India comprehends everything that is excluded and rejected by the British and comes to represent the intrepid adventures of the human mind and its discoveries.

A Passage to India is the triumphant expression of the British imagination exploring India. Forster's experience of India is translated into a vision which illuminates both her unique qualities and the more extensive meanings which her identity symbolizes. India's particular life-styles are woven into the context of a strange and equivocal atmosphere:

Going to hang up her cloak, she found that the tip of the peg was occupied by a small wasp... Perhaps he mistook the peg for a branch – no Indian animal has any sense of an interior. Bats, rats, birds, insects will as soon nest inside a house as out; it is to them a normal growth of the eternal jungle, which alternately produces houses trees, houses trees. There he clung asleep, while jackals in the plain bayed their desires and mingled with the percussion of drums. 'Pretty dear,' said Mrs Moore to the wasp. He did not wake, but her voice floated out, to swell the night's uneasiness.[44]

The tempo of existence intimates a concept of time unknown to the West: 'He called to Hassan to clear up, but Hassan, who was testing his wages by ringing them on the step of the veranda, found it possible not to hear him; heard and didn't hear, just as Aziz had called and hadn't called. "That's India all over ... how like us ... there we are..." He dozed again, and his thoughts wandered over the varied surface of life.'[45]

In the voyage from India the atmosphere alters with Egypt where 'clean sands heaped on each side of the canal, seemed to wipe off everything that was difficult or equivocal',[46] and seen from the Mediterranean and assessed by the human norm which it represents, India appears 'the strangest experience of all'.[47] The core of the novel is the cataclysmic discovery by two Englishwomen of a reality far beyond what life had hitherto taught them. For them, the passage to India is a journey into themselves and back to the spiritual memory of the race. Like the wilderness, the jungle and the desert, India who has mothered ambitious and daring philosophies of transcendence is the place and source of metaphysical revelations, inducing diabolical terror in some and bringing the peace that passeth understanding for others.

Mosque : The Secular and the Sacred

Lo Soul! seest thou not God's purpose from the first?
The earth to be spann'd, connected by net-work,
The people to become brothers and sisters,
The races, neighbors, to marry and be given in marriage.

Walt Whitman, Passage to India (1871)

I

From one aspect, Islam, a monotheistic system hospitable to mysticism, appears as the meeting-point between the West and the Orient. From another, the Moslems, despite pride in their distinctive Arabian origins and Moghul ancestry, are unmistakably Indian and it is as a branch of India and an expression of a singular temperament that Forster recreates their world. Theologically, Islam is as limited as Christianity: ' "There is no God but God" doesn't carry us far through the complexities of matter and spirit; it is only a game with words, really, a religious pun, not a religious truth.'[48] Still it nurtures in its adherents a responsiveness to the unseen. When Aziz, who is ill in bed, recites a poem to his Moslem friends it is an invitation to the sacred to enter and merge with their prosaic lives:

It had no connection with anything that had gone before, but it came from his heart and spoke to theirs... The squalid bedroom grew quiet; the silly intrigues, the gossip, the shallow discontent were stilled, while words accepted as immortal filled the indifferent air... The poem had done no 'good' to anyone, but it was a passing reminder, a breath from the divine lips of beauty, a nightingale between two worlds of dust. Less explicit than the call to Krishna, it voiced our loneliness nevertheless, our isolation, our need for the Friend who never comes yet is not entirely disproved.[49]

Forster is concerned with Islam as a culture rather than a religious creed, with its qualities and insufficiencies as a life-style and a home for the human spirit. Aziz's immersion in Islam involves more than his intellect:

A mosque by winning his approval let loose his imagination. The temple of another creed, Hindu, Christian, or Greek, would have bored him and failed to awaken his sense of beauty. Here was Islam, his own country, more than a Faith, more than a battle-cry, more, much more... Islam, an attitude towards life both exquisite and durable, where his body and his thoughts found their home.[50]

In Aziz's inner imaginative world his religion is in accord with his aesthetic sense and his emotional temper:

He dropped off to sleep amid the happier memories of the last two hours – poetry of Ghalib, female grace, good old Hamidullah, good Fielding, his honoured wife and dear boys. He passed into a region where these joys had no enemies but bloomed harmoniously in an eternal garden, or ran down watershoots of ribbed marble, or rose into domes whereunder were inscribed, black against white, the ninety-nine attributes of God.[51]

The passionate and volatile Aziz embodies both the quintessence of the Moslem disposition and the absorption of Islam into India. Voluble in his contempt for the flabby Hindus and proud of his Moghul ancestors who fought the British for control of India, it is he who protests at Adela Quested's approval of Akbar's new religion which was to serve all India: 'Nothing embraces the whole of India, nothing, nothing.'[52] Yet it seems that India does reach out to embrace everything. After Adela Quested's accusation of attempted rape and his trial, Aziz turns himself 'towards the vague and bulky figure of a mother-land. He was without natural affection for the land of his birth, but the Marabar Hills drove him to it. Half closing his eyes, he attempted to love India.'[53] Though this is alien to his nature he adopts a political posture: 'Of what help, in this latitude and hour, are the glories of Cordova and Samarcand? They have gone, and while we lament them the English occupy Delhi and exclude us from East Africa. Islam itself, though true, throws cross-lights over the path to freedom.'[54] Aziz manifests this will to identify with India in an illogical, unstable and contradictory way which is wholly consistent with his personality. He does not succeed in loving the motherland, 'the pathos of defeated Islam remained in his blood',[55] and he naturally continues to write poems lamenting the decay of the Moslem cause, while longing to compose a song of the future which would transcend creed and be acclaimed by the multitudes.

But he does escape from the English when he takes employment with a Hindu rajah in the princely state of Mau. As before, he finds Hindus quaint and incomprehensible: 'he felt bored, slightly cynical, like his own dear Emperor Babur, who came down from the north and found in Hindustan no good fruit, no fresh water or witty conversation, not even a friend.'[56] Yet Aziz, who so eloquently attests to India's divisions, also speaks of its unity. In Mau, both Hindus and Moslems worship at the shrines to a Moslem saint who, in obeying his mother's injunction to free prisoners, had lost his head. 'When Aziz arrived, and found that even Islam was idolatrous, he grew scornful, and longed to purify the place, like Alimgir. But soon he didn't mind, like Akbar.'[57] Like the mosque of Mau, 'a flat piece of ornamental stucco, with protuberances at either end to suggest minarets',[58] Islam has been transformed by India, so that the Moslem world in India appears as 'a strange outcome of the protests of Arabia'.[59] Aziz becomes assimilated into the paradox of India; standing motionless in Mau in the rain he thinks, 'I am an Indian at last',[60] and it is a process of absorption which he simultaneously invites and resists. His use of our and my and they and theirs when he is explaining the Hindu festival to Mrs Moore's son, Ralph, suggests his surrender to India and his need to retain an identity distinct from the Hindus:

This is our monsoon, the best weather. . . How I wish she could have seen them, our rains. Now is the time when all things are happy, young and old. They are happy out there with their savage noise, though we cannot follow them; the tanks are full so they dance, and this is India. I wish you were not with officials, then I would show you my country.[61]

The symmetrical injunctions of Islam, 'There is no God but God', melt in the mild air of Mau; India reaches out to contain the entire universe of men, objects and beliefs just as even 'tiny tazias after Mohurram'[62] feature as emblems of the all-inclusive, all-embracing God of the Hindus. Islam, then, is absorbed into India as an aspect

of its manifold nature while retaining a unique but deeply Oriental
cultural character, for while they do not seek union with God, the
Moslems' yearning for a vision of Him permeates their social
existence with an awareness and awe of the unknown:

> The banquet, though riotous, had been agreeable, and now the bless-
> ings of leisure – unknown to the West, which either works or idles –
> descended on the motley company. Civilization strays about like a ghost
> here, revisiting the ruins of empire, and is to be found not in great works
> of art or mighty deeds, but in the gestures well-bred Indians make when
> they sit or lie down. Fielding, who had dressed up in native costume, learnt
> from his excessive awkwardness in it that all his motions were makeshifts,
> whereas when the Nawab Bahadur stretched out his hand for food or
> Nureddin applauded a song, something beautiful had been accomplished
> which needed no development. This restfulness of gesture – it is the Peace
> that passeth Understanding, after all, it is the social equivalent of Yoga.
> When the whirring of action ceases, it becomes visible, and reveals a
> civilization which the West can disturb but will never acquire. The hand
> stretches out for ever, the lifted knee has the eternity though not the sad-
> ness of the grave.[63]

Aziz's professional skill as a doctor exists harmoniously with a
sensual nature and deference to things holy, and for him the passage
to intangibles is through 'the secret understanding of the heart'.[64]
'There are many ways of being a man; mine is to express what is
deepest in my heart.'[65] His roots in Islam and his acceptance, as
distinct from his approval, of all aspects of India, immunize him
against dislocation by Caves. Nevertheless, the experience changes
him, and his spiritual life, which has been characterized by a 'semi-
mystic, semi-sensuous overturn',[66] permitting him imaginative
flights away from the confines of the phenomenal environment, becomes more intense. Liberated from knowledge and habit he makes
a fleeting passage inwards, receiving into his being the unseen, the
unspoken and the uncanny. After meeting Fielding again in Mau
and hearing the name of Mrs Moore, Aziz is excited and happy:
' "Esmiss Esmoor . . ." – as though she was coming to help him.'[67]
In the presence of her son and spirit, Ralph, Aziz is possessed by a
guiding force to focus his heart 'on something more distant than the
caves, something beautiful'.[68] While he consciously rejects the

possibility of further friendship with the English, his hidden mind
goes out to Ralph Moore; while facts lead him to question his
gratitude to Mrs Moore – 'What did this eternal goodness of Mrs
Moore amount to? To nothing, if brought to the test of thought'[69] –
his instincts lead him to revere her: 'she had stolen to the depths of
his heart, and he always adored her'.[70]

As an act of homage to Mrs Moore's memory he takes Ralph out
in a boat to witness the Hindu ceremony. 'He knew with his heart
that this was Mrs Moore's son, and indeed until his heart was involved he knew nothing.'[71] On the waters of the great Mau tank in
the interstices of the chant, Radhakrishna Krishnaradha, he hears
'almost certainly, the syllables of salvation that had sounded during
his trial at Chandrapore'[72] when the Indian crowd had invoked Mrs
Moore as a goddess, Esmiss Esmoor.

II

When the Moslems discuss the chilly English, the cold and odd
nation whom Aziz thinks of as 'circulating like an ice-stream through
his land',[73] a wintry surface covers their conversation. By temperament and choice the Anglo-Indians are outsiders, hostile to India
whether it be Mosque, Caves or Temple, participating in none,
understanding none, resenting all.

We're out here to do justice and keep the peace. . . I am out here to
work, mind, to hold this wretched country by force. I'm not a missionary
or a Labour Member or a vague sentimental sympathetic literary man.
I'm just a servant of the Government. . . We're not pleasant in India, and
we don't intend to be pleasant. We've something more important to do.[74]

Ronny Heaslop, a Civilian and a natural recruit to Anglo-India, in
disputing the injunctions of his mother, Mrs Moore, to show kindness and love, is voicing the creed of utility and defending the means
of force. While profiting from the fear on which the Raj rests, the
Anglo-Indians are victims of a fear which India arouses in them.
They live amidst scenery they do not understand,[75] sense that
Indians hate them and feel India to be a poisonous country[76] intend-
ing evil against them.[77] Already coarsened by their status in India,
the crisis generated by Adela Quested's accusation against Aziz

hurls them into cruder demonstrations of their hostility, some demanding holocausts of natives, others longing to inflict humiliating punishment.

Furtive fantasies about Indians' sexuality and the proclivities of 'buck niggers'[78] come to the surface. The face of the police superintendent, McBryde, is 'inquisitive and slightly bestial'[79] when he finds a woman's photograph amongst Aziz's belongings, and on being told by Fielding that it is a picture of his wife, his unspoken reaction is, 'Wife indeed, I know those wives!'[80] During the trial he has the chance of expounding his views on the relationship of race and sex:

He wanted to keep the proceedings as clean as possible, but Oriental Pathology, his favourite theme, lay around him, and he could not resist it. Taking off his spectacles, as was his habit before enunciating a general truth, he looked into them sadly, and remarked that the darker races are physically attracted by the fairer, but not *vice versa* – not a matter for bitterness this, not a matter for abuse, but just a fact which any scientific observer will confirm.[81]*

The robust philistinism of Anglo-Indians is their protection against the dangerous territory they inhabit. In their gridiron of bungalows, within the arid tidiness of the Civil Station, they drink cocktails, smoke cigars and dress for dinner, 'and the menu was: Julienne soup full of bullety bottled peas, pseudo-cottage bread, fish full of branching bones, pretending to be plaice, more bottled peas with the cutlets, trifle, sardines on toast: the menu of Anglo-India . . . the food of exiles, cooked by servants who did not understand

* Following a review of *A Passage to India* in the *New Statesman*, a correspondent from Patna, E. A. Horne, offered this marvellously Anglo-Indian explanation of what had happened in the Caves: because of his sexual vanity and physical obsessions Aziz had been thrown off balance by Miss Quested's question on the number of his wives; it was he who experienced the hallucination of attempting to ravish Miss Quested, which he then communicated to her. *New Statesman*, 16 August 1924, p. 543. As Hamidullah, the Moslem lawyer and Aziz's friend, comments on overhearing Fielding and Miss Quested conjecturing about her experience and suggesting the guide's culpability, 'There are one hundred and seventy million Indians in this notable peninsula, and of course one or other of them entered the cave. Of course some Indian is the culprit, we must never doubt that' (p. 253).

it'.[82] As if alert to India's syncretic powers and the fate of previous conquerors, 'who also entered the country with intent to refashion it, but were in the end worked into its pattern and covered with its dust',[83] the Anglo-Indians have contrived to guard against absorption:

> Meanwhile the performance ended, and the amateur orchestra played the National Anthem. Conversation and billiards stopped, faces stiffened. It was the anthem of the Army of Occupation. It reminded every member of the club that he or she was British and in exile. It produced a little sentiment and a useful accession of will-power. The meagre tune, the curt series of demands on Jehovah, fused into a prayer unknown in England, and though they perceived neither Royalty nor Deity they did perceive something, they were strengthened to resist another day.[84]

The emblems of Anglo-India blazon a determination that they will not cross the threshold of any passage leading away from a censored consciousness into an emotional and spiritual anarchy: 'Ronny's religion was of the sterilized Public School brand, which never goes bad, even in the tropics. Wherever he entered, mosque, cave, or temple, he retained the spiritual outlook of the Fifth Form, and condemned as "weakening" any attempt to understand them.'[85]

III

It was from the Moslems, Aziz reminds Fielding, that the British conquered India, and it is the Moslems, precariously placed between the actually powerful British Raj and the potentially powerful Hindu majority, whom Forster shows as disturbed by the British intrusion into India. Aziz longs to shake the dust of Anglo-India off his feet: 'To escape from the net and be back among manners and gestures that he knew!'[86] The British Raj is a constant assault on his sensibilities, his dignity, his integrity, causing him to defy his masters and to fear the consequences: 'The complexion of his mind turned from human to political. He thought no longer, "Can I get on with people?" but "Are they stronger than I?" breathing the prevalent miasma.'[87] Heaslop's insolence at Fielding's tea-party provokes Aziz into being offensively friendly, impertinent, greasily confident, patronizing, shoddy and odious. The Nawab Bahadur, a wealthy land-owner, who is dignified and courtly in the company of Indians, appears silly and prolix in the presence of the uncomprehending English. The instincts of the Moslems flower through affectionate communion with those who behave as their brothers; gracious manners, loyalty to companions, generosity to dependants, hospitality conceived as a gift to the host, these suggest the priority they give to emotional fulfilment,* and it is appropriate that the Moslems should regret the lack of intimacy with the British and that Aziz should respond warmly to overtures of friendship from Fielding, Mrs Moore and Adela Quested, three people on the edge of Anglo-India. With the Hindus as onlookers – Professor Godbole accepts invitations from the British but remains detached from the events at which he is present† – this group attempts to create relationships in the uninhabited territory between India and Anglo-India, and the human tragedy of the British–Indian encounter is acted out between English and Moslem with Aziz as the martyr.

Fielding, the principal of the college at Chandrapore, is a humanist, a rational and enlightened man who thinks himself free of race feelings and who believes the world to be 'a globe of men who are trying to reach one another and can best do so by the help of goodwill plus culture and intelligence – a creed ill suited to Chandrapore'.[88] He mistrusts cant and trusts in education to develop the individual's capacity for civilized social intercourse. Both Adela Quested, an honest and sensible girl who is visiting India to decide whether she will marry Ronny Heaslop, and Heaslop's mother, Mrs Moore, who has accompanied her, are in their separate ways responsive to fresh surroundings and open to new experiences. Thus,

* As if to emphasize the spiritual ambitions of the Hindus in the novel, Forster pays little attention to their social existence outside of their communal religious activities. Thus affection, generosity and courtesy, which Forster knew both Moslems and Hindus possessed in abundance, are represented as an essential feature of the Indian temperament by Moslems.

† At the official 'bridge-party' Adela Quested and Mrs Moore solicit an invitation from some Indian guests, the Bhattacharyas. Always courteous and complaisant the Bhattacharyas 'did not dispute' the arrangements which the English ladies suggested but nor did they send their carriage as promised, an expedient which permitted them to pay lip-service to English etiquette while ignoring its content, perhaps even an instance of polite passive resistance.

while the Anglo-Indians make obeisance to the formal meeting of the races in their grudgingly given 'bridge-parties', at which Indians cluster on one side of the lawn and the English remain on the other, Fielding, Adela Quested and Mrs Moore expect the sort of relationships they had known in England.

The beginnings are propitious; it is the time of the cool weather. The moon, in Indian mythology the symbol of the life-giving principle, watches benignly over the attempts of these men and women to initiate and crystallize their own unity. Mrs Moore and Aziz first meet by chance in the Mosque illuminated by full moonlight, and later that evening Mrs Moore knows a sense of kinship with the heavenly bodies: 'She watched the moon, whose radiance stained with primrose the purple of the surrounding sky. In England the moon had seemed dead and alien; here she was caught in the shawl of night together with earth and all the other stars.'[89]

At Fielding's tea-party, his contribution to introducing the ladies to India in the persons of Aziz and the Brahman Professor Godbole, Aziz's spirits soar as he chatters excitedly with his new friends.

The arrival of Professor Godbole quieted him somewhat, but it remained his afternoon. The Brahman, polite and enigmatic, did not impede his eloquence, and even applauded it... The ladies were interested in him, and hoped that he would supplement Dr Aziz by saying something about religion. But he only ate – ate and ate, smiling, never letting his eyes catch sight of his hand.[90]

To impress the ladies with his Oriental munificence, rather than as a practical proposal, Aziz invites those at the party to visit the Marabar Caves as his guests, an expedition which does take place but without the presence of Professor Godbole.

Adela Quested's acquaintance with Aziz does not go beyond formalities; they converse earnestly and at length but neither their minds nor their hearts are in sympathy. But between Mrs Moore and Aziz there is so strong and enduring a link that they can communicate in ellipses; theirs is more than a social encounter and it does not terminate with Mrs Moore's death. It is the relationship of Aziz and Fielding which reveals the pleasures of friendship and poses the dilemmas. Delicate and highly charged as relations are between members within a community, these are made yet more fragile, more explosive when men meet in the no-man's-land where they must create anew the conditions for communion. Their friendship is disturbed by differences in precepts and values, by clashing standards of beauty and propriety. Fielding's censure, 'You are so fantastic... Your emotions never seem in proportion to their objects', is answered by an irate Aziz: 'Is emotion a sack of potatoes, so much the pound, to be measured out? Am I a machine? I shall be told I can use up my emotions by using them next.'[91] Their intercourse is interrupted by tangles: 'A pause in the wrong place, an intonation misunderstood, and a whole conversation went awry.'[92] It was as if 'something racial intruded – not bitterly but inevitably'.[93] Ultimately their relationship is tainted by the context of their encounter.* Fielding is instinctively patronizing, as befits an Englishman in India – 'the scale, the scale. You always get the scale wrong, my dear fellow'[94] – and Aziz, who craves an intimacy which Fielding is temperamentally incapable of meeting, is in turn importunate and easily offended, the occupational hazards of those obliged to be clients of a master-race. The tensions caused by disparate motives, unequal emotional appetites and different sources of satisfaction, are exacerbated in this meeting of men from opposite sides of the colonial barrier. Misunderstandings fracture their association; Fielding draws back from the emotional demands Aziz makes on him; Aziz suspects Fielding's probity, believing that his motive in persuading him to renounce the compensation money from Miss Quested was that Fielding could return to England and marry her.

Yet they had known an interlude of friendship. Fielding had stood by Aziz after Miss Quested's accusation, incurring the scorn and insults of his countrymen, openly aligning himself with the Indians in what had become a racial confrontation. But after the

* Arnold Kettle, in *An Introduction to the English Novel* (1953), draws attention to the political pressures distorting the relationship: 'Forster, despite all his emphasis on personal relationships, is far too sensible and far too worldly to attempt to abstract relationships from their actual contexts... Both Aziz and Fielding are subjected to a strain so profound that their relationship can scarcely survive, even with all arbitrariness, all casual forms of misunderstanding removed, and the strain is the strain of the actual situation in which they exist, the strain of imperialism ... which corrupts all it touches' (pp. 153-4).

crisis each retreats to his own community, Aziz recognizing his
identity as an Indian and Fielding, who has married Heaslop's half-
sister and Mrs Moore's daughter, Stella, throwing in his lot with
Anglo-India: 'he was acquiring some of its limitations, and already
felt surprise at his own past heroism'.[95] A letter from Heaslop to
Fielding which Aziz reads suggests the extent of his apostasy to his
former ideals:

I quite agree – life is too short to cherish grievances, also I'm relieved
you feel able to come into line with the Oppressors of India to some extent.
We need all the support we can get. . . You are lucky to be out of British
India at the present moment. Incident after incident, all due to propaganda, but we can't lay our hands on the connecting thread. The longer
one lives here, the more certain one gets that everything hangs together.
My personal opinion is, it's the Jews.[96]

When the friendship of Aziz and Fielding is healed it is a symbolic
reconciliation, not an attainment of inter-racial harmony: 'socially
they had no meeting-place',[97] and they are aware that they can meet
no more. On their last ride in the Mau jungles they recapture the
intimacy they had sporadically known in the past, declaring that they
are now partisans in the struggle between India and Britain, recognizing that the time and the place forbids their friendship. They
wrangle about politics, about Indian ineptitude and British insolence,
and Fielding derides Aziz's prediction of an Indian nation:

And Aziz in an awful rage danced this way and that, not knowing what
to do, and cried: 'Down with the English anyhow. That's certain. Clear
out, you fellows, double quick, I say. We may hate one another, but we
hate you most. If I don't make you go, Ahmed will, Karim will,* if it's
fifty [or]† five-hundred years we shall get rid of you, yes, we shall drive
every blasted Englishman into the sea, and then' – he rode against him
furiously – 'and then,' he concluded, half kissing him, 'you and I shall be
friends.'[98]

---

* Aziz's sons.

† See Oliver Stallybrass, 'Forster's "Wobblings": The Manuscripts of *A
Passage to India*' in *Aspects of E. M. Forster*, in which he points out errors in
the published texts of the novel, p. 154.

E. M. FORSTER: 'A PASSAGE TO INDIA'

Caves : The Return to the Ancestral Mind

The past! the dark, unfathom'd retrospect! ...
Passage indeed, O soul, to primal thought!

Walt Whitman, Passage to India

I

In his study of Forster, *The Cave and the Mountain*, Wilfred Stone approaches the caves within the Marabar Hills, the mountain and its hollow core, as 'archetypal picturings of life's origin, of the primal inside and outside from which creation springs... They are the primal womb from which we all came and the primal tomb to which we all return; they are the darkness before existence itself.'[99] Their universal symbolic meaning, Stone suggests, is preserved and venerated by the Hindus, who are closest to elemental knowledge and the meaning of ancient myth, in the architecture of their temple, 'a temple which Forster later learned symbolised the World Mountain'.* Yet it is difficult to associate Caves with the Hindu mind and sensibility for they seem to be the expression of an aboriginal philosophy over whose tenets the Aryan invaders of India had triumphed, assimilating aspects but rejecting the whole in their creation of Brahmanical Hinduism.

During Aziz's trial McBryde produces a map of the Marabars on which a specimen cave had been lettered as Buddhist Cave and he is corrected by Mr Das, 'Not Buddhist, I think, Jain... All the Marabar Caves are Jain.'† Although Hinduism had scratched and

---

* 'The architecture of *Passage* is the architecture of this temple. At the centre is that "small, secret and dark" inner core – the ur-temple, the ultimate darkness – around which is clustered all the complexity of the daylight world of appearance. On the inside is the anonymous, humourless region of the "subconscious", of those primal forces antecedent to character and the source of experience Forster calls "prophecy". On the outside is the world of ego, of consciousness and history, life in its tragedy, comedy, absurdity, abundance and mess. Connecting the two is a simple, doorless corridor, inviting men to travel freely in either direction as they will. Although the World Mountain retains the old dichotomies between body and soul, seen and unseen, the connection between them is made superlatively easy' (p. 302).

† Characteristically, Mr McBryde retorts, 'Mr Lesley says they're Buddhist and he ought to know' (p. 232).

plastered a few rocks of the Marabars, the shrines are unfrequented: 'Some saddhus did once settle in a cave, but they were smoked out, and even Buddha, who must have passed this way down to the Bo Tree of Gya, shunned a renunciation more complete than his own, and has left no legend of struggle or victory in the Marabar.'[100] Pressed by Aziz at Fielding's tea-party, Godbole had declined to affirm that the caves were immensely holy and indeed his reticent replies denied all attributes to them. But disowned by Hinduism and Buddhism, the caves have been claimed by one of India's religions and in them we meet with an aspect of the Indian mind rooted in the forgotten life of the race but remembered and perpetuated by those sects who claim that they are the inheritors and guardians of the true, original and eternal religion of mankind. In 'Caves' Forster summons the profoundly pessimistic vision at the heart of Jainism, an ascetic tradition and a spiritual experience founded on a cosmology immeasurably older than the Ancient Night of Godbole's memory which is the Hinduism of Aryan India. The archetypal quality of the Marabars is matched by the archaic mind they reawaken and the ancestral voices which the caves echo. Their mood is that of the human soul plunged in a dark night of despair.*

---

* The meanings of caves have been variously interpreted by critics. Gertrude M. White, 'A Passage to India: Analysis and Revaluation', PMLA, Vol. LXVIII, September 1953, analyses the novel's dialectical pattern and suggests that the Marabar Caves are the very voice of that union which is the opposite of divine; the voice of evil and negation; of the universe which is "older than all spirit" ' (p. 647). Glen O. Allen, 'Structure, Symbol and Theme in E. M. Forster's A Passage to India', PMLA, Vol. LXX, December 1955, suggests that caves, mosque and temple represent some kind of religion: 'It is easier to understand Forster's treatment of mosque, caves and temple if we accept as his basic categories the emotional nature, the intellect, and the capacity for love.' Caves stand for the intellect and Forster represents as the religion of caves 'devotion to reason, form, and the sense of purpose as the sine qua non of right behaviour and attitude... It is not surprising that India, which, according to Forster, "mirrors the universe" and likewise has no unity itself, should in the history of its religious philosophy have embraced an approximation of each one of these "attitudes towards life" as a way of salvation' (pp. 936, 937). Louise Dauner, 'What Happened in the Caves? Reflections on A Passage to India' (1961), disputes propositions which approach caves as rational elements: 'the

A post-Vedic heterodoxy which originated in the same regions as Buddhism and during the same era, *circa* fifth century B.C., Jainism is an atheistic system and a world-rejecting philosophy which postulates the duality of soul and matter. Zimmer considers that Jainism is akin to the other ascetic strains within the Indian tradition, none of which derives from Brahman sources, 'being rooted in the same subsoil of archaic metaphysical speculation as Yoga, Sankhya and Buddhism, the other non-Vedic systems'.[101] Confined to India, Jainism has survived as a small sect whose influence is disproportionate to its numbers, and their doctrine of *ahimsa*, harmlessness or non-violence, which stems from the belief that all matter contains a living soul, is their special contribution to Indian thought and has been absorbed into Hinduism.* In Jain cosmology the whole world is alive; all matter, even to the tiniest particle, contains an imprisoned soul, a life-monad or *jiva*; entangled in matter, the soul of the phenomenal individual experiences the world as a place of pain and terror and only on releasing itself through prolonged austerities will it 'regain its pristine purity and enjoy omniscient, self-sufficient bliss for all eternity'.[102] Relationships of the flesh and deference to human values are disparaged as involvements which keep the life-monad tied to the material universe and the endless round of transmigration. The Jain goal therefore is to strive for liberation from bondage to the world, to attain that supreme state of sterile isolation whereby the soul, purged of all matter and life-processes, rises like a bubble of air to the summit of the cosmos there to exist for eternity in a state of absolute emptiness.

The scoured-out cavity of a Marabar cave is both the unfertilized womb of the race and the Nothing to which the Jain aspires.[103]

---

caves are not only the setting for *irrational* experience, but they are themselves archetypal. We mean by this first that the caves function in a situation involving elements which derive, not from Forster's rational or conscious mind, or even from Adela's conscious mind, but from the dark ambiguous soil of the unconscious, which disguises its meanings in symbols, as in myths, fantasies, fairy tales; and second, that the cave, *as cave*, is itself a primordial image in mythology and psychology, hence as an archetype it is a constituent of the collective unconscious and not of the purely personal and conscious psyche' (pp. 259-60).

* Gandhi was a notable adherent of this creed; he grew up in an area where Jains were numerous.

Nothing, nothing attaches to them. . . Nothing is inside them, they were sealed up before the creation of pestilence or treasure; if mankind grew curious and excavated, nothing, nothing would be added to the sum of good or evil. One of them is rumoured within the boulder that swings on the summit of the highest of the hills; a bubble-shaped cave that has neither ceiling nor floor, and mirrors its own darkness in every direction infinitely. If the boulder falls and smashes, the cave will smash too – empty as an Easter egg. The boulder because of its hollowness sways in the wind, and even moves when a crow perches upon it: hence its name and the name of its stupendous pedestal: the Kawa Dol.[104]*

Enclosing the cave's emptiness, which is the condition preceding life and the Jain image of the liberated soul, is the granite, matter imprisoning those life-monads whose presence is momentarily illuminated in the light of a match which itself entangles a fire-being:

These are dark caves. Even when they open towards the sun, very little light penetrates down the entrance tunnel into the circular chamber. There is little to see, and no eye to see it, until the visitor arrives for his five minutes, and strikes a match. Immediately another flame rises in the depths of the rock and moves towards the surface like an imprisoned spirit: the walls of the circular chamber have been most marvellously polished. The two flames approach and strive to unite, but cannot, because one of them breathes air, the other stone. A mirror inlaid with lovely colours divides the lovers, delicate stars of pink and grey interpose, exquisite nebulae, shadings fainter than the tail of a comet or the midday moon, all the evanescent life of the granite, only here visible. Fists and fingers thrust above the advancing soil – here at last is their skin, finer than any covering acquired by the animals, smoother than windless water, more voluptuous than love. The radiance increases, the flames touch one another, kiss, expire. The cave is dark again, like all the caves.[105]†

* Zimmer in *Philosophies of India* discusses Jain imagery: 'The metaphor of the bubble is one that is used frequently in the Jaina texts. The life-monad rises, passing through the celestial regions of the gods where radiant beings still burdened by the weight of virtuous karma enjoy the fruits of former lives of benignant thought and action. Self-luminous, transparent, the balloon ascends to the dome of the world – that highest sphere . . . which is whiter than milk and pearls, more resplendent than gold and crystal, and has the shape of a divine umbrella' (p. 258).

† Basham in *Sources of Indian Tradition* gives this account of the Jain teaching

The voice which Mrs Moore hears in the cave speaks to her of a total despair at the nature of the world; it is a message which annihilates all human values and robs man's mortal existence of any meaning except the need to escape from its coils. To the modern sensibility a philosophy which describes the temporal universe as a place of imprisonment, which degrades human effort and aspiration within the world, is a vision of depletion and bereavement. In a state of supersensuous consciousness, the ordinary modes of cognition suspended by the effect of a cave, Mrs Moore, now deprived of the supports of acquired habit and learned responses, is overwhelmed by the panic and terror which Dravidian India, the primal universe, inspires in the soul of modern man. As if reliving one of the crucial Indian experiences of facing the harsh struggle to survive in such a world, Mrs Moore takes on the stance of a world-weary ascetic and loses her will to live.

II

Adela Quested and Mrs Moore had hoped to know India through 'Mosque', Miss Quested imploring information from Aziz and expecting that he would unlock the country for her, and Mrs Moore after her encounter with Aziz in the Mosque of Chandrapore being refreshed by a 'sudden sense of unity, of kinship with the heavenly bodies'.[106] They are destined to know India in 'Caves', confronting an altogether darker and more remote aspect of India, and because of this are overpowered by sensations outside the range of their ordinary experience. From the moment of their arrival, the two women, in their respective ways both seekers, had been obscurely affected by India. Adela Quested, an avowedly secular girl who trusts in information and believes the whole stream of events to be important and interesting, is determined to see 'the *real* India' and she approaches the adventure as an academic exercise to be systematically organized.

---

on life-monads incarcerated in matter: 'In every stone on the highway a soul is locked, so tightly enchained by matter that it cannot escape the careless foot that kicks it or cry out in pain, but capable of suffering nevertheless. When a match is struck a fire-being, with a soul which may one day be reborn in a human body, is born, only to die a few moments afterwards. In every drop of rain, in every breath of wind, in every lump of clay, is a living soul' (p. 50).

Yet the sight of the distant Marabar Hills containing the extra-ordinary caves disturbs her mental equilibrium and brings her a prevision of life as a member of Anglo-India:

> Colour would remain – the pageant of birds in the early morning, brown bodies, white turbans, idols whose flesh was scarlet or blue – and movement would remain as long as there were crowds in the bazaar and bathers in the tanks. Perched up on the seat of a dogcart, she would see them. But the force that lies behind colour and movement would escape her even more effectually than it did now. She would see India always as a frieze, never as a spirit.[107]

Mrs Moore's arrival in India coincides with an oncoming spiritual crisis. Her instincts guide her to acknowledge mysteries and ghosts, she thinks of herself as a Christian, and it is her hope that men will venerate the sacred and translate this reverence into their everyday behaviour:

> The English *are* out here to be pleasant [she tells her son]. Because India is part of the earth. And God has put us on earth in order to be pleasant to each other. God ... is ... love... God has put us on earth to love our neighbours and to show it, and He is omnipresent, even in India, to see how we are succeeding.[108]

As she grew older she found it more difficult to avoid talking of God, 'and he had been constantly in her thoughts since she entered India, though oddly enough he satisfied her less and less... Outside the arch there seemed always an arch, beyond the remotest echo a silence.'[109] The sight of the Indian moon revitalizes her, the Ganges fills her with wonder and terror and she finds in India that 'a new feeling, half languor, half excitement, bade her turn down any fresh path'.[110]

After Fielding's tea-party Adela Quested had sunk into living at half-pressure despite the interesting events in which she was participating. 'I feel I haven't been – frank enough, attentive enough, or something. It's as if I got everything out of proportion.'[111] Her disquiet is understood by Mrs Moore who communicates rather than explicitly states that her bothers are mixed up with India: 'It's partly the odd surroundings; you and I keep on attending to trifles instead of what's important.'[112]

India acts on these two uneasy women with the power of an hallucinogenic drug, rearranging their senses, extending the limits of their perceptions and depriving them of the power of choice. The expedition to the caves happens as if independently of human will and in obedience to the dictates of destiny: 'no one was enthusiastic, yet it took place.'[113] The cycle of the Indian seasons has reached the hot weather, the time of annihilation when humanity flees from the destructive power of the sun: 'April, herald of horrors, is at hand.'[114] During the journey to the caves Adela Quested is distressed because the new scenes and situations fail to bite into her mind, and Mrs Moore feels herself being withdrawn from the world of personal relationships. 'It so happened that Mrs Moore and Miss Quested had felt nothing acutely for a fortnight. Ever since Professor Godbole had sung his queer little song, they had lived more or less inside cocoons, and the difference between them was that the elder lady accepted her own apathy, while the younger resented hers.'[115] As they move away from the familiarity of the civil station at Chandrapore, the Englishwomen are cut off from the security of their milieu, separated even from the comprehensible world of Mosque.

In the Marabars they are returning to the primal shambles, to a timeless place before birds, men and gods.

They are older than anything in the world. No water has ever covered them, and the sun who has watched them for countless aeons may still discern in their outlines forms that were his before our globe was torn from his bosom. If flesh of the sun's flesh is to be touched anywhere, it is here, among the incredible antiquity of these hills. Yet even they are altering. As Himalayan India rose, this India, the primal, has been depressed, and is slowly re-entering the curve of the earth... They are sinking beneath the newer lands. Their main mass is untouched, but at the edge their outposts have been cut off and stand knee-deep, throat-deep, in the advancing soil. There is something unspeakable in these outposts. They are like nothing else in the world, and a glimpse of them makes the breath catch. They rise abruptly, insanely, without the proportion that is kept by the wildest hills elsewhere, they bear no relation to anything dreamt or seen. To call them 'uncanny' suggests ghosts, and they are older than all spirit.[116]

Such can be the effect of proximity to the Marabars; yet seen by the British characters from suitable distances and in certain lights, strictures which are repeated whenever their beauty is noted, the hills appear lovely, romantic and finite.[117] Viewed from the train approaching their cosmos, 'the Marabars were gods to whom earth is a ghost'.[118] Appearances, then, are relative, sensory cognition is unreliable; as the aspect alters, so does our recognition of that fragment of reality which is available to our view. To modern Western man, who is intent on discerning truth through information and reasoning, this uncertainty, this relativity, is experienced as a perilously dislocating confusion.

When the party nears the Marabars

a new quality occurred, a spiritual silence which invaded more senses than the ear. Life went on as usual, but had no consequences, that is to say, sounds did not echo or thoughts develop. Everything seemed cut off at its root, and therefore infected with illusion. For instance, there were some mounds by the edge of the track, low, serrated, and touched with whitewash. What were these mounds – graves, breasts of the goddess Parvati? The villagers gave both replies.[119]

Adela sees a thin, dark object reared at the farther side of a watercourse and exclaims that it is a snake; Aziz and the villagers agree; she re-examines it through field-glasses and sees it as a stick, but the villagers and Aziz persist in accepting it as a snake. Graves or breasts of a goddess, snake or stick, Indians do not insist on a clear-cut answer, they can accept the blurring of boundaries, the inevitability of ambiguities.* The Marabars which abolish the categories of animate and inanimate, where the whole universe seems alive, present a landscape congenial to Indians who can adjust to hylozoistic

* In 'The Nine Gems of Ujjain (Adrift in India)' (1914), in *Abinger Harvest*, Forster describes a visit to ruins: 'The track we were following wavered and blurred and offered alternatives; it had no earnestness of purpose like the tracks of England... There was no place for anything and nothing was in its place. All the small change of the north rang false, and nothing remained certain but the dome of the sky and the disk of the sun... One confusion enveloped Ujjain and all things. Why differentiate? I asked the driver what kind of trees those were, and he answered: "Trees"; what was the name of that bird, and he said "Bird"; and the plain, interminable, murmured, "Old buildings are buildings, ruins are ruins" ' (pp. 324, 327).

concepts. To the British they are the source of a profound mental and emotional disorder. 'The assemblage [of hills], ten in all, shifted a little as the train crept past them, as if observing its arrival';[120] an elephant appears 'grey and isolated, like another hill'; the train wobbles away, 'turning its head this way and that like a centipede'; the counterpoises of wells produce a movement 'as of antennae'.[121] 'A patch of field would jump as if it were being fried, and then lie quiet';[122] 'the boulders said, "I am alive," the small stones answered, "I am almost alive." Between the chinks lay the ashes of little plants. They meant to climb to the rocking-stone on the summit, but it was too far, and they contented themselves with the big group of caves.'[123]

The intense experience of the Marabars is known by Adela Quested and Mrs Moore, products of the modern West, who have to a lesser or greater extent been programmed to receive the stimuli selected by their own society. Exposed to India they are disoriented, turned back in Caves to a past condition of man, they are cut off from the supports and constraints of their society and their slumbering spirits awaken with catastrophic impact. Their states of super-sensuous awareness are visitations of perceptions which their conscious minds could not have distinguished; their experiences are encounters between the civilized mind and the primitive memories dormant in man. The Marabars compel the decent and honest Adela Quested, flat-chested, plain and sensually underdeveloped, to acknowledge her atrophied sexuality, a confrontation which is in itself an assault on her being. The very shapes and contours of the hills and caves are emblems of the male and female principles which work their way into her consciousness, anticipating her sensation of rape. The hill whose outer shoulder she and Aziz climb in their search for interesting caves is the Kawa Dol, the highest of the Marabars: 'It shot up in a single slab, on whose summit one rock was poised – if a mass so great can be called one rock. Behind it, recumbent, were the hills that contained the other caves.'[124] When Adela recalls her experience of an attempted assault in a cave, she remembers 'there was this shadow, or sort of shadow, down the entrance tunnel, bottling me up'.[125] She flees from the cave, flings herself down a precipitous slope covered in cactuses which enter her body as if repeating the travesty of a sexual encounter.

Now Adela Quested is possessed; her feelings, behaviour and speech are those of one transformed by an hallucinogenic agent. Tended by solicitous ladies in the safety of an Anglo-Indian bungalow, she lies

passive beneath their fingers, which developed the shock that had begun in the cave. Hitherto she had not much minded whether she was touched or not: her senses were abnormally inert and the only contact she antici- pated was that of the mind. Everything now was transferred to the surface of her body, which began to avenge itself and feed unhealthily. People seemed very much alike, except that some would come close while others kept away. 'In space things touch, in time things part,' she repeated to herself while the thorns were being extracted – her brain so weak that she could not decide whether the phrase was a philosophy or a pun.[126]

Logical thought processes are suspended, the senses are alerted. She vibrates between hard common sense and hysteria; the echo she had heard in a cave rages up and down 'like a nerve in the faculty of her hearing';[127] she tries to think the incident out, declares her wish that the assailant be punished, suffers grief and the need to abase herself. 'After one of these bouts, she longed to go out into the bazaars and ask pardon from everyone she met, for she felt in some vague way that she was leaving the world worse than she found it. She felt that it was her crime, until the intellect, reawakening, pointed out to her that she was inaccurate here, and set her again upon her sterile round.'[128]

Implicit in her derangement is a recognition, new to Adela Quested's normally well-ordered mind, that reality is subtle, com- plex and uncertain – 'I shouldn't mind if it had happened anywhere else; at least I really don't know where it did happen'[129] – and an insight, previously alien to her concerns, into the tragedy of her incompleted nature:

What is the use of personal relationships when everyone brings less and less to them? I feel we ought all to go back into the desert for centuries and try and get good. I want to begin at the beginning. All the things I thought I'd learnt are just a hindrance, they're not knowledge at all. I'm not fit for personal relationships.[130]

Adela Quested is on a journey away from easy certainties – her belief in 'the sanctity of personal relationships'[131] – into a reality below the surface of life.

The peak of her agonizing but fruitful dislocation comes during the trial when her hidden mind, now liberated from all restrictions, relives what had happened in the cave:

A new and unknown sensation protected her, like magnificent armour. She didn't think what had happened, or even remember in the ordinary way of memory, but she returned to the Marabar Hills, and spoke from them across a sort of darkness to Mr McBryde. The fatal day recurred, in every detail, but now she was of it and not of it at the same time, and this double relation gave it indescribable splendour.[132]

Guided by Mrs Moore's spirit, as if wafted by the airs sent swirling by the punkah-wallah, she knows that Aziz is innocent and withdraws the charge. She had passed from despair and confusion to a moment of illumination, and then she reverts to normal consciousness: 'Though the vision was over, and she had returned to the insipidity of the world, she remembered what she had learnt.'[133] Having reached into herself and seen her own deficiencies, she accepts the trip beyond the boundaries of logic and the senses as entering a region which she cannot inhabit: 'the vision disappeared whenever she wished to interpret it.'[134] But she has been stretched and reshaped, and her conversations with Fielding, who questions what *had* happened in the cave, show that she has acquired a more subtle sensibility: 'It will never be known. It's as if I ran my finger along that polished wall in the dark, and cannot get further. I am up against something, and so are you. Mrs Moore – she did know.'

Mrs Moore's experience of Caves is larger than the awakening of her unconscious for she is possessed by a vision emanating from a tradition alien to her culture and nature. The voice of the caves is transmitted through her as it had spoken to aboriginal man looking out on the primordial abyss. The echo of a Marabar cave is entirely without distinction: 'Whatever is said, the same monotonous noise replies. . . "Boum" is the sound as far as the human alphabet can express it, or "bou-oum," or "ou-boum," – utterly dull. Hope, politeness, the blowing of a nose, the squeak of a boot, all produce "boum." '[135] To Mrs Moore, fatigued and in poor health, an old woman approaching the end of her natural life-span and aware of the irreversible passage towards death, the cave murmurs, 'Pathos, piety, courage – they exist, but are identical, and so is filth. Everything exists, nothing has value.'[136] From a state of terror about her own being and the universe she passes into apathy and cynicism as she surrenders to her vision:*

What had spoken to her in that scoured-out cavity of the granite? What dwelt in the first of the caves? Something very old and very small. Before time, it was before space also. Something snub-nosed, incapable of generosity – the undying worm itself. Since hearing its voice, she had not entertained one large thought, she was actually envious of Adela. All this fuss over a frightened girl! Nothing had happened, 'and if it had,' she found herself thinking with the cynicism of a withered priestess, 'if it had, there are worse evils than love.' The unspeakable attempt presented itself to her as love: in a cave, in a church – Boum, it amounts to the same.[137]

Thoughts foreign to her character as it had formerly been now flood her mind and she experiences an overwhelming contempt for

---

* 'She had come to that state where the horror of the universe and its smallness are both visible at the same time – the twilight of the double vision in which so many elderly people are involved ... in the twilight of the double vision a spiritual muddledom is set up for which no high-sounding words can be found; we can neither act nor refrain from action, we can neither ignore nor respect infinity' (p. 216). Mrs Moore's experience exists on many levels; it resembles the 'panic fear' described by James as a form of melancholy and has affinities with what he has called a diabolical mysticism, 'a sort of religious mysticism turned upside down' which occurs in delusional insanity: 'the emotion is pessimistic: instead of consolations we have desolations'. See *The Varieties of Religious Experience*, p. 410. Her vision is also strikingly like a 'mood of pessimistic meditation' recorded by Bertrand Russell in 1968: 'Formerly, the cruelty, the meanness, the dusty fretful passion of human life seemed to me a little thing, set, like some resolved discord in music, amid the splendour of the stars and the stately procession of geological ages. What if the universe was to end in universal death? It was none the less unruffled and magnificent. But now all this has shrunk to be no more than my own reflection in the windows of the soul through which I look out upon the night of nothingness... There is darkness without, and when I die there will be darkness within. There is no splendour, no vastness, anywhere; only triviality for a moment, and then nothing. Why live in such a world? Why even die?' Bertrand Russell, *Autobiography* (1968), pp. 158–9.

the pursuits and concerns of men. Like Adela Quested, she is visited by strange feelings and speaks in unaccustomed cadences:

'My body, my miserable body,' she sighed. 'Why isn't it strong? Oh, why can't I walk away and be gone? Why can't I finish my duties and be gone? Why do I get headaches and puff when I walk? And all the time this to do and that to do and this to do in your way and that to do in her way, and everything sympathy and confusion and bearing one another's burdens. Why can't this be done and that be done in my way and they be done and I at peace? Why has anything to be done, I cannot see. Why all this marriage, marriage? . . . The human race would have become a single person centuries ago if marriage was any use. And all this rubbish about love, love in a church, love in a cave, as if there is the least difference, and I held up from my business over such trifles!'[138]

When Mrs Moore speaks to Adela Quested and her son in this vein 'her mind seemed to move towards them from a great distance and out of darkness'.[139] What she expresses is the weariness of ascetics longing to escape from the world of men: 'Oh, how tedious . . . trivial. . . Oh, why is everything still my duty? when shall I be free from your fuss? Was he in the cave and were you in the cave and on and on . . . and Unto us a Son is born, unto us a Child is given . . . and am I good and is he bad and are we saved? . . . and ending everything the echo.'[140]* Forces are now battling within Mrs Moore; she is the selfish and petulant old lady bereft of her former Christian faith and denied the solace of heaven who abdicates all responsibility to her friends. And she is an imprisoned soul longing for release from the coils of the phenomenal world, in Indian terms yearning for *moksha*, liberation, a goal which in the Jain teachings is to be attained through quietism and whose end is not a merging through annihilation with an Absolute but a state of complete isolation beyond all transactions with the world of man and matter. Here the mimicry of Mrs Moore's passage to becoming a Jain Saviour, a

* 'A basic fact generally disregarded by those who "go in" for Indian wisdom is this one of the total rejection of every last value of humanity by the Indian teachers and winners of redemption from the bondages of the world . . . for the Indian sages and ascetics, the Mahatmas and enlightened Saviours, "humanity" was no more than the shell to be pierced, shattered and dismissed.' Zimmer, *Philosophies of India*, pp. 231, 232.

Maker of the River-Crossing, ends. She dies at sea on her way back to England, is buried in the Indian Ocean and is claimed by Hindu India as a goddess or aspect of a goddess, just as parts of the pre-Vedic ascetic traditions of India were absorbed by Hinduism. Assimilated into India, Mrs Moore acquires the powers of a redeemer who intercedes as a benign force in the affairs of men. So it is that the chanting of her name, Esmiss Esmoor, by the Indian crowd during the trial leads Adela Quested along the path of truth to retract her accusation against Aziz. Later in time, when Aziz 'almost certainly' hears the Hindus of Mau invoking her, he is moved to a symbolic reconciliation with those whom he had shunned as his enemies. In her children, Ralph and Stella, whose restlessness is soothed by Hinduism, Mrs Moore's spirit has found a mortal home, in India an eternal one. Because Mrs Moore is a vessel who receives all the aspects of India, her spiritual journey is consummated. From dissatisfaction with the limitations of Christianity she passes effortlessly to Mosque whose shallow arcades do initially seem to offer a refuge to her soul – even in the shadow of the Marabars she is made suddenly young and vital by Aziz reminding her of their Mosque. Then, as she surrenders to the pessimistic message of Caves, she is possessed by their life-denying vision. On her last journey across India she is revived by manifestations of man's creative imagination, 'the indestructible life of man and his changing faces, and the houses he has built for himself and God'.[141] Buried in the Indian Ocean, she is taken into India and through Godbole's intercession, when his soul is surging to be reunited with God, she is impelled 'by his spiritual force to that place where completeness can be found. Completeness, not reconstruction.'[142] Through Mosque, Caves and Temple Mrs Moore has been worked into India's pattern and dust and added to her myriad of gods.

III

Caves intrude into the existence of Adela Quested and Mrs Moore with a life-shattering impact; others they discompose only slightly and some not at all. Fielding, a self-assured and mature man of independent outlook who values clarity and definition, finds India a muddle and dismisses mystery as a high-sounding name for muddle. When he returns to Europe he is moved by the beauty of form in the Mediterranean, 'the harmony between the world of man and the earth that upholds them, the civilization that has escaped muddle, the spirit in a reasonable form'.[143] Fielding is worldly and tolerant, his humanism is robust rather than sentimental, he is not a seeker, and he finds his satisfactions wholly within society. His reactions to the caves are appropriate to his temperament: when invited to join the expedition he agrees out of courtesy but without enthusiasm, 'caves bored him',[144] and when he arrives late after he and Godbole had missed the train, he cuts sight-seeing to a minimum: 'Fielding ran up to see one cave. He wasn't impressed.'[145]

Yet the Marabars do act obliquely on him, disturbing his equanimity:

It was the last moment of the light and as he gazed at the Marabar Hills they seemed to move graciously towards him like a queen, and their charm became the sky's. At the moment they vanished they were everywhere, the cool benediction of the night descended, the stars sparkled, and the whole universe was a hill. Lovely, exquisite moment – but passing the Englishman with averted face and on swift wings. He experienced nothing himself; it was as if someone had told him there was such a moment, and he was obliged to believe. And he felt dubious and discontented suddenly, and wondered whether he was really and truly successful as a human being.[146]

Surveying his life and his achievements, how he had developed his personality, explored his limitations and controlled his passions, he feels that his efforts had been misdirected and that he should have been working at something else, 'he didn't know at what, never would know, never could know, and that was why he felt sad'.[147]

Although he immediately regains his equipoise, he will again momentarily know discomposure and lose his usual sane view of human intercourse; and while he becomes in time sterner about education and duty, he has also been made more aware of a universe he had missed or rejected and his atheism becomes moderated by doubt: 'There is something in religion that may not be true, but has not yet been sung... Something that the Hindus have perhaps found.'[148] After his marriage to Mrs Moore's daughter, Stella, and their return to India, his sense of Hinduism's mystery, to which

Stella and Ralph are drawn, is intensified: 'I can't explain, because it isn't in words at all, but why do my wife and her brother like Hinduism, though they take no interest in its forms?'[149] Through India, Fielding, like Adela Quested, has been brought face to face with an enigma which reason cannot ravish: 'Not for them was an infinite goal behind the stars, and they never sought it. But wistfulness descended on them now . . . the shadow of the shadow of a dream fell over their clear-cut interests, and objects never seen again seemed messages from another world.'[150]

The return journey which Aziz makes when visiting the caves is to the sixteenth century. Entertaining his guests places him in the position of his adored Moghul emperors whose munificence he wishes to emulate, and throughout the expedition he remains preoccupied with acquitting himself honourably as a host, noticing nothing of his extraordinary surroundings. He is totally uninterested in caves; even as they depart he asks his relative, Mohammed Latif, 'What is in these caves, brother? Why are we going to see them?'[151] When he accompanies Adela Quested to a group of caves, his deeper thoughts are with the breakfast. The Marabars strike at Aziz as if punishing him for his ignorance and because of them he refashions his life; but they bring no psychological dislocation. Because Aziz is immersed in Islam and unconcerned with other creeds – 'I study nothing, I respect'[152] – he had 'no notion how to treat this particular aspect of India'.[153] But he is a native of India and no aspect of India presents the challenge of the alien for him.

When Aziz and Adela Quested had pressed Professor Godbole to tell them about the caves, 'Aziz realized that he was keeping something back'.[154] Godbole accepts the invitation to join the expedition but misses the train through miscalculating the length of a prayer, so that no Brahman is present – the cook who had been specially hired to cater for Godbole is left behind at the railway siding to await the party's return. After the calamity, at a moment which seems grotesquely inappropriate to Fielding, Godbole asks him whether he had visited any of the interesting Marabar antiquities and if he had seen the tank by the usual camping ground. On being told by a distracted Fielding that he had, Godbole is pleased and proceeds to relate the legend of the Tank of the Dagger, of how an evil act committed by a rajah was later expiated by the performance of a good one, winning him redemption. A ruined tank holding a little stagnant water reputedly built by the rajah to commemorate his salvation, symbolizes the affirmative stance of Brahmanical Hinduism to which Godbole adheres and measures his distance from the world-negating, value-annihilating outlook of Caves. Godbole's Ancient Night is the Vedic tradition of his Aryan ancestors who invaded Dravidian India and triumphed over the aboriginal religions, while absorbing aspects into their own developing philosophies.* As a devotee of *bhakti* yoga, the discipline or yoking of the mind to believing love, it is Godbole's ambition to reunite the Self with the Absolute through surrender to the Lord Krishna. This was the Brahmanical tradition with which Forster was familiar through his months in Dewas Senior,† and it is a creed within Hinduism which presents a powerful

* 'It was in the great paradoxes of the epoch-making *Bhagavad Gita* that the non-Brahmanical, pre-Aryan thought of aboriginal India became fruitfully combined and harmonized with the Vedic ideas of the Aryan invaders. In the eighteen brief chapters was displayed a kaleidoscopic interworking of the two traditions that for some ten centuries had been contending for the control and mastery of the Indian mind . . . the non-Aryan systems which included Jainism . . . were characterized by a resolutely logical, theoretical dichotomy, which insisted on a strict distinction between the two spheres, that of the life-monad . . . and that of matter . . . the pure and crystal-like immaterial essence of the pristine individual and the polluting, darkening principle of the material world. . . Contrast with this the vigorous, tumultuous, and joyous life-affirmative of the Vedic Hymn of Food. The new thing that the Brahmans brought to India was a jubilant, monistic emphasis on the sanctity of life: a powerful and persistent assertion that the One Thing is always present as two. "I am both," asserts the Lord of Food; "I am the two: the life-force and the life-material – the two at one."' Zimmer, *Philosophies of India*, pp. 378, 379–80. The *Bhagavad Gita* is the source of the Krishna-worship which Godbole follows.

† Forster, in *The Hill of Devi*, writes that, between them, the Maharajah of Dewas Senior and the Maharajah of Chhatarpur, who both followed the path of Krishna-worship, helped to illuminate Indian religion for him. A letter written from Dewas in 1913 explains the Maharajah's creed: 'He believes that we – men, birds, everything – are part of God, and that men have developed more than birds because they have come nearer to realising this. This isn't so difficult; but when I asked why we had any of us ever become severed from God, he explained it by God becoming unconscious that we were parts of him, owing to his energy at some time being concentrated elsewhere. . . Salvation . . . is the thrill which we feel when God again becomes conscious of us, and all our life we must train

antithesis to the voice of Caves. In 'Temple' there is a bursting of light, a flooding of noise, a joyous celebration of the Divine's all-inclusiveness which succeeds, but does not annihilate, the barren silence of Caves in which the soul spends its dark nights.

Temple : The Affirmative Stance of Hinduism

The world, in spite of its pain, is as it were enraptured by itself, and does not count the hurts that go with the procedure. . . Everything depends on where one puts the emphasis. That of the Hymn of Food [a Vedic Hymn] is on the dionysiac aspect of the world. A continuous blending and transformation of opposites through a relentless vital dynamism – even asking for pains, to balance and enhance the intensity of delight – goes spontaneously, powerfully, and joyously with this terrific Oriental acceptance of the whole dimension of the universe. And this wild affirmative is one that is eminently characteristic . . . of Hinduism.

Zimmer, *Philosophies of India*

Not you alone, proud truths of the world!
Nor you alone, ye facts of modern science!
But myths and fables of old – Asia's, Africa's fables!
The far-darting beams of the spirit! – the unloos'd dreams!
The deep diving bibles and legends;
The daring plots of the poets – the elder religions;
– O you temples fairer than lilies, pour'd over by the rising sun!
O you fables, spurning the known, eluding the hold of the
  known, mounting to heaven!

Walt Whitman, *Passage to India*, p. 350

our perceptions so that we may be capable of feeling when the time comes. . . I expect that as I have tried to describe it to you, this reads more like philosophy than religion, but it is inspired by his belief in a being who, though omnipresent, is personal, and whom he calls Krishna' (pp. 29, 30). During a Krishna conversation with the Maharajah of Chhatarpur in the same year, Forster asked if he could forget his troubles when he meditated: 'Oh, no, not at all, they come in with me always unless I can meditate on love, for love is the only power that can keep thought out. I try to meditate on Krishna. I do not know that he is a God, but I love Love and Beauty and Wisdom, and I find them in his history. I worship and adore him as a man. If he is divine he will notice me for it and reward me; if he is not, I shall become grass and dust like the others' (pp. 30–31). See also J. R. Ackerley, *Hindoo Holiday* (1952), for information on the Maharajah of Chhatarpur.

E. M. FORSTER: 'A PASSAGE TO INDIA'

I

On her last journey across India and to her death in India Mrs Moore had seen the life-loving, world-accepting Indian imagination in the creative works of her peoples, Hindu and Moslem:

> She watched the indestructible life of man and his changing faces, and the houses he has built for himself and God, and they appeared to her not in terms of her own trouble but as things to see... 'I have not seen the right places,' she thought... She would never visit Asirgarh or the other untouched places; neither Delhi nor Agra nor the Rajputana cities nor Kashmir, nor the obscurer marvels that had sometimes shone through men's speech: the bilingual rock of Girnar, the statue of Shri Belgola, the ruins of Mandu and Hampi, temples of Khajraha, gardens of Shalimar.[155]

After Caves and a fleeting respite in the Mediterranean clarity, the novel returns to India, and the Mediterranean interposes a standard of normality by which India's intricacies and extremities may be measured: 'When men leave that exquisite lake, whether through the Bosphorus or the Pillars of Hercules, they approach the monstrous and extraordinary; and the southern exit leads to the strangest experience of all.'[156] The dichotomies and contradictions of the universe, of man's nature and existence, are swallowed and digested by Hinduism's ecstatic affirmation that all share in the Divine, and in 'Temple' Forster shows Hinduism, which expresses a philosophy, a spiritual discipline and an attitude towards life, as a mirror-image of India, blending diversity, containing opposites and spanning a continuum from mud to mystery.

'Temple' opens with the celebration of Krishna's birth in the princely state of Mau, the festival of Gokul Ashtami* where every

---

* 'It is (or was) celebrated throughout India, often under the name of Jamnashtami – the Eight Days of the Birth. But I had never heard of it being celebrated so sumptuously. It had been appropriated and worked up by the Dewas dynasty.' *The Hill of Devi*, pp. 116–17. Forster explains that the literary authorities for the Krishna birth stories are the *Bhagavad Purana* and the *Vishnu Purana*. In *Sources of Indian Tradition*, V. Raghavan discusses the Purana of the Lord, *Bhagavata Purana*, which gained an extraordinary popularity within Hinduism: 'This Purana deals with the incarnations that the Lord repeatedly takes to restore the balance of values in the world, by putting down evil and reviving virtue. The book is noteworthy for its own unique way of dealing with

aesthetic presumption of the West is overturned, for without form
and despite disorder, there is beauty:

When the villagers broke cordon for a glimpse of the silver image, a
most beautiful and radiant expression came into their faces. . . They sang
not even to the God who confronted them, but to a saint; they did not
one thing which the non-Hindu would feel dramatically correct; this
approaching triumph of India was a muddle (as we call it), a frustration
of reason and form. Where was the God Himself, in whose honour the
congregation had gathered? Indistinguishable in the jumble of His own
altar, huddled out of sight amid images of inferior descent, smothered
under rose-leaves, overhung by oleographs, outblazed by golden tablets
representing the Rajah's ancestors, and entirely obscured, when the wind
blew, by the tattered foliage of a banana.[157]

In worshipping Krishna, the Hindus of Mau are following the
path of *bhakti* yoga, adoration and surrender to the Divine, a popular
religion in which music, dance and drama are an integral part of the
quest to unite with the Absolute conceived as the Lord of the Universe.* The symbols, emblems, imitations and substitutions of the
festival indicate the universal, all-inclusive and eternal qualities of God:
the chain of sacred sounds is kept unbroken; an inscription of God's
attributes appears in English, 'God si [sic] love'; tiny tazias from
the Moslem festival of Mohurram are dedicated; merry acts are performed – 'All spirit as well as all matter must participate in salvation,

the story of the Lord in His incarnation as Krishna and the ecstatic type of
devotion exemplified by the cowherd lasses (*gopis*) for the Lord. There is the
Supreme Being, the Brahman, of which the Personal God is a form assumed
freely for blessing the universe. That one omniscient, omnipotent God, transcendent as well as immanent, takes for the further benefit of humanity manifold
forms and incarnations through His mystic potency (*maya*)' (pp. 328–9).

* R. N. Dandekar, in *Sources of Indian Tradition*, shows how the teachings
of the *Bhagavad Gita*, the cornerstone of Krishna-worship, differ from the
Upanishads: 'Whereas the Vedic ritual practices were exclusive in character,
Krishna sponsors a way of spiritual life in which all can participate. It is the
yoga of devotion (*bhakti yoga*). . . This way of devotion presupposes the recognition of a personal god – in the present context, of course, Krishna himself
– who is regarded as being responsible for the creation, preservation, and
destruction of the universe. The devotee serves that God like a loyal servant,
always craving some kind of personal communion with Him' (pp. 281–2).

and if practical jokes are banned, the circle is incomplete'[158]* –
sensual joys are celebrated: 'It was their duty to play various games
to amuse the newly born God, and to simulate his sports with the
wanton dairymaids of Brindaban.'[159] A devotee praises God as she
apprehends Him without attributes: 'Others praised Him with†
attributes, seeing Him in this or that organ of the body or manifestation of the sky.'[160] The hills of Mau are covered with temples of over
two hundred gods, 'who visited each other constantly, and owned
numerous cows, and all the betal-leaf industry, besides having shares
in the Asirgarh motor omnibus'.[161]

At the height of the festival the Sweepers' Band arrives:

Playing on sieves and other emblems of their profession, they marched
straight at the gate of the palace with the air of a victorious army. All
other music was silent, for this was ritually the moment of the Despised
and the Rejected: the God could not issue from his temple until the unclean
Sweepers played their tune, they were the spot of filth without which the
spirit cannot cohere.[162]

When Professor Godbole is aspiring to a mystical union with the
Divine, he smears on his forehead a fragment of mud adhering to
one of His emblems, ceremonially acknowledging that they are one.
Hinduism embraces all of life for its adherents, the secular and the
sublime are intertwined, the whole universe and the entire man are
participants in the Absolute, and therefore the spectrum of experience known by the body, the senses and the mind can be brought
together and symbolically expressed: a Saivite temple invites to lust,
'but under semblance of eternity, its obscenities bearing no relation
to those of our flesh and blood'.[163] When God's birth is staged at the
climax of Gokul Ashtami, 'Infinite Love took upon itself the form
of SHRI KRISHNA, and saved the world. All sorrow was annihilated,
not only for Indians, but for foreigners, birds, caves, railways, and

* In *The Hill of Devi* Forster remarks on the gap in Christianity: 'the canonical
gospels do not record that Christ laughed or played. Can a man be perfect if
he never laughs or plays? Krishna's jokes may be vapid, but they bridge a gap'
(p. 119).

† This appears in all texts as 'without attributes'; given the context this is
surely a misprint. See Stallybrass, *op. cit.*, p. 154.

the stars; all became joy, all laughter; there had never been disease nor doubt, misunderstanding, cruelty, fear.'[164]

In contradistinction to the Christian conception of divine hospitality which assumes the need to 'exclude someone from our gathering, or we shall be left with nothing',[165] the Hindu tradition proclaims that salvation is open to all forms of existence, to plants, stones, the elements and even artefacts. If Forster chides the earnest missionaries for the entrance requirements they would impose on those seeking admission to the mansions of the Father's house, he recognizes that exclusion might be the price of certain forms of excellence and restrictions the cost of order: 'Trees of a poor quality bordered the road, indeed the whole scene was inferior, and suggested that the countryside was too vast to admit of excellence. In vain did each item in it call out, "Come, come." There was not enough god to go round.'[166] The reckless generosity of Hinduism requires a total emotional commitment of its participants and Forster makes a gasping withdrawal from the enormity of feeling and suffering which the Indian sensibility admits:

> How indeed is it possible for one human being to be sorry for all the sadness that meets him on the face of the earth, for the pain that is endured not only by men, but by animals and plants, and perhaps by the stones? The soul is tired in a moment, and in fear of losing the little she does understand, she retreats to the permanent lines which habit or chance have dictated, and suffers there.[167]

Forster both celebrates the indiscriminate opening of the gates of salvation and intimates the inevitability of their closing.

Less audacious than that furthest ambition postulated in the last period of Vedic thought by Sankara (who taught that it is man's purpose to attain 'the identity of the individual life-monad with Brahman, which is of the nature of pure consciousness or pure spirituality')[168]* *bhakti* yoga, an internal yoking of the mind to a

---

* Zimmer, *Philosophies of India*: 'the goal of the "Way of Devotion" (*bhakti-marga*) has to be transcended by the student of Vedanta. The loving union of the heart with its highest personal divinity is not enough. The sublime experience of the devotee beholding the inner vision of his God in concentrated absorption is only a prelude to the final ineffable crisis of complete illumination, beyond the spheres even of the divine form' (pp. 417–18).

divine principle, is nevertheless a spiritual and emotional discipline whose goal is to surmount the limitations of the egocentric awareness and to reach a state of superconsciousness beyond logic and sensory apprehensions. Thus can man realize the true dimensions of his Self in becoming reintegrated with the Brahman. The interrelated notion of the Self, the Atman, and the Brahman poses an idea of man's nature, potentialities and goals so remote from Western notions that, without an interpretation of its meaning, it is difficult to understand the antics of the seemingly quaint and opaque Professor Godbole, nor indeed of the peoples of Mau at prayer.

This is Zimmer's explanation of the Atman–Brahman conception:

> The supreme and characteristic achievement of the Brahman mind (and this has been decisive, not only for the course of Indian philosophy, but also for the history of Indian civilization) was its discovery of the Self (*atman*) as an independent, imperishable entity, underlying the conscious personality and the bodily frame. Everything that we normally know and express about ourselves belongs to the sphere of change, the sphere of time and space, but this Self (*atman*) is forever changeless, beyond time, beyond space and the veiling net of causality, beyond measure, beyond the dominion of the eye. The effort of Indian philosophy has been, for millenniums, to know this adamantine Self and to make the knowledge effective in human life. And this enduring concern is what has been responsible for the supreme morning calm that pervades the terrible histories of the Oriental world... Through the vicissitudes of physical change a spiritual footing is maintained in the peaceful-blissful ground of Atman; eternal, timeless, and imperishable Being... Brahman properly is that which lies beyond the sphere and reach of intellectual consciousness, in the dark, great, unmeasured zone of height beyond height, depth beyond depth. Brahman, then, the highest, deepest, final, transcendental power inhabiting the visible, tangible levels of our nature, transcends both the so-called 'gross body'... and the inner world of forms and experiences – the notions, ideas, thoughts, emotions, visions, fantasies, etc. – of the 'subtle body'... As the power that turns into and animates everything in the microcosm as well as in the outer world, it is the divine inmate of the mortal coil and is identical with the Self (*atman*).[169]

The rituals of Gokul Ashtami, the main event of the religious year, act on the Hindus of Mau as if to release them from imprisonment in their separate forms: 'The assembly was in a tender, happy state unknown to an English crowd, it seethed like a beneficent potion.'[170] When the villagers gaze on the sacred image of the Lord their faces take on an expression of beauty and radiance, 'a beauty in which there was nothing personal, for it caused them all to resemble one another during the moment of its indwelling, and only when it was withdrawn did they revert to individual clods'.[171] The effect of their participating in the worship of Krishna awakens in each one according to his capacity 'an emotion that he would not have had otherwise'.[172]

Appropriately, the inducement of rapture and the authority of ecstasy over the persons possessed is closely observed in the mystical experience of the Brahman Professor Godbole. The rhythm of the music invokes inner images for the worshippers who summon for a moment 'scraps of their past, tiny splinters of detail'[173] to be merged with the universal warmth:

Thus Godbole, though she was not important to him, remembered an old woman he had met in Chandrapore days. Chance brought her into his mind while it was in this heated state, he did not select her, she happened to occur among the throng of soliciting images, a tiny splinter, and he impelled her by his spiritual force to that place where completeness can be found. Completeness, not reconstruction. His senses grew thinner, he remembered a wasp seen he forgot where, perhaps on a stone. He loved the wasp equally, he impelled it likewise, he was imitating God. And the stone where the wasp clung – could he . . . no, he could not, he had been wrong to attempt the stone, logic and conscious effort had seduced, he came back to the strip of red carpet and discovered that he was dancing upon it.[174]*

* 'I have never seen religious ecstasy before and don't take to it more than I expected I should, but he [the Maharajah of Dewas] manages not to be absurd. Whereas the other groups of singers stand quiet, he is dancing all the time, like David before the ark, jigging up and down with a happy expression on his face, and twanging a stringed instrument that hangs by a scarf round his neck. At the end of his two hours he gets wound up and begins composing poetry . . . and yesterday he flung himself flat on his face on the carpet. Ten minutes afterwards I saw him as usual, in ordinary life. . . I cannot see the point of this, or rather in what it differs from ordinary mundane intoxication. I suppose that if you believe your drunkenness proceeds from heaven it becomes more enjoyable. Yet I am very much muddled in my own mind about it all, for H.H. has what one understands by the religious sense and it comes out all through his life.' *The*

Through religious ecstasy Professor Godbole develops once more the life of his spirit. Strange thoughts are evoked, and Godbole again sees Mrs Moore as if surrounded by forms of trouble:

> It was his duty, as it was his desire, to place himself in the position of the God and to love her, and to place himself in her position and to say to the God, 'Come, come, come, come.' This was all he could do. How inadequate! But each according to his own capacities, and he knew that his own were small. 'One old Englishwoman and one little, little wasp,' he thought. . . 'It does not seem much, still it is more than I am myself.'[175]

Godbole has attempted a passage to the core of his being in search of that essence lodged in man. All matter and all spirit share in the Divine but only man through discipline and exertion can realize the identity of the Atman–Brahman and experience his own fusion with the Absolute.

Forster in 'Temple' explores the pursuit of metaphysical revelations, but at the climactic moment, when Universal Love in the form of Krishna saves the world, the agnostic's cry for validation is heard:

> the human spirit had tried by a desperate contortion to ravish the unknown, flinging down science and history in the struggle, yes, beauty herself. Did it succeed? Books written afterwards say 'Yes.' But how, if there is such an event, can it be remembered afterwards? How can it be expressed in anything but itself? Not only from the unbeliever are mysteries hid, but the adept himself cannot retain them. He may think, if he chooses, that he has been with God, but as soon as he thinks it, it becomes history, and falls under the rules of time.[176]

What Forster has affirmed through Hinduism is the possibility of inducing intense awareness and comprehensions which are unrelated to experiences known through the rational consciousness and sensory organs, that is, mystical states which deviate from what is

---

Hill of Devi, p. 106. This extract is from a letter written during his months in Dewas Senior; when writing the book Forster asks further questions on the Maharajah's feelings when he danced before the altar: 'He felt as King David and other mystics have felt when they are in the mystic state. He presented well-known characteristics. He was convinced that he was in touch with the reality he called Krishna. And he was unconscious of the world around him... He was in an abnormal but recognisable state; psychologists have studied it.' *ibid.*, p. 115.

considered normal and open out new dimensions to the experiential range.*

II

The paradox of India's being is given a living form in the person of Professor Godbole. Even his appearance suggests the happy blending of opposites: 'He wore a turban that looked like pale purple macaroni, coat, waistcoat, dhoti, socks with clocks. The clocks matched the turban, and his whole appearance suggested harmony – as if he had reconciled the products of East and West, mental as well as physical, and could never be discomposed.'[177] Godbole is the product of an ancient religion and a petrified social order, the paradigm of a philosophical stance and the emissary of metaphysical forces. Aloof, tranquil and apparently remote from the complexities of the transient world – he can neither catch a train nor run a school – this enigmatic Deccani Brahman is not indifferent to human needs and mortal concerns. It is his way of interceding which departs radically from expected means. At Fielding's tea-party, when Ronny Heaslop's intrusion generates a sudden ugliness – Heaslop fuming, Aziz provocative, Miss Quested puzzled – Godbole observes all three, 'but with downcast eyes and hands folded, as if nothing was noticeable'.[178] Aware that evil is abroad, he acts by calling on Krishna to come and through his presence combat and dispel what can exist

* Mystical states brought about through the use of plants, and more recently chemicals and gases, approximate to those achieved through yogic practices. To take an example from an established authority, consider William James's account of the effects of inhaling nitrous oxide, which suggest how closely his sensations resemble those of a Hindu devotee knowing fusion with the Brahman: 'Depth beyond depth of truth seems revealed to the inhaler... Looking back on my experiences, they all converge toward a kind of insight to which I cannot help ascribing some metaphysical significance. The keynote of it is invariably a reconciliation. It is as if the opposites of the world, whose contradictoriness and conflict make all our difficulties and troubles, were melted into unity.' *The Varieties of Religious Experience*, pp. 373-4. In *Soma: Divine Mushroom of Immortality*, R. Gordon Wasson advances the hypothesis that Soma, the deified plant of the Vedic hymns, is the hallucinogenic fly-agaric mushroom: 'The fly-agaric appears to have given those who ate it (or drank its juice) a feeling of elation, of ecstasy, so powerful that they felt they were sharing, for the nonce, the life of the immortals.' The inference which Wasson draws is that 'a plant with properties that could be plausibly named the Herb of Immortality re-

only in his absence. For Godbole God expresses the whole of the universe and is the source of everything in the cosmos both benign and malevolent. Because man partakes in the divine essence, it is within his capacities to commit good and evil actions:

nothing can be performed in isolation. All perform a good action when one is performed, and when an evil action is performed, all perform it. They [good and evil] are not what we think them, they are what they are, and each of us has contributed to both. . . Good and evil are different, as their names imply. But, in my own humble opinion, they are both of them aspects of my Lord. He is present in the one, absent in the other, and the difference between presence and absence is great, as great as my feeble mind can grasp. Yet absence implies presence, absence is not non-existence, and we are therefore entitled to repeat, 'Come, come, come, come.'[179]

Godbole, who must eat apart from the outcastes, from all who are not Brahman, who must purge himself of their touch by bathing,

---

sponded to one of man's deepest desires in the early stages of his intellectual development. The superb fly-agaric gave him a glimpse of horizons beyond any that he knew in his harsh struggle for survival, of planes of existence far removed and above his daily round of besetting cares. It contributed to the shaping of his mythological world and his religious life' (pp. 209–10). Wasson suggests that Soma was known at first hand to the poets of the subtle and sophisticated Vedic hymns, people who had brought from their northern homeland a cult of the sacred fly-agaric; but as the Indo-Aryans spread out all over India supplies of the mushrooms, which grow only beneath pines, firs and birches, became un-available and the divine inebrient was reduced to a fading sacerdotal memory, in time sublimated as a moon god. 'The sublime adventure of religious contemplation, the mystical experience, which the priestly caste (and perhaps others) of the Indo-Aryans had known through the mediation of the fly-agaric, could now only be achieved through regulated austerity and mortification of the flesh, and the Hindus, who had known to the full the bliss that contemplation can give, made themselves the masters of those techniques' (p. 70). See also Wendy Doniger O'Flaherty, 'The Post-Vedic History of the Soma Plant', in Wasson's book: 'The history of the search for Soma is, properly, the history of Vedic studies in general, as the Soma sacrifice was the focal point of the Vedic religion. Indeed, if one accepts the point of view that the whole of Indian mystical practice from the Upanishads through the more mechanical methods of yoga is merely the attempt to recapture the vision granted by the Soma plant, then the nature of that vision – and of that plant – underlies the whole of Indian religion, and everything of a mystical nature within that religion is pertinent to the identity of the plant' (p. 95).

who lives within the sects and clans of Hinduism and observes its subtle network of social discrimination, responds warmly to Aziz's enlightened poem acclaiming internationality: 'Ah, that is bhakti; ah, my young friend, that is different and very good. Ah, India, who seems not to move, will go straight there while the other nations waste their time.'[180] Imitations and substitutions, rituals, ceremonials, symbolic acts, these speak of a philosophical and religious system which is rooted in and perpetuates an immobile society. Experimentation with the psyche, the pursuit of fusion with the One, these passages to self-transcendence short-circuit a scientific exploration of the material world and a systematic re-ordering of the natural and man-created environments. In rhythm with the movements of nature, tied to the soil, in accord with their social order, in harmony with God, the Hindus of Mau have avoided the dismemberment of personality and the moral confusions besetting modern urbanized man. But do they through the experiences they seek and the comprehensions which reach them totally fulfil their potentailities?

If Forster laments the loss of sustenance when men are separated from roots in nature, he makes no sentimental concessions to the natural order. This he shows to be benign and malevolent, able to inspire peace in the soul of man and at the same time a threat to his already tenuous command over his own existence:

It matters so little to the majority of living beings what the minority, that calls itself human, desires or decides. Most of the inhabitants of India do not mind how India is governed. Nor are the lower animals of England concerned about England, but in the tropics the indifference is more prominent, the inarticulate world is closer at hand and readier to resume control as soon as men are tired.[181]

Hinduism lies at the heart of India because it is appropriate to agriculture and has accommodated to nature, but it is also the outcome of interferences with the natural order, of rejecting her domination, and providing for its adherents a faith, a life-style and a complex of social institutions. The entire Hindu community of Mau joins together in celebrating the birth of Krishna: 'Hindus, Hindus only, mild-featured men, mostly villagers, for whom anything outside their village passed in a dream. They were the toiling ryot, whom some call the real India. Mixed with them sat a few tradesmen out of the little town, officials, courtiers, scions of the ruling house.'[182]

Do such harmony, confinement and inertia have as high a price as that paid by men of industrialized societies in the attenuation of their personalities?* When Forster approaches India as a social entity he does in fact refer to her poverty and the circles of her humanity 'grading and drifting beyond the educated vision'.[183] Through the metaphors of dust and mud both the people's closeness to their soil and the punishments which nature and society inflict on them are made vivid: the inhabitants of Chandrapore appear as mud moving; the villagers of the Marabars seem to be the scurf of life, the Hindus of Mau resemble clods. Yet even within a social order so apparently unchanging, so securely static, there are portents of change: the Indian crowds who apparently have no identity distinct from their natural and religious environment disclose a will to defy their situation – during Aziz's trial the moving mud is stirred to anger and the Sweepers go on strike leaving the commodes of Chandrapore unattended: 'A new spirit seemed abroad, a rearrangement, which no one in the stern little band of whites could explain.'[184] Perhaps unchanging India is in flux – a little group of Indian ladies attend the 'bridge-party': 'The sight was significant: an island bared by the turning tide, and bound to grow';[185] on the Maidan of

* It is interesting to compare Forster's remarks in an essay 'Art For Art's Sake', *Two Cheers For Democracy* – 'How can man get into harmony with his surroundings when he is constantly altering them? The future of our race is, in this direction, more unpleasant than we care to admit, and it has sometimes seemed to me that its best chance lies through apathy, uninventiveness and inertia' (p. 100) – with those of Rabindranath Tagore who well knew the outcome of such a chance: 'How is it possible for men to live in such unlovely, unhealthy, squalid, neglected surroundings? The fact is we are so used to bear everything hands down – the ravages of Nature, the oppression of rulers, the pressures of our Shastras [religious injunctions] to which we have not a word to say while they keep eternally grinding us down.' *Glimpses of Bengal: Selected from the Letters of Sir Rabindranath Tagore, 1885–1895* (1921), p. 133. In *Appearances: Being Notes of Travel* (1914), Goldsworthy Lowes Dickinson described Indians as 'patient, beautiful people who labour without hope, while universal Nature, symbolised by Shiva's foot, presses heavily on their heads, and forbids them the stature of men' (p. 10).

Chandrapore some bazaar youths, weedy and knock-kneed, are training: 'Training for what?'[186]* Perhaps Hinduism, which has grown through absorbing the customs and beliefs of the indigenous peoples and cushioning the onslaught of invaders by subtly altering their influences, perhaps Hinduism will also accommodate the changes demanded by the modern world.

All the attributes of India and all her enigmas are embraced by Hinduism and the contradictions and resolutions, the muddles and the triumphs of the hundred Indias are symbolically posed and ritually enacted in Temple. It is as if India through her very nature and existence presented the challenge that truth is not a monolith, that reality is not a fixed quantity but a dialectical process, and Hinduism has accepted the validity of such claims. Just as good and evil are acknowledged by Hinduism as being aspects of the Absolute, so are Mosque, Caves and Temple accommodated as facets of the One reality:

The secret of Maya is this identity of opposites. Maya is a simultaneous and successive manifestation of energies that are at variance with each other, processes contradicting and annihilating each other: creation *and* destruction, evolution *and* dissolution, the dream-idyll of the inward vision of the god *and* the desolate nought, the terror of the void, the dread infinite. Maya is the whole cycle of the year, generating everything *and* taking it away. This 'and' uniting incompatibles, expresses the fundamental character of the Highest Being who is Lord and Wielder of Maya, whose energy is Maya. Opposites are fundamentally of the one essence.[187]

Yet, just as Professor Godbole welcomes the abstraction of internationality while rigorously observing caste restrictions, so does Hinduism implore fusion without being able to effect it. Hinduism remains the expression of a magnificent ambition, an emblem of 'a passage not easy, not now, not here, not to be apprehended except when it is unattainable'.[188] If the divisions of daily life are to be

* In 'India Again' (1946), *Two Cheers For Democracy*, written after a visit to India in 1945, Forster records his impressions and sensations of India as he then experienced it: 'There is still poverty, and, since I am older today and more thoughtful, it is the poverty, the malnutrition, which persists like a ground-swell beneath the pleasant froth of my immediate experience. I do not know what political solution is correct. But I do know that people ought not to be so poor and to look so ill' (p. 328).

obliterated, if Universal Love is to be realized, then man will have to make a voyage out to join with other men beyond creeds and nations, as well as the journey inwards in search of his share in the cosmic essence.

Conclusions : Passage to More than India

Passage to more than India!
Are thy wings plumed indeed for such far flights?
O Soul, voyagest thou indeed on voyages like these? ...
Sail forth! steer for the deep waters only!
Reckless, O soul, exploring, I with thee, and thou with me;
For we are bound where mariner has not yet dared to go,
And we will risk the ship, ourselves and all.

Walt Whitman, *Passage to India*

Just as the air of Mau is thick with religion and rain, so are the last pages of *A Passage to India* thick with symbols and omens of reconciliation, fertilization and salvation, and of their opposites, divisions, death and annihilated human hopes. Nature and artefacts intercede to proclaim Infinite Love and universal redemption, and to prophesy that these are unattainable. Mosque was watched over by the moon, Caves retreated from the demolishing force of the sun, and Temple is bathed in water, the Indian symbol both of the source and sustainer of life and of the dreaded grave.* The Indian awareness of a self-generating, self-destroying cosmos, sustained by an endless

---

* Zimmer, in *Myths and Symbols*, points to the dual import of the images: 'In this Indian conception of the process of destruction, the regular course of the Indian year – fierce heat and drought alternating with torrential rains – is magnified to such a degree that instead of sustaining, it demolishes existence. The warmth that normally ripens and moisture that nourishes, when alternating in beneficent co-operation, now annihilate.' Vishnu in the form of a cloud sheds torrential rains to quench the burning earth, which is destroyed and taken back 'into the primal ocean from which it arose at the universal dawn. The fecund-water-womb receives again into itself the ashes of all creation. The ultimate elements melt into the undifferentiated fluid out of which they once arose. The moon, the stars, dissolve' (pp. 36, 37). This is the night of Brahma, to be followed by the irreversible passage of the universe reborn, deteriorating, disintegrating and then annihilated, only to be born again, a cycle conceived as a biological process. For an illuminating discussion of the latent mythology in *A Passage to India*, see Stone, *op. cit.*, pp. 311–17.

cycle of things new-born, decaying and dying, enters the novel as the heart-beat of its existence. As with the circulation of Aziz's emotions, 'Nothing stayed, nothing passed that did not return',[189] everything is conceived as in flux, sometimes imperceptible as in the geological evolution of India, sometimes visual as in the contours of Chandrapore, the Marabars and India itself which swell and shrink, rise and fall. Here, in 'Temple', the cycle is telescoped; the season of monsoon both promises new birth and augurs a time for dying – Stella Fielding has conceived and the Rajah of Mau has died.

Krishna is born in the pouring wet morning; Aziz recognizes his Indian identity as he stands in the rain; lakes appear in the countryside around Mau; the sky is filled with bellyfuls of rain, the earth is pocked with pools of water, and the great Mau tank is full. When Fielding and Aziz meet again in Mau both are wary and belligerent and Fielding demands of Aziz why he had not answered his letters, 'going straight to the point, but not reaching it, owing to buckets of rain'.[190] Mistaking Ralph Moore for Adela Quested's brother, Aziz is aggressive: ' "I'm only Ralph Moore," said the boy, blushing, and at that moment there fell another pailful of the rain, and made a mist around their feet.'[191] These portents of peace and emblems of concord emanate from the deities summoned by the Hindus, from Krishna the Lord of the Universe and from the newly assimilated lesser goddess, Esmiss Esmoor. God is born. Infinite Love in the form of Krishna issues from His Temple carried in a palanquin, and escorted by the whole power of the state of Mau proceeds to the jail there to free one prisoner as a token of His will to save the whole world. As the guns go off signalling the ceremonial release of the prisoner, Aziz's harsh words to Ralph Moore – 'No, of course, your great friend Miss Quested did me no harm at the Marabar'[192] – are drowned. 'It was the halfway moment; God had extended His temple, and paused exultantly. Mixed and confused in their passage, the rumours of salvation entered the Guest House.'[193] Here they are heard by Aziz and Ralph Moore, and as Aziz listens to the choir reiterating and inverting the names of the deities, Radhakrishna, Krishnaradha, he is moved beyond anger, takes Ralph out in a boat on the Mau tank to witness the procession and in the interstices of the chanting hears again Mrs Moore's name, Esmiss Esmoor, and knows that she had saved him at his trial. Into the dark waters of the tank, in the midst of a storm, the substitute image of God is ritually thrown, just as He was thrown year after year, signalling the closing of the gates of salvation. As this ceremony is enacted, the boat rowed by Aziz collides with that of Fielding and his wife Stella Moore: 'The shock was minute, but Stella, nearest to it, shrank into her husband's arms, then reached forward, then flung herself against Aziz, and her motions capsized them.'[194] After this symbolic immersion in the waters of Mau Aziz and Fielding recapture their old relationship and at their final meeting – 'myriads of kisses around them as the earth drew the water in'[195] – Aziz speaks of his wish to do kind actions and wipe out for ever the wretched business of the Marabar and Fielding tells him that Stella, who has found in Hinduism 'some solution of her queer troubles',[196] believes too that the Marabars have been wiped out.

But emblems finally are only emblems; rituals can appease longings and symbols can presage possibilities, but they cannot eliminate barriers, desolation or despair. Temple has vanquished Caves but the Marabars have not been wiped out, and omens of doom appear together with those of promise. The scenery through which Aziz and Fielding ride, though it smiled, 'fell like a gravestone on any human hope. . . They splashed through butterflies and frogs; great trees with leaves like plates rose among the brushwood. The divisions of daily life were returning, the shrine had almost shut.'[197] Ralph and Stella Moore, who as Mrs Moore's children incarnate her redemptive powers and stand for love and reconciliation, are also Ronny Heaslop's half-brother and half-sister, and through him are related to the exclusiveness and brutality of Anglo-India. The separations persist, communities which provide the base and security for man's endeavours are also prisons and fortresses. Were Godbole again to sing his haunting invocation to Krishna, only the Hindu servants would understand it; when Englishmen go to bed, those who wake up are still 'people whose emotions they could not share, and whose existence they ignored'.[198] That is why the passage inwards to the hidden mind and the silenced psyche must be accompanied by a passage outwards to understanding and empathizing with versions of human nature and forms of society different from those within which the individual has developed. If Aziz and Fielding cannot yet be friends, this is because men have failed to consummate either journey.

Essentially a speculative novel, *A Passage to India* explores means and assesses ends but is silent about the consummation of goals. It intimates illimitable desires and recognizes, indeed even protests, the limitations ordained by man's estate. 'There was death in the air, but not sadness; a compromise had been made between destiny and desire, and even the heart of man acquiesced.'[199] Expectations bring disappointments in their wake; invitations are met with rejections, conquests are not crowned, disillusion follows victory. The visitors to the Marabars await the miracle of dawn: 'But at the supreme moment, when night should have died and day lived, nothing occurred. It was as if virtue had failed in the celestial fount... The sun rose without splendour.'[200] The Hindus celebrate the birth of God but the longing for miracles is unassuaged: 'The revelation was over, but its effect lasted, and its effect was to make men feel that the revelation has not yet come. Hope existed despite fulfilment, as it will be in heaven.'[201] The scapegoats and husks, thrown into the waters with the substitute image of God, are emblems of 'a passage not easy, not now, not here, not to be apprehended except when it is unattainable'.[202] The earth and sky reflected in the Mau tank which seem about to clash in ecstasy finally intrude as portents of separation. Aziz promises that one day he and Fielding shall be friends; meanwhile Fielding's plea that they be friends now is answered by nature, beasts and the works of man who join in proclaiming that fusion cannot be accomplished at that time nor in that place:

But the horses didn't want it – they swerved apart; the earth didn't want it, sending up rocks through which the riders must pass single file; the temples, the tank, the jail, the palace, the birds, the carrion, the Guest House, they came into view as they issued from the gap and saw Mau beneath; they didn't want it, they said in their hundred voices, 'No, not yet,' and the sky said, 'No, not there.'[203]*

* White, *op. cit.*, describes the festival celebrating God's birth as a prophetic vision: 'for what happens in "Temple" is reconciliation on the human level, the cancelling of the effects of the Marabar. Reconciliation, not real union; that is not possible on earth, whatever may be the truth about that universe of which earth is only an atom. The hundred voices of India say, "No, not yet," and the sky says, "No, not there"... But the most painful human differences are soothed'

A Passage to India is a vision of existence which assesses what man appears to be and asserts what he might become and it is a vision rooted in those concentrated moments of extraordinary and illuminating experience which focus man's true experiential range and capacities. Forster has reached to communicate the ineffable, to intimate mystery as an inexpressible quality which makes itself known to men but remains unknowable. 'Mrs Moore shivered. "A ghost!" But the idea of a ghost scarcely passed her lips. The young people did not take it up, being occupied with their own outlooks, and deprived of support it perished, or was reabsorbed into the part of the mind that seldom speaks.'[204] Adela Quested suggests that telepathy enabled Mrs Moore to know what had happened in the cave, and the 'pert, meagre word fell to the ground'.[205] Fielding struggles to tell Aziz about the liking Stella and Ralph Moore have for Hinduism, 'I can't explain, because it isn't in words at all'.[206] The accretions which words have gathered make them insensitive transmitters of sensations so elusive yet momentous and to state explicitly that which isn't in words at all is to risk misconstruction, a peril which Forster almost entirely avoids, although phrases such as 'syllables of salvation' and 'Something – not a sight, but a sound flitted past him'[207] are open to interpretations critically different from that which the total text supports.

Through India Forster's imagination followed those paths which the human mind and spirit can travel to destinations the contemporary Western sensibility did not acknowledge as attainable or worth reaching. His mediation of those evanescent but intensely living experiences when man's imagination breaks through the crust of automatic perceptions to comprehend as a revelation his own essential being as identical with the One, be it humanity, the universe or a divinity, restores to them that reality which modern civilization would deny.

(p. 652). See, too, V. A. Shahane, 'Symbolism in *A Passage to India*: "Temple"', reprinted from *English Studies*, December 1963, in his *Perspectives on E. M. Forster's 'A Passage to India'*, who concludes that the effects of the episodes in 'Temple' are not everlasting. 'Other elements of actualities of existence intervene.' But the end of the novel is not defeatist, since it shows Forster as a moral realist: 'His key symbols visualise what life ought to be, his social comedy modifies the conceptual vision and shows what life really is' (p. 150).

References

INTRODUCTION

1. O. Mannoni, *Prospero and Caliban: The Psychology of Colonization* (1956), p. 23.
2. Jawaharlal Nehru, *An Autobiography* (1936), p. 428.
3. Rudyard Kipling, 'A Song of the English', *Rudyard Kipling's Verse* (1885–1918), p. 194.
4. *ibid.*
5. See Bhupal Singh, *A Survey of Anglo-Indian Fiction* (1934).
6. For an analysis of themes in British fiction about India, see Allen J. Greenberger, *The British Image of India: A Study in the Literature of Imperialism, 1880–1960* (1969).

CHAPTER 1: *The British–Indian Encounter*

1. Opinion on the economic advantages which the British derived from her Indian Empire is divided. For a recent sceptical assessment, see Max Beloff, *Imperial Sunset*, Vol. I: *Britain's Liberal Empire, 1897–1921* (1969), pp. 31–2.
2. See A. K. Cairncross, *Home and Foreign Investment, 1870–1913: Studies in Capital Accumulation* (1953), p. 183.
3. Sarvepalli Gopal, *Modern India* (1967), p. 7.
4. Vera Anstey, *The Economic Development of India* (1929) (ref. to revised 1957 edn), pp. 62–5.
5. N. V. Sovani, 'The British Impact on India', *Journal of World History*, Vol. I, No. 4, 1955 and Vol. II, No. 1, 1956.
6. For an analysis of the evolution of British thinking about India, see Francis G. Hutchins, *The Illusion of Permanence: British Imperialism in India* (1967).
7. For an analysis of agrarian policy and its effects, see T. R. Metcalf, 'The British and the Moneylenders in Nineteenth Century India', *Journal of Modern History*, Vol. XXXIV, No. 4, 1962.
8. Raghavan Iyer, 'Utilitarianism and All That: The Political Theory of British Imperialism in India', *St Antony's Papers*, No. 8, 1960, *South Asian Affairs*, No. 1.
9. *ibid.*, p. 57.
10. 'The Foundations of the Government of India', *The Nineteenth Century*, Vol. LXXX, 1883, p. 566.

11. Sir John Strachey, *India: Its Administration and Progress* (1888) (ref. to 1911 edn), pp. 189, 432.

12. Sir Alfred Lyall, *The Rise and Expansion of British Dominion in India* (1894) (ref. to 1920 edn), p. 354.

13. Lord Roberts of Kandahar, *Forty-One Years in India* (1897) (ref. to 1901 edn), p. 251.

14. See A. P. Thornton, *The Imperial Idea and Its Enemies* (1959).

15. See Hannah Arendt, *The Origins of Totalitarianism* (1951).

16. Quoted in George Bennett, *The Concept of Empire* (1953), p. 315.

17. Sir Lepel Griffin, 'Indian Princes at Home', *Fortnightly Review*, Vol. XXXIV, 1883, p. 495.

18. Sir Richard Temple, *Men and Events in My Time in India* (1882), p. 494.

19. Sir Andrew H. L. Fraser, *Among Rajahs and Ryots* (1911), pp. 270, 271.

20. *Indian Planter's Gazette and Sporting News*, 8 September 1885, pp. 218–19; 3 August 1886, p. 11.

21. Jubilee Pamphlet of the *Englishman*, 20 February 1887.

22. S. R. Mehrotra, *India and the Commonwealth, 1885–1929* (1965), p. 37. I have followed Mehrotra's lucid account and analysis of the Congress struggle and the British response during these years.

23. Quoted by Mehrotra, *ibid.*, p. 35. An important aspect of Mehrotra's argument is that British policy towards the development of nationalism had not been thought out in fundamental terms.

24. *ibid.*, p. 47.

25. Quoted in *ibid.*, p. 76.

26. Quoted in *ibid.*, p. 103.

27. Ravindar Kumar, 'Liberalism and Reform in India', *Journal of World History*, Vol. VII, No. 4, 1963, pp. 909–10.

28. Fraser, *op. cit.*, p. 311.

29. Sir Michael O'Dwyer, *India As I Knew It* (1925).

30. Sir Evan Maconochie, *Life in the Indian Civil Service* (1926), p. 2.

31. *ibid.*, p. 249.

32. Sir Walter Lawrence, *The India We Served* (1928), p. 122.

33. Al. Carthill, *The Lost Dominion* (1924), p. 88.

34. *ibid.*, p. 236.

35. Sir Walter Lawrence, 'The Indian Civil Service', in *Fifty Years* (1932), p. 167.

36. Dennis Kincaid, *British Social Life in India, 1608–1937* (1938), p. 279.

37. L. S. S. O'Malley, *The Indian Civil Service* (1931); Sir Edward Blunt, *The Indian Civil Service* (1937).

38. Philip Mason, *The Men who Ruled India* (1953–4). This work appeared under Mason's pen-name, Woodruff. For another recent account which focuses on the disinterested services performed by the I.C.S., see Maurice and Taya Zinkin, *Britain and India: Requiem for Empire* (1964). Zinkin was a member of the I.C.S.

39. Mannoni, *op. cit.*, Foreword, pp. 11–12.
40. Leonard Woolf, *Autobiography, Vol. II: Growing* (1961), p. 111.
41. *ibid.*, pp. 113–14.
42. *ibid.*, p. 48.
43. George Orwell, 'Shooting an Elephant' (1936), *Selected Essays* (1957), pp. 91, 95.
44. See *Statesman's Year Book* (1914), p. 130. The figures of the 1911 Census list the total number of European males as 143,974 and females as 55,862. See *Statistical Abstract Relating to British India, 1908-9 and 1918-19*, Cmd 725, p. 7.
45. A. Claude Brown, *The Ordinary Man's India* (1927), pp. 21, 23.
46. Michael Malim, *The Pagoda Tree* (1963), p. 58.
47. Barbara Wingfield-Stratford, *India and the English* (1922).
48. See Private Frank Richards, *Old Soldier Sahib* (1936). Richards joined the Army in 1900, was drafted to India in 1902 and spent six and a half years in the East.
49. Sir Edward Wakefield, *Past Imperative: My Life in India, 1927–1947* (1966), p. 2.
50. Fraser, *op. cit.*, p. 360.
51. Lawrence, *The India We Served*, p. 82.
52. See Bernard S. Cohn, 'The British in Benares: A Nineteenth Century Colonial Society', *Comparative Studies in Society and History*, Vol. VI, 1961-2, pp. 169–99. See also R. Pearson, *Eastern Interlude: A Social History of the European Community in Calcutta* (1930).
53. Colin Cross, *The Fall of the British Empire, 1918–1968* (1968), p. 51.
54. O. Douglas, *Olivia in India* (1913), pp. 80–81.
55. Sir Malcolm Darling, *Apprenticeship to Power: India, 1904–1908* (1966), p. 98.
56. For a dictionary of the patois evolved by the British in India, see *Hobson-Jobson: A Glossary of Anglo-Indian Colloquial Words and Phrases*, by Henry Yule and A. C. Burnell, first published 1886, edited by William Crooke in 1902, reprinted 1968.
57. Michael Edwardes, *Bound to Exile: The Victorians in India* (1969), p. 23. For an account of British social life in India during an earlier period, see Percival Spear, *The Nabobs: A Study of the Social Life of the English in Eighteenth Century India* (1932).
58. Edwardes, *op. cit.*, p. 38.
59. *ibid.*, p. 64.
60. *ibid.*, p. 65.
61. Kincaid, *op. cit.*, p. 244.
62. Maud Diver, *The Englishwoman In India* (1909), p. 36.
63. Douglas, *op. cit.*, p. 69.
64. *ibid.*
65. *Indian Planter's Gazette*, 1 September 1885, pp. 198–9.

66. Blunt, *op. cit.*, p. 202.

67. Diver, *op. cit.*, p. 33.

68. Major-General L. C. Dunsterville, *Stalky's Reminiscences* (1929), p. 115.

69. Sir Robert Baden-Powell, *Indian Memoirs: Recollections of Soldiering, Sport etc.* (1915).

70. Diver, *op. cit.*, p. 129.

71. Wakefield, *op. cit.*, p. 154.

72. Dunsterville, *op. cit.*, p. 119.

73. Baden-Powell, *op. cit.*, p. 93.

74. Alan Butterworth, *The Southlands of Siva: Some Reminiscences of Life in Southern India* (1923), pp. 6, 116, 209.

75. Robert Wallace, *Contemporary Review*, Vol. LXXV, June 1899.

76. N. Macnicol, 'The Future of India', *Contemporary Review*, Vol. XCIV, July 1908, p. 76.

77. Reginald Reynolds, *The White Sahibs in India* (1937).

78. H. N. Brailsford, *Subject India* (1941), pp. 34-5.

79. *ibid.*, p. 36.

80. *ibid.*, p. 34.

81. Wingfield-Stratford, *op. cit.*, p. 40.

82. *ibid.*, p. 221.

83. Diver, *op. cit.*, pp. 87-8.

84. Quoted in F. H. Skrine, *The Life of Sir William Wilson Hunter* (1901), pp. 382-3. The review appeared in *The Academy*, September 1888.

85. R. D. Osborn, 'Representative Government for India', *Contemporary Review*, Vol. LXII, December 1882, pp. 931, 953.

86. Quoted in Lord Beveridge's biography of his parents, Henry and Annette Beveridge, *India Called Them* (1947), p. 96.

87. *ibid.*, p. 44, quoted from 'Christianity in India', *The Theological Review*, October 1869.

88. *ibid.*, p. 251.

89. 'The Anglo-Indian Creed', *Contemporary Review*, Vol. LXXVI, August 1899.

90. W. Bonnar, 'The English in India', *Contemporary Review*, Vol. LXVIII, October 1895.

91. J. Chartres Molony, *A Book of South India* (1926), pp. 59-60.

92. Darling, *op. cit.*, p. 118.

93. Sir Henry Cotton, *Indian and Home Memoirs* (1911).

94. *ibid.*, p. 269.

95. *ibid.*, p. 258.

96. Baden-Powell, *op. cit.*, p. 17.

97. Maconochie, *op. cit.*, p. 250.

98. *Lord Curzon in India: Being a Selection from his Speeches as Viceroy and Governor-General of India, 1898–1905* (1906), p. 491.

99. Beveridge, *op. cit.*, p. 99.

100. Chartres Molony, *op. cit.*, pp. 66–7, 114.
101. Kincaid, *op. cit.*, p. 254.
102. Chartres Molony, *op. cit.*, p. 88.
103. John Morris, *Eating the Indian Air: Memories and Present Day Impressions* (1968), pp. 14–15.
104. O'Dwyer, *op. cit.*, p. 451.
105. Lawrence, *The India We Served*, pp. 68, 70, 276.
106. *ibid.*, p. 100.
107. R. Carstairs, *The Little World of an Indian District Officer* (1912), p. 92.
108. *ibid.*, pp. 50, 52.
109. See Fraser, *op. cit.*; also Sir Valentine Chirol, *India* (1926), p. 111. Chirol, author and journalist, reported on India for *The Times* on numerous occasions.
110. *The Civilian's South India* (1921).
111. Brown, *op. cit.*, pp. 144, 193.
112. *ibid.*, p. 193.
113. O'Dwyer, *op. cit.*, pp. 113–14.
114. J. R. Ackerley, *Hindoo Holiday: An Indian Journal* (1932/52), p. 22.
115. Baden-Powell, *op. cit.*, p. 257.
116. Butterworth, *op. cit.*, p. 239.
117. Martin Gilbert, *Servant of India: A Study of Imperial Rule from 1905 to 1910 as told through the correspondence and diaries of Sir James Dunlop Smith* (1966), p. 37. Smith went to India in 1878 as a soldier and served both in a military and civilian capacity in the Punjab and the Native States for twenty-two years.
118. J. Campbell Oman, *The Brahmans, Theists and Muslims of India* (1907), p. 236.
119. Mason, *op. cit.*, Vol. 2, p. 76.
120. *ibid.*, pp. 172–3.
121. See Chapter 7 below.
122. 'Notes on the Interaction of English and Indian Thought in the Nineteenth Century', *Journal of World History*, Vol. IV, No. 4, 1958, p. 833. Pocock's concern in this article is with the Indian side of the relationship and the English inheritance while stated is not developed.
123. 'The Historical Context of Encounters Between Asia and Europe' in *The Glass Curtain Between Asia and Europe: A Symposium on the Historical Encounters and the Changing Attitudes of the Peoples of the East and the West*, ed. Raghavan Iyer (1965), pp. 48–9.
124. See Michael Edwardes, *British India, 1772–1947: A Survey of the Nature and Effects of Alien Rule* (1967), who considers that 'the influence of things Indian on Europeans, and in particular, British life seems very small for so long a connection' (p. 312).
125. Review of Anglo-Indian novels, entitled 'The Romance of India', *Quarterly Review*, Vol. CXCVI, July 1902, pp. 50, 51.

126. Kumar, *op. cit.*, argues that the policy-makers and administrators did not necessarily understand the core and ramifications of the structure on which they were imposing change. See also, T. R. Metcalf, *op. cit.*, and S. P. Sen, 'Effects on India of British Law and Administration in the Nineteenth Century', *Journal of World History*, Vol. IV, No. 4, 1958.

127. Sir Alfred Lyall, *Asiatic Studies* (1882; revised edn, 1907).

128. Oman, *op. cit.*, p. 271.

129. *ibid.*, pp. 16, 22.

130. Heinrich Zimmer, *Myths and Symbols in Indian Art and Civilization* (1946; ref. to 1962 edn), p. 215.

131. Louis Dumont, 'Introductory Note: Change, Interaction and Comparison', *Contributions to Indian Sociology*, No. VII, March 1964, p. 16. In this connexion, note the information provided by G. M. Carstairs in his Introduction to *The Twice-Born: A Study of a Community of High-Caste Hindus* (1957), where he states the salient facts of his background and beliefs: 'the bulk of my data consists in the record of conversations with my informants; and what emerges in these exchanges was a function of my personality as well as theirs. In this circumstance, to claim personal objectivity of observations would be unwarranted' (p. 17).

132. Edward Hyams, 'Problems of Communication', *New Statesman*, 2 February 1968, p. 148.

133. Goldsworthy Lowes Dickinson, *An Essay on the Civilisations of India, China and Japan* (1914), p. 12.

134. *ibid.*, p. 40.

135. *ibid.*, p. 16.

136. V. S. Naipaul, *An Area of Darkness: An Experience of India* (1964). Naipaul's Brahman grandparents had emigrated from India to Trinidad and this book is an account of his first visit to India.

137. Sasthi Brata, *My God Died Young* (1968).

138. Dom Moraes, *My Son's Father: An Autobiography* (1968).

139. Nirad C. Chaudhuri, *The Continent of Circe: An Essay on the Peoples of India* (1965), p. 94.

140. See G. T. Garratt, *An Indian Commentary* (1928).

141. Oman, *op. cit.*, pp. 243, 246–7.

142. Sir George MacMunn, *The Underworld of India* (1932), p. 27.

143. *ibid.*, p. 96.

144. *ibid.*, p. 97.

145. *ibid.*, p. 199.

146. *ibid.*, p. 201.

147. *ibid.*, p. 202.

148. *ibid.*, pp. 202, 203–4.

149. Katherine Mayo, *Mother India* (1927), p. 29. In 1929 a further work by Miss Mayo also purporting to be an exposure of Hinduism was published, *Slaves of the Gods*.

150. Douglas, *op. cit.*, pp. 83, 95.
151. Diver, *op. cit.*, p. 5.
152. *ibid.*, p. 74.
153. *ibid.*, p. 75.
154. *ibid.*, p. 82.
155. Maconochie, *op. cit.*, p. 6.
156. Leonard Handley, *Time's Delinquency* (1935). It has not been possible to locate biographical information on Handley other than that which he provides incidentally in the book; from this it appears that he served in the Indian Army.
157. Lawrence, *The India We Served*, pp. 42, 43.
158. Jon and Rumer Godden, *Two Under the Indian Sun* (1966), pp. 73, 81.
159. Jawaharlal Nehru, *The Discovery of India* (1946), pp. 30, 37–8, 485.
160. Zimmer, *op. cit.*, pp. 12, 18–19.
161. 'India: What Can it Teach Us?', *Edinburgh Review*, Vol. CLXI, April 1885, p. 491.
162. Heinrich Zimmer, *Philosophies of India*, ed. Joseph Campbell (1952; ref. to 1967 edn), p. 4.

CHAPTER 2: *The Romancers: Five Lady Novelists*

1. Mannoni, *op. cit.*, p. 200.
2. Fanny Penny, *Caste and Creed* (1890; ref. to 1906 edn), p. 192.
3. *ibid.*, p. 193.
4. *ibid.*
5. *ibid.*, p. 199.
6. Fanny Penny, *The Swami's Curse* (1929), p. 47.
7. *ibid.*, p. 48.
8. *ibid.*, p. 62.
9. *ibid.*, pp. 61–2.
10. *ibid.*, p. 11.
11. *ibid.*, p. 40.
12. *ibid.*, p. 279.
13. *ibid.*, p. 267.
14. Alice Perrin, *East of Suez* (1901; ref. to 1926 edn), p. 107.
15. *ibid.*, p. 111.
16. *ibid.*
17. B. M. Croker, *A Family Likeness: A Sketch in the Himalayas* (1901; ref. to undated edn), p. 205.
18. *ibid.*, p. 215.
19. *ibid.*
20. Alice Perrin, *The Anglo-Indians* (1912), p. 271.
21. Alice Perrin, *The Stronger Claim* (1903; ref. to 1925 edn), p. 142.
22. *ibid.*, p. 245.
23. *ibid.*, p. 251.

24. *The Stronger Claim*, p. 159.
25. *ibid.*, p. 240.
26. B. M. Croker, *The Company Servant: A Romance of Southern India* (1907), p. 127.
27. Penny, *The Swami's Curse*, p. 8.
28. Maud Diver, *Lilamani* (1910; ref. to 1935 edn), pp. 130–31.
29. *ibid.*, p. 133.
30. *ibid.*
31. *ibid.*, p. 254.
32. *ibid.*, p. 339.
33. Maud Diver, *Far to Seek* (1920; ref. to 1921 edn), p. 298.
34. *ibid.*
35. I. A. R. Wylie, *The Daughter of Brahma* (1912), p. 397.
36. *ibid.*, p. 115.
37. *ibid.*, p. 112.
38. *ibid.*, p. 119.
39. *ibid.*
40. *ibid.*, pp. 44–5.
41. *ibid.*, p. 46.
42. *ibid.*, p. 115.
43. *ibid.*, p. 388.
44. *ibid.*, p. 394.
45. *ibid.*, p. 147.
46. *ibid.*
47. *ibid.*
48. *ibid.*, p. 111.
49. *ibid.*, p. 200.
50. *ibid.*, p. 356.
51. *ibid.*, p. 68.
52. *ibid.*, p. 302.
53. *ibid.*, p. 399.
54. *ibid.*, p. 90.
55. *ibid.*, p. 92.
56. *ibid.*
57. *ibid.*, p. 319.
58. *ibid.*, p. 351.
59. *ibid.*, p. 148.
60. *ibid.*, p. 60.
61. *ibid.*, p. 390.
62. *ibid.*, p. 156.
63. Diver, *Lilamani*, p. 94.
64. Maud Diver, *Captain Desmond, V.C.* (1907), p. 8.
65. Maud Diver, *Candles in the Wind* (1909), p. 34.
66. Maud Diver, *Desmond's Daughter* (1916), p. 23.

67. *ibid.*, p. 29.
68. *ibid.*, p. 31.
69. *ibid.*, p. 566.
70. Diver, *Lilamani*, p. 128.
71. Diver, *Far to Seek*, p. 325.
72. Wylie, *The Daughter of Brahma*, p. 4.
73. Perrin, *The Anglo-Indians*, pp. 15–16.
74. Diver, *Far to Seek*, p. 227.
75. *ibid.*, p. 359.
76. Maud Diver, *Ships of Youth* (1931), p. 30.
77. Perrin, *The Anglo-Indians*, pp. 148–9.
78. Croker, *A Family Likeness*, p. 25.
79. Perrin, *The Anglo-Indians*, pp. 170–71.
80. Alice Perrin, *The Woman in the Bazaar* (1914), pp. 43–4.
81. Diver, *Desmond's Daughter*, p. 49.
82. Diver, *Far to Seek*, p. 312.
83. *ibid.*, p. 328.
84. B. M. Croker, *Her Own People* (1903), p. 25.
85. Croker, *The Company Servant*, pp. 84, 85, 86.
86. Diver, *Captain Desmond*, p. 56.
87. Diver, *Candles in the Wind*, p. 34.
88. Maud Diver, *The Englishwoman in India* (1909), p. 82.
89. Diver, *Far to Seek*, p. 315.
90. Wylie, *The Daughter of Brahma*, p. 60.
91. Penny, *The Swami's Curse*, p. 165.
92. Perrin, *The Anglo-Indians*, p. 119.
93. *ibid.*, pp. 25–6.
94. *ibid.*, p. 25.
95. *ibid.*, p. 275.
96. Perrin, *The Woman in the Bazaar*, p. 125.
97. Perrin, *The Anglo-Indians*, pp. 115–16.
98. *ibid.*, p. 172.
99. *ibid.*, p. 174.
100. Diver, *Desmond's Daughter*, p. 358.
101. Wylie, *The Daughter of Brahma*, p. 67.
102. *ibid.*, p. 65.
103. *ibid.*, p. 105.
104. Q. D. Leavis, *Fiction and the Reading Public* (1932), p. 62.
105. Alice Perrin, *Government House* (1925), p. 151.
106. *ibid.*, p. 153.

REFERENCES

CHAPTER 3: *Flora Annie Steel, 1847–1929*

1. Preface to *The Law of the Threshold* (1924). All references to Mrs Steel's works are to Heinemann editions unless otherwise stated.
2. *The Garden of Fidelity: Being the Autobiography of Flora Annie Steel* (1929), p. 133.
3. *On the Face of the Waters* (1896; ref. to 1987 edn), p. 9.
4. *India* (1905), pp. 109–10.
5. *Review of Reviews*, Vol. XVI, 1897, p. 163.
6. *The Garden of Fidelity*, p. 248.
7. *India*, p. 6.
8. *The Garden of Fidelity*, p. 1.
9. Dated 15 April 1929. Quoted in Daya Patwardhan, *A Star of India: Flora Annie Steel, Her Works and Times* (1963), p. 41. Other reviews to which Mrs Patwardhan refers compare her with Kipling, praise her writing for being charged with the mystery of the East, and remark on her deep understanding of India. Mrs Patwardhan's study, while containing a great deal of information, lacks a critical focus.
10. E. F. Oaten, *A Sketch of Anglo-Indian Literature* (1908), p. 197. Mrs Steel won sterner praise from Sir Alfred Lyall who in assessing *On the Face of the Waters* appreciatively notes her character drawings of Indians and her imaginative vigour while criticizing her sacrificing verisimilitude to historical accuracy. 'The Anglo-Indian Novelist', *Edinburgh Review*, Vol. 190, 1899, pp. 415–39; reprinted in Lyall, *Studies in Literature and History* (1915).
11. *The Potter's Thumb* (1894; ref. to 1900 edn), p. 313.
12. 'Gunesh Chand' in *From the Five Rivers* (1893; ref. to 1897 edn), p. 34.
13. *ibid.*, pp. 56–7.
14. 'Harvest' (1894) in *The Indian Scene* (1933).
15. *On the Face of the Waters*, p. 158.
16. *The Hosts of the Lord* (1900; ref. to undated edn), p. 32.
17. *ibid.*, p. 62.
18. *ibid.*, p. 32.
19. *ibid.*, p. 201.
20. *ibid.*, p. 53.
21. *The Law of the Threshold*, p. 40.
22. *ibid.*, p. 125.
23. *ibid.*, p. 145.
24. *ibid.*, pp. 188–9.
25. 'On the Second Story' in *In the Permanent Way* (1897; ref. to 1898 edn), p. 49.
26. *ibid.*, p. 50.
27. *ibid.*, p. 52.
28. 'The Blue-throated God' in *In the Permanent Way*.
29. 'Ramchunderji' in *The Indian Scene*.
30. 'The Squaring of the Gods' in *In the Guardianship of God* (1900).

31. *On the Face of the Waters*, p. 102.
32. *The Law of the Threshold*, pp. 11–12.
33. *ibid.*, p. 42.
34. *ibid.*, p. 27.
35. *ibid.*, p. 25.
36. 'On the Second Story', p. 57.
37. *The Law of the Threshold*, p. 10.
38. *ibid.*, p. 256.
39. 'A Maiden's Prayer' in *The Indian Scene*, p. 624.
40. *ibid.*, p. 625.
41. *ibid.*, p. 626.
42. *ibid.*, p. 630.
43. *On the Face of the Waters*, p. 72.
44. *ibid.*, pp. 97–8.
45. *The Potter's Thumb*, pp. 29–30.
46. *ibid.*, p. 27.
47. *ibid.*
48. *The Law of the Threshold*, p. 37.
49. *ibid.*, p. 210.
50. *ibid.*, p. 285.
51. *ibid.*, p. 23.
52. *ibid.*, p. 300.
53. *ibid.*, p. 304.
54. *ibid.*, p. 300.
55. *ibid.*, p. 195.
56. 'The Sorrowful Hour' in *In the Permanent Way*, p. 208.
57. *The Hosts of the Lord*, p. 297.
58. *ibid.*, p. 348.
59. *ibid.*, p. 342.
60. *ibid.*, p. 368.
61. See Surendra Nath Sen, *Eighteen Fifty-Seven* (1957); T. R. Metcalf, *The Aftermath of Revolt: India, 1857–1870* (1965); Edward Thompson, *The Other Side of the Medal* (1924).
62. *On the Face of the Waters*, p. 156.
63. S. N. Sen, *op. cit.*, p. 414.
64. *On the Face of the Waters*, p. 157.
65. *ibid.*, p. 307.
66. *ibid.*, p. 178.
67. *ibid.*
68. *ibid.*, p. 197.
69. *ibid.*, p. 198.
70. *ibid.*, p. 183.
71. *ibid.*, p. 181.
72. *ibid.*, p. 263.

73. *On the Face of the Waters*, p. 179.
74. *ibid.*, p. 106.
75. *ibid.*, p. 264.
76. *ibid.*, p. 279.
77. *ibid.*, p. 228.
78. *ibid.*, p. 431.
79. *The Law of the Threshold*, p. 146.
80. *On the Face of the Waters*, p. 60.
81. *The Potter's Thumb*, p. 1.
82. *ibid.*, p. 40.
83. *ibid.*, p. 45.
84. *ibid.*, p. 46.
85. *On the Face of the Waters*, p. 35.
86. *ibid.*, p. 37.
87. *ibid.*, p. 324.
88. *ibid.*, p. 9.
89. *Miss Stuart's Legacy* (1893; ref. to 1913 edn), p. 7.
90. *ibid.*, p. 98.
91. *The Potter's Thumb*, p. 126.
92. *ibid.*, p. 286.
93. *ibid.*, p. 243.
94. *The Hosts of the Lord*, p. 3.
95. *ibid.*, p. 359.
96. *ibid.*, p. 340.
97. *The Law of the Threshold*, p. 293.
98. *ibid.*, p. 188.
99. *ibid.*, pp. 267–8.
100. *On the Face of the Waters*, p. 21.
101. *ibid.*, p. 135.
102. *ibid.*, p. 134.
103. *The Law of the Threshold*, p. 305.
104. *The Hosts of the Lord*, p. 93.
105. *The Law of the Threshold*, p. 25.
106. *ibid.*, pp. 211–12.
107. *ibid.*, pp. 205–6.
108. *The Garden of Fidelity*, p. 226.
109. *On the Face of the Waters*, p. 233.
110. *ibid.*, p. 278.
111. *ibid.*, p. 359.
112. *ibid.*, p. 356.
113. *ibid.*
114. *The Garden of Fidelity*, p. 191.

REFERENCES

CHAPTER 4: *Edmund Candler, 1874–1926*

1. *Youth and the East: An Unconventional Autobiography* (1924; ref. to 1932 edn), p. 22. The chapters comprising the book initially appeared anonymously in *Blackwood's Magazine*.
2. *ibid.*, p. 113.
3. Biographical information from the Introductory Memoir written by Candler's brother, Henry, in the 1932 edn of *Youth and the East*.
4. *Youth and the East*, p. 56.
5. *ibid.*, p. 58.
6. *A Vagabond in Asia* (1900), p. 6.
7. *ibid.*, p. 169.
8. *ibid.*, p. 170.
9. *ibid.*, p. 169.
10. *ibid.*, p. 25.
11. *The Mantle of the East* (1910), p. 15.
12. *ibid.*, p. 6.
13. *ibid.*, p. 28.
14. *ibid.*, pp. 28–9.
15. *ibid.*, p. 13.
16. *Youth and the East*, p. 51.
17. *ibid.*, p. 53.
18. *ibid.*, p. 54.
19. *Abdication* (1922), p. 216.
20. *Youth and the East*, p. 203.
21. *ibid.*, p. 205.
22. *ibid.*, p. 215.
23. *ibid.*, pp. 212–13.
24. *Abdication*, pp. 113–14.
25. *The Mantle of the East*, p. 243.
26. *ibid.*, p. 57.
27. *ibid.*, p. 111.
28. *ibid.*, pp. 120–21.
29. *ibid.*, p. 227.
30. *Youth and the East*, pp. 146–7.
31. *ibid.*, pp. 192–3.
32. *The Mantle of the East*, pp. 182, 183, 198.
33. *Youth and the East*, pp. 188–9.
34. *ibid.*, pp. 180–81.
35. *ibid.*, p. 181.
36. *ibid.*
37. *ibid.*, p. 182.
38. Henry Candler's Introductory Memoir to *Youth and the East*, pp. xv–xvi.
39. 'Probationary' in *The General Plan* (1911), p. 23.

40. 'Probationary'.
41. *ibid.*, p. 36.
42. *ibid.*, p. 31.
43. *ibid.*, p. 35.
44. *ibid.*, p. 42.
45. *ibid.*, p. 58.
46. 'At Galdang Tso' in *The General Plan*, p. 234.
47. *Youth and the East*, p. 63.
48. 'At Galdang Tso', p. 246.
49. 'The Testimony of Bhagwan Singh' in *The General Plan*, p. 190.
50. *ibid.*, pp. 190–91.
51. *ibid.*, p. 191.
52. *ibid.*
53. 'Père Ailland' in *The General Plan*, p. 262.
54. *ibid.*, p. 278.
55. *ibid.*, p. 277.
56. *ibid.*, p. 280.
57. 'A Break in the Rains' in *The General Plan*, p. 99.
58. *ibid.*, p. 109.
59. *ibid.*, p. 111.
60. *ibid.*, p. 112.
61. *ibid.*, pp. 112–13.
62. *ibid.*, p. 116.
63. *ibid.*
64. *ibid.*, p. 120.
65. *ibid.*, pp. 120–21.
66. *ibid.*, p. 121.
67. *ibid.*, p. 124.
68. *ibid.*
69. *ibid.*, pp. 112–13.
70. *Siri Ram: Revolutionist* (1912), p. 275.
71. For analysis of the political tendencies, see S. R. Mehrotra, *India and the Commonwealth, 1885–1929* (1965).
72. *Siri Ram: Revolutionist*, p. 206.
73. *ibid.*, p. 138.
74. *ibid.*, p. 208.
75. *Abdication*, p. 11.
76. *Siri Ram: Revolutionist*, p. 50.
77. *ibid.*, p. 255.
78. *ibid.*, p. 271.
79. *ibid.*, p. 304.
80. *ibid.*, p. 305.
81. *ibid.*, p. 232.
82. *ibid.*, p. 41.

83. *ibid.*, p. 83.
84. *ibid.*, p. 274.
85. *ibid.*, p. 84.
86. *ibid.*, p. 80.
87. *ibid.*, pp. 81-2.
88. *ibid.*, p. 83.
89. *ibid.*, pp. 243-4.
90. *ibid.*, final unnumbered page.
91. *Abdication*, p. 116.
92. *ibid.*, p. 39.
93. *ibid.*, p. 263.
94. *ibid.*, p. 280.
95. *Siri Ram: Revolutionist*, p. 21.
96. *ibid.*, pp. 98, 99.
97. *ibid.*, p. 99.
98. *Abdication*, pp. 43-4.
99. *ibid.*, p. 235.
100. *ibid.*, p. 3.
101. *Youth and the East*, p. 89.
102. *ibid.*, pp. xxvii-xxviii.
103. *Abdication*, p. 221.
104. *ibid.*, p. 205.
105. *ibid.*, p. 198.
106. *Siri Ram: Revolutionist*, pp. 237-8.
107. *ibid.*, p. 298.
108. *Abdication*, p. 209.
109. *ibid.*, pp. 52-3.
110. *ibid.*, p. 134.
111. *ibid.*, p. 136.
112. *ibid.*, p. 237.
113. *ibid.*, p. 319.
114. *ibid.*, p. 201.
115. *ibid.*, p. 227.
116. *ibid.*, p. 208.
117. *ibid.*, p. 238.
118. *Youth and the East*, p. xxxv.
119. *ibid.*, p. 113.
120. *The Mantle of the East*, p. 156.
121. *ibid.*, p. 171.
122. *Abdication*, p. 2.
123. *Siri Ram: Revolutionist*, pp. 26-7.

REFERENCES

CHAPTER 5: *Edward J. Thompson, 1886–1946*

1. Undated letter, which Mrs Thompson estimates was written in 1942, to S. K. Ratcliffe (1868–1958), author of books on India and acting editor of a Calcutta newspaper, the *Statesman*, from 1903–6.
2. Information from Mrs Thompson and *DNB*, 1941–50.
3. *The Reconstruction of India* (1930), p. 279.
4. Letter to Canton, dated 20 October 1911.
5. Introduction to *Srikanta* (1922), translated by K. C. Sen and Theodosia Thompson, by Sarat Chandra Chatterji (1876–1938).
6. *Rabindranath Tagore: Poet and Dramatist* (1926; ref. to 1940 edn), p. 262.
7. *The Reconstruction of India*, pp. 254–5.
8. *The Other Side of the Medal* (1926 edn).
9. *The Reconstruction of India*, p. 256.
10. E. J. Thompson and G. T. Garratt, *The Rise and Fulfilment of British Rule in India* (1934), p. 655. Garratt (1888–1942) served in the I.C.S. from 1913 to 1923; thereafter he was a journalist and author of histories and political commentary; he organized welfare work in Bengal and was Political Secretary to the Indian Round Table Conferences. He shared many ideas and dispositions with Thompson; see, for example, *An Indian Commentary* (1928).
11. The Report to the Rhodes Trustees is in Thompson's papers.
12. *The Reconstruction of India*, p. 106.
13. *ibid.*, p. 268.
14. *ibid.*, p. 159.
15. Letter dated 26 June 1924.
16. *The Other Side of the Medal* (1925), p. 29.
17. *ibid.*, p. 36.
18. *ibid.*
19. *ibid.*, p. 38.
20. *ibid.*, pp. 131–2.
21. *ibid.*, p. 131.
22. *Atonement* (1924), p. 105.
23. *ibid.*, p. 156.
24. *ibid.*, p. 185.
25. Letter to S. K. Ratcliffe, undated and thought by Mrs Thompson to have been written in 1942.
26. *An Indian Day* (1927; ref. to 1938 edn), p. 46.
27. *ibid.*, p. 91.
28. *ibid.*, p. 34.
29. *ibid.*, p. 89.
30. *ibid.*, p. 15.
31. *ibid.*, p. 189.
32. *ibid.*, p. 190.

33. *ibid.*
34. *ibid.*, p. 25.
35. *ibid.*, p. 29.
36. *ibid.*, p. 30.
37. *ibid.*, p. 182.
38. *ibid.*
39. *ibid.*, p. 57.
40. *ibid.*, p. 250.
41. *ibid.*, p. 116.
42. *ibid.*, p. 233.
43. *ibid.*, p. 155.
44. *ibid.*, pp. 155, 233.
45. *ibid.*, p. 70.
46. *ibid.*, pp. 167–8.
47. *ibid.*, pp. 113–14.
48. *ibid.*, p. 126.
49. *ibid.*, p. 149.
50. *ibid.*, p. 146.
51. *ibid.*, pp. 247–8.
52. *ibid.*, p. 75.
53. *ibid.*, p. 270.
54. *ibid.*, pp. 272–3.
55. *ibid.*, p. 272.
56. *ibid.*, p. 218.
57. *ibid.*, p. 49.
58. *ibid.*, p. 52.
59. *A Farewell to India* (1931), p. 90.
60. *ibid.*, p. 78.
61. *ibid.*, p. 79.
62. *ibid.*, p. 81.
63. S. R. Mehrotra, *India and the Commonwealth, 1885–1929* (1965), pp. 138–9.
64. *A Farewell to India*, p. 132.
65. *ibid.*, p. 189.
66. *ibid.*, pp. 233–4.
67. *ibid.*, pp. 162–3.
68. *ibid.*, p. 162.
69. *ibid.*, p. 166.
70. *ibid.*, pp. 88–9.
71. *ibid.*, p. 272.
72. *ibid.*, p. 271.
73. *An Indian Day*, pp. 96, 117, 119.
74. *ibid.*, p. 120.
75. *ibid.*, p. 279.
76. *ibid.*, p. 280.

77. *An Indian Day*, p. 91.
78. *ibid.*, p. 62.
79. *ibid.*, p. 254.
80. *ibid.*, p. 261.
81. *An End of the Hours* (1938), p. 123.
82. *ibid.*, p. 39.
83. *ibid.*, pp. 109–10.
84. *ibid.*, p. 125.
85. *ibid.*, p. 247.
86. *ibid.*
87. *ibid.*, p. 5.
88. *ibid.*, p. 44.
89. *ibid.*, p. 227.
90. *ibid.*, p. 228.
91. *ibid.*, pp. 233–4.
92. *ibid.*, p. 217.
93. *ibid.*, p. 260.
94. *ibid.*, p. 288.
95. *ibid.*, p. 272.
96. *ibid.*, p. 261.
97. *ibid.*, p. 270.
98. *ibid.*, p. 180.
99. Thompson and Garratt, *op. cit.*, Preface.
100. *Atonement*, p. 122.
101. *ibid.*, pp. 59, 61.

CHAPTER 6: *Rudyard Kipling, 1865–1936*

1. W. T. Stead, editor of the *Pall Mall Gazette*; the article on Kipling appeared in *Review of Reviews*, 15 April 1899. Herbert Spencer's article is cited in Jonah Raskin's essay, 'Imperialism: Conrad's *Heart of Darkness*' in *Journal of Contemporary History*, Vol. II, No. 2, 1967, *Literature and Society*, p. 130. For a survey and selection of critical opinion see Elliott L. Gilbert (ed.), *Kipling and the Critics* (1965).
2. An interesting exception is C. A. Bodelsen, author of *Studies in Mid-Victorian Imperialism* (1924), whose *Aspects of Kipling's Art* (1964) deals entirely with the later tales.
3. J. M. S. Tompkins, *The Art of Rudyard Kipling* (1959).
4. Bonamy Dobrée, 'Rudyard Kipling' in *The Lamp and the Lute* (1921); revised version reprinted in *Kipling and the Critics*, p. 43.
5. Alan Sandison, *The Wheel of Empire* (1967), pp. 60, 195. Parts of this chapter, 'The Imperial Simulacrum', appeared in an earlier essay, 'Kipling: The Artist and the Empire' in Andrew Rutherford (ed.), *Kipling's Mind and Art* (1964).

6. In addition to the works already cited, there is Louis L. Cornell, *Kipling in India* (1966); T. R. Henn, *Kipling* (1967). In 1960, *English Fiction in Transition* (now appearing as *English Literature in Transition*) published an annotated bibliography of writings about Kipling, Vol. III, Nos. 3, 4 and 5, to which a First Supplement in two parts has since been added, Vol. VIII, Nos. 3 and 4, 1965. The journal has published numerous original essays on Kipling. The strength of the current flowing in favour of Kipling may be gauged from the tone of essays and articles which appeared in newspapers, weeklies and critical journals during the centenary year, as well as from the serious consideration given by reviewers to new appraisals. In the *Morning Star*, 30 January 1967, a reviewer referred to Kipling as 'social critic and humanist'.

7. See T. S. Eliot's introductory essay to *A Choice of Kipling's Verse* (1941). Also Edmund Wilson's essay, 'The Kipling That Nobody Read' (1941), George Orwell's essay, 'Rudyard Kipling' (1942), and Lionel Trilling's essay, 'Kipling' (1943), which are reprinted in *Kipling's Mind and Art*.

8. Sandison, 'Kipling: The Artist and the Empire', p. 149.

9. For analyses which do consider the role of imperialism in the structure of his ideas, see Noel Annan, 'Kipling's Place in the History of Ideas', and George Shepperson, 'The World of Rudyard Kipling', both in *Kipling's Mind and Art*.

10. *Something of Myself: The Autobiography of Rudyard Kipling* (1937), p. 149. 'My use to him was mainly as a purveyor of words; for he was largely inarticulate. After the idea had been presented – and one had to know his code for it – he would say: "What am I trying to express? Say it, *say* it" ' (pp. 173-4).

11. *Something of Myself*, p. 2.

12. *ibid.*, pp. 41, 42, 43. See also Charles Carrington, *Rudyard Kipling: His Life and Work* (1955).

13. Cornell, *op. cit.*, p. 157. This aspect is examined in some depth by Alan Sandison in the works cited.

14. 'At the End of the Passage' (1890) in *Life's Handicap* (1891), p. 185. All references to Kipling's writings are to the Macmillan uniform edition unless otherwise stated.

15. 'Venus Annodomini' (1886) in *Plain Tales from the Hills* (1888), p. 257.

16. 'The Education of Otis Yeere' (1888) in *Under the Deodars* (1888), p. 20.

17. 'William the Conqueror' (1895) in *The Day's Work* (1898), p. 179.

18. 'Beyond the Pale' (1888) in *Plain Tales from the Hills*, p. 173.

19. 'The Mark of the Beast' (1890) in *Life's Handicap*, pp. 240, 244.

20. 'Miss Youghal's Sais' (1887) in *Plain Tales from the Hills*, p. 34.

21. 'To be Filed for Reference' (1888) in *Plain Tales from the Hills*, p. 332.

22. *ibid.*, pp. 335-6.

23. *ibid.*, pp. 358-9.

24. See Cornell, *op. cit.*, for a discussion of Kipling's published and uncollected newspaper writings.
25. First printed in the *Pioneer*, 2 March 1888; see Cornell, *op. cit.*, Appendix I. Collected in *From Sea to Sea, Letters of Travel* (1899), Vol. II, pp. 205-6.
26. For a discussion of the Calcutta community, see Pearson, *op. cit.*
27. First printed in the *Pioneer*, 18 February 1888, collected in *From Sea to Sea*, Vol. II (1899), p. 219.
28. *Indian Planter's Gazette*, 5 October 1886, p. 357.
29. 'The Head of the District' (1891) in *Life's Handicap*, p. 147.
30. 'The Enlightenment of Pagett M.P.' in the *Contemporary Review*, September 1890, Vol. LVIII, pp. 352, 353. The doctor's tone is remarkably similar to that adopted by a real American lady writing in the 1920s; see Chapter 1 for reference to Katherine Mayo's books.
31. E. M. Forster, 'The Boy Who Never Grew Up' (review of *Letters of Travel*), *Daily Herald*, 9 June 1920, p. 7.
32. 'The Man Who Would Be King' (1888) in *The Phantom Rickshaw* (1888), p. 214.
33. *ibid.*
34. *ibid.*, p. 218.
35. See *From Sea to Sea*, Vol. I, p. 167.
36. See *Military Memoirs of Mr George Thomas* (1803), Compiled and Arranged from Mr Thomas's Original Documents by William Francklin. For later accounts, see H. Compton's *A Particular Account of the European Military Adventures of Hindustan from 1784 to 1803* (1893) and *European Adventures of Northern India, 1785 to 1849* (1929), by C. Grey, edited by H. L. O. Garrett.
37. 'The Man Who Would Be King', pp. 213-14.
38. Paul Fussell, in 'Irony, Freemasonry and Humane Ethics in Kipling's "The Man Who Would Be King" ', *English Literary History*, Vol. 25, 1958, pp. 216-33, points out that the symbolism of Freemasonry was derived from Near Eastern cults.
39. 'The Man Who Would Be King', p. 228.
40. *ibid.*, pp. 238-9.
41. *ibid.*, p. 207.
42. *ibid.*, p. 215.
43. *ibid.*, p. 230.
44. *ibid.*, p. 234.
45. *ibid.*, p. 250.
46. 'The Tomb of his Ancestors' (1897) in *The Day's Work*, p. 114.
47. 'The Man Who Would Be King', p. 242.
48. 'The Mark of the Beast' (1890) in *Life's Handicap*, p. 240.
49. 'Beyond the Pale', p. 171.
50. *The Naulahka* (1892), p. 78.

51. *ibid.*, p. 58.
52. *ibid.*, p. 117.
53. *ibid.*, p. 272.
54. *ibid.*, p. 331.
55. *ibid.*, p. 212.
56. *ibid.*, p. 163.
57. *ibid.*, p. 164.
58. *ibid.*, p. 166.
59. *ibid.*, p. 170.
60. *ibid.*, p. 171.
61. *ibid.*, p. 162.
62. *ibid.*, p. 275.
63. 'The Bridge-Builders' (1893) in *The Day's Work*, p. 5.
64. *ibid.*, p. 3.
65. *ibid.*, p. 41.
66. *ibid.*, p. 9.
67. *ibid.*, p. 7.
68. *ibid.*, p. 10.
69. *ibid.*, p. 9.
70. *ibid.*, p. 20.
71. *ibid.*, p. 25.
72. *ibid.*, p. 24.
73. *ibid.*, p. 32.
74. *ibid.*, p. 33.
75. *ibid.*, p. 38.
76. *ibid.*, p. 28.
77. *ibid.*, p. 35.
78. *ibid.*, p. 31.
79. *ibid.*, p. 33.
80. *ibid.*, pp. 34-5.
81. *ibid.*, p. 37.
82. *ibid.*, p. 36.
83. *ibid.*, p. 37.
84. *ibid.*, p. 38.
85. *ibid.*, p. 39.
86. *ibid.*, pp. 39, 40.
87. *ibid.*, p. 40.
88. *ibid.*, p. 41.
89. *ibid.*, p. 42.
90. *ibid.*, p. 43.
91. *ibid.*, p. 44.
92. *ibid.*, p. 5.
93. *ibid.*, p. 2.
94. 'On the City Wall' (1888) in *In Black and White* (1888), p. 322.

95. 'On the City Wall', p. 326.
96. *ibid.*, p. 329.
97. *ibid.*, p. 327.
98. *ibid.*, p. 335.
99. *ibid.*, p. 338.
100. *ibid.*, p. 352.
101. *ibid.*, p. 324.
102. *ibid.*, p. 346.
103. Zaehner, *op. cit.*, p. 7.
104. *Kim* (1901), pp. 13–14.
105. *ibid.*, pp. 89, 103.
106. *ibid.*, p. 81.
107. *ibid.*, p. 86.
108. *ibid.*, p. 88.
109. *ibid.*, p. 131.
110. *ibid.*, p. 360.
111. *ibid.*, pp. 411, 412.
112. *ibid.*, p. 412.
113. *Bhagavad Gita*, translated by Swami Prabhavananda and Christopher Isherwood (1954), Part III, p. 44.
114. *Kim*, p. 303.
115. *ibid.*, p. 56.
116. *ibid.*, p. 302.
117. *ibid.*, p. 210.
118. *ibid.*, p. 4.
119. *ibid.*, p. 52.
120. *ibid.*, p. 67.
121. *ibid.*, p. 321.
122. *ibid.*, p. 73.
123. *ibid.*, pp. 403–4.
124. *ibid.*, p. 168.
125. *ibid.*, p. 193.
126. *ibid.*, p. 178.
127. *ibid.*, p. 211.
128. *ibid.*, p. 271.
129. *ibid.*, pp. 104–5.
130. *ibid.*, p. 167.
131. *ibid.*, p. 204.
132. *ibid.*, p. 197.
133. *ibid.*, p. 413.
134. E. M. Forster, 'That Job's Done' (review of *Something of Myself*) in the *Listener*, Supplement III, March 1937.
135. For discussions of Kipling's ideas, see *Kipling's Mind and Art*, especially the essay by Noel Annan, 'Kipling's Place in the History of Ideas'.

136. 'Without Benefit of Clergy: A Farewell to Ritual' in *Kipling and the Critics*, p. 182.
137. Sir Michael O'Dwyer, 'Kipling – Some Recollections', *Saturday Review*, 25 January 1936, p. 105.
138. *Something of Myself*, p. 170.
139. *ibid.*, p. 117.
140. *ibid.*, p. 128.
141. *ibid.*, p. 132.
142. *ibid.*, p. 224.

CHAPTER 7: *E. M. Forster:* A Passage to India

1. *Spectator*, 28 June 1924, pp. 1048–50.
2. *Nation and Athenaeum*, 14 June 1924, p. 354.
3. For a survey and discussion of some critical reactions, see V. A. Shahane's Introduction to the collection of essays which he edited, *Perspectives on E. M. Forster's 'A Passage to India'* (1968). The major study of Forster's art and vision is Wilfred Stone's *The Cave and the Mountain* (1966). Amongst other important works are F. C. Crews, *E. M. Forster: The Perils of Humanism* (1962); K. W. Gransden, *E. M. Forster* (1962); James H. McConkey, *The Novels of E. M. Forster* (1957); Lionel Trilling, *E. M. Forster* (1944); George H. Thomson, *The Fiction of E. M. Forster* (1967).
4. *A Passage to India* (1924), p. 101.
5. *ibid.*, p. 139.
6. *ibid.*, p. 273.
7. *ibid.*, p. 120.
8. *The Hill of Devi* (1953), p. 175.
9. *Goldsworthy Lowes Dickinson* (1934).
10. Programme notes to the dramatized version of *A Passage to India*, adapted by Santha Rama Rau and quoted by her in an essay in *E. M. Forster: A Tribute* (1964), edited by K. Natwar-Singh, p. 50.
11. *A Passage to India*, p. 40.
12. *ibid.*
13. *ibid.*, p. 300.
14. *The Hill of Devi*, p. 43.
15. *ibid.*, p. 99.
16. *A Passage to India*, p. 84.
17. *ibid.*, p. 111.
18. *ibid.*, p. 299.
19. *ibid.*, p. 90.
20. *ibid.*, p. 122.
21. *ibid.*, p. 151.
22. *ibid.*, p. 76.
23. *ibid.*, p. 288.

24. *A Passage to India*, p. 274.
25. *ibid.*, pp. 142–3.
26. *ibid.*, p. 218.
27. *ibid.*, p. 9.
28. *ibid.*, p. 218.
29. *ibid.*, p. 226.
30. *ibid.*
31. See 'Indian Entries', selections from Forster's Journal kept during the visit, *Encounter*, Vol. XVIII, No. 1, January 1962, pp. 20–27.
32. *The Hill of Devi*, p. 10.
33. *ibid.*, pp. 59, 64.
34. *ibid.*, p. 127.
35. 'The Emperor Babur' in *Abinger Harvest* (1934; ref. to 1967 edn), p. 323.
36. 'Pan' (1922) in *Abinger Harvest*, p. 343.
37. 'Mohammed Iqbal' in *Two Cheers for Democracy* (1953), pp. 297, 298.
38. *The Hill of Devi*, p. 118.
39. *ibid.*, p. 62.
40. *ibid.*, p. 155.
41. H. A. Smith, 'Forster's Humanism and the Nineteenth Century' in *Forster: A Collection of Critical Essays* (1966), edited by Malcolm Bradbury. For an analysis of Forster's two voices and *A Passage to India*, see Malcolm Bradbury, 'Two Passages to India: Forster as Victorian and Modern' in *Aspects of E. M. Forster*.
42. Smith, *op. cit.*, p. 109.
43. *ibid.*, pp. 112–13.
44. *A Passage to India*, pp. 37–8.
45. *ibid.*, p. 105.
46. *ibid.*, p. 276.
47. *ibid.*, p. 293.
48. *ibid.*, p. 287.
49. *ibid.*, pp. 110, 111.
50. *ibid.*, p. 21.
51. *ibid.*, pp. 127–8.
52. *ibid.*, p. 151.
53. *ibid.*, p. 279.
54. *ibid.*
55. *ibid.*, p. 306.
56. *ibid.*, p. 318.
57. *ibid.*, p. 308.
58. *ibid.*, p. 309.
59. *ibid.*
60. *ibid.*, p. 305.
61. *ibid.*, p. 325.
62. *ibid.*, p. 328.

63. *ibid.*, p. 261.
64. *ibid.*, p. 22.
65. *ibid.*, p. 280.
66. *ibid.*, p. 333.
67. *ibid.*, p. 315.
68. *ibid.*, p. 324.
69. *ibid.*, p. 325.
70. *ibid.*
71. *ibid.*, p. 327.
72. *ibid.*
73. *ibid.*, p. 75.
74. *ibid.*, p. 53.
75. *ibid.*, p. 188.
76. *ibid.*, p. 179.
77. *ibid.*, p. 193.
78. *ibid.*, p. 225.
79. *ibid.*, p. 180.
80. *ibid.*
81. *ibid.*, p. 227.
82. *ibid.*, pp. 50, 51.
83. *ibid.*, p. 220.
84. *ibid.*, p. 28.
85. *ibid.*, p. 267.
86. *ibid.*, p. 20.
87. *ibid.*, p. 63.
88. *ibid.*, p. 65.
89. *ibid.*, p. 32.
90. *ibid.*, p. 76.
91. *ibid.*, p. 264.
92. *ibid.*, p. 285.
93. *ibid.*, p. 271.
94. *ibid.*, p. 283.
95. *ibid.*, p. 332.
96. *ibid.*, pp. 320–21.
97. *ibid.*, p. 332.
98. *ibid.*, pp. 335–6.
99. *The Cave and the Mountain*, pp. 301, 307.
100. *A Passage to India*, p. 130.
101. Zimmer, *Philosophies of India*, p. 217.
102. Basham, *op. cit.*, p. 49.
103. cf. Glen O. Allen, *op. cit.*, who finds the source of the symbolism of the Caves in Hindu scriptures and practice, i.e. in Brahmanical systems.
104. *A Passage to India*, pp. 130, 131–2.
105. *ibid.*, p. 131.

106. *A Passage to India*, p. 32.
107. *ibid.*, p. 50.
108. *ibid.*, pp. 54–5.
109. *ibid.*, pp. 55–6.
110. *ibid.*, p. 73.
111. *ibid.*, p. 102.
112. *ibid.*, pp. 102–3.
113. *ibid.*, p. 135.
114. *ibid.*, p. 120.
115. *ibid.*, p. 139.
116. *ibid.*, pp. 129–30.
117. *ibid.*, pp. 48–9, 132, 168, 199.
118. *ibid.*, p. 143.
119. *ibid.*, p. 147.
120. *ibid.*, p. 143.
121. *ibid.*, p. 146.
122. *ibid.*, p. 147.
123. *ibid.*, p. 157.
124. *ibid.*, p. 143.
125. *ibid.*, p. 202.
126. *ibid.*, p. 201.
127. *ibid.*, p. 202.
128. *ibid.*
129. *ibid.*, p. 208.
130. *ibid.*, p. 205.
131. *ibid.*, p. 88.
132. *ibid.*, pp. 236–7.
133. *ibid.*, p. 239.
134. *ibid.*, p. 250.
135. *ibid.*, p. 154.
136. *ibid.*, p. 156.
137. *ibid.*, p. 217.
138. *ibid.*, p. 210.
139. *ibid.*, pp. 213–14.
140. *ibid.*, pp. 214–15.
141. *ibid.*, p. 218.
142. *ibid.*, p. 298.
143. *ibid.*, p. 293.
144. *ibid.*, p. 132.
145. *ibid.*, p. 166.
146. *ibid.*, p. 199.
147. *ibid.*
148. *ibid.*, p. 288.
149. *ibid.*, p. 333.

150. *ibid.,* p. 275.
151. *ibid.,* p. 138.
152. *ibid.,* p. 304.
153. *ibid.,* p. 148.
154. *ibid.,* p. 75.
155. *ibid.,* p. 218.
156. *ibid.,* p. 293.
157. *ibid.,* pp. 296, 297.
158. *ibid.,* p. 301.
159. *ibid.*
160. *ibid.,* p. 327.
161. *ibid.,* p. 310.
162. *ibid.,* p. 318.
163. *ibid.,* p. 335.
164. *ibid.,* pp. 299–300.
165. *ibid.,* p. 41.
166. *ibid.,* p. 92.
167. *ibid.,* p. 257.
168. Zimmer, *Philosophies of India,* p. 417.
169. *ibid.,* pp. 3, 79.
170. *A Passage to India,* p. 296.
171. *ibid.*
172. *ibid.,* p. 302.
173. *ibid.,* p. 298.
174. *ibid.*
175. *ibid.,* p. 303.
176. *ibid.,* p. 300.
177. *ibid.,* p. 76.
178. *ibid.,* p. 81.
179. *ibid.,* pp. 185–6.
180. *ibid.,* p. 306.
181. *ibid.,* p. 119.
182. *ibid.,* pp. 295–6.
183. *ibid.,* p. 40.
184. *ibid.,* p. 223.
185. *ibid.,* p. 44.
186. *ibid.,* p. 60.
187. Zimmer, *Myths and Symbols,* p. 46.
188. *A Passage to India,* p. 328.
189. *ibid.,* p. 59.
190. *ibid.,* p. 312.
191. *ibid.,* p. 314.
192. *ibid.,* p. 323.
193. *ibid.*

194. *A Passage to India*, p. 328.
195. *ibid.*, p. 332.
196. *ibid.*
197. *ibid.*, pp. 334–5.
198. *ibid.*, p. 104.
199. *ibid.*, p. 319.
200. *ibid.*, p. 144.
201. *ibid.*, p. 316.
202. *ibid.*, p. 328.
203. *ibid.*, p. 336.
204. *ibid.*, p. 101.
205. *ibid.*, p. 273.
206. *ibid.*, p. 333.
207. *ibid.*, pp. 327, 333.

Bibliography

INTRODUCTION and CHAPTER 1

George Aberigh-Mackay, *Twenty-One Days in India: Being the Tour of Sir Ali Baba, K.C.B.* (Calcutta: Thacker, Spink, 1898).

J. R. Ackerley, *Hindoo Holiday: An Indian Journal* (London: Chatto & Windus, 1932; revised edn, 1952).

Vera Anstey, *The Economic Development of India* (London: Longmans Green, 1929; revised edn, 1957).

Hannah Arendt, *The Origins of Totalitarianism* (London: Allen & Unwin, 1951).

Sir Robert Baden-Powell, *Indian Memoirs: Recollections of Soldiering, Sport, Etc.* (London: Herbert Jenkins, 1915).

Michael Banton, *Race Relations* (London: Tavistock, 1967).

A. L. Basham, *The Wonder That Was India* (London: Sidgwick & Jackson, 1954; revised edn, 1967).

—, contributions to Wm. Theodore de Bary (ed.), *q.v.*

Henri Baudet, *Paradise on Earth: Some Thoughts on European Images of Non-European Man* (New Haven: Yale University Press, 1965).

George Bearce, *British Attitudes Towards India, 1784–1858* (Oxford: O.U.P., 1961).

Mira Behn (Madeleine Slade), *The Spirit's Pilgrimage* (London: Longmans, 1960).

Max Beloff, *Imperial Sunset*, Vol. I: *Britain's Liberal Empire, 1897–1921* (London: Methuen, 1969).

George Bennett, *The Concept of Empire: Burke to Attlee 1774–1947* (London: Black, 1953).

Annie Besant, *India: Bond or Free?* (New York: Putnam, 1926).

Lord Beverdge, *India Called Them* (London: Allen & Unwin, 1947).

Agehananda Bharati, *The Tantric Tradition* (London: Rider, 1965).

Sir Edward Blunt, *The Indian Civil Service* (London: Faber & Faber, 1937).

Rev. W. Bonnar, 'The English in India', *Contemporary Review*, Vol. LXVIII, October 1895.

H. N. Brailsford, *Subject India* (London: Left Book Club, 1941).

Sasthi Brata, *My God Died Young* (London: Hutchinson, 1968).

A. Claude Brown, *The Ordinary Man's India* (London: Cecil Palmer, 1927).

D. H. Buchanan, *The Development of Capitalist Enterprise in India* (New York: Macmillan, 1934).

A. Butterworth, *The Southlands of Siva: Some Reminiscences of Life in Southern India* (London: John Lane The Bodley Head, 1923).

BIBLIOGRAPHY

A. K. Cairncross, *Home and Foreign Investment, 1870–1913: Studies in Capital Accumulation* (Cambridge: C.U.P., 1953).

G. Morris Carstairs, *The Twice-Born: A Study of a Community of High-Caste Hindus* (London: Hogarth Press, 1957).

R. Carstairs, *The Little World of an Indian District Officer* (London: Macmillan, 1912).

Al. Carthill (pseudonym of Bennet Christian Huntingdon Calcraft-Kennedy), *The Lost Dominion* (London: Blackwood, 1924).

Nirad C. Chaudhuri, *The Continent of Circe: An Essay on the Peoples of India* (London: Chatto & Windus, 1965).

Sir Valentine Chirol, *Indian Unrest* (London: Macmillan, 1910).

—, *India* (London: Benn, 1926).

'Civilian', *The Civilian's South India* (London: John Lane The Bodley Head, 1921).

Bernard S. Cohn, 'The British in Benares: A Nineteenth Century Colonial Society', *Comparative Studies in Society and History*, Vol. VI, 1961–2.

Sir Henry Cotton, *Indian and Home Memoirs* (London: T. Fisher Unwin, 1911).

Colin Cross, *The Fall of the British Empire, 1918–1968* (London: Hodder & Stoughton, 1968).

Lord Curzon in India: Being a Selection from his Speeches as Viceroy and Governor-General of India, 1898–1905, introduced by Sir Thomas Raleigh (London: Macmillan, 1906).

Sir Malcolm Darling, *Apprenticeship to Power: India, 1904–1908* (London: Hogarth Press, 1966).

Wm. Theodore de Bary (ed.), *Sources of Indian Tradition* in series, *Records of Civilization, Sources and Studies* (Oxford: O.U.P., 1958).

Goldsworthy Lowes Dickinson, *An Essay on the Civilisations of India, China and Japan* (London: Dent, 1914).

—, *Appearances: Being Notes of Travel* (London: Dent, 1914).

Maud Diver, *The Englishwoman in India* (London: Blackwood, 1909).

O. Douglas, *Olivia in India* (London: Hodder & Stoughton, 1913).

Louis Dumont, 'Introductory Note: Change, Interaction and Comparison', *Contributions to Indian Sociology*, No. VII, March 1964.

Major-General L. C. Dunsterville, *Stalky's Reminiscences* (London: Cape, 1929).

R. Palme Dutt, *India Today* (London: Left Book Club, 1940).

Edinburgh Review, unsigned article, 'India: What Can it Teach Us?', Vol. CLXI, April 1885.

Michael Edwardes, *British India, 1772–1947: A Survey of the Nature and Effects of Alien Rule* (London: Sidgwick & Jackson, 1967).

—, *Bound to Exile: The Victorians in India* (London: Sidgwick & Jackson, 1969).

Thomas Edwardes, 'Christian Effort in India', *Calcutta Review*, Vol. CXL, 1880.

EHA (pseudonym of Edward Hamilton Aitkin), *Behind the Bungalow*, illustrations by F. C. Macrae (Calcutta: Thacker, Spink, 1889).

BIBLIOGRAPHY

Englishman, Jubilee Pamphlet, 20 February 1887.

Erik H. Erikson, *Gandhi's Truth: On the Origins of Militant Non-Violence* (New York: Norton, 1969).

Richard Faber, *The Vision and the Need: Late Victorian Imperialist Aims* (London: Faber & Faber, 1966).

Frantz Fanon, *Black Skin, White Masks* (New York: Grove Press, 1967; first published in France, 1952).

—, *A Dying Colonialism* (New York: Monthly Review Press, 1965; first published in France, 1959).

—, *The Wretched of the Earth* (London: MacGibbon & Kee, 1965; first published in France, 1961).

E. M. Forster, *The Hill of Devi* (London: Arnold, 1953).

Sir Andrew H. L. Fraser, *Among Rajahs and Ryots: A Civil Servant's Recollections and Impressions of Thirty-Seven Years of Work and Sport in the Central Provinces and Bengal* (London: Seeley, 1911).

Friends' Foreign Mission Association, Reports.

G. T. Garratt, *An Indian Commentary* (London: Cape, 1928).

Martin Gilbert, *Servant of India: A Study of Imperial Rule from 1905 to 1910 as Told through the Correspondence and Diaries of Sir James Dunlop Smith* (London: Longmans, 1966).

Jon and Rumer Godden, *Two Under the Indian Sun* (London: Macmillan, 1966).

Norman Goodall, *A History of the London Missionary Society 1895-1945* (Oxford: O.U.P., 1954).

Ram Gopal, *British Rule in India: An Assessment* (London: Asia Publishing House, 1963).

Sarvepalli Gopal, *Modern India* (London: Historical Association, 1967).

Allen J. Greenberger, *The British Image of India: A Study in the Literature of Imperialism, 1880-1960* (Oxford: O.U.P., 1969).

Sir Lepel Griffin, 'Indian Princes at Home', *Fortnightly Review*, Vol. XXXIV, October 1883.

Sir Percival Griffiths, *The British in India* (London: Hale, 1946).

—, *The British Impact on India* (London: Cass, 1965).

Leonard Handley, *Time's Delinquency* (London: Hutchinson, 1935).

'A Heretic', 'The Anglo-Indian Creed', *Contemporary Review*, Vol. LXXVI, August 1899.

Sir Claude H. Hill, *India: Stepmother* (London: Blackwood, 1929).

Richard Hoggart, 'Literature and Society', *The American Scholar*, Vol. 35, No. 2, Spring 1966.

Susanne Howe, *Novels of Empire* (New York: Columbia University Press, 1949).

Sir William Wilson Hunter, *The Old Missionary* (London: Henry Froude, 1896).

Francis G. Hutchins, *The Illusion of Permanence: British Imperialism in India* (Princeton: Princeton University Press, 1967).

Edward Hyams, 'Problems of Communication', *New Statesman*, 2 February 1968.

Indian Planter's Gazette and Sporting News.

Harold Isaacs, *Scratches on Our Minds: American Images of China and India* (New York: John Day, 1958).

Christopher Isherwood (ed.), *Vedanta for the Western World* (New York: Viking Press, 1960).

—, edited and translated with Swami Prabhavananda, *Bhagavad Gita* (New York: Mentor, 1954).

Raghavan Iyer, 'Utilitarianism and All That: The Political Theory of British Imperialism in India', *St Antony's Papers*, No. 8, 1960.

— (ed.), *The Glass Curtain Between Asia and Europe: A Symposium on the Historical Encounters and the Changing Attitudes of the Peoples of the East and the West* (Oxford: O.U.P., 1965).

Journal of Contemporary History, 'Literature and Society', Vol. 2, No. 2, 1967.

—, Colonialism and Decolonisation, Vol. 4, No. 1, 1969.

Michael Kidron, *Foreign Investment in India* (Oxford: O.U.P., 1965).

V. G. Kiernan, *The Lords of Human Kind: European Attitudes Towards the Outside World in the Imperial Age* (London: Weidenfeld & Nicolson, 1969).

C. A. Kincaid, *Forty-Four Years a Public Servant* (London: Blackwood, 1934).

Dennis Kincaid, *British Social Life in India, 1608–1937* (London: Routledge, 1938).

—, *Cactus Land* (London: Chatto & Windus, 1934).

—, *The Final Image* (London: Routledge, 1939).

Ravindar Kumar, 'Liberalism and Reform in India', *Journal of World History*, Vol. VII, No. 4, 1963.

Sir Walter Lawrence, *The India We Served* (London: Cassell, 1928).

—, 'The Indian Civil Service', in *Fifty Years: A Composite Picture of the Period 1882–1932 by Twenty-Seven Contributors to 'The Times'* (London: Thornton Butterworth, 1932).

Q .D. Leavis, *Fiction and the Reading Public* (London: Chatto & Windus, 1932).

Sir Alfred Comyns Lyall, *Asiatic Studies* (London: John Murray, 1882; revised edn, 1907).

—, *Studies in Literature and History* (London: John Murray, 1915).

—, *The Rise and Expansion of British Dominion in India* (London: John Murray, 1894; ref. to 1920 edn).

—, *Verses Written in India* (London: Kegan Paul, Trench & Trübner, 1896).

Lieutenant-General Sir George MacMunn, *The Underworld of India* (London: Jarrolds, 1932).

N. Macnicol, 'The Future of India', *Contemporary Review*, Vol. XCIV, July 1908.

Sir Evan Maconochie, *Life in the Indian Civil Service* (London: Chapman & Hall, 1926).

Michael Malim, *The Pagoda Tree* (London: Kenneth Mason, 1963).

O. Mannoni, *Prospero and Caliban: The Psychology of Colonization* (New York: Praeger, 1956; first published in France, 1950).

BIBLIOGRAPHY

Sir John A. R. Marriott, *The English in India: A Problem of Politics* (Oxford: O.U.P., 1932).

Juan Mascaró (ed.), *The Upanishads* (Harmondsworth: Penguin Books, 1965).

—, *The Bhagavad Gita* (Harmondsworth: Penguin Books, 1966).

Katherine Mayo, *Mother India* (London: Cape, 1927).

—, *Slaves of the Gods* (London: Cape, 1929).

S. R. Mehrotra, *India and the Commonwealth, 1885–1929* (London: Allen & Unwin, 1965).

T. R. Metcalf, 'The British and the Moneylenders in Nineteenth Century India', *Journal of Modern History*, Vol. XXXIV, No. 4, 1962.

—, *The Aftermath of Revolt: India, 1857–1870* (Oxford: O.U.P., 1965).

J. Chartres Molony, *A Book of South India* (London: Methuen, 1926).

Dom Moraes, *My Son's Father: An Autobiography* (London: Secker & Warburg, 1968).

James Morris, *Pax Britannica: The Climax of an Empire* (London: Faber & Faber, 1968).

John Morris, *Eating the Indian Air: Memories and Present Day Impressions* (London: Hamish Hamilton, 1968).

V. S. Naipaul, *An Area of Darkness: An Experience of India* (London: Deutsch, 1964).

Jawaharlal Nehru, *An Autobiography* (London: John Lane The Bodley Head, 1936).

—, *The Discovery of India* (New York: Meridian, 1946).

—, *A Bunch of Old Letters: Mostly Written to Jawaharlal Nehru and Some Written by Him* (Bombay: Asia Publishing House, 1960).

Arthur H. Nethercot, *The Last Four Lives of Annie Besant* (London: Hart-Davis, 1963).

Beverley Nichols, *Verdict on India* (London: Cape, 1944).

Sister Nivedita (Margaret Noble), *The Web of Indian Life* (1904) (Calcutta: Advaita Ashrama edn, 1955).

E. F. Oaten, *A Sketch of Anglo-Indian Literature* (London: Kegan Paul & Trübner, 1908).

Sir Michael O'Dwyer, *India As I Knew It* (London: Constable, 1925).

L. S. S. O'Malley, *The Indian Civil Service* (London: John Murray, 1931).

J. Campbell Oman, *The Brahmans, Theists and Muslims of India* (London: Fisher Unwin, 1907).

George Orwell, 'Shooting an Elephant' (1936), *Selected Essays* (Harmondsworth: Penguin, 1957).

—, *Burmese Days* (London: Gollancz, 1935).

Lieutenant-Colonel R. D. Osborn, 'Representative Government in India', *Contemporary Review*, Vol. LCII, December 1882.

K. M. Panikkar, *The Foundations of New India* (London: Allen & Unwin, 1963).

R. Pearson, *Eastern Interlude: A Social History of the European Community in Calcutta* (Calcutta: Thacker, Spink, 1930).

BIBLIOGRAPHY

D. F. Pocock, 'Notes on the Interaction of English and Indian Thought in the Nineteenth Century', *Journal of World History*, Vol. IV, No. 4, 1958.

Quarterly Review, unsigned article, 'The Romance of India', Vol. CXCVI, July 1902.

S. Radhakrishnan, *Indian Philosophy* (London: Allen & Unwin, 1923).

—, *Eastern Religions and Western Thought* (Oxford: O.U.P., 1939; ref. to 1958 edn).

K. Rahman, *Race Relations in Indian Fiction Between 1919 and 1939 with particular reference to India and South East Asia*, unpublished Ph.D. thesis, Birmingham University, 1962.

H. Rawlinson, *India: A Short Cultural History* (1937) (London: Cresset Press edn, 1965).

Sir Robert Reid, *Years of Change in Bengal and Assam* (London: Benn, 1966).

Reginald Reynolds, *The White Sahibs in India* (London: Secker & Warburg, 1937).

Private Frank Richards, *Old Soldier Sahib* (London: Faber & Faber, 1936).

Lord Frederick Sleigh Roberts of Kandahar, *Forty-One Years in India* (London: Macmillan, 1897; ref. to 1901 edn).

K. M. Sen, *Hinduism* (Harmondsworth: Penguin Books, 1961).

S. N. Sen, *Eighteen-Fifty-Seven* (Delhi: Publications Division, Ministry of Information and Broadcasting, Government of India, 1957).

S. P. Sen, 'Effects on India of British Law and Administration in the Nineteenth Century', *Journal of World History*, Vol. IV, No. 4, 1958.

Robert Sencourt (pseudonym of R. E. Gordon George), *India in English Literature* (London: Simpkin, Marshall, Hamilton, Kent, 1923).

Edward Shils, 'The Intellectual between Tradition and Modernity: The Indian Situation', *Comparative Studies in Society and History*, Supplement I, 1961.

Bhupal Singh, *A Survey of Anglo-Indian Literature* (Oxford: O.U.P., 1934).

F. H. Skrine, *The Life of Sir William Wilson Hunter* (London: Longmans Green, 1901).

N. V. Sovani, 'The British Impact on India', *Journal of World History*, Vol. I, No. 4, 1955; Vol. II, No. 1, 1956.

Percival Spear, *The Nabobs: A Study of the Social Life of the English in Eighteenth Century India* (1932) (Oxford: O.U.P. edn, 1963).

—, *India: A Modern History* (University of Michigan Press, 1961).

— (ed.), *The Oxford History of Modern India, 1740–1947* (Oxford: O.U.P., 1964) (being a reprint of the *Oxford History of India*, 1958, originally compiled by Vincent Smith).

— *A History of India* (Harmondsworth: Penguin Books, 1965).

M. N. Srinivas, *Caste in Modern India* (Bombay: Asia Publishing House, 1962).

James FitzJames Stephen, 'The Foundations of the Government of India', *The Nineteenth Century*, Vol. LXXX, October 1883.

Eric Stokes, *The English Utilitarians and India* (Oxford: O.U.P., 1959).

Sir John Strachey, *India: Its Administration and Progress* (London: Macmillan, 1888; ref. to 1911 edn).

Rabindranath Tagore, *Glimpses of Bengal: Letters, 1885–95* (London: Macmillan, 1921).

Sir Richard Temple, *Men and Events in My Time in India* (London: John Murray, 1882).

E. J. Thompson and G. T. Garratt, *The Rise and Fulfilment of British Rule in India* (London: Macmillan, 1934).

H. P. Thompson, *Into All Lands: A History of the Society for the Propagation of the Gospel in Foreign Parts, 1701–1950* (London: S.P.C.K., 1951).

A. P. Thornton, *The Imperial Idea and Its Enemies* (London: Macmillan, 1959).

—, *Doctrines of Imperialism* (New York: Wiley, 1965).

—, *For the File on Empire: Essays and Reviews* (London: Macmillan, 1968).

Sir Edward Wakefield, *Past Imperative: My Life in India, 1927–1947* (London: Chatto & Windus, 1966).

Robert Wallace, 'The Seamy Side of "Imperialism" ', *Contemporary Review*, Vol. LXXV, June 1899.

Barbara Wingfield-Stratford, *India and the English* (London: Cape, 1922).

Philip Woodruff (pseudonym of Philip Mason), *The Men Who Ruled India* (London: Cape, 1953–4; ref. to 1963 edn).

—, *Call the Next Witness* (London: Cape, 1945).

—, *The Wild Sweet Witch* (London: Cape, 1947).

Leonard Woolf, *Growing*: Vol. II of his Autobiography (London: Hogarth Press, 1961).

—, *The Village in the Jungle* (1913) (London: Chatto & Windus in association with Hogarth Press edn, 1951).

—, *Diaries in Ceylon 1908–1911: Records of a Colonial Administrator and Stories from the East* (London: Hogarth Press, 1963).

Francis Yeats-Brown, *Bengal Lancer* (London: Gollancz, 1930).

—, *Lancer at Large* (London: Gollancz, 1936).

Henry Yule and A. C. Burnell, *Hobson-Jobson: A Glossary of Anglo-Indian Colloquial Words and Phrases* (1886; reprinted 1902, ed. William Crooke; reprinted Routledge & Kegan Paul, 1968).

R. C. Zaehner, *Hinduism* (Oxford: O.U.P., 1966).

Heinrich Zimmer, *Myths and Symbols in Indian Arts and Civilization*, ed. Joseph Campbell (New York: Bollingen Foundation, 1946; ref. to 1962 edn).

—, *Philosophies of India*, ed. Joseph Campbell (New York: Bollingen Foundation, 1952; ref. to Routledge & Kegan Paul edn, 1967).

Maurice and Taya Zinkin, *Britain and India: Requiem for Empire* (London: Chatto & Windus, 1964).

CHAPTER 2

B. M. Croker, *A Family Likeness: A Sketch in the Himalayas* (1901; ref. to Modern Library edn, n.d.).

BIBLIOGRAPHY

B. M. Croker, *Her Own People* (London: Hurst & Blackett, 1903).

—, *The Company Servant: A Romance of Southern India* (London: Hurst & Blackett, 1907).

Maud Diver, *Captain Desmond V.C.* (London: Blackwood, 1907).

—, *The Great Amulet* (London: Blackwood, 1908).

—, *Candles in the Wind* (London: Blackwood, 1909).

—, *Lilamani* (London: Blackwood, 1910).

—, *Desmond's Daughter* (London: Blackwood, 1916).

—, *Far to Seek* (London: Blackwood, 1920; ref. to Houghton, Mifflin edn, 1921).

—, *The Singer Passes* (London: Blackwood, 1931).

—, *Ships of Youth* (London: Blackwood, 1931).

F. E. Penny, *Caste and Creed* (1890; ref. to Chatto & Windus edn, 1906).

—, *The Rajah* (London: Chatto & Windus, 1911).

—, *Southern India* (Painted by Lady Lawley, Described by F. E. Penny) (London: Black, 1914).

—, *The Swami's Curse* (London: Hodder & Stoughton, 1929).

Alice Perrin, *East of Suez* (1901; ref. to Staple Inn edn, 1926).

—, *The Stronger Claim* (1903); ref. to Harrap edn, 1925).

—, *The Anglo-Indians* (London: Methuen, 1912).

—, *The Woman in the Bazaar* (London: Cassell, 1914).

—, *Government House* (London: Cassell, 1925).

I. A. R. Wylie, *The Daughter of Brahma* (London: Mills & Boon, 1912).

—, *My Life With George* (New York: Random House, 1940).

CHAPTER 3

Daya Patwardhan, *A Star of India: Flora Annie Steel, Her Works and Times* (Bombay, 1963).

Flora Annie Steel, *Miss Stuart's Legacy* (London: Heinemann, 1893; ref. to 1913 edn).

—, *From the Five Rivers* (London: Heinemann, 1893; ref. to 1897 edn).

—, *The Potter's Thumb* (London: Heinemann, 1894; ref. to 1900 edn).

—, *On the Face of the Waters* (London: Heinemann, 1896; ref. to 1897 edn).

—, *In the Permanent Way* (London: Heinemann, 1897; ref. to 1898 edn).

—, *The Hosts of the Lord* (London: Heinemann, 1900; ref. to Nelson edn, n.d.).

—, *In the Guardianship of God* (London: Heinemann, 1900; ref. to 1903 edn).

—, *India* (Paintings by Mortimer Menpes, Text by Flora Annie Steel) (London: Black, 1905).

—, *The Law of the Threshold* (London: Heinemann, 1924).

—, *The Garden of Fidelity: Being the Autobiography of Flora Annie Steel* (London: Macmillan, 1929).

—, *The Indian Scene* (London: Arnold, 1933).

CHAPTER 4

Edmund Candler, *A Vagabond in Asia* (London: Greening, 1900).

—, *The Mantle of the East* (London: Blackwood, 1910).

—, *The General Plan* (London: Blackwood, 1911).

—, *Siri Ram: Revolutionist* (London: Constable, 1912).

—, *Abdication* (London: Constable, 1922).

—, *Youth and the East: An Unconventional Autobiography* (1924; ref. to Blackwood edn, 1932).

CHAPTER 5

Edward John Thompson, Papers in possession of the author's widow, Mrs T. Thompson.

—, *Atonement* (London: Benn, 1924).

—, *The Other Side of the Medal* (London: L. & V. Woolf, 1925).

—, *Rabindranath Tagore: Poet and Dramatist* (Oxford: O.U.P., 1926; revised edn, 1940).

—, *Suttee: A Historical and Philosophical Enquiry into the Hindu Rite of Widow-Burning* (London: Allen & Unwin, 1928).

—, *An Indian Day* (1927; ref. to Penguin edn, 1938).

—, *The Reconstruction of India* (London: Faber & Faber, 1930).

—, *A Farewell to India* (London: Benn, 1931).

—, *A Letter from India* (London: Faber & Faber, 1932).

—, *An End of the Hours* (London: Macmillan, 1938).

—, *You Have Lived Through All This: An Anatomy of the Age* (London: Gollancz, 1939).

—, with G. T. Garratt, *The Rise and Fulfilment of British Rule in India* (London: Macmillan, 1934).

CHAPTER 6

C. A. Bodelsen, *Aspects of Kipling's Art* (Manchester: Manchester University Press, 1964).

Hilton Brown, *Rudyard Kipling* (London: Hamish Hamilton, 1945).

Robert Buchanan, 'The Voice of the Hooligan', *Contemporary Review*, Vol. LXXVI, 1899.

Charles Carrington, *Rudyard Kipling: His Life and Work* (London: Macmillan, 1955).

Nirad C. Chaudhuri, 'The Finest Story About India in English', *Encounter*, April 1957.

Herbert Compton, *A Particular Account of the European Military Adventurers of Hindustan from 1784 to 1803* (London: Unwin, 1893).

Stanley Cooperman, 'The Imperial Posture and the Shrine of Darkness: Kipling's *The Naulahka* and E. M. Forster's *A Passage to India*', *English Literature in Transition*, Vol. VI, No. 1, 1963.

Louis L. Cornell, *Kipling in India* (London: Macmillan, 1966).

Bonamy Dobrée, 'Rudyard Kipling' in *The Lamp and the Lute* (Oxford: O.U.P., 1921).

BIBLIOGRAPHY

Bonamy Dobrée, *Rudyard Kipling* (London: British Council, 1951).

—, *Rudyard Kipling: Realist and Fabulist* (Oxford: O.U.P., 1967).

English Literature in Transition (formerly *English Fiction in Transition*), 'Rudyard Kipling: An Annotated Bibliography of Writings About Him', *EFT*, Vol. III, Nos. 3, 4 and 5, 1960, and *ELT*, Vol. VIII, Nos. 3 and 4, 1965.

E. M. Forster, 'The Boy Who Never Grew Up', a review of *Letters of Travel* in the *Daily Herald*, 9 June 1920.

—, 'That Job's Done', a review of *Something of Myself* in the *Listener*, Supplement III, March 1937.

Paul Fussell, 'Irony, Freemasonry and Humane Ethics in Kipling's "The Man Who Would Be King"', *English Literary History*, Vol. 25, 1958.

Elliot L. Gilbert (ed.), *Kipling and the Critics* (New York: New York University Press, 1965).

C. Grey, *European Adventurers of Northern India, 1785 to 1849*, ed. H. L. O. Garrett (Lahore, 1929).

T. R. Henn, *Kipling* (Edinburgh: Oliver & Boyd, 1967).

Syed Sajjed Husain, *Kipling and India: An Inquiry into the Nature and Extent of Kipling's Knowledge of the Indian Sub-continent* (Dacca: University of Dacca, 1964).

The *Kipling Journal*, published by the Kipling Society.

Rudyard Kipling (unless otherwise stated, Kipling's writings are published by Macmillan), *Plain Tales from the Hills* (1888).

—, *In Black and White* (1888).

—, *Under the Deodars* (1888).

—, *The Phantom Rickshaw* (1888).

—, *Wee Willie Winkie* (1888).

—, 'The Enlightenment of Pagett M.P.', *Contemporary Review*, Vol. LVIII, 1890.

—, *Life's Handicap* (1891).

—, *The Naulahka* (1892).

—, *Many Inventions* (1893).

—, *The Day's Work* (1898).

—, *From Sea to Sea and Other Sketches* (1899).

—, *Kim* (1901).

—, *Verse*, Inclusive Edition, 1885–1918 (London: Hodder & Stoughton).

—, *The Eyes of Asia* (New York: Doubleday, 1919).

—, *Something of Myself* (1937).

Richard le Gallienne, *Rudyard Kipling: A Criticism* (London: John Lane, 1900).

John Munro, 'Kipling's *Kim* and Co-existence', *English Literature in Transition*, Vol. VII, No. 4, 1964.

Jeffrey Myers, 'The Idea of Moral Authority in "The Man Who Would Be King"', *Studies in English Literature*, Vol. VIII, No. 4, Autumn 1968.

K. Bhaskara Rao, *Rudyard Kipling's India* (University of Oklahoma Press, 1967).

BIBLIOGRAPHY

Andrew Rutherford (ed.), *Kipling's Mind and Art* (Edinburgh: Oliver & Boyd, 1964).

Alan Sandison, *The Wheel of Empire* (London: Macmillan, 1967).

—, 'Kipling: The Artist and the Empire', in Andrew Rutherford (ed.), *q.v.*

Edward Shanks, *Rudyard Kipling: A Study on Literature and Political Ideas* (London: Right Book Club, 1940–41).

J. I. M. Stewart, *Rudyard Kipling* (London: Gollancz, 1966).

George Thomas, *Military Memoirs of Mr George Thomas*, Compiled and Arranged from Mr Thomas's Original Documents by William Francklin (Calcutta, 1803).

J. M. S. Tompkins, *The Art of Rudyard Kipling* (London: Methuen, 1959).

H. L. Varley, 'Imperialism and Rudyard Kipling', *Journal of the History of Ideas*, Vol. XIV, January 1953.

CHAPTER 7

Glen O. Allen, 'Structure, Symbol and Theme in E. M. Forster's *A Passage to India*', *PMLA*, Vol. LXX, December 1955.

John Beer, *The Achievement of E. M. Forster* (London: Chatto & Windus, 1962).

Malcolm Bradbury (ed.), *Forster: A Collection of Critical Essays* (New York: Prentice Hall, 1966).

Nirad C. Chaudhuri, 'Passage to and from India', *Encounter*, June 1954.

Malcolm Cowley (ed.), *Writers at Work* (London: Secker & Warburg, 1958).

F. C. Crews, *E. M. Forster: The Perils of Humanism* (Oxford: O.U.P., 1962).

Louise Dauner, 'What Happened in the Caves? Reflections on *A Passage to India*', *Modern Fiction Studies*, Vol. VII, Autumn 1961.

E. M. Forster, *A Passage to India* (London: Arnold, 1924).

—, *Goldsworthy Lowes Dickinson* (London: Arnold, 1934).

—, *Abinger Harvest* (London: Arnold, 1934; ref. to 1967 Penguin edn).

—, *Two Cheers for Democracy* (London: Arnold, 1953).

—, 'Indian Entries', *Encounter*, January 1962.

K. W. Gransden, *E. M. Forster* (Edinburgh: Oliver & Boyd, 1962).

Stuart Hampshire, 'Two Cheers for Mr Forster', *New York Review of Books*, 12 May 1966.

William James, *The Varieties of Religious Experience: A Study in Human Nature* (1902; ref. to Fontana edn, 1968).

W. A. S. Keir, '*A Passage to India* Reconsidered', *Cambridge Journal*, 1952.

Arnold Kettle, *An Introduction to the English Novel*, Vol. 2 (London: Hutchinson, 1953).

R. D. Laing, *The Politics of Experience* and *The Bird of Paradise* (Harmondsworth: Penguin Books, 1967).

F. R. Leavis, 'E. M. Forster', in *The Common Pursuit* (London: Chatto & Windus, 1953).

BIBLIOGRAPHY

James H. McConkey, *The Novels of E. M. Forster* (Ithaca: Cornell University Press, 1957).

Hugh MacLean, 'The Structure of *A Passage to India*', *University of Toronto Quarterly*, Vol. XXII, January 1953.

K. Natwar-Singh, *E. M. Forster: A Tribute* (New York: Harcourt Brace, 1964).

D. S. Savage, 'E. M. Forster', in *The Withered Branch* (London: Eyre & Spottiswoode, 1950).

V. A. Shahane, *E. M. Forster: A Reassessment* (Delhi: Kitab Mahal, 1963).

— (ed.), *Perspectives on E. M. Forster's 'A Passage to India': A Collection of Critical Essays* (New York: Barnes & Noble, 1968).

Ranjee G. Shahani, 'Some British I Admire', *Asiatic Review*, Vol. XLII, July 1946.

Oliver Stallybrass (ed.), *Aspects of E. M. Forster* (London: Arnold, 1969).

Wilfred Stone, *The Cave and the Mountain: A Study of E. M. Forster* (Oxford: O.U.P., 1966).

George H. Thomson, *The Fiction of E. M. Forster* (Wayne State University Press, 1967).

Lionel Trilling, *E. M. Forster* (London: Hogarth Press, 1944).

R. Gordon Wasson, *Soma: Divine Mushroom of Immortality* (New York: Harcourt Brace, 1968).

Gertrude M. White, '*A Passage to India*: Analysis and Revaluation', *PMLA*, Vol. LXVIII, September 1953.

Index

'q' following a page number means that the reference is to a quoted passage; the actual title or author indexed may not appear on the page.

Handley, L., 66q
Hardinge, Lord, 23
Hartley, L. P., 260
Her Own People, 93
Hesse, Hermann, 56n.
Hill, Sir Claude H., 64n.
Hill of Devi, The, 262, 264, 269ff.,
302n., 304n., 306n., 309–10n.
Hinduism, British attitudes to, 3–4,
55ff.; their obsession with Hindu
sexuality, 60ff.; interpretations of
Hindu philosophy and outlook,
55–6, 68–9, 231n., 233n., 234n.,
235n., 236n., 243n., 245n., 248n.,
249n., 250n., 264n., 265n., 268n.,
302n., 303, 305n., 307n., 308; as seen
and portrayed by romantic novelists,
71ff., 82ff., 90; by Flora Annie
Steel, 108–12, 115–17; by Candler,
136, 139, 140, 143–4, 145ff.; by
Thompson, 172, 189–90, 195, 199–
200; by Kipling, 230–38, 242–55; by
Forster, 264, 303–16; *see also* Tantric tradition
Horne, E. A., 280n.
Hosts of the Lord, The, 107, 113, 117,
124q, 126q
Howard's End, 273
Hunter Commission of Inquiry, 174
Hunter, Sir William Wilson, 3n., 42
Hutchins, Francis G., 241n.
Hyams, E., 57q

I.C.S., *see* Indian Civil Service
'If–', 256
If . . . (film), 256 and n.
imperialism in India, economic, 9–11,
14, 15; British justifications of imperial domination, 15–17, 22, 25–9;
repudiation of these, 30–1; attitudes and relationships in the imperialist context, 1–3, 29, 33, 54, 65,
281–5; modern defences of imperialism, 203–7. *See also* racialism:

Western-centric conceptions of
India
In Black and White, 'On the City Wall',
239–42
In the Guardianship of God, 110q
In the Permanent Way, 109q, 117q
India, 103q
Indian Army, 9, 11, 17, 23, 32, 34
Indian Civil Service (I.C.S.), 12–13,
15, 26ff., 37, 41
Indian Day, An, 181–91, 194–6
Indian National Congress, 21–3, 24–5,
165
Indian Planter's Gazette, 19–20q, 37,
213 and n.
Indian Scene, The, 106q, 110q
Indian Unrest, 86, 120n., 152
Iqbal, Mohammed, 270–71
Irwin, Viceroy, 24
Isaacs, Harold, 172n.
Isherwood, Christopher, 233n., 235n.
Islam (Moslems), British preference
for, 49–50; expressed by Flora
Annie Steel, 100; by Candler, 139;
Moslems as portrayed by Flora
Annie Steel, 113ff., 117ff.; by
Candler, 145; by Kipling, 239–41,
253; Forster's attitudes to, 264,
269; in *A Passage to India*, 275ff.
Iyer, Raghavan, 14, 15, 205n.

Jainism, Candler's perception of, 161;
ideas and imagery in *A Passage to
India*, 286ff., 298; concepts, 288–90
James, William, 262n., 297n., 311n.
Jews, Anglo-Indian attitudes to, 114n.,
137, 258

Kabir, Humayum, 174n.
Kali, 21n., 55, 62, 82, 90, 94, 107,
109ff., 120n., 121, 141, 227n., 231
Kettle, Arnold, 284n.
Kidron, M., 10n.
Kiernan, V. G., 222n.

INDEX

imperialism in India; Western-
centric conceptions of India
Radhakrishnan, S., 237n., 247n.
Rajah, The, 74n., 79
Rajputs, 50, 80, 94, 139
Ramayana, 232n.
Raghavan, V., 304n.
Ratcliffe, S. K., 177
Rawlinson, H. G., 237n.
Ray, Satyajit, 169n.
rebellion (1857), 9, 20, 118ff., 170,
176–7, 178
Reconstruction of India, The, 166n.,
169q, 184n.
Reynolds, Reginald, 40, 166n.
Rhodes, Cecil, 207, 220, 258
Rhodes Trustees, 170
Richards, Private Frank, 34
*Rise and Expansion of British Dominion
in India, The*, 17
*Rise and Fulfilment of British Rule in
India, The*, 170q, 200q
Roberts of Kandahar, Lord Frederick
Sleigh, 17 and n., 177n.
romantic novelists, the (B. M. Croker,
Maud Diver, F. E. F. Penny, Alice
Perrin, I. A. R. Wylie), 70–99 *pas-
sim*: obsession with Indian sen-
suality, 71–3, 75–6, 84–5; defence
of aloofness from India, 73, 93–5;
India as place of mystery and horror,
74–5, 82, 87–8, 93–4; abhorrence of
inter-racial relationships, 76–82;
celebration of Anglo-Indian virtue,
88ff., 92–3; conceptions of Indians,
71ff., 82ff., 95–6; the spell of India,
96ff.
Round Table Conferences, 24–5, 171n.
Rowlatt Acts (1919), 91, 155
Rushbrook, L. F., 64n.
Russell, Bertrand, 297n.

Sandison, Alan, 204, 214n., 237n.
Savakar, V. D., 177n.

Scott, Paul, 260n.
Seeley, John, 18 and n.
Sen, Dinesh Chandra, 169n.
Sen, K. M., 116n., 231n.
Sen, Surendra Nath, 118q, 119q
Shahane, V. A., 320n.
Shils, Edward, 59n.
Ships of Youth, 91q
Shivaji-worship, 21n.
Sikhism, 50, 139
Simla, 36, 37, 209
Singer Passes, The, 79n.
Siri Ram: Revolutionist, 133, 149–58,
161n, 162–3q
Slade, Madeleine (Mira Behn), 33
Smith, H. A., 272
Smith, Sir James Dunlop, 50
*Soma: Divine Mushroom of Immortal-
ity*, 311n.–312
Something of Myself, 208q, 255q, 258q
Sovani, N. V., 11q
Spear, Percival, 65n.
Spencer, A. M., 169n.
Spencer, Herbert, 137, 203
Spirit's Pilgrimage, The, 33n.
Srinivas, M. N., 60n.
Stalky & Co., 38n.
Stallybrass, Oliver, 285n.
Stead, W. T., 203
Steel, Flora Annie, 6, 7, 65, 100–130
passim: autobiography, 101, 102,
104, 129; her life in India, 100–102;
qualities and deficiencies as a writer,
103–6, 128–9; conceptions of Indian
secular and religious life, 106–16;
Indians in grip of tradition, 106–7,
109; her view of lust and violence as
central to Indian character, 110–12,
114, 117–21; on Moslem depravity,
113–14; arcane India, 115–16; on
instinctive withdrawal of British
from India, 121–5; on Anglo-
Indian displacement in India, 125–6;
on Anglo-Indians as defenders of